P9-DMB-989

Judges of the Christian Research Foundation presented Dr. John E. Steely an award for the high quality of his efforts. The author approved the translation and made available changes and additions which make this, in essence, a revised edition.

the author

WALTER SCHMITHALS, well-known New Testament scholar, is a professor at the University of Marburg in Germany. Another of his books, *The Theology of Rudolf Bultmann*, has recently been published in an English translation.

the translator

JOHN E. STEELY is professor of historical theology, Southeastern Baptist Theological Seminary, Wake Forest, North Carolina. The Christian Research Foundation presented him with awards both for the translation of this work and for the translation of Wilhelm Bousset's *Kyrios Christos*.

the office
of apostle
in the
early church

the office of apostle in the early church

WALTER SCHMITHALS Translated by John E. Steely

ABINGDON PRESS   Nashville and New York

THE OFFICE OF APOSTLE IN THE EARLY CHURCH

Originally published as *Das kirchliche Apostelamt.*
Translation from the German language with the approval of
the Publishing House Vandenhoeck & Ruprecht, Goettingen.
© Vandenhoeck & Ruprecht, Goettingen.

Standard Book Number: 687-28399-x
Library of Congress Catalog Card Number: 73-84724

SET UP, PRINTED, AND BOUND BY THE
PARTHENON PRESS, AT NASHVILLE,
TENNESSEE, UNITED STATES OF AMERICA

TRANSLATOR'S PREFACE

The role of the translator is a modest one, and a preface from the translator's pen may be correspondingly brief. There is good reason, however, to make some explanatory comments here and to express thanks for assistance in this work.

Professor Schmithals has reviewed the translation and has revised the work at several points. Hence the English edition has the character of a revised edition. These revisions involve some modifications, some rearrangements of the text, and some additions. The additions are to be found in the text, in some expanded footnotes, and in some new footnotes. Hence the reader who wishes to compare this translation with the German edition is invited to use the rather full table of contents, since even the footnote numbers will not correspond in the two editions in many places.

Where it was possible to do so, I have given the page references to English translations of works used by the author, rather than the German originals. In addition, I have made a translation of other materials which he has cited in German, though quotations in Greek or Latin have been left in those languages.

I should like to express my thanks to Professor Schmithals for his kindness and generosity in making possible this publication in revised form, and for his labor in reading the typescript. The responsibility for any failure to capture his meaning is, of course, my own.

Thanks must be expressed also to the Christian Research Foundation, Inc., who awarded a prize for this translation in the 1965-66 competition, and to my friend, Dr. William C. Strickland, for his assistance at many points along the way. My last and warmest word of thanks must go to my family for their support and understanding.

John E. Steely

Wake Forest, North Carolina

CONTENTS

INDEX TO LITERATURE

The works listed here are cited in the study only with the author's name and *op. cit.* If several works of the same author are listed in this index, they are cited in the sequence given below with [1], [2], [3], etc. My own works are at times cited only by title. Works that are used only once or rarely are listed in the footnotes.

Adam, A.: "Erwägungen zur Herkunft der Didache," ZKG (1957), pp. 1-47.
Ashcraft, M.: "Paul's Understanding of Apostleship," *Review and Expositor,* LV (1958), 400-412.
Bammel, E.: "Herkunft und Funktion der Traditionselemente in I Kor. 15,1-11," ThZ, XI (1955), 401-19.
Barrett, C. K.: "The Apostles in and after the New Testament," *Svensk Exegetisk Årsbok,* XXI (1956), 30-49.
————. "Paul and the Pillar Apostles," in *Studia Paulina,* 1953.
Barth, M.: *Der Augenzeuge,* 1946.
Battifol, P.: "L'apostolat," RevBibl NS, III (1906), 520 ff.
Bauer, W. [1]: *Rechtgläubigkeit und Ketzerei im ältesten Christentum,* 1934.
————. [2]: *Griechisch-deutsches Wörterbuch zum Neuen Testament, s. v.* "ἀπόστολος."
————. [3]: *Das Johannesevangelium,* HNT, VI (3rd ed., 1933).
Baur, F. C. [1]: "Über die Ekstasen des Apostels," TheolJb (1850), pp. 182 ff.
————. [2]: "Über das Auctoritätsprinzip des Apostels," *ibid.* (1852), pp. 32 ff.
Becker, H.: *Die Reden des Johannesevangeliums und der Stil der gnostischen Offenbarungsrede,* FRLANT NF, L (1956).
Betz, H. D.: *Nachfolge und Nachahmung Jesu Christi im Neuen Testament,* BhTh, XXXVII (1967).
Bieder, W.: *Die Berufung im Neuen Testament,* AThANT, XXXVIII (1961).
Bornkamm, G.: *Mythos und Legende in den apokryphen Thomasakten,* FRLANT NF, XXXI (1933).
Bultmann, R. [1]: *Theology of the New Testament,* 1951, 1955.
————. [2]: "Die Bedeutung der neuerschlossenen mandäischen und manichäischen Quellen für das Verständnis des Johannesevangeliums," ZNW, XXIV (1925), 100 ff.
————. [3]: *Das Evangelium des Johannes,* 12th ed., 1952.
Burton, E. de Witt: *A Critical and Exegetical Commentary on the Epistle to the Galatians,* 1921.
Campenhausen, H. v. [1]: "Der urchristliche Apostelbegriff," StudTheol, I (1948), 96-130.

————. [2]: *Kirchliches Amt und geistliche Vollmacht in den ersten drei Jahrhunderten*, BhTh, XIV (1953).

————. [3]: "Lehrerreihen und Bischofsreihen im 2. Jahrhundert," in: *In memoriam Ernst Lohmeyer* (1951), pp. 240-49.

————. [4]: *Die Begründung kirchlicher Entscheidungen beim Apostel Paulus*, SAH (1957), 2.

Cerfaux, L.: "Pour l'histoire du titre Apostolos dans le Nouveau Testament," RechdeSciRel, XLVIII (1960), 76-92.

Clemen, C.: "Die Missionstätigkeit der nichtchristlichen Religionen," ZMR, XLIV (1929), 225 ff.

Colson, J: *Les fonctions ecclésiales aux deux premiers siècles*, 1956.

Conzelmann, H.: *The Theology of St. Luke*, 1960.

Cullmann, O. [1]: "Le caractère eschatologique du devoir missionaire et de la conscience apostolique de Saint Paul," RHPhR, XVI (1936), 210 ff.

————. [2]: *Peter: Apostle, Disciple, Martyr*, 1953.

Deissmann, A.: *Paul*, 2nd ed., 1926.

Deissner, K.: "Das Sendungsbewusstsein der Urchristenheit," ZsTh, VII (1929-30), 772 ff.

Denis, A. M. [1]: "L'investiture de la fonction apostolique par 'Apocalypse.' " Étude thématique de Gal. 1,16. RevBibl, LXIV (1957), 335-62; 492-515.

————. [2]: "La fonction apostolique et la liturgie nouvelle en esprit," RSciPhTh, XLII (1958), 401-36.

Dobschütz, E. v. [1]: *Die Thessalonicherbriefe*, 1909.

————. [2]: *Probleme des apostolischen Zeitalters*, 1904.

Dupont, J.: "Pierre et Paul à Antioche et à Jérusalem," RechdeSciRel, XLV (1957), 42-60; 225-39.

Ehrhardt, A.: *The Apostolic Succession in the First Two Centuries of the Church*, 1953.

Epictetus. *Dissertationes*, ed. H. Schenkl, Leipzig, 2nd ed., 1916.

Fridrichsen, A.: "The Apostle and his Message," *Uppsala Universitets Årsskrift* (1947), Heft 3.

Gaechter, P.: *Petrus und seine Zeit* (1958), esp. pp. 338-450.

Gavin, F.: "Shaliach and Apostolos," AnglTheolRev, IX (1927), 250 ff.

Georgi, D.: *Die Gegner des Paulus im Zweiten Korintherbrief*, WMANT, XI (1964).

Gerhardsson, B.: "Die Boten Gottes und die Apostel Christi," *Svensk Exegetisk Årsbok*, XXVII (1962), 89-131.

Goguel, M. [1]: *The Life of Jesus*, 1933.

————. [2]: *The Primitive Church*, 1947 (1964).

Goppelt, L.: *Die apostolische und nachapostolische Zeit*, [n. d.].

Greeven, H.: "Propheten, Lehrer, Vorsteher bei Paulus," ZNW, XLIV (1952), 1 ff.

Gressmann, H. [1]: "Heidnische Mission in der Werdezeit des Christentums," ZMR, XXXIX (1924), 10-24.

————. [2]: "Jüdische Mission in der Werdezeit des Christentums," ZMR, XXXIX (1924).

Grundmann, W.: "Die Apostel zwischen Jerusalem und Antiochien," ZNW, XXXIX (1940), 110-37.

Güttgemanns, E. [1]: *Der leidende Apostel und sein Herr*, FRLANT, XC (1966).

————. [2]: "Literatur zur neutestamentlichen Theologie," VF, XII/2 (1967), 61 ff.

Haase, F.: "Apostel und Evangelisten in den orientalischen Überlieferungen," *Neutestamentliche Abhandlungen* IX, 1-3 (1922).

Haenchen, E.: *Die Apostelgeschichte*, 1956.

Hahn, F.: *Das Verständnis der Mission im Neuen Testament*, WMANT, XIII (1963).

Hanson, S.: *The Unity of the Church in the New Testament*, 1946.

Harlé, P. A.: "Perspectives nouvelles sur le Ministère de Saint Paul," *Études Theol. et Rel.*, XXXII (1957), 199-212.

Harnack, A. v. [1]: *The Mission and Expansion of Christianity*, 2 vols. (2nd ed., 1908).

————. [2]: *Beiträge zur Einleitung in das Neue Testament*, VI: Die Entstehung des

Neuen Testaments und die wichtigsten Folgen der neuen Schöpfung (1914).
———. [3]: *Lehre der Zwölf Apostel*, 1884.
Haupt, E.: *Zum Verständnis des Apostolats im Neuen Testament*, 1896.
Héring, J.: *La seconde Épitre de Saint Paul aux Corinthiens* (1958), pp. 107-11: Remarques sur les origines de l'apostolat d'après le Nouveau Testament.
Holl, K. [1]: "Der Kirchenbegriff des Paulus in seinem Verhältnis zu dem der Urgemeinde," SAB (1921), pp. 920-47.
———. [2]: "Die schriftstellerische Form des griechischen Heiligenlebens," NJbchKlAlt, XXIX (1912), 406 ff.
Jeremias, J.: *Jesus' Promise to the Nations*, 1958.
———. *Imago Dei*, FRLANT NF, LVIII (1960).
The Jewish Encyclopaedia, s. v. "ἀπόστολος."
Käsemann, E. [1]: *Das wandernde Gottesvolk*, FRLANT NF, XXXVII (2nd ed., 1957).
———. [2]: "Die Legitimität des Apostels," ZNW, XLI (1942), 33 ff.
Kattenbusch, F.: "Die Vorzugsstellung des Petrus und der Charakter der Urgemeinde zu Jerusalem," in *Festgabe, Karl Müller zum 70. Geburtstag* (1922), pp. 322 ff.
Kinder-Perels-Sommerlath: *Apostolat und Amt*, 1953.
Kirk, K. E.: *The Apostolic Ministry*, 1946.
Klebba, E.: *Des heiligen Irenäus 5 Bücher gegen die Häresien*, BKV, III-IV (1912).
Klein, G.: *Die Zwölf Apostel, Ursprung und Gehalt einer Idee*, FRLANT NF, LIX (1961).
Knox, J.: *Marcion and the New Testament*, 1942.
Köppel: *Ursprung des Apostolats*, StKr (1889), pp. 313 ff.
Kramer, W.: *Christus, Kyrios, Gottessohn*, AThANT, XLIV (1963).
Kredel, E. M.: "Der Apostelbegriff in der neueren Exegese," *Zeitschrift für katholische Theologie*, LXXVIII (1956), 169 ff.; 257 ff.
Krauss, S.: "Die jüdischen Apostel," JQR, XVII (1905), 370 ff.
Kümmel, W. G.: *Kirchenbegriff und Geschichtsbewusstsein in der Urgemeinde und bei Jesus*, 1943.
Lake, K.: "The Twelve and the Apostles," in *The Beginnings of Christianity*, Part I, V, 37 ff.
Lamers, B. J.: "Der Apostel Thomas in Südindien," *Zeitschrift für Missionswissenschaft*, XIV (1958), 15 ff.
Leuba, J. L.: *Institution und Ereignis*, 1957.
Lidzbarski, Mark, ed. *Ginza*. 1925.
———, ed. *Das Johannesbuch der Mandäer*. 1915.
Lietzmann, H.: *An die Römer*, HNT, VIII (4th ed., 1933).
Lightfoot, J. B.: *St. Paul's Epistle to the Galatians*, 1890.
Linton, O.: *Das Problem der Urkirche in der neueren Forschung*, 1932.
Lohse, E. [1]: "Ursprung und Prägung des christlichen Apostolates," ThZ, IX (1953). 259 ff.
———. [2]: *Die Ordination im Spätjudentum und im Neuen Testament*, 1951.
Lührmann, D.: *Das Offenbarungsverständnis bei Paulus und in den paulinischen Gemeinden*, WMANT, XVI (1965).
Margot, J. C.: "L'apostolat dans le Nouveau Testament et la succession apostolique," *Verbum Caro*, XI (1957), 213-25.
Meyer, E.: *Ursprung und Anfänge des Christentums*, I (1921), 264 ff.; III (1923), 255 ff.
Michaelis, W.: *Die Erscheinungen des Auferstandenen*, 1944.
Michel, O.: *Der Brief an die Hebräer*, 1949.
Monnier, H.: *La notion de l'apostolat des origines à Irénée*, 1903.
Morenz, S.: "Der Apostel Andreas als νέος Σάραπις," ThLZ (1947), col. 295.
Mosbech, H. [1]: "Apostolos in the New Testament," StudTheol, II (1949), 166-200.
———. [2]: "ἀπόστολος hos Paulos," in *Studier tilegnede Fr. Buhl*, 1925.
Moule, C. F. D.: *The Epistles of Paul the Apostle to the Colossians and to Philemon* (1957), Excursus, pp. 155-59.
Munck, J. [1]: "Paul, the Apostles and the Twelve," StudTheol, III (1950), 96-110.

————. [2]: *Paul and the Salvation of Mankind*, 1959.

————. [3]: "La vocation de l'Apôtre Paul," StudTheol, I (1948), 131-45.

————. [4]: "Paulus' Apostolat og Apostelbegrebet i det Ny Testament," *Dansk teologisk tidsskrift*, XI (1948), 141 ff.

Nagel, W.: *Der Begriff des Apostolischen in der christlichen Frühzeit bis zur Kanonbildung*, Habilitationsschrift (Leipzig, 1958).

Nägeli, T.: *Der Wortschatz des Paulus* (1905), s. v. "ἀπόστολος."

Nielen: "Nachfolger und Nachahmer Gottes," in *Heilige Überlieferung*, Ildefons Herwegen dargeboten von Odo Casel, 1938.

Norden, E. [1]: "Beiträge zur Geschichte der griechischen Philosophie," JbKlPhil, XIX (1893), 365 ff.

————. [2]: *Agnostos Theos*, 4th ed., 1956.

Odland, S.: *Apostolatets begreb og oprindelse* (Oslo, 1897).

Oepke, A.: *Die Missionspredigt des Apostels Paulus*, 1920.

Pax, E.: ΕΠΙΦΑΝΕΙΑ (München, 1955).

Reitzenstein, R.: *Die hellenistischen Mysterienreligionen*, 3rd ed., 1927.

Rengstorf, K. H. [1]: Article, "ἀπόστολος" in TDNT I, 407 ff.

————. [2]: *Apostolat und Predigtamt*, 2nd ed., 1954.

Roloff, J.: *Apostolat—Verkündigung—Kirche*, 1965.

Rudolph, K.: *Die Mandäer* I, FRLANT NF, XVI (1960).

Sabbe, M.: "Enkele Aspecten van het apostolaat bij Paulus," Coll Brug Gand, III (1957), 507-21.

Sass, G. [1]: *Apostolat und Kirche*, 1939.

————. [2]: "Der Apostel in der Didache," in *In Memoriam E. Lohmeyer*, 1951.

Schelkle, K. H.: *Jüngerschaft und Apostelamt*, 1957.

Schille, G.: *Liturgisches Gut im Epheserbrief*, Dissertation (Göttingen, 1953).

————.: *Die urchristliche Kollegialmission*, AThANT, XLVIII (1967).

Schlier, H.: *Die Brief an die Galater*, 1949.

Schmithals, W.: *Die Gnosis in Korinth*, FRLANT NF, XLVIII (1956; 2nd ed., 1965).

————.: "Die Häretiker in Galatien," ZNW, XLVII (1956), 25-67; in *Paulus und die Gnostiker*, 1965.

Schoeps, H. J.: *Urgemeinde—Judenchristentum—Gnosis*, 1956.

Schürer, E.: *Geschichte des jüdischen Volkes*, III (1909).

Schütz, R.: *Apostel und Jünger*, 1921.

Schwartz, J.: "A propos du statut personnel de l'apôtre Paul," RHPhR, XXXVII (1957), 91-96.

Schweizer, E.: *Church Order in the New Testament*, 1961.

————.: review in TLZ (1962), cols. 837-40.

Seufert, W.: *Der Ursprung und die Bedeutung des Apostolates in der christlichen Kirche der ersten zwei Jahrhunderte*, 1887.

Söder, R.: *Die apokryphen Apostelschriften und die romanhafte Literatur der Antike*, 1932.

Staerk, W. [1]: *Soter* I, 1933.

————. [2]: *Soter* II, 1938.

Stauffer, E.: "Zur Vor- und Frühgeschichte des Primatus Petri," ZKG, LXII (1943-44), 3 ff.

Stegemann, V.: *Die Gestalt Christi in den koptischen Zaubertexten* (Heidelberg, 1934).

Stirnimann, H.: "Apostelamt und apostolische Überlieferung," Freiburger ZPhTh (1957), pp. 129-47.

Strack, H. L., and Billerbeck, P.: *Kommentar zum NT aus Talmud und Midrasch*, 2nd ed., 1956.

Verheul, A., OSB: "Apostolaat en Verrijzenis, onderzoek naar de inhoud van het Apostelbegrip in I Cor.," StudCath, XXVI (1951).

————.: "De moderne exegese over ἀπόστολος," *Sacris Erudiri*, I (1948), 380-90.

————.: "Kent Sint Paulus buiten de 'Twaalf' nog andere apostelen?" StudCath, XXII (1947), 65-75; XXIII (1948), 147-57, 217-28.

Vogelstein, H. [1]: "Die Entstehung und Entwicklung des Apostolats im Judentum," MGWJ, XLIX (1905), 427 ff.

——. [2]: "The Development of the Apostolate in Judaism and its transformation in Christianity," HbrUnCollAnn, II (1925).

Wagenmann, J.: *Die Stellung des Apostels Paulus neben den Zwölf in den ersten zwei Jahrhunderten*, 1926.

Warneck, J.: *Paulus im Lichte der heutigen Heidenmission*, 2nd ed., 1914.

Weizsäcker, C.: *Das apostolische Zeitalter der christlichen Kirche*, 3rd ed., 1902.

Wellhausen, J.: *Einleitung in die drei ersten Evangelien* (2nd ed., 1911), pp. 138 ff.

Wendland, P.: *Die hellenistisch-römische Kultur in ihren Beziehungen zu Judentum und Christentum* (1907), esp. pp. 39 ff.

Wernle, P. [1]: *Die Anfänge unserer Religion*, 2nd ed., 1904.

——. [2]: *Paulus als Heidenmissionar*, 2nd ed., 1909.

Wetter, G. P.: *Der Sohn Gottes*, FRLANT NF, IX (1916).

Widengren, G. [1]: *The Great Vohu Manah and the Apostle of God*, 1945.

——. [2]: *The Ascension of the Apostle and the Heavenly Book*, 1950.

——. [3]: *Muhammad, the Apostle of God, and His Ascension*, 1955.

——. [4]: *Mesopotamian Elements in Manichaeism*, 1946.

——. [5]: "Stand und Aufgaben der iranischen Religionsgeschichte," *Numen*, I (1954), 48 ff.; II (1955), 51 ff.; 151 ff.

Wikenhauser, A.: Article "Apostel" in RAC.

Windisch, H.: *Paulus und Christus*, 1934.

Zahn, T. [1]: *Apostel und Apostelschüler in der Provinz Asien*, 1900.

——. [2]: *Skizzen aus dem Leben der alten Kirche*, 1894.

List of Abbreviations

AAB	Abhandlungen der Preussischen Akademie der Wissenschaften zu Berlin	BENT	Beiträge zur Einleitung in das Neue Testament
Act. Andr.	Acta Andreae	Br.	Berakhoth
Act. Paul.	Acta Pauli	BGU	Berliner Griechische Urkunden
Act. Petr.	Acta Petri	BhTh	Beiträge zur historischen Theologie
Act. Thom.	Acta Thomae		
Adv. Haer.	Adversus Haereses	BKV	Bibliothek der Kirchenväter
Adv. Marc.	Adversus Marcionem	B. M.	Baba Metzia
AThR.	Anglican Theological Review	B. Q.	Baba Qamma (Kamma)
		BZNW	Beihefte zur Zeitschrift für die neutestamentliche Wissenschaft und die Kunde der Älteren Kirche
Ant.	Antiquities of the Jews (Josephus)		
Ap. Const.	Apostolic Constitutions		
Apoc. Abr.	Apocalypse of Abraham	Chag.	Chagiga (Hagigah)
Apoc. Bar.	Apocalypse of Baruch	I Clem.	The First Epistle of Clement
Apoc. Mos.	Apocalypse of Moses	Clem. Alex. Strom.	Clement of Alexandria Stromateis
Asc. Jes.	Ascensio Jesaiae		
AThANT	Abhandlungen zur Theologie des Alten und Neuen Testaments	Coll Brug Gand	Collationes brugenses et gandavenses
		Corp. Herm.	Corpus Hermeticum
		Demosth. Or.	Demosthenes, Orationes
b	Babylonian Talmud	Did.	Didache
B. B.	Baba Bathra	Dion. Hal. Ant. Rom.	Dionysius of Halicarnassus, Antiquitates Romanae
Barn.	Epistle of Barnabas		

ABBREVIATIONS

Diss.	Dissertation (s)	LXX	Septuagint
En.	Book of Enoch	Lys. Or.	Lysias, Orationes
Ep. Ap.	Epistula Apostolorum	Mart. Petr.	Martyrium Petri
Epiph. Haer.	Epiphanius, Haereses	Mart. Petr.	Martyrium Petri et Pauli
Eth.	Ethiopic	et Paul.	
Eus. CH	Eusebius, Church History	Mart. Polyc.	Martyrium Polycarpi
Ev. Theol.	Evangelische Theologie	Meg.	Megillah
Exc. ex Theod.	Excerpta ex Theodoto	Men.	Menahoth (Menachot)
FRLANT NF	Forschungen zur Religion	M. Ex.	Mekilta (Mechilta) Exodus
	und Literatur des Alten	MGWJ	Monatsschrift für Geschich-
	und Neuen Testaments,		te und Wissenschaft des
	Neue Folge		Judentums
GCS	Die griechischen christlichen	Mid. Ps.	Midrash on Psalms
	Schriftsteller der ersten	MSG	Migne, Patrologia Series
	drei Jahrhunderte		Graeca
GGA	Göttingische Gelehrte	MSL	Migne, Patrologia Series
	Anzeigen		Latina
Git.	Gittin	Ned.	Nedarim
Gn r	Genesis rabba	NGG	Nachrichten der Gesellschaft
Hdt.	Herodotus		der Wissenschaften zu
Pseud. Hdt.	Pseudo-Herodotus		Göttingen
Vita Hom.	Vita Homeri	NJbKlAlt	Neue Jahrbücher des Klas-
Herm.	Shepherd of Hermas		sichen Altertums
Mand.	Mandates	NRTh	Nouvelle Revue Theologique
Sim.	Similitudes	N. S.	New Series
Vis.	Visions	NTD	Das Neue Testament
Hipp.	Hippolytus		Deutsch
HNT	Handbuch zum Neuen	NTS	New Testament Studies
	Testament	Od. Sol.	Odes of Solomon
Hor.	Horayoth	Orig.	Origen
HThR	Harvard Theological	Cels.	(contra) Celsum
	Review	de Prin.	de Principiis
Ign.	Ignatius	Pes.	Pesahim (Pesachim)
Magn.	to the Magnesians	Philo	Philo of Alexandria
Philad.	to the Philadelphians	Leg. Gaj.	Legatio ad Gajum
Polyc.	to Polycarp	Mig. Abr.	de Migratione Abrahami
Smyrn.	to the Smyrneans	Rer. Div.	Quis Rerum Divinarum
Trall.	to the Trallians	Her.	Heres sit
Iren.	Irenaeus	Spec. Leg.	de Specialis Legibus
j	Jerusalem Talmud	Pist. Soph.	Pistis Sophia
JbfKlPhil	Jahrbuch für Klassische	Plat., Ep.	Plato, Epistulae
	Philologie	Polyc.	Polycarp
Jeb.	Jebamot (Yebamoth)	P. Oxy.	Oxyrhynchus Papyri
Jes. Sir.	Jesus Sirach	Ps.-Cl.	Pseudo-Clement
Joma	Joma (Yoma)	Hom.	Homilies
Jos. Ant.	Josephus, Antiquitates	Rec.	Recognitions
JQR	Jewish Quarterly Review	Qid.	Qiddushin (Kiddushin)
JThS	Journal of Theological	RAC	Reallexikon für Antike und
	Studies		Christentum
Jul. Ep.	Julian, the Emperor,	RechdeSciRel	Recherches de Science Re-
	Epistulae		ligieuse
Just.	Justin Martyr	RevBibl	Revue Biblique
Apol.	Apology	RevSciPhTh	Revue des Sciences Philo-
Dial.	Dialogue with Trypho		sophiques et Théologiques
Kid.	Kiddushin		

ABBREVIATIONS

RGG	Die Religion in Geschichte und Gegenwart	Test	Testament
R. H.	Rosh ha-Shanah	TheolJb	Theologisches Jahrbuch
RHPhR	Revue d'Histoire et de Philosophie Religieuses	ThLZ	Theologische Literaturzeitung
SAB	Sitzungsberichte der Preussischen Akademie der Wissenschaften zu Berlin	ThR	Theologische Rundschau
		ThZ	Theologische Zeitschrift
SAH	Sitzungsberichte der Akademie der Wissenschaften zu Heidelberg	TU	Texte und Untersuchungen zur Geschichte der altchristlichen Literatur
Sanh.	Sanhedrin	VF	Verkündigung und Forschung
Sir.	Sirach	VigChr	Vigiliae Christianae
Slav.	Slavonic	WBG	Wissenschaftliche Buchgesellschaft
SNu	Sifre Numeri	Wisd. Sol.	Wisdom of Solomon
StBTh	Studies in Biblical Theology	WMANT	Wissenschaftliche Monographien zum Alten und Neuen Testament
StKr	Theologische Studien und Kritiken		
Str.-B.	H. L. Strack—Paul Billerbeck, Kommentar zum Neuen Testament aus Talmud und Midrasch	WZKM	Wiener Zeitschrift für die Kunde des Morgenlandes
		ZKG	Zeitschrift für Kirchengeschichte
Strom.	Stromateis	ZMR	Zeitschrift für Missionskunde und Religionswissenschaft
StudCath	Studia Catholica		
StudTheol	Studia Theologica		
T	Tosefta	ZNW	Zeitschrift für die Neutestamentliche Wissenschaft und die Kunde der älteren Kirche
Taan.	Taanith		
TDNT	Theological Dictionary of the New Testament, Gerhard Kittel, ed.; trans. by Geoffrey W. Bromiley		
		ZPhThF	Zeitschrift für Philosophie und Theologie, Freiburg
Ter.	Terumoth	ZsTh	Zeitschrift für systematische Theologie
Tert.	Tertullian		
adv. Marc.	adversus Marcionem	ZThK	Zeitschrift für Theologie und Kirche
carn.	de carne Christi		
de praescr.	de praescriptione	ZwTh	Zeitschrift für wissenschaftliche Theologie
haer.	haereticorum		

INTRODUCTION

The question as to the origin and nature of the apostolate in the early church appears remarkably late among the problems with which scientific theology of the nineteenth century began to come to terms. Once propounded, however, this question was then discussed with ever-increasing intensity, and this has continued to be true even to the present day.

If I understand it aright, it was the gifted J. B. Lightfoot who in his commentary on Galatians[1] (1st ed., 1865) was the first to lay hold in a fundamental way upon this problem, which is presented as "The Name and Office of an Apostle." His excursus under this title is lacking in any reference to earlier literature, and it is indeed true that before him people did not sense the difficulties which are bound up in the concept of the apostolic in the early days of the church,[2] difficulties with which every student of the New Testament and of early church history today sees himself confronted: When were the twelve disciples of Jesus recognized as apostles? How is their apostolate related to that of Paul? Whence came the concept and the content of the apostolate? How wide was the circle of the apostles at the time of Paul? What led to the later narrowing of the apostolic circle to the twelve and Paul? Where are the beginnings of the apostolic succession?

J. B. Lightfoot's achievement was not only that he posed these questions. Indeed, he also gave answers which for the majority of investigators even to this day have lost none of their persuasive power. It was Lightfoot who pointed to שליח, the Jewish equivalent of ἀπόστολος; he drew the other apostles, along with Paul and the twelve, into his studies and attempted to

---

[1] 10th ed., 1890, with reprints in 1892 and 1896.

[2] F. C. Baur still constructs his picture of the development of the early church on the basis of the conception, come down from the time of the earliest church fathers and never called in question, that there were thirteen apostles in primitive Christianity: the twelve (Judaistic) apostles in Jerusalem and the apostle Paul. Cf. F. C. Baur, *Kirchengeschichte der ersten drei Jahrhunderte* (3rd ed., 1863), pp. 44-62; W. Seufert, *op. cit.*, pp. 1-2.

determine the relationship of this wider apostolic circle to the narrower one. His research provided the foundation—which, though considerably enlarged, has hardly needed serious correction—for the great number of later works on the figure of the apostle and on the concept of the apostolic.

The debate over our problem is, of course, still a long way from being concluded. K. H. Rengstorf's comprehensive article ἀπόστολος in TDNT, I, 398-447 brings together in independent reworking the results of earlier studies, but precisely against the chief result of his research, the derivation of the primitive Christian apostolate from the late Jewish legal institution of the "Schaliach," objection has been raised in increasing measure.[3] Still unexplained is the question as to where and why the apostolate was restricted to the twelve disciples of Jesus (and Paul), all the more since the opinions sharply diverge over the question of when the members of the circle of the twelve were named apostles at all. How did it happen that, of the other apostles, only Paul's claim besides theirs continued to be recognized as valid? [4]

In the comprehensive literature on our theme all the sources have been investigated from every side; the viewpoints which have been brought forward are constantly repeated, without bringing an end of the discussion any nearer.[5] Only new sources, which are hardly to be expected, or essentially new ideas offer any hope for real progress.[6]

The hope of reviving the discussion through some such new ideas, and here and there of laying a different foundation, is the thrust of the following investigation.

[3] See p. 110, n. 64.

[4] The fact that today less than ever can one speak of assured results of the investigation of the Christian apostolate is shown, for example, by the extremely cautious and often too vaguely handled article "Apostel" in the third ed. of RGG (H. Riesenfeld).

[5] E. Haupt's judgment (op. cit., p. 1) of 1896 is thoroughly relevant: "The question of the origin and the concept of the apostolate currently belongs to the most complicated and most difficult problems of New Testament scholarship."

[6] The work of G. Klein, Die zwölf Apostel, FRLANT NF, LIX (1961), marks an important new beginning. Klein's work grew out of his use of the present investigation, which was already completed in 1956. Cf. Klein, op. cit., pp. 62 ff. I have taken Klein's work into detailed account esp. in the notes and in Part Four, V.

PART ONE
The Apostolate of Paul

In his praiseworthy prizewinning work on "Der Ursprung und die Bedeutung des Apostolates in der christlichen Kirche der ersten zwei Jahrhunderte," W. Seufert begins with Paul's concept of apostle. This is the only sensible beginning point for any investigation of the primitive Christian apostolate. There are no earlier sources than the Pauline for the office of apostle in the Christian community; but further, there are no other sources that are more immediate or more immune to criticism on the topic of the apostolate in the early time of the church; and most of all, no other source is as fruitful and comprehensive as the Pauline epistolary literature.

If the Pauline letters offer basic and clear information concerning *any* theologoumenon of the apostle, it is that concerning his view of the apostolic office. In view of the relatively brief compass of the Corpus Paulinum this assertion may be surprising, and, in fact, of the undoubtedly genuine Pauline letters, Romans, Philippians, I Thessalonians, and Philemon are hardly of any significance for our problem which was still quite peripheral in such congregational or private letters. All the more, however, in the two Corinthian epistles and in Galatians Paul concerns himself with his own position as the ἀπόστολος Ἰησοῦ Χριστοῦ. The reason is not difficult to recognize: In Galatia as well as in Corinth people were denying his right to be called an apostle and were seeking thereby to brand his message as unapostolic and therefore reprehensible. For the sake of his message Paul is compelled to defend his apostolic rights.[7] This he does in Gal. 1-2, and particularly in II Cor., especially in the section 2:14–7:16[8] as well as in the concluding chapters 10-13, with great explicitness.[9]

---

[7] Thus it is probably true that Paul is not at all interested in a doctrine of the apostolic office in itself (H. v. Campenhausen [1], p. 111). The extent of the apologetic reference to his office in the one passage mentioned above can, however, hardly be overestimated.

[8] With the exception, above all, of the section 6:14–7:1, which is not original here; see the commentaries.

[9] This argument already begins to be heard in I Cor. 9:1 ff. also.

21

What is the nature of the apostolic office according to Paul? [10]

1. First of all, the office of the apostle does not bestow upon the bearer any kind of spiritual quality which elevates him above the congregation[11]; he is and remains a member of this congregation.[12]

The congregation must concern itself with being found ἐν Χριστῷ (Phil. 4:1), but the apostle no less so (Phil. 3:8-9). All must be made manifest before the judgment seat of Christ (II Cor. 5:10), even the apostle (I Cor. 3:13). Congregation and apostle alike live by the grace of God (Phil. 1:7). They share the situation of those who have not yet apprehended, but have been apprehended (Phil. 3:12 ff.; I Cor. 13:12).

The special commission and the special authority which the apostles receive are functions of the congregation[13]; for God set ἐν τῇ ἐκκλησίᾳ first apostles, second prophets, third teachers, then workers of miracles, and so on (I Cor. 12:28). By no means are all members of the congregation apostles, yet all apostles are obviously members of the congregation (I Cor. 12:29). τὸ ἓν καὶ τὸ αὐτὸ πνεῦμα provides the charisma for the apostolate no less than all the other charismata in the congregation (I Cor. 12:7-11). No charisma, however, essentially elevates its bearer out of the community.

In that hour when all tongues shall confess that Christ is Lord, all the gifts of grace of this time will cease. Along with all others the apostles will reign in the kingdom of God (I Cor. 4:8), and all the saints will judge the world (I Cor. 6:2). Then, "in Christ," not only the distinctions between Jew and Greek, bond and free, will have ceased (I Cor. 12:13), but also apostles and prophets, πνευματικοί and νήπιοι (I Cor. 3:1) will be the *one* Christ (Gal. 3:28; Col. 3:11), or will be "*one* in Christ." The apostle is therefore a member of the community, commissioned for the time up until the parousia of Christ.[14]

2. The commission of the apostle consists in the fact that the mission is entrusted to him. He is to preach Christ: ἀπέστειλέν με Χριστὸς . . .

[10] The essay of J. Cambier, "Paul, apôtre du Christ et prédicateur de l'évangile" (NRTh, LXXXI [1959], 1009-28), contains no new information.

[11] Cf. E. Haupt, *op. cit.*, p. 136.

[12] Note how in the headings of his letters Paul always associates himself as an apostle with other brethren; see H. Schlier, *op. cit.*, p. 4.

[13] I thereby make the function of the apostle neither "the function of the other charismata nor the general function of the 'soma Christou,'" as E. Güttgemanns ([1], p. 325; [2], pp. 65-66) suggests, and even less a function granted *by the community*. I am only affirming that the apostle as such does not stand *over against* the community but *with* the other charismatics and *like* them performs his ministry as a member of the community.

[14] Cf. G. Sass [1], p. 69.

εὐαγγελίζεσθαι (I Cor. 1:17). For such preaching a sending forth is required: πῶς δὲ κηρύξωσιν ἐὰν μὴ ἀποσταλῶσιν (Rom. 10:15). It is the apostle who declares: Ὑπὲρ Χριστοῦ οὖν πρεσβεύομεν ὡς τοῦ θεοῦ παρακαλοῦντος δι' ἡμῶν· δεόμεθα ὑπὲρ Χριστοῦ, καταλλάγητε τῷ θεῷ (II Cor. 5:20). Paul is an ἐθνῶν ἀπόστολος (Rom. 11:13; Gal. 2:8), and this means that through his preaching among the heathen the ὑπακοὴ πίστεως (Rom. 1:5) is to be accomplished.[15]

Now all this is so obvious that it would be superfluous to cite further passages. The choice of the words ἀπόστολος and ἀποστέλλειν adequately shows that the "sending forth," the mission, was the special assignment of the apostle.

However, this by no means fully describes the nature of the apostolic office. Apostles are indeed always missionaries, but not all missionaries are also apostles. Timothy (Rom. 16:21; I Cor. 16:10; II Cor. 1:19) and Titus (II Cor. 2:13; Gal. 2:1-2) are associates in the mission work with Paul, but are not apostles.[16] Apollos is a missionary completely independent of Paul (I Cor. 3:3 ff.; 4:6; 16:12), but apparently not an apostle. Paul testifies to the Thessalonians that from them ὁ λόγος τοῦ κυρίου has sounded forth in Macedonia and Achaia (I Thess. 1:8), but this missionary service performed by the Thessalonians certainly was not done by them in direct apostolic authority. The foundation of the congregation in Rome, to take a further example, may also have been laid without a regular apostolic mission.

With this collection of evidence, however, the problematic of the concept of apostle has already appeared. There were missionaries who were apostles, and there were others who could not bear, or did not bear, this designation.[17] This did not mean that any significant distinction is to be established between the task of the apostles and that of the nonapostolic missionaries, nor did it mean that the apostle generally exhibited a more extensive or more successful activity than did the other missionaries; for such a noteworthy figure of early Christianity as for example Apollos[18] was in his missionary activity doubtless more significant than the numerous unknown

---

[15] In various ways Paul emphasizes the fact that he is a missionary to the *Gentiles*. However, this apparently is not a characteristic mark of the apostolate as such; for Paul knows that Peter is an apostle to the *Jews* (Gal. 2:8-9). D. Georgi (*op. cit.*, p. 41) oddly asserts that Paul is, in his own opinion, the *only* apostle to the Gentiles. On the contrary, Paul never asserts this.

[16] Cf. K. H. Rengstorf [1], p. 423.

[17] "εὐαγγελιστής" is, no less than "ἀπόστολος," a special term in primitive Christianity for a missionary; see TDNT, II, 736-37, and below, p. 226.

[18] Acts 18:24; 19:1; I Cor. 1:12; 3:4 ff., 22; 4:6; 16:12; (Titus 3:13).

apostles, some of whose names have been preserved for us merely by accident.[19]

What is the special distinguishing mark of that missionary who bears the official designation of ἀπόστολος?

3. The apostle receives his commission and charisma οὐκ ἀπ' ἀνθρώπων οὐδὲ δι' ἀνθρώπου ἀλλὰ διὰ 'Ιησοῦ Χριστοῦ καὶ θεοῦ πατρὸς τοῦ ἐγείραντος αὐτὸν ἐκ νεκρῶν (Gal. 1:1). Marcion omits καὶ θεοῦ πατρός, apparently as a result of the correct observation that Paul usually traced the call to apostleship back solely to Christ. But with the reference to God in Gal. 1:1, Paul intends to say nothing other than that which is clearly expressed in the opening of both Corinthian letters: ἀπόστολος 'Ιησοῦ Χριστοῦ διὰ θελήματος θεοῦ (cf. Eph. 1:1; Col. 1:1; II Tim. 1:1); the call to become an apostle of Christ comes in conformity to the will of God (Gal. 1:15), whose gospel the apostle is, indeed, to proclaim (Rom. 1:1; Gal. 1:16; Rom. 15:16).[20] Yet the placing of Christ and God on the same footing in Gal. 1:1 indicates that Paul apparently had no interest in restricting the call particularly to Christ. The grounding of apostleship upon the call from Christ therefore does not rest upon certain theological requirements, but is simply determined by the event of the call itself or by Paul's traditional understanding of it.

That it is Christ who calls is witnessed to in numerous passages. In Rom. 1:4-5 Paul speaks of Jesus Christ δι' οὗ ἐλάβομεν χάριν καὶ ἀποστολήν. He speaks of himself as (κλητὸς) ἀπόστολος 'Ιησοῦ Χριστοῦ in I Cor. 1:1; II Cor. 1:1; I Thess. 2:7; cf. Eph. 1:1; Col. 1:1; I Tim. 1:1; II Tim. 1:1; Titus 1:1. The title is employed polemically in II Cor. 11:13. In I Cor. 1:17 Paul declares: ἀπέστειλέν με Χριστὸς . . . εὐαγγελίζεσθαι. In I Cor. 9:1 he defends his apostleship with the argument, οὐχὶ 'Ιησοῦν τὸν κύριον ἡμῶν ἑόρακα? According to Gal. 1:15-16 God is the source of the calling through Christ; it pleased him ἀποκαλύψαι τὸν υἱὸν αὐτοῦ ἐν ἐμοί, ἵνα εὐαγγελίζωμαι αὐτὸν ἐν τοῖς ἔθνεσιν; and since for Paul to be entrusted with the gospel is the same as to receive the apostleship,[21] Gal. 1:12 is relevant here: οὐδὲ γὰρ ἐγὼ παρὰ ἀνθρώπου παρέλαβον αὐτὸ οὔτε ἐδιδάχθην, ἀλλὰ δι' ἀποκαλύψεως 'Ιησοῦ Χριστοῦ. Likewise in I Cor. 15:7-8, where Paul adduces the "vocational vision" of the whole apostolic company (τοῖς ἀποστόλοις πᾶσιν) as proof of the resurrection of Jesus, the calling by Christ is presupposed as obvious, and Paul calls himself the ἐλάχιστον τῶν ἀποστόλων, to whom Christ appeared ὡσπερεὶ τῷ ἐκτρώματι.

---

[19] Rom. 16:7.
[20] Cf. H. Schlier, op. cit., p. 4.
[21] See Gal. 2:7-8, and below, pp. 30 ff.

This last passage shows, as do the Galatian passages, the still noteworthy fact that the calling of the apostle obviously comes from the *exalted* Christ.[22] For Paul there exists no connection of any kind between the "historical Jesus" and the apostolate.[23] The *resurrected* One appeared to *all* the apostles at the time of their call (I Cor. 15:7 ff.).

Paul does not give any information about the "how" of the calling through Christ. In view of this lack, one must guard against the tendency either uncritically or critically to draw on the reports of the book of Acts[24] as a substitute for such direct information. It may be that certain recollections about the context of Paul's calling, for example with regard to the place and time of the event, have been deposited in the accounts in Acts; the historicity of the core of the narrative cannot be made out as likely.[25] Every attempt to offer information about this core remains fantasy, no matter whether one builds his fantasy historically, source-critically, or psychologically.[26]

But also in connection with the remarks which Paul makes about his call any set formulations and fixed phrases are lacking which might allow the deduction that a firm tradition existed for telling in detail the commissioning of an apostle by Christ. Precisely in connection with the apostolate such fixed phrases are often employed, but here they are completely lacking.[27]

Present are only some technical terms which Paul uses in the description of the process of his call. In Gal. 1:12 it is ἀποκάλυψις, in Gal. 1:16 ἀποκαλύπτειν. The active ὁράω appears in I Cor. 9:1, and corresponding to it the passive ὤφθην in I Cor. 15:7. This latter expression appears to have been, for Paul, the broader concept and to have designated *every* appearance of the resurrected One. In I Cor. 15:5-8 it appears four times, among them the primitive-church formula of v. 5. The concept ἀποκάλυψις on the other hand may have been more closely connected with the apostolate, indeed, as a *terminus technicus;* for in Gal. 1:12 and 16, ἀποκαλύπτειν apparently describes the calling to apostleship and signifies therefore something other than the impartation of a hidden knowledge or of an unknown decree, as Paul ordinarily used the concept.

---

[22] G. Sass [1], p. 34.

[23] *Contra* Acts 1:21-22. That the book of Acts may not be employed to present the Pauline concept of the apostle probably no longer requires any special demonstration.

[24] Acts 9:1-9; 22:3-16; 26:9-20.

[25] Cf. E. Haenchen, *op. cit.,* p. 284; *ibid.,* in ZThK (1955), pp. 210 ff.

[26] W. Grundmann, *op. cit.,* p. 111, is of the opinion that in II Cor. 4:6 Paul is also thinking of the Damascus vision. This is not to be ruled out entirely. In any case he is correct in the statement that the conversion of Paul was more an inward event than an outward one, such as the book of Acts portrays.

[27] See pp. 36, 57.

More than this certainly cannot be inferred from the brief remarks of Paul; yet there remains the striking fact that even where in his epistles to Galatia and Corinth Paul desperately contends for the recognition of his apostleship and does not spare with his arguments (*vide infra*), he does not make even the slightest attempt to support the bold assertion of his call by any more precise portrayal of the event of the call itself. What could have hindered him from saying more here? Was he *unable* to say anything more precise, or was he simply *unwilling?*

The fact that Paul did not separate or even distinguish between the calling to the apostolic office and the visionary "revelation of Jesus Christ" has been rightly established by many investigators.[28] I Cor. 15:8-9 shows this clearly enough. While G. Sass ([1], p. 37) acknowledges this with reference to the person of Paul, he goes on, inconsistently and without foundation, to say, "Fundamentally, according to his [Paul's] opinion, manifestation and calling appear not to be identical" (*ibid.*). In this, H. v. Campenhausen ([1], p. 113) concurs.[29] But according to I Cor. 15:7 *all* the apostles have seen the Lord (*vide infra*, pp. 74 ff.). Further, I Cor. 9:1 ff. presupposes that every apostle is a witness to the resurrection.[30] Thus the fact that Paul has seen the Lord brings to his apostolic rank nothing special or extraordinary, as H. v. Campenhausen ([1], p. 113, n. 2) asserts, but is constitutive for this rank. Otherwise the allusion to the resurrection appearance would have no meaning in a context such as I Cor. 9:1 ff., where the issue is the validity of his claim to apostleship.[31] Finally, Gal. 1–2 also shows that an ἀποκάλυψις Ἰησοῦ Χριστοῦ constitutes the apostolic office; for with reference to such "revelation" Paul justifies his claim to apostleship.

One must ask after all with what right and in what sense one can speak, with reference to Paul, of an actual *calling* apart from the "manifestation of Christ." In Rom. 1:1 and I Cor. 1:1 [32] Paul indeed calls himself κλητὸς ἀπόστολος, but Rom. 1:6-7 (ἐν οἷς ἐστε καὶ ὑμεῖς κλητοὶ Ἰησοῦ

---

[28] G. Sass [1], p. 37; H. Schlier, *op. cit.*, p. 26, n. 4; J. C. Margot, *op. cit.*, pp. 219-20.

[29] Also—without giving his own reasons—G. Klein, *op. cit.*, p. 44, n. 179. In any case, the correct principle that not all witnesses to the resurrection also became apostles (*vide infra*), does not justify Klein's conclusion that not all the apostles had to be witnesses to the resurrection.

[30] Cf. H. Mosbech [1], p. 170. In I Cor. 9:1 ff. Paul refutes two charges of his (Gnostic) opponents: (1) that he was not ἐλεύθερος, and (2) that he was not an apostle, He goes into this second charge more in detail and offers a double justification of his apostolic rights: by means of a reference to his vision of Christ, and by means of an appeal to the success of his labors (*vide infra*, pp. 33 ff.). Over against this, G. Klein's comments on I Cor. 9:1 ff. (*op. cit.*, p. 44, n. 179) are in error.

[31] "It is clear that the third and fourth assertions are intended to attest to the second" (A. v. Harnack [1], I, 322, n. 2).

[32] Here, however, not certainly attested.

Χριστοῦ) shows that in these two passages one may not understand κλητός too exclusively as a technical designation for the event of an apostolic call. Fundamentally Paul never speaks of such an event. He is indeed always conscious of having received the office from Christ (Rom. 1:5; Gal. 1:1), but when he wishes to tell of the calling, he only refers to the ἀποκάλυψις Ἰησοῦ Χριστοῦ or the ὅρασις κυρίου. When it pleased God ἀποκαλύψαι τὸν υἱὸν αὐτοῦ ἐν ἐμοί, ἵνα εὐαγγελίζωμαι αὐτὸν ἐν τοῖς ἔθνεσιν, εὐθέως . . . ἀπῆλθον εἰς Ἀραβίαν (Gal. 1:15 ff.; cf. I Cor. 9:1). One must therefore guard against too close a comparison of the calling of Paul for example with that of Jeremiah, with whom some like to compare Paul.[33] In Gal. 1:15, as is well known, Paul plays upon Jer. 1:5 [34]; but it is all the more noteworthy that the decisive thing in the call visions in the Old Testament (and in the Synoptics)[35]—the command of sending one forth—is completely lacking in Paul.[36] While in the Old Testament the vision is supposed only to make possible the decisive act of sending forth, which is then explicitly reported,[37] Paul knows only of the vision itself, upon which he directly bases his service. This fact is so extraordinary and unprecedented that it is hardly adequately explained by the words of G. Sass: "When God reveals His Son to him [Paul], the one born to death, the persecutor of the churches, what other meaning can that have than that the intensity of opposition is to be changed, and must be changed, into a positive readiness now to work *for* this Son" ([1], p. 37). At any rate, Paul himself has nowhere said any such thing.

The blending together of manifestation and calling becomes still more noteworthy when one considers that in fact by no means did all those who had seen the resurrected One also become apostles (cf. I Cor. 15:5 ff.). Wherein then lies the actual impetus to apostleship among the witnesses to the resurrection? Karl Holl ([1], p. 930) calls for a "commission formally issued by Christ." He sharply criticizes (*ibid.*, p. 929) Wellhausen, who had asserted that "in the case of the apostles, vision and calling come . . . together,"[38] because in fact the more than five hundred brethren of I Cor. 15:6 still had not become apostles. But to the degree that this last assertion is correct, one is unable with the postulate that a special calling must have

[33] See K. H. Rengstorf [1], pp. 439 ff.; J. Wellhausen, NGG (1907), p. 3.
[34] Cf. also I Cor. 9:16 with Jer. 20:9.
[35] Mark 6:7 ff.; Matt. 10:1, 5 ff.; 28:18 ff.; Luke 9:1-5.
[36] In this connection I Cor. 9:16-17 is worthy of note. It is striking that in this passage, in which Paul refers to the compulsion which stands back of his εὐαγγελίζεσθαι, any reference to a vocational commandment is lacking. The ἀνάγκη apparently consists in an inner necessity, similar to that of Jer. 20:9.
[37] E.g., Isa. 6:8 ff.; Jer. 1:4 ff.; Ezek. 2–3; Amos 7:15.
[38] NGG (1907), p. 3.

occurred, to avoid the fact that Paul himself says nothing of it, but knows himself only to have been called through the manifestation and to have been separated from his mother's womb.

It necessarily follows from this unity of the vision of the resurrected One and the calling to apostleship that one can receive the office of apostle at no other point of time than at that of the manifestation. We shall have to return to this problem at a later point.

This, then, distinguishes the apostle in every case from the other missionaries of primitive Christianity: The apostle is called to his missionary service by the exalted Lord through an ἀποκάλυψις. This special character of the apostolate, which at least makes understandable the use of a special term, even though it does not explain it, does not however establish a special *function* of the apostle. The distinctive form of the calling does not lead the apostle into any other kind of service than that of every other primitive Christian missionary. By no means, then, may one see the special task of the apostle in the fact that he is a witness of the resurrection.[39] Paul can naturally refer to the apostles as witnesses of the resurrection, as indeed he does in I Cor. 15:7-8, where it is his concern to make as complete a list of witnesses as possible. But precisely this list shows that it did not require the apostles for testimony to the resurrection of Christ; and how little it belonged to the *essence* of the apostolate to be active in such witnessing service is shown by the fact that outside I Cor. 15 Paul nowhere combines the fact of the resurrection and the apostolic office, although he does speak of them both quite often. Even in I Cor. 15 the message of the resurrection is not proclaimed as strictly an *apostolic* message. To be sure an apostle has brought it to Corinth (I Cor. 15:1), and it is naturally proclaimed by all apostles (I Cor. 15:11), but for the rest, it is quite "nonapostolic" that Χριστὸς κηρύσσεται ὅτι ἐκ νεκρῶν ἐγήγερται (I Cor. 15:12), and when Paul says with respect to the preaching of the resurrection, "Therefore whether it was I or they, *so* we preach and *so* you have believed" (I Cor. 15:11), the "they" embraces apostles and nonapostles without distinction. The resurrected Lord calls the apostle and for this reason testifies for him. This is characteristic for the apostolate. Paul does not however conversely represent the apostle as resurrection witness. The apostle proclaims the message of the resurrection of Jesus and the general resurrection of the dead which is thereby introduced, but he does this with an authority that is not at all different from that of every other proclaimer.[40]

[39] Thus K. H. Rengstorf [1], pp. 430-31; Acts 1:22; 2:32; 3:15; 4:33; 5:32; 10:41; 13:31.
[40] On the whole preceding section, cf. P. Gaechter, *op. cit.*, pp. 338-450, who seeks to show that Paul according to his own conviction was firmly rooted in the tradition which

Still more misleading than the assertion that the apostle is *the* witness to the resurrection appears the other assertion that Christ has his word to come to his community in general only through apostles. When E. Güttgemanns, who with an appeal to E. Lohmeyer advocates this interpretation ([1], pp. 324 ff.), interprets Rom. 10:14-17 in passing to mean that "faith is elicited only by apostolic preaching" (p. 325), it must be objected that in this passage it is said of preaching in general and not of preaching of apostles in particular that it establishes faith. And how Güttgemanns can draw the conclusion, from the undoubted fact that *Paul's* communities were founded by an apostle, that in Paul's opinion *all* Christians were converted by apostles remains incomprehensible. The alternative, that Christ either works through apostles or else bypasses preaching, is an arbitrary one (p. 326, n. 30). I Cor. 15:1 ff., for example, shows clearly how little the fundamental Christian preaching for Paul necessarily proceeds from apostles; here, as often in Paul, other proclaimers stand *alongside* the apostles, and in the numerous instances in which Paul refers to traditions, he never reflects upon their apostolicity. The "brothers of the Lord" and Peter (I Cor. 9:5) certainly do not preach with any less authority than the apostles named along with them, and nowhere does Paul make the charge against the false teachers in his congregations that they are neither apostles nor sent by apostles. Thus one may not reverse the correct principle that an apostle always preaches the gospel into the affirmation that the true gospel is always of apostolic origin. Even though already in the second Christian generation the apostolate was presented in this way (Luke; Eph.), still one may not overlook the fact that such a concept of the apostle is never found in Paul. This must also be said *contra* J. Roloff (*op. cit.,* pp. 83 ff.), who attaches to one another the apostolate and the gospel as well as the apostolate and the church exclusively, which would not be possible in a somewhat complete and appropriate interpretation of the Pauline texts.

Only in Gal. 1:17 ff. does Paul seem to assume that the fundamental ecclesiastical tradition as such represents an originally *apostolic* tradition. This idea however is not found elsewhere in Paul and, as is yet to be shown, may have been prompted by the peculiar apologetic situation of Gal. 1:17 ff. Possibly in it there is disclosed an already given concept of the apostolic which Paul does not elsewhere utilize. In this connection we ought to note W. Kramer's sufficiently successful proof that the concept and idea of the apostle on the one hand, and the basic concepts of the primitive Christian proclamation of the gospel (πίστις/πιστεύειν; κήρυγμα/κηρύσσειν;

---

came from Peter and the twelve. As much as Gaechter's individual observations deserve attention, a refutation would not be rewarding.

εὐαγγέλιον/εὐαγγελίζεσθαι; the title "Christ" and the pre-Pauline formulas of faith of Hellenistic Jewish Christian origin) on the other hand, were not originally connected. That it was Paul who first made this connection, as Kramer presumes, indeed appears to me to be very questionable, but he may be altogether correct in his statement that the Hellenistic Jewish Christian *kerygma*, to which even Paul undoubtedly owes the foundation of his preaching, was not propounded as *apostolic* kerygma. One then can easily understand that Paul generally can in no way characterize the preaching of the gospel exclusively as apostolic.

4. It has already been shown[41] that for Paul the call to become an apostle (and thus the manifestation of Christ) is to be equated with the reception of the message. Calling and conversion are consequently a single event.[42] This point emerges most clearly in the Galatian epistle. There can be no doubt that in Gal. 1:1, 11-12, and 15-16 Paul is speaking of the selfsame event, of the one fundamental ἀποκάλυψις ᾽Ιησοῦ Χριστοῦ. While according to Gal. 1:1 Paul was called to be an apostle through this revelation, according to Gal. 1:11-12 he received through this revelation τὸ εὐαγγέλιον τὸ εὐαγγελισθὲν ὑπ᾽ ἐμοῦ (Gal. 1:11). Gal. 1:16 then combines the two, gospel and apostleship: ἵνα εὐαγγελίζωμαι αὐτὸν ἐν τοῖς ἔθνεσιν. In Gal. 2:7-8 gospel and apostleship are also similarly interchangeable: ἰδόντες ὅτι πεπίστευμαι τὸ εὐαγγέλιον τῆς ἀκροβυστίας καθὼς Πέτρος τῆς περιτομῆς, ὁ γὰρ ἐνεργήσας Πέτρῳ εἰς ἀποστολὴν τῆς περιτομῆς ἐνήργησεν καὶ ἐμοὶ εἰς τὰ ἔθνη, an argument which presupposes that the reception of the message and that of the office of messenger coincide.

From this perspective it must be regarded as most unlikely that "a canon of the Lord's sayings as well as probably also a stock of Jesus narratives" were "common to all apostles" (J. Roloff, *op. cit.*, p. 92), and in view of the Pauline literature it proves to be an untenable assertion which Roloff does not even document but only repeats with the curious assertion that in Paul the gospel literature *apparently* recedes thus noticeably into the background (*op. cit.*, p. 94). If such an apostolic kerygma is altogether "based on the eye-witness qualification of the apostles" (*op. cit.*, p. 93), one would like to know from Roloff to what extent then Paul was an eye-witness of the Jesus narratives and the Jesus logia. Nowhere does Paul indicate even the slightest connection between the apostolate and the historical Jesus.

[41] P. 24.
[42] Cf. M. Dibelius, *Botschaft und Geschichte*, II, 158. E. Haenchen (NTS, VII [1961], 187) correctly writes: "Neither Paul himself nor the book of Acts speaks of his 'conversion,'" but only of the call.

Thus it appears also to be a characteristic of the apostolate that with the ἀποκάλυψις Ἰησοῦ Χριστοῦ both are given: the message and the office. This is by no means to be taken as a matter of course. Just as likely, indeed even likelier, would be the supposition that the commissioning with the office of apostle could follow not only in the moment of conversion but at any and every time.[43] But for the apostle apparently three occurrences are indissolubly bound together, and are in fact the same event: the manifestation of Christ, the reception of the gospel, which corresponds to conversion, and the call to the apostolic office.[44]

5. From this follows what in Gal. 1:11-12 is explicitly affirmed, that Paul has received his gospel, no less than his office, directly from Jesus Christ. H. Schlier[45] appropriately remarks: "The gospel which is preached by Paul is for this reason not a 'human' one, because it has its origin in the event of the total and direct disclosure of Jesus Christ himself to the apostle, an event which anticipated the eschatological disclosure, and was not granted to him in the form of a tradition which is appropriated through instruction." It therefore belongs to the nature of the apostolate that the apostle is the *direct* mediator between Christ and the congregation.[46] From this unique self-understanding we must understand such passages, as, for example, I Cor. 11:23 [47]: Ἐγὼ γὰρ παρέλαβον ἀπὸ τοῦ κυρίου, ὃ καὶ παρέδωκα ὑμῖν; II Cor. 5:20: Ὑπὲρ Χριστοῦ οὖν πρεσβεύομεν ὡς τοῦ θεοῦ παρακαλοῦντος δι' ἡμῶν; perhaps II Cor. 4:6: ὁ θεὸς . . . ἔλαμψεν ἐν ταῖς καρδίαις ἡμῶν πρὸς φωτισμὸν τῆς γνώσεως τῆς δόξης τοῦ θεοῦ ἐν προσώπῳ Χριστοῦ; in any case also the expression τὸ εὐαγγέλιόν μου in Rom. 2:16; 16:25; I Thess. 1:5; cf. II Tim. 2:8.

Paul can even equate the gospel revealed to him with the living Christ himself. Gal. 1:16: ἀποκαλύψαι τὸν υἱὸν αὐτοῦ ἐν ἐμοί, ἵνα εὐαγγελίζωμαι αὐτὸν ἐν τοῖς ἔθνεσιν; that is, Paul proclaims the Christ revealed to him as the gospel. Likewise Gal. 1:6: The Galatians have turned from Christ to another gospel; thus Christ is himself the revealed gospel. In this connection belong also the numerous passages in which Paul joins to the verbs of proclamation as object "Christ." [48] This usage shows that in the ἀποκάλυψις Ἰησοῦ Χριστοῦ object and subject are identical: Christ reveals, and what he reveals is nothing other than himself. The genitive Ἰησοῦ Χριστοῦ can

[43] Thus, e.g., A. Ehrhardt (StudTheol, XII [1958], 77) conceives it, when he writes: "His [sc. Paul's] apostleship was confirmed upon him in the course of his ministry."

[44] Cf. H. v. Campenhausen [1], p. 112.

[45] H. Schlier, *op. cit.*, p. 20.

[46] Cf. I Cor. 11:1.

[47] On the idea of tradition in this passage, see p. 210, n. 486.

[48] See H. Schlier, *op. cit.*, pp. 13-14.

hardly be identified more precisely as either objective or subjective genitive.[49]

On the other hand, one notes that Paul constantly makes use with unconstrained obviousness of various traditions from the community, before him and contemporary with him, and even—as for example in I Cor. 15:1 ff.—imparts the gospel to the community explicitly as that which he also has received from the tradition. Thus in general he places no special value on the possibility, which is sketched in his concept of the apostle, of being able as an apostle to make the claim to be a direct recipient of revelation. Only in Galatians does he expressly appeal to this aspect of the apostolic self-understanding, and this in fact is obviously because the stout contesting of his gospel provoked such an appeal. When some time later, when he has to defend himself in II Cor. against no less vigorous attacks on his message and his apostleship, he does not again seize upon this argument used in Galatians but defends himself differently, one might conclude that it is not the direct imparting of the revelation to the apostle as such but the appeal to it in order to defend the truth of his words that has in the meantime become suspect for him.

6. a) The attacks which the opponents of Paul in Galatia and Corinth direct against his claim to be an apostle compel Paul to make a defense of his apostleship. It is interesting to observe the arguments of his apology. The first step is always to declare that he has been called by Christ himself to this service. This is true in the Galatian letter, which is content with this argument, as well as in the Corinthian letters, which discuss the problem far more comprehensively, in epistolary address and refutation.

Even in the Galatian letter, however, it was evident that to establish the point thus would not suffice: Paul is able indeed to assert the decisive fact of the unique call, but not to prove it—and this all the less because, strangely, he cannot underscore (cf. pp. 25-26) his assertion with an account of his call as is done in Acts 22:1 ff. He therefore attempts, through the adducing of various pieces of peripheral evidence, to verify his assertion which is found in Gal. 1:1, 11-12, and 15-16. The consistent argument of Gal. 1:8-9 should be convincing. After that Paul points to his honesty as δοῦλος Χριστοῦ, which forbids him to seek by means of untruthfulness to persuade men (or God), or to speak for the sake of pleasing men (Gal. 1:10). Further, the fact, well-known to the Galatians, that Paul had been a very zealous persecutor of the church of Christ and had been suddenly converted

---

[49] One may, to be sure, classify the uses: the *formula* ἀποκάλυψις ᾽Ιησοῦ Χριστοῦ apparently speaks of the revelation in which Jesus Christ is revealed; Paul uses it to designate the revelation which Jesus Christ allotted to him. The crucial point is that therewith he does not rule out the duality of meaning but—intentionally or unconsciously—includes it.

is a proof of the nonhuman origin of this conversion (= calling) (Gal. 1:13 ff., 22 ff.). Still more explicitly Paul adduces the negative proof: After his calling he had formed no connection at all with those who would have been able to communicate the gospel to him; he must therefore have received it from Christ himself (Gal. 1:16-24). In the later encounters with the "original" apostles he not only preserved the independence of his apostleship (Gal. 2:1-5), but the "pillars" in Jerusalem even confirmed to him expressly that his apostleship was to be esteemed no differently from that of Peter (Gal. 2:6-10), a fact to which the episode in Antioch also bears eloquent witness (Gal. 2:11 ff.).

In the Galatian letter, with the reference to the calling by Christ which establishes his apostleship, Paul apparently uses the traditional proof for the claim to apostleship; in the Corinthian letters also this motif stands at the beginning of his apology (*vide infra*). At the same time however this argument involves him in the unique difficulty of having to cite a means of proof which itself in turn demands proof, and yet such proof is simply not available to him.[50] These facts which Paul enumerates in order to make evident his calling by Christ may for us have their convincing power—whoever basically contested Paul's trustworthiness, as did the disputants of his apostolic rights in Galatia and Corinth, will not have let himself be influenced by them. Why did Paul not refrain from using this questionable proof? Apparently none other was at his disposal. Then, however, it is strange that the "apostolic tradition" could offer him only a kind of proof citation which at least to *him* was unsatisfactory.[51]

b) But Paul appears to have had another proof available to him, one of which he made abundant use in the Corinthian letters. In I Cor. 9:1-3 he defends himself against those who accuse him: ἡ ἐμὴ ἀπολογία τοῖς ἐμὲ ἀνακρίνουσίν ἐστιν αὕτη (9:3).[52] The accusation charges that Paul is not an apostle.[53] The accused counters: οὐχὶ Ἰησοῦν τὸν κύριον ἡμῶν ἑόρακα? This is the traditional citation of proof explicitly attempted in Gal. 1-2:

[50] See H. Schlier, *op. cit.,* p. 18; E. Haupt, *op. cit.,* p. 132.

[51] From the fact that Paul, who wishes to prove his apostolic rights with a reference to his having been called by Christ, gives no particulars as to the course of events in the call, we probably may conclude that such particulars were not at his disposal. Otherwise why should he have remained silent? Naturally they would not have saved the proof, but this awareness did not restrain him from the use of other statements in his attempt at proof. Moreover, he had no unconquerable reservations requiring him to keep silent about supersensual experiences and encounters with the exalted Lord, as, e.g., II Cor. 12:1-10 shows. Apparently the experience of the call was lacking any vividness.

[52] That this verse is related to the preceding, in spite of the incorrect separation in Nestle and the uncertainty of the commentators, is clear from the fact that in the following verses no charges of any kind against Paul are mentioned.

[53] Cf. p. 26, n. 30.

I am an apostle, for I have seen Christ. Now here, to be sure, this proof is brought forward in almost exaggerated brevity. Nothing is said of "calling" or "receiving" or "revealing"; only the fact of a vision of Christ is established. Then, apparently conscious of the inadequacy of such argumentation, he passes over at once to a new proof: οὐ τὸ ἔργον μου ὑμεῖς ἐστε ἐν κυρίῳ; εἰ ἄλλοις οὐκ εἰμὶ ἀπόστολος, ἀλλά γε ὑμῖν εἰμί. ἡ γὰρ σφραγίς μου τῆς ἀποστολῆς ὑμεῖς ἐστε ἐν κυρίῳ. In three short sentences the point is made three times that Paul, sent to the Corinthians and received by them, has preached the gospel to them with success. Thereby, at least for the Corinthians, the apostolic claim of Paul is confirmed—sealed, as Paul says in a traditional image[54]—even if no advance σημεῖον legitimized the apostle. The Lord himself [55] has set forth Paul as a called messenger when he blessed his message. This "dialectical" method of proof is probably originally Pauline: the gospel is verified by faith, the messenger legitimized by his being accepted.[56]

This basic thought especially dominates the conflict over apostleship in II Cor.[57] One who observes that the related sections II Cor. 2:14–6:13 and 10–13, which are studded with polemic and apology, were called forth almost exclusively by the attacks upon Paul's apostolic rights,[58] encounters in these sections the afore-mentioned argument step by step: Christ leads about his apostle with him in the triumphant procession of the gospel (2:14-17)[59]; the congregation in Corinth is itself the epistle of Christ, which commends Paul before all men as an apostle (3:1-3); Paul has his authority from God (3:4 ff.), and through proclamation, in such authority unintimidated, he commends himself before men and before God (4:1-2), who himself illumines men through this proclamation (4:3-6); Paul hopes to be "evident" to the Corinthians as an apostle by the fact that he performs the solemn ministry of the proclamation (5:11-15)[60]; the apostle is a messenger in Christ's stead (5:18 ff.), and is commended as such in

[54] Cf. H. Lietzmann in HNT, IX (4th ed., 1949), on I Cor. 9:2.

[55] Note the repeated ἐν κυρίῳ (I Cor. 9:1 and 2).

[56] Cf. E. Haupt, op. cit., pp. 132 ff.; H. v. Campenhausen [4], pp. 32 ff. Naturally I do not mean to assert, as J. Roloff (op. cit., p. 54) thinks, that in this line of argument Paul ignores the calling by the resurrected One. Of course I would understand dialectically what Roloff, by objectivizing, pulls apart: "The attestation of the resurrection" is not "presupposed" as a "point of departure"; rather the resurrected One is witnessed to *in* the faith-forming preaching of the apostle.

[57] Cf. E. Käsemann [2], pp. 59 ff.

[58] Cf. R. Bultmann, *Exegetische Probleme des Zweiten Korintherbriefes* (Uppsala, 1947), p. 13. H. Lietzmann, HNT on II Cor. 2:14-17.

[59] Cf. W. G. Kümmel in Lietzmann, HNT, IX on p. 108, l. 20.

[60] On the interpretation of this passage, cf. Bultmann, op. cit. (see n. 58, above), pp. 12 ff.; and my *Die Gnosis in Korinth* (2nd ed., 1965) pp. 177 ff.

that he gives no offense which could make his message untrustworthy (6: 1 ff.); the standard, appointed by God, by which the Corinthians are to measure the apostleship of Paul, is that Paul has come to Corinth in the gospel of Christ (10:12-18); and so on.

I said above that it *appears* that with this argument Paul has in hand still another means of proof for his apostleship in addition to that inadequate reference to his (unprovable) call. In fact, the argument just considered is only an apparent proof for the claim of Paul to apostleship. Not because this dialectical adducing of proof in the nature of things cannot convince the unbeliever; Paul indeed speaks especially to the believing community, which lives in the faith that is self-confirming. Rather because Paul indeed can thereby substantiate before the community the truth of his message and the genuineness of his missionary service, but is not able in particular to establish his right to be called an *apostle*. The proof which is particularly brought forward in II Cor. can be taken over unaltered by *every* missionary. Paul can hardly have failed to see this. It is certainly no accident that in the corresponding sections of II Cor. the concept of "apostle" is lacking and is replaced by general paraphrases: φανεροῦν τὴν ὀσμὴν τῆς γνώσεως τοῦ Χριστοῦ (2:14); λαλοῦμεν ἐν Χριστῷ (2:17); ἐπιστολὴ Χριστοῦ διακονηθεῖσα ὑφ' ὑμῶν (3:3); τῇ φανερώσει τῆς ἀληθείας συνιστάνομεν ἑαυτούς (4:2); κηρύσσομεν (4:5); ἀνθρώπους πείθομεν (5:11); πρεσβεύομεν (5:20); παρακαλοῦμεν (6:1), and so on. Thus in the decisive conflict over his apostleship Paul places himself in the midst of all the other messengers of the gospel. To him it is sufficient to be recognized as a witness to the truth. The fact that he is an *apostle* who has been called by Christ himself becomes, by comparison, a matter of indifference, and in fact the corresponding assertion apparently has, even in the Galatian letter, only the purpose of substantiating the message as such, not of attesting the messenger's preferential place.

Thus Paul himself confirms the evidence which we have already seen that an apostle possesses no function which *only he* of all the primitive Christian missionaries can exercise. In spite of his well-known special position which is grounded in the form of his call, his service is the same as that performed by the other missionaries who are not called apostles.

The concluding point, that the proof adduced in this section cannot possibly have been joined originally with the apostolate, demands no more special proof after what has been said.

c) To be sure, we still have not exhausted the number of arguments which Paul brings forth for the defense of his office. The ψευδαπόστολοι in Corinth (II Cor. 11:13) measure Paul by the standards of *their* apostolic

35

consciousness and, in view of the critical situation in the Corinthian congregation, compel him against his will to accept these Corinthian standards and to demonstrate that he also fulfills the conditions which are set for an apostle in *Corinth*. Thus comes about his foolish self-praise, the ἀφροσύνη which Paul never tires of pointing out (II Cor. 11:1, 16 ff., 21; 12:1, 11). Only: ὑμεῖς με ἠναγκάσατε . . . ἐπεὶ πολλοὶ καυχῶνται κατὰ τὴν σάρκα, κἀγὼ καυχήσομαι (II Cor. 12:11; 11:18).

The totality of reproaches cast upon Paul in Corinth are calculated to contest his claim to the apostolic office; but it is questionable whether with all his counterarguments Paul either can or wishes to assure his apostleship. If for example one shows that Paul is a σαρκικός (II Cor. 10:2), then he certainly could no longer be considered an apostle; but does the demonstration of Paul that in truth he is a πνευματικός show the Corinthian teachers of error the justification of his apostolic claims? Or: Paul will certainly lose his apostolic authority if he is not "of Christ" (II Cor. 10:7); but does he gain it back in the eyes of his opponents by showing that he is indeed τοῦ Χριστοῦ?

The facts of the case are unmistakable in II Cor. 12:11-12, where Paul takes up a *special* argument for his claim to apostleship: οὐδὲν γὰρ ὑστέρησα τῶν ὑπερλίαν ἀποστόλων, εἰ καὶ οὐδέν εἰμι. τὰ μὲν σημεῖα τοῦ ἀποστόλου κατειργάσθη ἐν ὑμῖν ἐν πάσῃ ὑπομονῇ, σημείοις τε καὶ τέρασιν καὶ δυνάμεσιν. There are then definite signs which signify an apostle. This authentication, to which Paul finds himself compelled to appeal, appears elsewhere to have been quite widespread. In any case a glance at Rom. 15:19; Heb. 2:4; II Thess. 2:9; Acts 2:22, and other passages shows that a stereotyped formula existed for the enumeration of the σημεῖα τοῦ ἀποστόλου,[61] which later found a varied application. Paul is content with merely citing the formula. This is noteworthy. Thus to him at least no weight is placed upon confirming his claim to apostleship through σημεῖα τε καὶ τέρατα καὶ δυνάμεις. It is possible that he does not even connect with this formula —at least in connection with apostleship—any further concrete conception. At any rate, it is hardly possible for us to answer with certainty the question as to wherein, for Paul, the "signs and wonders and mighty acts" consist.[62]

To think about miracles such as the book of Acts reports[63] concerning the apostles appears to me to be a mistake.[64] Apart from this formula, the

---

[61] The formula has its origins in the Old Testament (cf., e.g., Deut. 7:19; Jer. 39:21 LXX) as also in secular literature (see Bauer's Lexicon on σημεῖον).

[62] G. Sass [1], p. 127.

[63] Heinrici in Meyer's *Kommentar* (8th ed., 1900), *ad loc.*; P. Schmiedel, *Handkommentar, ad loc.*

[64] Of course the book of Acts possibly used the old formula in order to describe the miraculous deeds of the apostles (Acts 2:22; 2:43; 4:30; 5:12; 6:8; 14:3; 15:12).

Pauline epistles contain no sort of suggestion that Paul was such a miracle-worker,[65] or that he practiced healings and exorcisms, or "mighty acts over the world of demons which is at enmity with God."[66] The formula itself indeed originally has in view pneumatic-ecstatic wonder-signs,[67] but the apparently Pauline addition ἐν πάσῃ ὑπομονῇ fits in with this even less well than with miracles.[68] Most likely in this "apostolic" connection is the position that Paul here thought of the wondrous effect of the Word (cf. I Cor. 2:4; I Thess. 1:5),[69] but the possibility must remain open that he simply refused to take the trouble to fill the traditional form of the expanded formula with specific content.

But whether Paul here deliberately formulates or casually cites the formula —the fact that he must force himself to use this all-too-bare allusion to the σημεῖα τοῦ ἀποστόλου shows that he has no fundamental hesitation about using it but nevertheless possesses no inclination to this manifestly widespread method of proof for his office.[70] This must however give food for thought and will engage our attention later on.

An argument in particular for the genuineness of the apostleship seems to come up for discussion in II Cor. 12:1-10. Here Paul concerns himself with his ὀπτασίαι καὶ ἀποκαλύψεις κυρίου, which according to the view of his opponents in Corinth are an apparently essential characteristic sign of apostolic authority.[71] The privilege of such visions and revelations is at

---

[65] G. Sass [1], p. 127.

[66] Thus E. Käsemann [2], p. 63.

[67] Cf. p. 213; P. Wernle [1], p. 120; E. Käsemann [2], p. 35.

[68] It is clear that Paul does not place his just portrayed journey to heaven under the caption of σημεῖα τοῦ ἀποστόλου.

[69] H. Lietzmann, HNT on I Cor. 2:4; in my *Paulus und die Gnostiker*, see "Die Häretiker in Galatien," n. 42.

[70] Thus H. v. Campenhausen [1], p. 111, is incorrect in his comment on the basis of II Cor. 12:12 that the performance of miracles is "for the most eminent representative of the mission, the apostle, a matter of course."

[71] To be sure, H. Windisch (in Meyer's *Kommentar, in loc.*) thinks that in II Cor. 12:1-10, Paul is glorying in wholly personal advantages beside which his opponents can place nothing comparable, and H. Lietzmann *in loc.* considers it at least not *necessary* to assume that in Corinth also some appealed to visions. But this assumption is absolutely indispensable. For it is unqualifiedly certain from 12:1 and 12:11 that Paul is *compelled* to refer to his trances. If in 12:1 ff. he had wished to adduce a unique personal argument with which he would overtrump all the arguments of his opponents, he would have had to do everything to extend the meaning of this experience for his apostolic office which was at stake. But instead, he strives in every way to minimize this experience and to make it irrelevant for the question of his apostolic rights (*vide infra*). But this is the way one handles only an argument which is forced from him by an opponent because the latter himself has employed the same argument.

Moreover, II Cor. 5:11 ff. leaves no doubt, in a suitable interpretation of the passage, that for the community the ecstasies adduced belonged to the favorite means of propaganda of Paul's opponents (cf. Bultmann's *Exegetische Probleme des Zweiten Korintherbriefes* [1947], pp. 12 ff.; *Die Gnosis in Korinth* [2nd ed., 1965], pp. 177 ff.).

any rate not allotted to all members of the congregation, and just how closely these ecstatic experiences are related to the apostolate is shown by the fact that Paul uses the same terms in the picturing of his call: ἀποκά-λυψις (Gal. 1:12, 16); ὁρᾶν (I Cor. 9:1; 15:7-8).[72] To be sure, it is note-worthy that in spite of the similarity of terminology, Paul does not here think of mentioning his call, when he after all is taking up the challenge of his opposition. Apparently the conversion experience had for him a wholly different character from that which happened to the ἄνθρωπος ἐν Χριστῷ fourteen years earlier. The former he reports most reluctantly; but he calls on the latter without hesitation. Now the antipathy of Paul to the portrayal of his ecstatic experience is quite comprehensible from the stand-point of his understanding of Christian existence: ὅταν γὰρ ἀσθενῶ, τότε δυνατός εἰμι (II Cor. 12:10b). That his apostolic rights should be de-pendent upon the "visions and revelations" is to him so little comprehensible that he does all in his power to depreciate his experience. The knowledge that in the eyes of his opponents, the false apostles, exactly the opposite was true, will turn out to be a significant fact for the explanation of the primitive Christian apostolate.

7. From the indissoluble connection between genuineness of apostleship and immediacy of message must now actually follow that the apostle can prove the truth of his proclamation by establishing his apostolic rights; and conversely, he must have the genuineness of his apostleship confirmed by the proof that the gospel which he proclaims is traced back directly to Christ.

The opponents of Paul in Galatia and Corinth apparently can argue in this fashion. They are willing, for example, to recognize Paul as an apostle only after he has proved that Christ actually speaks in him (ἐπεὶ δοκιμὴν ζητεῖτε τοῦ ἐν ἐμοὶ λαλοῦντος Χριστοῦ, II Cor. 13:3), in other words, if the truth of his message is no longer "hidden" (II Cor. 4:3) but "open" (II Cor. 5:11). Conversely, they contest the genuineness of his proclama-tion in principle because he is no apostle: This is the dominant form of the conflict in Galatians and I and II Corinthians. The charges which above all Paul has to refute in II Cor. are indeed directed not against the content of his message, but against his office. In Corinth it apparently was not neces-sary to contradict the gospel of Paul so long as one could dispute his apostolic rights: the message stands or falls with the office.

Now it is interesting that Paul does not take over this form of argument, even though from the beginning point of his concept of the apostle he would have been in a position to do so—indeed, from this beginning point

[72] See p. 25.

such an argument would only have been consistent; for even for him office and message coincide. But Paul *cannot* objectively guarantee his apostolic rights with a reference to his gospel, and this, as we have already shown,[73] for a twofold reason. In the first place, there is no objective measure for the truth of his message, and in the second place, not every true messenger is also thereby an apostle.[74] And Paul apparently *does not wish* to adduce the converse proof—to verify the disputed truth of his proclamation by means of the legitimacy of his office.

To be sure, Paul defends, in Gal. 1–2, his apostolic rights which are being contested, but he does not in the least think of demanding obedience to the gospel which he thereafter cites in Gal. 3 ff. simply because it is he, *the apostle,* who proclaims this message. Similarly, in I Cor. 9:1 ff. the brief defense of his apostleship is not the foundation or presupposition of the proclamation in I Cor. And when he later remarks that he is to vindicate his apostolic claim only in order that through his office the truth of his gospel may be proved, he still utterly refuses to adduce any other argument for his apostleship than the truth and convincing power of his message itself. This situation appears in II Cor. and has already been described. Only at the climax of the conflict in II Cor. 10–13 [75] does he allow himself to be forced into following the pattern of argument of his opponents and seeking to show that he can fulfill all the demands which are set up in Corinth for an apostle whose message is to be accepted (II Cor. 11–12). But the form in which Paul clothes this proof, the constant reference to his foolishness in this proceeding, to the compulsion under which he stands, to the unseemliness of such an undertaking,[76] shows more plainly than anything else that he considers wrong in principle an attempt to guarantee the truth of his message by a prior demonstration of the genuineness of his office.

This is entirely self-evident from the perspective of Paul's interpretation of the Word of God. For Paul indeed the gospel is not a transmitted doctrine whose credibility is dependent upon the trustworthiness of the teacher; for even he himself had received no doctrine through the ἀποκάλυψις ᾽Ιησοῦ Χριστοῦ. The evangelical message is rather first of all kerygma, address, summons, and for this reason it demands, not agreement, but the obedience of faith. Such believing obedience however responds only to the

---

[73] See p. 34.

[74] Differently in Corinth, apparently, where the false missionaries as a group are called apostles: II Cor. 11:13.

[75] I regard it as an assured result of New Testament research that these chapters do not belong with II Cor. 1–9, but are the torso of a separate epistle which is later than the polemical parts of II Cor. 1–9.

[76] See n. 71.

content of the message, not to the person of the messenger. It clearly shows that he did not simply use office and message interchangeably, as did his opponents; yet there remains the noteworthy fact that the Pauline interpretation of the apostolate also is aimed at such an exchange from the start, because even for Paul calling and conversion by Christ himself were a *single* event.

8. To sum up, for Paul the authority of the apostle is absolute; it rests however not in the office itself but in the message which is proclaimed by the office. This authority finds its stoutest expression in the solemn adjuration and warning to the Galatians: "If we, or an angel from heaven, should preach to you a gospel other than that which we have preached to you, let him be accursed. As we have already said to you, so I say once again: if anyone preaches to you a gospel other than what you have received, let him be accursed." It is erroneous to say that Paul in this passage pushes "passionately aside every apostolic authority, even his own," in order to let the gospel alone be determinative (H. v. Campenhausen [1], p. 123). Paul rather is establishing precisely this, his apostolic authority, by defending *his* gospel.

At the same time, however, it is clear in this passage *why* Paul can speak such an authoritative anathema: The Galatians have turned away from Christ and to another gospel,[77] although there is in fact no other gospel but only the gospel of Christ which some have perverted. Paul has the only true gospel, received from Christ himself, to proclaim; therefore he can condemn all other messages which do not agree with his gospel. That is to say, Paul himself does not dare to say anything which οὐ κατειργάσατο Χριστὸς δι᾽ ἐμοῦ εἰς ὑπακοήν (Rom. 15:18). He distinguishes himself from the false apostles: οὐ γάρ ἐσμεν ὡς οἱ πολλοὶ καπηλεύοντες τὸν λόγον τοῦ θεοῦ, ἀλλ᾽ ὡς ἐξ εἰλικρινείας, ἀλλ᾽ ὡς ἐκ θεοῦ κατέναντι θεοῦ ἐν Χριστῷ λαλοῦμεν (II Cor. 2:17; cf. II Cor. 4:2). Only because he keeps pure the gospel which he received from Christ, he can refute with unconditional authority every false message. Indeed he does not dare λογίσασθαί τι ὡς ἐξ ἑαυτῶν (II Cor. 3:5), and because he faithfully clings to the revelation given directly to him, his ἱκανότης is ἐκ τοῦ θεοῦ (II Cor. 3:5).

There is therefore no apostolic authority which the apostle might possess apart from his message.[78] Because, and insofar as, the κύριος speaks through him, his word is obligatory (I Cor. 7:10). Because, and insofar as, he exhorts ὑπὲρ Χριστοῦ, one must give heed to him (II Cor. 5:20). Whatever

[77] "Ἀπὸ τοῦ καλέσαντος ὑμᾶς ἐν χάριτι Χριστοῦ εἰς ἕτερον εὐαγγέλιον" (Gal. 1:6); observe how Paul here equates Christ and the gospel!
[78] H. v. Campenhausen, correctly: "Ultimately the foundation laid by the apostles must also support the apostles, . . . and not vice versa" ([1], p. 123).

he says that is not expressly covered by the Lord who is the gospel (I Cor. 7:12), he can say only with the same authority of all others: δοκῶ δὲ κἀγὼ πνεῦμα θεοῦ ἔχειν (I Cor. 7:40). Conversely, however, all those who preach the one gospel can also speak with "apostolic" authority (Phil. 3:17); for even if Paul does possess the—undemonstrable—priority of having received this gospel "first-hand," the authority still rests only in the Word itself. Thus Christ is the authority[79] with which the apostle preaches.[80] Therefore Paul never plays off a "higher" authority against the "lower" one of the congregation.[81]

Related to this is the fact that Paul comes "to speak of his apostolic authority only infrequently; and, to be more precise, this is generally only when he is on the defensive" (H. v. Campenhausen [1], p. 111). The "only infrequently" is to be further qualified, but it is correct to say that Paul affirms his office only where he must defend himself against the charge that his message is invalid because he is not an apostle. This compels him to set forth his apostleship in order to gain a hearing for his proclamation, which gets him into the already described difficult position of having to prove his office for the sake of his message, an office which still is nothing at all without the message. If we possessed only the passages from the genuine Pauline epistles in which Paul comes to speak of his apostolic rank *of his own accord*, we would not know much more about the Pauline apostolate than the fact that for its bearer it was without any particular meaning.

This last assertion to be sure must be expanded and thus in a certain sense must also be corrected. There is in Paul still another line of apostolic authority than that of the Word. Twice Paul speaks in very similar-sounding words of the ἐξουσία which the Lord has given to him εἰς οἰκοδομὴν καὶ οὐκ εἰς καθαίρεσιν (II Cor. 10:8; 13:10; cf. II Cor. 10:4). He hopes not to have put his ἐξουσία to the test with the Corinthians. Wherein this consists can hardly be decided on the basis of these two passages.

---

[79] In Gal. 4:14 Paul can say that people have accepted him ὡς Χριστὸν Ἰησοῦν. Whether that is his own formulation or, as I should surmise, a traditional one—it is clear that in the message of the apostle Christ himself establishes his authority.

[80] On this, cf. H. v. Campenhausen's splendid study [4], esp. pp. 29-34.

[81] The anathema in Gal. 1:8-9 in fact does not apply to the person who is preaching otherwise than the apostle Paul preaches—Paul himself would be subject to this anathema —but to one who is preaching a false gospel, whoever he may be. Therefore it is not clear to me how Gal. 1:8-9 is supposed to establish a "unique position of Paul" (H. D. Betz, *op. cit.*, pp. 179-80). Naturally the "uniqueness" of Paul can easily be shown historically—the apostle himself was not unaware of it (I Cor. 15:9-10); it is however simply a historical phenomenon and in no way given by a unique consciousness of office and ministry.

R. Reitzenstein[82] rightly asserts that one may not limit this ἐξουσία to the rights of the apostle to the exclusion of the congregation. For actually this authority is given for οἰκοδομή. The apostolic *exousia*, as Paul claims it in these two passages, is not however exactly identical with the authority of the proclaimed Word.

This is plainly shown in the unparalleled passage of I Cor. 5:3 ff., in which Paul apparently describes an exercise of his authority.[83] The manifold problems of this passage are not to engage us here. It is plain enough that Paul does not exclude the evildoer from the community,[84] but wishes him to be destroyed as to his σάρξ, so that his πνεῦμα may be saved. This happens in the presence of the community by the πνεῦμα of Paul which is bound up with the δύναμις of Christ. How this judging and saving act took place is simply beyond our knowledge. The dualism of σάρξ and πνεῦμα here presupposed is alien to Paul elsewhere[85] and stems from Gnosticism, in which also ἐξουσία in the sense employed in II Cor. 10:8; 13:10 is at home.[86] Therefore when Paul calls on his ἐξουσία in this case he stands in a tradition which is quite far removed from his theological intention. This warns us to be cautious in interpreting the passages here referred to.

Still, I Cor. 5:3 ff. shows with sufficient clarity that (and this corresponds to the Gnostic tradition) the ἐξουσία does not pertain to the apostle in particular but to the "pneumatic," the spirit-filled one in general and to the apostle only for the reason that he also is naturally a "pneumatic."

Evidently Paul knows a double authority. In the foreground stands the authority that resides in the Word which he has to proclaim. Alongside this, however, he does not disdain to point also to the ἐξουσία which rests upon the πνεῦμα he possesses. The first authority he shares with all true preachers, the second with all "pneumatics."

In every case his authority, however, is absolute: Whoever accepts Paul accepts Christ (Gal. 4:14); whoever hears him hears Christ (II Cor. 5:20); whoever rejects him is accursed (Gal. 1:8-9).[87] And no wonder that things stand thus; for "the Lord is the spirit" (II Cor. 3:17), and the Lord is at the same time the gospel (Gal. 1:12, 16). The Lord himself is thus the authority of the pneumatic and of the preacher.

9. Several times Paul set himself up as an example for the congregation,

---

[82] *Op. cit.*, p. 363.

[83] Thus, correctly, R. Reitzenstein, *op. cit.*, pp. 363-64.

[84] This is here as elsewhere a matter for the community itself (I Cor. 5:2, 7 ff.).

[85] See R. Bultmann [1], I, 208.

[86] See R. Reitzenstein, *op. cit.*, pp. 362 ff.

[87] See G. Sass [1], pp. 78 ff.

and the frequency of the passages as well as the similarity of terminology points to the fact that here we have to do with a feature which traditionally belongs to the nature of the apostolate. The fact that one is to take the apostle as an example is described with the technical terms μιμέομαι, μιμητής, or συμμιμητής.[88] In profane Greek this word group signifies in a bad sense a counterfeit, a slavishly dependent copy; in a good sense it means taking something for an example, emulation, in order to come to one's self.[89] Paul naturally uses the word in the latter sense when (II Thess. 3:7, 9; Phil. 3:17; I Cor. 4:16; 11:1; I Thess. 1:6) he offers himself to the community as an example.

W. Michaelis attempts to establish distinctions in the use of the concept in these passages, but the arguments which he offers are artificial. In all the passages Paul intends to express what he says in Gal. 4:12 with the greatest possible brevity: γίνεσθε ὡς ἐγώ.[90] Paul desires for the community his faith, his love, his hope, his glory, his weakness, and so on.[91] W. Michaelis is greatly reluctant to admit that Paul here sets himself forth actually in his personal existence as an example worthy of imitation; rather, the congregations are to be μιμηταί above all in that they heed the instructions of Paul and bow to the authority of his word (*op. cit.*, IV, 672; 670). But that is not included in the meaning of the word group μιμέομαι, etc., nor do the passages cited presuppose such an understanding.[92] Obedience to the word of Paul is only indirectly included in the μίμησις, insofar as Paul became a μίμημα through the fact that he himself grounds his exemplary existence in the Word which he repeats.

The afore-mentioned reluctance of W. Michaelis may have grown out of the correct impression that it actually is not in accord with the nature of Paul to place himself in the foreground.[93] But one should not, in the light of this knowledge, misinterpret the relevant expressions of Paul, but rather

[88] The pertinent passages have recently been examined by D. M. Stanley, " 'Become Imitators of Me': The Pauline Conception of Apostolic Tradition" (*Biblica*, XL [1959], 859-77), with reference to the "apostolic tradition" encountered in them.

[89] Cf. W. Michaelis in TDNT, IV, 659 ff.

[90] Strange to say, according to W. Michaelis in TDNT, IV, 671, n. 29, this passage presents no parallel to the other passages.

[91] That in the mimesis conception it is a matter of "the authoritative maintenance of the Christ tradition" or of "the recollection of the apostolic doctrinal tradition" (thus J. Roloff, *op. cit.*, p. 119) is imputed to the texts and certainly is not to be inferred from I Cor. 4:16 and I Thess. 1:6, the passages cited by Roloff as proof. In I Thess. 1:6 Paul mentions "the word (of the Lord)," and in I Cor. 4:16-17 "my ways in Christ Jesus." We can by no means deduce from these texts that they refer to a fixed complex of inherited, specifically apostolic and authoritative doctrinal tradition.

[92] Cf. W. G. Kümmel in Lietzmann, HNT, IX, 21, 1. 46.

[93] Cf. e.g., II Cor. 4:5; 5:12; 10:12; I Cor. 3:5.

first should inquire after the tradition in which he apparently stands with his μίμησις conception. If this inquiry is pursued further, then those other passages also are to be drawn in, in which not the apostle but the congregation (I Thess. 2:14) or the Lord himself (I Cor. 11:1; I Thess. 1:6; cf. Eph. 5:1) is the example; for the similarity of terminology may point to a connection of all these passages.

10. The apostle is in a special way an eschatological figure.[94] This "in a special way" suggests that with the apostolate an eschatological conception is bound up, which includes more than the obvious fact that the apostle is entrusted with the eschatological message: the proclamation of the end of the world which has broken in with the death and resurrection of Jesus Christ.[95] That quite special conception is found in its clearest form in Rom. 15:19 ff. Paul first declares that he has filled with the gospel of Christ the lands of a great crescent extending from Jerusalem to Illyricum.[96] The road led from East to West and now leads on logically beyond Rome to Spain. The remarkable thing here is that Paul is convinced that he has now performed his service in these areas. In Rom. 15:23 he can even say: νυνὶ δὲ μηκέτι τόπον ἔχων ἐν τοῖς κλίμασι τούτοις . . . ! It appears to be the task of the apostle to establish in every country some support points for the larger missionary work and, having done this, to consider his commission in this area completed. Connected with this is the oft-mentioned prescription for the apostle to εὐαγγελίζεσθαι only where the name of Christ has not yet been called (Rom. 15:20), and in no case to build upon another man's foundation (Rom. 15:20-21; II Cor. 10:15-16)—something that is not wrong in general (on the contrary—see I Cor. 3:6 ff.), but simply is not to be the task of the apostle.[97]

Naturally opinions have been formed about the origin of this particular characteristic of the apostolate. The usual explanation points to the awareness of Paul that the parousia was imminent, and to the consequent urgency to bring the gospel to as many men as possible. Therefore it would be

---

[94] A. Fridrichsen begins his study of "The Apostle and His Message" with the words: "When Paul in Romans introduces himself as a κλητὸς ἀπόστολος he characterizes himself as an eschatologic person. He is a man who has been appointed to a proper place and a peculiar task in the series of events to be accomplished in the final days of this world."

[95] In this sense G. Sass, e.g., speaks of the eschatological commission of the apostle ([1], pp. 27-28). But in this connection it is to be observed that such eschatological definiteness is nothing specifically apostolic, but simply belongs to the Christian kerygma.

[96] This evidently presupposed that "Jerusalem" and "Illyria" belong to the lands that are "filled."

[97] Paul is disturbed over the invasion by his opponents into his missionary territory in Corinth (and Galatia) mainly because they call themselves apostles (II Cor. 10:15). Basically Paul could only welcome the fact when the gospel was proclaimed by all sorts of men (Phil. 1:18).

"superfluous and a waste of time" (G. Sass [1], p. 131) to preach in alien missionary territories. According to this view, Paul believes himself "to be the last messenger of God before the dawning of the day of the Lord" (*ibid.*).

However, it seems that Paul's missionary work is hardly characterized by any special urgency. He can stay for years in a place like Ephesus or Corinth, and several times his road goes back to Jerusalem and to the well-established congregations. At no point in his missionary activity does one gain the impression that Paul was in very much of a hurry.

Also, nowhere in his epistles does Paul himself speak of the return of Christ in such a way as to suggest that the imminence of the Parousia spurs him on to a particularly urgent proclamation. Indeed, Rom. 11:25-26, seems to preclude any such urgency, because according to the will of God first of all the "fullness of the Gentiles" must be converted and then also Israel will be saved, before the end comes. In other words, this mysterious plan of God does not provide for the Parousia until the mission sooner or later has reached its divinely appointed goal.[98]

Finally, in the passage now under discussion, Rom. 15:19 ff., there is totally lacking any indication of a pressure of time under which Paul could stand. The expressions about the sphere of action of his apostleship are completely lacking in any temporal category. This is all the more striking since Paul in fact counted on an early end of the world and thus of missionary preaching. It would have been understandable if in view of the advanced time he had been in great haste to save as many as possible.[99]

Instead of this, the spatial category remains the only decisive one. It concerns a definite space or area which is to be filled with the gospel.[100] This

[98] In this connection one cannot refer to the indeed interesting but little convincing thesis of O. Cullmann ([1]; cf. *ibid.*, "Eschatology and Missions in the NT," in the Dodd *Festschrift* [1956], pp. 409-21, esp. 417 ff.; this thesis was taken over, e.g., by J. Munck), that in II Thess. 2:7, by ὁ κατέχων Paul is meant, while in II Thess. 2:6, by τὸ κατέχον his message is meant. This is impossible because according to II Thess. 2 the removal of the κατέχων will have as a consequence the emergence of lawlessness, but according to Rom. 11:25 the success of the entire Gentile mission will result in the conversion of the Jews.

[99] The following statement of K. Deissner (*op. cit.*, p. 776) therefore cannot be documented by any passage of Paul's epistles: "The view of the immediately imminent end, of the in-breaking βασιλεία τοῦ θεοῦ with its judgment and its salvation signifies for the first emissaries . . . greatest exertion of energies. The earliest mission takes place under the viewpoint that the whole world must receive the message before the end, which is to be expected *momentarily*, comes." The same holds true for J. Munck's judgment concerning Paul, "who in his aroused hope in the nearness of the end of the world could not hurry fast enough from country to country" ([2], p. 45).

[100] That Paul thinks "in terms of peoples" is, as over against this, incorrect, at least in expression (P. Wernle, *Paulus als Heidenmissionar*, p. 31). Cf. J. Munck [2], p. 45; P. Althaus in NTD, VI, on Rom. 15:19.

has happened when missionary centers have been established at reasonable distances from one another.[101] Then the apostle seeks a new area of work in which up to this point no proclamation may have taken place. This is a fixed pattern, and O. Michel (*Der Brief an die Römer*, p. 330) probably is right in supposing that πληρῶσαι τὸ εὐαγγέλιον τοῦ Χριστοῦ (Rom. 15:19; Col. 1:25) is also a fixed and established expression within this tradition. Any setting of a goal in terms of time, on the other hand, is lacking.[102] The spatial way of considering things is in harmony with Rom. 11:25-26: If first the "fullness of the Gentiles" must be converted, then it is not the hurried proclamation of the message that is demanded, but the comprehensive, extensive proclamation. A certain tension does exist, however, between Rom. 11:25 ff. and passages such as Rom. 13:11 ff. and I Thess. 5:1 ff.: The day of the Lord comes as a thief in the night.

11. The apostle is called to his service for a lifetime. This is so obvious that Paul does not allude to this fact either for himself or for any other of the apostles. Thus it is inconceivable that the apostle could, for example, give back his commission.

The lifelong office, however, also apparently presupposes lifelong service. One cannot be an apostle without rendering the service of an apostle. The apostle is not an officeholder who could retire to private life. This too is left unsaid by Paul; but why should he reflect over things which lie outside the circle of his vision and which are not points of controversy between himself and his opponents? The apostleship of Paul apart from apostolic service is, in any case, inconceivable.

12. From this it follows that the question of the support and livelihood of the apostle is posed and demands a ruling. Basically, Paul is of the opinion that the preacher of the gospel may also live of the gospel. An explicit command of the Lord says this: οὕτως καὶ ὁ κύριος διέταξεν τοῖς τὸ εὐαγγέλιον καταγγέλλουσιν ἐκ τοῦ εὐαγγελίου ζῆν (I Cor. 9:14). Besides, there are the reasons drawn from general custom: The soldier has a right to his pay; the vineyard keeper lives from the produce of his vineyard; the shepherd drinks milk from the cattle.[103] These reasons are further covered by the authority of the Scripture, for when it says: "Thou shalt not muzzle the ox that threshes the grain," this means—so Paul allegorizes

[101] Therefore the focus of Paul's missionary work lies in the great cities and on the main traffic arteries (A. Deissmann, *op. cit.*, pp. 174-75).

[102] There is also no basis for the assumption that "after his journey to Spain Paul was aware that he had reached the goal of his commission" (G. Sass [1], p. 130).

[103] I Cor. 9:7.

—that every man is to live from the fruits of his labor (I Cor. 9:8 ff.). Other reasons are given in I Cor. 9:1 ff.[104]

This right to support is valid for all "servants of the Word" [105] and thus holds true for apostles. The λοιποὶ ἀπόστολοι, as well as the brothers of the Lord and Peter, apparently lay claim to this right for themselves (I Cor. 9:5).

Paul, on the other hand, and Barnabas, who in I Cor. 9:6 apparently is counted among the apostles, renounce their right. There are, to be sure, exceptions to this renunciation, as Paul shows in connection with the Corinthians themselves (II Cor. 11:8-9), and as clearly appears in Phil. 4:10 ff. Thus Paul had no major objections to accepting gifts for his own support from established congregations. But in order not to appear as one of the traveling exorcists who sponged off the people, he ordinarily earned his living with his own hands, "so that we give no one occasion to be offended at the gospel of Christ" (I Cor. 9:12).

This is a strange state of affairs. The apostle has the right to live off the gospel, because he is a preacher of it; at the same time, however, it is precisely the apostolic office itself which requires him to renounce his right in order not to give offense.

13. It belongs to the nature of the apostolate that the apostle must suffer. Suffering is naturally decreed for the whole congregation of Christ. Whoever is baptized into Christ is συμμορφιζόμενος τῷ θανάτῳ αὐτοῦ, and consequently lives in the κοινωνία παθημάτων αὐτοῦ, in order also to have a share in his ἐξανάστασις (Phil. 3:10). The Christian who takes upon himself his sufferings experiences therein the certainty of communion with Christ. To this extent suffering is necessary for salvation. This is the basic idea in the Pauline theology of suffering.[106] In addition to this, he knows still other reasons for the positive evaluation of suffering: Rom. 5:3 ff. ("We glory in tribulation, for we know that tribulation produces patience"); II Cor. 12:9 ("In the weakness of men the power of God is made perfect").

It has long been recognized, however, that the suffering of the apostle is contrasted with the suffering of the community in general, that the apostolic suffering stands in a special connection with the apostolic *service*. This may be seen in many affirmations of Paul. One notes, for example, I Cor. 4:9 ff.: "It appears to me that God has exhibited us apostles as last

---

[104] On the whole matter, cf. E. Käsemann, "Eine paulinische Variation des 'amor fati,' " ZThK, LVI (1959), 138-54.

[105] H. v. Campenhausen ([1], p. 112) rightly asserts: "Thus here one may not speak of special 'apostolic rights.' "

[106] Cf. Bultmann [1], I, 345 ff.; Dibelius, *Botschaft und Geschichte*, II, 144-45.

of all, like condemned lawbreakers; for we have become a spectacle for the
world, for angels and for men. . . . We have become, and are down to the
present, the refuse of the world, every man's offscourings." Similarly
I Cor. 15:30 ff. pertains in a special way to the apostle: "I die daily." Also in
connection with the special apostolic suffering we note the catalog of
pressures in II Cor. 11:23 ff., which enumerates the professional (or vocational) sufferings of the apostle from the daily experience of being besieged
all the way up to martyrdom. G. Sass ([1], p. 87) is right when he remarks:
"After all, Paul mentions his personal suffering so frequently only because
it is vocational suffering." This is true also of II Cor. 6:3 ff., where Paul
enumerates the life situations in which he as apostle gives offense to no one,
and therefore first and most explicitly describes the situations of suffering.

That this suffering actually means more than the suffering of Christians
generally and is a necessary part of apostolic ministry is shown by the
rationale which Paul gives for the θλίψεις of the apostle and which in this
form otherwise is not valid for the distresses of the believers: It is for the
sake of the people to whom he is sent that the apostle suffers.[107]

This reasoning is supported by two different motifs. According to II Cor.
1:3 ff. the apostle experiences in his suffering the comfort of God: εἰς τὸ
δύνασθαι ἡμᾶς παρακαλεῖν τοὺς ἐν πάσῃ θλίψει διὰ τῆς παρακλήσεως
ἧς παρακαλούμεθα αὐτοὶ ὑπὸ τοῦ θεοῦ; thus, "if we suffer, it is for your
comfort and salvation" (II Cor. 1:6).

Along with this is found another explanation of the necessary suffering of
the messenger of salvation for the salvation of the hearer: ἀεὶ γὰρ ἡμεῖς οἱ
ζῶντες εἰς θάνατον παραδιδόμεθα διὰ Ἰησοῦν, ἵνα καὶ ἡ ζωὴ τοῦ Ἰησοῦ
φανερωθῇ ἐν τῇ θνητῇ σαρκὶ ἡμῶν (II Cor. 4:11). The thought which
finds expression in this declaration begins with the observation that the
apostle bears his message in the earthen vessel of his body; that is, that he
proclaims it against the background of his own weakness.[108] Thereby it is
made plain to the hearer that the power of this message comes from God
and not ἐξ ἡμῶν.[109] For this reason, the more the death of Jesus takes form
in the life of the apostle, the more powerfully must the proclamation of the
gospel distinguish itself from human weakness and thus make its way with

---

[107] Thus not: The exercise of the apostolic ministry leads to especially numerous sufferings (naturally this also is true), but: The apostle must suffer for the sake of the proper
exercise of his ministry. I do not understand how E. Güttgemanns ([1], p. 28, n. 136),
referring to the foregoing statements, can give it as my opinion that the specific apostolic
sufferings are "a result of the apostolic ministry."

[108] Cf. Gal. 4:13 ff.

[109] Cf. Dibelius, Botschaft und Geschichte, II, 144-45.

the hearers. The suffering of the apostle is the negative presupposition for the success of his preaching.[110]

In comparison with II Cor. 1:3 ff., this is a quite complicated bit of reasoning to explain the apostolic suffering, and one which is not wholly satisfying.[111] Fundamentally, it is quite difficult to understand how the convincing power of a message to be delivered can be heightened by the physical weakness of the messenger. One wonders whether, in his arguments in II Cor. 4:7 ff., Paul perhaps stands in a tradition which he is unable to accept without a break. The fact that in II Cor. 1:3 ff. he gives another, simpler, apparently personal explanation for the meaning of apostolic suffering suggests such a surmise.

[110] To speak here of "vicarious suffering" of the apostle is mistaken, at least as far as the language is concerned (G. Sass [1], p. 89); for the apostle's suffering indeed is in no way a substitute for the suffering of the community, even if it is "for," i.e. for the benefit of, the community that it happens.

[111] I take note with some disbelief of the view that, of all things, with my exposition of II Cor. 4:7 ff. the *theologia crucis* is in principle eliminated (thus E. Güttgemanns [1], p. 97, n. 25; p. 98, n. 30; p. 125 *et passim*). It is even more astounding to me that therewith I am said to despair of understanding the Pauline train of thought; why should an exposition which does not conform to that of Güttgemanns represent a refusal to undertake an exposition? Güttgemanns himself interprets the passage to mean that Paul in his suffering makes the crucified One immediately manifest. The suffering of Jesus is, so to speak, repeated in the suffering of his apostle. Güttgemanns can therefore speak of a "demonstration of identity" (p. 119) or can say that Paul at one stroke (!) is defending his Christology along with his apostolic rights (p. 117, n. 135). The sufferings of the apostle are to be characterized as a "christological epiphany" (p. 195), the bodily existence of the apostle takes on "christological relevance" (p. 134). Therewith the apostle emerges from within the community and with Christ becomes an entity over against the community (pp. 195, 324 ff.).

Now here I would speak of an at least *threatening* elimination of the *theologia crucis*. For, if one does not, with Güttgemanns, make this into a merely formal principle, it is constituted by the unrepeatable "once-for-all" of Jesus' suffering, which in its uniqueness can be present solely in the proclamation, never in the achievement of existence of some distinguished Christian officeholders. The variation of the *Christus prolongatus* offered by Güttgemanns, consciously following mystical-Gnostic ideas of identity (p. 139), makes it appear on the other hand as in principle irrelevant whether the glory of God is beheld in the sufferings of Jesus or in the sufferings of his apostle, and the allegedly radical contrast of this concept of the apostle with Gnosticism (p. 139) is in fact only a very relative one.

Meanwhile Paul defends himself in II Cor. 4:7 ff. precisely against the demand of his Gnostic opponents that he exalt the apostolate in a christological way, and he does this by affirming that the *true* proclaimers of the gospel (Paul is by no means speaking in II Cor. 4 of the apostles exclusively, as Güttgemanns assumes) bear this treasure in earthen vessels, hence it must be clear to everyone that the superabundant power of this gospel comes absolutely from God and does not at all stem from the existence of the apostle (4:7) —*that* is theologia crucis which is man's undoing, and does not make him the bearer of an epiphany of Deity. This denies neither an interconnection of weakness and gospel nor a positive function of weakness for the gospel, as Güttgemanns incomprehensibly charges against me (p. 97, n. 25). It rather is definitely the connection of the two, to be sure in the way required by the text itself and the context of Pauline theology. Güttgemanns converts both—I return his charge (p. 97, n. 25)—into the opposite.

A thought similar to that of II Cor. 4:11 may stand behind Col. 1:24,[112] where Paul [113] speaks of τοῖς παθήμασιν ὑπὲρ ὑμῶν, with which he intends to fulfill the still incomplete sufferings of Christ for the community. I consider it completely mistaken to suppose that here Paul is thinking that the apostle must bear for the community[114] a part of the representative suffering of Christ (II Cor. 5:21), or that Paul here picks up the old ideas of Jewish apocalyptic about the messianic woes.[115] The former idea would be, for Paul, utterly inconceivable; Lohmeyer's interpretation overlooks the fact that the messianic woes are in no sense the sufferings of the Messiah himself. Further, these thoughts are wholly alien to the "mystical" or Gnostic[116] tradition, according to which Col. 1:24 is formulated. Without prejudice to the fact that the tradition employed in Col. 1:24 is purely mythological, the meaning of the passage in Colossians may be the same as that of II Cor. 4:7 ff.: The sufferings of the messenger allow the message itself to become more effective for the edifying of the community.

The expression τὰ παθήματα τοῦ Χριστοῦ in II Cor. 1:5 and similarly Col. 1:24 [117] makes even plainer than do the words of Paul in II Cor. 4:10-11 that in the tradition employed here Christ and the apostles were set side by side. The apostolic suffering is the same as the suffering of Christ and in the same class with it. This approximate identification of Christ and his apostles has already come to our view frequently in the context of our observations.

14. Closely bound up with the apostolate is the concept μυστήριον as a designation of the Christ kerygma as a whole or of individual hidden truths. In this connection pseudo-Paul becomes clearest in Eph. 3:1-6. In this passage, Paul is introduced as the apostle to the Gentiles, and to him κατὰ ἀποκάλυψιν ἐγνωρίσθη τὸ μυστήριον . . . ὃ ἑτέραις γενεαῖς οὐκ ἐγνωρίσθη τοῖς υἱοῖς τῶν ἀνθρώπων ὡς νῦν ἀπεκαλύφθη τοῖς ἁγίοις ἀποσ-τόλοις αὐτοῦ καὶ προφήταις ἐν πνεύματι. "Apostles and prophets possess a spiritual insight into the mystery of Christ which distinguishes them from

---

[112] On this passage, cf. the able work of Jacob Kremer, *Was an den Leiden Christi noch mangelt*, Bonn, 1956.

[113] Or one of his pupils. In this case it is immaterial, since the equation of the suffer-ings of Christ and of the apostle which is the basis of Col. 1:24 is also found in II Cor. 1:5, where Paul calls his sufferings παθήματα τοῦ Χριστοῦ.

[114] Thus G. Sass [1], p. 89.

[115] Thus E. Lohmeyer in Meyer's *Kommentar, in loc.*; E. Lohse, *Märtyrer und Gottes-knecht*, pp. 201 ff.; cf. E. Käsemann in ThLZ (1957), col. 695.

[116] See my *Die Gnosis in Korinth*, first ed., p. 123; the tradition is that of the σῶμα Χριστοῦ concept.

[117] Cf. I Pet. 4:13; 5:1.

the rest of the community." [118] Apostles and prophets are the "spiritual officeholders," who receive knowledge concerning the μυστήρια through an ἀποκάλυψις.[119]

In the writings of Paul himself this conception is no longer found so explicitly as in the traditions which the author of Ephesians reworked. That Paul, however, stands in this tradition is not to be doubted. The ἀποκάλυψις in Eph. 3:3, which mediates the μυστήρια, is certainly a revelation of the same kind as that to which Paul owes his gospel (Gal. 1:12) and in which God ἀπεκάλυψεν διὰ τοῦ πνεύματος (I Cor. 2:10) to him the μυστήρια (I Cor. 2:7). This fundamental ἀποκάλυψις, however, made Paul an οἰκονόμος μυστηρίων θεοῦ (I Cor. 4:1; cf. Eph. 3:2). Before this μυστήριον was revealed to the apostle κατὰ ἀποκάλυψιν, it had been concealed χρόνοις αἰωνίοις (Rom. 16:25; I Cor. 2:6-7; cf. Eph. 3:9: ἡ οἰκονομία τοῦ μυστηρίου τοῦ ἀποκεκρυμμένου ἀπὸ τῶν αἰώνων).

If the content of the mystery proclaimed in Eph. 3:6 is that the Gentiles are fellow heirs of the promise, then this content in Rom. 11:25 is only slightly shifted: τὸ μυστήριον τοῦτο contains the knowledge that Israel is in part hardened, *until the fullness of the Gentiles is saved,* in order then to be saved also. The thought of the Gentile mission generally tends to be bound together with the concept of the apostolic mystery, as Rom. 16:25 ff. also shows. It may also lie behind such other passages as I Cor. 2:7; Eph. 1:9; 6:19; Col. 1:26 ff.[120] In I Cor. 15:51 the mystery has a different content; in I Cor. 2:1 [121], 13:2, and 14:2 the expression remains quite indefinite.

I Cor. 14:2 however shows plainly that the "pneumatic" knows about the secrets of God. All the passages in which Paul speaks of the μυστήρια move in the context of this conception, which in Eph. 3:5 is only somewhat more precisely expressed when apostles and prophets are specifically named. For Paul, therefore, the knowledge of the μυστήρια necessarily belongs to the apostle, who through an ἀποκάλυψις κυρίου was called to be a steward of the divine secrets. He shares this special knowledge, of course, with the προφήτης.

15. This leads us to still another characteristic of the apostolate: Closely and almost indissolubly bound together with the apostle is the figure of the prophet, and this pair of officeholders is frequently enlarged, by the addition of the teacher, to a triad. The conjunction of ἀπόστολος and

[118] G. Bornkamm in TDNT, IV, 821.
[119] Cf. Eph. 6:19-20.
[120] Here the mystery is "Christ is in you," but "in you" indeed means "in you Gentiles."
[121] μυστήριον may be the better reading here; see the commentaries.

προφήτης is so firmly anchored in the tradition that to ascertain the source of the one figure would suffice to answer the question as to the origin of the other.

The most important relevant passages may be cited in brief compass.[122] I Cor. 12:28-29: God has set in the church "first apostles, second prophets, third teachers. . . . Are all apostles? Are all prophets? Are all teachers?" In this connection Paul does not name other officeholders, but only *functions* of offices: δυνάμεις, χαρίσματα ἰαμάτων, ἀντιλήμψεις, and so on. This shows how closely bound up together this triad is, and how it is at the same time set off from all else.[123] According to Eph. 2:20 the church is built ἐπὶ τῷ θεμελίῳ τῶν ἀποστόλων καὶ προφητῶν, for the mystery of the kingdom of Christ was revealed τοῖς ἁγίοις ἀποστόλοις αὐτοῦ καὶ προφήταις (Eph. 3:5), and God himself has placed apostles and prophets at the head of the "hierarchy" (Eph. 4:11).[124] In Rev. 18:20, among the heavenly saints who rejoice over the downfall of Babylon, οἱ ἀπόστολοι καὶ οἱ προφῆται are specifically named, as officeholders "who have already fallen victims to the persecutions." [125] A large part of the Didache treats περὶ τῶν ἀποστόλων καὶ προφητῶν (Did. 11:3),[126] and occasionally here the διδάσκαλος is placed alongside the prophets (Did. 13:1-2; 15:1). The Didache therefore still knows about the "very ancient triad." [127] In this same connection belongs also the Shepherd of Hermas, although in this writing only apostles and teachers regularly appear together (Sim. IX, 15:4; 16:5; 25:2; Vis. III, 5:1), a phenomenon which is duplicated in the Pastoral Epistles (I Tim. 2:7; II Tim. 1:11). Harnack ([1], p. 340) rightly recognizes, along with others, that in these passages the omission of any reference to the primitive Christian prophets is a deliberate one. This avoidance on the part of Hermas is hardly to be explained by saying that he himself was a prophet[128]; rather, Hermas and the author of the Pastorals no longer recognize any Christian prophets, among the leaders of the congregation,

---

[122] The source material is almost completely assembled in A. v. Harnack [1], I, 343 ff.

[123] Cf. H. v. Campenhausen [2], p. 65. According to G. Sass ([1], p. 105), in I Cor. 12:28 Paul "is thinking only of missionaries of the community," and the concept of the apostle here is wholly different from that which Paul claims for himself. But this interpretation is not admissible. The congregational apostles certainly do not belong at the head of the congregational authorities.

[124] "And he made some apostles, some prophets, others evangelists, and still others pastors and teachers." This list shows that the teachers, even where they are named, do not unconditionally have to stand in the third place.

[125] P. Ketter, *Die Apokalypse* (Freiburg, 1953), *in loc.*

[126] See R. Knopf in HNT on Did. 11:3 ff.

[127] See *ibid., in loc.*

[128] Thus Harnack [1], I, 340, who correctly rejects Lietzmann's (GGA [1905], p. 486) explanation that Hermas was familiar with a prophetic office only in the Old Testament.

because the prophet had become the foremost holder of the pneumatic office in Gnosticism.[129] Precisely this shows these authors to be witnesses to the earlier triad. Perhaps one may also compare Acts 13:1, where prophets and teachers send out Paul and Barnabas as apostles. In any case, the designation of Polycarp as διδάσκαλος ἀποστολικὸς καὶ προφητικός belongs in this connection.[130] In the pseudo-Clementines also prophets and apostles appear side by side (Rec. 4:35; Hom. 11:35). In Eus., CH IV, 22, false Christs, false apostles, and false prophets of the Gnostics are introduced.[131]

If one surveys these testimonies to an original connection between apostles and prophets, then, preliminary to any investigation into the nature and origin of this conjunction, one must clearly see that the concept of the apostolic in primitive Christianity is not comprehended and explained unless at the same time the concept of the prophetic is clarified and, additionally, that of teaching.

16. It appears to have been an ancient custom that the apostles always traveled in pairs. This shows up in Mark 6:7: καὶ ἤρξατο αὐτοὺς ἀποστέλλειν δύο δύο. This stipulation perhaps belongs to the section of an ancient church order which is handed down by Mark in the following verses. The source of this feature remains uncertain. One might refer to Deut. 19:15 [132] or Eccl. 4:9.[133] The arrangement of sending out in pairs appears also in Luke 10:1:[134] the 72 (or 70) disciples were sent out ἀνὰ δύο.[135] More important for us is the fact that at first Paul appears to have followed this arrangement. According to Acts 13–15 Paul together with Barnabas formed such an apostolic pair, and this tradition is systematically confirmed by Gal. 2:1, 9. Acts 15:36 ff. may also rely in this point upon a trustworthy tradition: When Paul and Barnabas separate, Barnabas takes Mark with him, while Paul goes on the so-called second missionary journey accompanied by Silas.[136] To be sure, it is possible that Silas was not an apostle,[137] but the traditional arrangement nevertheless is preserved.[138] The later de-

---

[129] See E. Fascher, *Prophetes*, pp. 190-224; Origen, Cels., VII, 8 ff.; *vide infra*, p. 226, n. 538; Herm. Mand., XI and Dibelius in HNT, *in loc.*

[130] Mart. Pol., 16.2; Eus., CH IV, 15.39.

[131] Cf. also the passages from the Mandaean literature cited on p. 185; cf. p. 226, n. 538.

[132] H. J. Holtzmann, *Handkommentar* on Mark 6:7.

[133] E. Lohmeyer in Meyer's *Kommentar* on Mark 6:7.

[134] Andronicus and Junias also form such a pair of apostles (Rom. 16:7).

[135] According to Luke 7:18, John the Baptist sends two disciples to Jesus.

[136] Cf. II Cor. 1:19.

[137] See pp. 65 ff.

[138] Other examples of this two-by-two appearance of primitive Christian missionaries or messengers perhaps are Aquila and Priscilla (Acts 18:26) and Gaius and Aristarchus (Acts

velopment, which made necessary a larger number of fellow workers because of the number of congregations founded by Paul and still requiring assistance, and which at the same time elevated Paul to a singular position among the missionaries, caused the erosion of the ancient custom. Still, the fact that Paul always retained an especially close associate—after Silvanus apparently came Timotheus[139]—is certainly a relic of that ancient arrangement of the sending forth δύο δύο.[140]

17. It is further worthy of note that there is for the apostle a genuine καύχημα, which neither is excluded from the Christian existence as sin (Rom. 3:27), nor is permitted to be mentioned only when he "plays the fool" (II Cor. 11–12), but which serves some purpose in the day of the Lord. This genuine glorying boasts ὅτι οὐκ εἰς κενὸν ἔδραμον οὐδὲ εἰς κενὸν ἐκοπίασα (Phil. 2:16). τίς γὰρ ἡμῶν ἐλπὶς ἢ χαρὰ ἢ στέφανος καυχήσεως —ἢ οὐχὶ καὶ ὑμεῖς—ἔμπροσθεν τοῦ κυρίου ἡμῶν Ἰησοῦ ἐν τῇ αὐτοῦ παρουσίᾳ ὑμεῖς γάρ ἐστε ἡ δόξα ἡμῶν καὶ ἡ χαρά (I Thess. 2:19-20). How little this resembles a glorying in his own privileges is shown in II Cor. 1:14: "We are your glory just as you are our glory in the day of our Lord Jesus." If Paul glories in the congregations in the same way that they glory in him, then the ground even of his glory cannot ultimately be his own work, but rather the spirit of God, who gave to him the churches out of the same grace through which the apostle was given to the churches. I Cor. 9:16 agrees with this: ἐὰν γὰρ εὐαγγελίζωμαι, οὐκ ἔστιν μοι καύχημα. And further I Cor. 15:10: "By the grace of God I am what I am [i.e., a

---

19:29); but in any case Zenas–Apollos (Titus 3:13), Tychicus–Onesimus (Col. 4:7 ff.), and Titus and an unnamed brother (II Cor. 12:18). Aristarchus and Secundus, Gaius and Timothy, and Tychicus and Trophimus (Acts 20:4), who were messengers sent with money, are to be mentioned here only with some qualifications. Cf. W. Hartke, "Die Sammlung und die ältesten Ausgaben der Paulusbriefe," Diss. (Bonn, 1917), p. 22; J. Jeremias, "Paarweise Sendung im Neuen Testament," in the Manson *Festschrift* (1959), pp. 136 ff.

[139] Rom. 16:21; Phil. 1:1.

[140] O. Bauernfeind ("Die Begegnung zwischen Paulus und Kephas Gal. 1, 18-20," ZNW, XLVII [1956], 268-76) has shown with some persuasive force that Paul, in his portrayal of his first visit to Jerusalem, did not intend to prove that this visit had been too *short* for him, Paul, to have been given his gospel in Jerusalem. Instead, Paul intends to say plainly that among the apostles, about whom alone he is concerned according to Gal. 1:17*a*, he has met only Peter, unless one also wishes to count James among the apostles (1:19), which Paul apparently prefers not to do.

Since one can hardly doubt that Paul's biographical accounts from Gal. 1:11 onward are intended unequivocally to confirm what Paul presents in 1:11-12 as his theme, i.e., "My gospel does not come from men," Paul's comment that on his first visit to Jerusalem he had seen *only* the apostle Peter ought to mean that this encounter did not suffice to communicate to him the gospel in an obligatory way. This curious logic may be related to the observation that for Paul the apostles preach always at least in two's.

successful apostle], and his grace to me was not in vain." [141] According to Rom. 15:18, Paul glories only in that "which Christ accomplishes through me" (cf. I Cor. 15:31).

18. Finally we must refer to the remark of I Cor. 1:17: οὐ γὰρ ἀπέστει-λέν με Χριστὸς βαπτίζειν ἀλλὰ εὐαγγελίζεσθαι. This ἀποστέλλεσθαι is above all else the origin of the apostolic office, and the commission to this office is εὐαγγελίζεσθαι (Gal. 1:16). Paul does not by any means depreciate baptism as such, as is shown in numerous passages in his epistles where he speaks of the significance of baptism, but only leaves it for his fellow workers to perform.[142] Therefore the commission not to baptize but to evangelize must have been limited to a narrower circle of missionaries, that is, to the apostles. Consequently it is not traditionally the task of the apostle to baptize.

Conclusion of Part One

With these points the basic characteristics of the Pauline concept of apostleship are set forth. The presentation naturally could be expanded without difficulty in several different directions. One could examine the apostolic *message* in particular; or one could investigate the circle of hearers from among Jews and Gentiles and their relationship to each other and to the apostle; and the concern of the apostle for the established congregations would be worth consideration. Especially could one investigate the question of how Paul operated with his ministry in the already given context of the apostolic office,[143] how he filled the already present form with his spirit. But all this and much else does not belong to the specific traits of the traditional apostolate.

It is, after all, very easy to fall into the danger of referring general Christian thoughts and patterns of relationship to the apostolate in particular. Thus, I am unable to persuade myself that there was a special apostolic blessing.[144] Equally false, it appears to me, is the frequently[145] encountered argument that Paul had a *prophetic* concept of the apostle. "Prophetic" is certainly a comprehensive designation. But if it is intended to say that a close relationship existed between the apostle and the Old Testament

---

[141] "He does not earn God's favour by the results of his missionary work, but *vice versa*." Bultmann, TDNT, III, 650.

[142] Paul cannot recall having himself baptized anyone but Crispus, Gaius, and the house of Stephanus during a stay of several years in Corinth! (I Cor. 1:14 ff.).

[143] On this, cf. the splendid presentation by H. v. Campenhausen [2], pp. 32-58.

[144] Thus G. Sass [1], pp. 77-78.

[145] G. Sass [1], pp. 40-41; K. H. Rengstorf [1], pp. 440 ff.; H. Windisch, *op. cit.*, pp. 150-51; E. Lohmeyer, *Grundlagen paulinischer Theologie* (1929), pp. 201-2.

prophets, then it is out of place. Naturally there are some obvious points in common: The apostle preaches the same gospel as do the prophets (Rom. 1:1-7); with his proclamation to the Gentiles he continues the line of the prophetic words to the nations[146]; his word is often granted no acceptance (Rom. 10:16); and so on. Above all else, in both cases it is the word that determines the office. From this, however, one cannot derive a special line from prophet to apostle. On the contrary, it is striking to note how little Paul thinks of adducing, for the presentation of his ministry, the manifold and often even insistently obvious connections which exist between his office and that of the Old Testament prophets. Only in Gal. 1:15 do we find a clear echo of the prophetic self-consciousness (cf. Jer. 1:5). Paul explicitly compares the office of the apostle (and of the other messengers of the gospel) with that of Moses[147] (II Cor. 3:4-18), but this comparison depends upon the *differences* of the present ministry. We have already noted that, in contrast to the prophets, Paul can relate no experience of his call. It is true that the message of Paul, like that of the prophets, has the unmediated character of a revelation, but the typical prophetic "thus saith the Lord" is completely lacking in Paul. The New Testament apostolate does not find its explanation in the Old Testament prophetic office.[148]

When one summarizes the result of our investigation so far, one point emerges with unconditional clarity: The primitive Christian apostolate, as it is presented in the figure of the apostle Paul, is not an original creation of Pauline Christianity, but must have been taken over by Paul from a religious movement whose position did not allow him to accomplish this assimilation intact. Certain discontinuities have come to our attention at many points: The apostle is a missionary like all other missionaries, but not every missionary is an apostle. The apostle has seen the resurrected One, but not every witness to the resurrection becomes an apostle. Paul was conscious of having been called by an appearance of the resurrected One, but was unable to depict the calling itself.[149] He wishes to insure his apostolic rights by means of a ὅρασις κυρίου, although the ὅρασις itself first demands a proof of its own.[150] He asserts that he has received his message directly, and yet he lives consciously in the traditions of the community. The funda-

---

[146] G. Sass [1], p. 41.

[147] In late Judaism Moses frequently is regarded as a prophet; cf. H. J. Schoeps, *Theologie und Geschichte des Judenchristentums* (1949), pp. 87 ff.

[148] Thus correctly also J. Munck [2], p. 30, who considers rather the possibility of a comparison of Exod. 3:1-4:17 (esp. 3:10 LXX) with the Pauline concept of the apostle.

[149] It is precisely in such a portrayal that the prophets and apostles of the oriental and Hellenistic environment are generally most at home.

[150] Unless the apostle produces his trances in public—but this is just what Paul in II Cor. 5:11 ff. refuses to do (see p. 37, n. 71).

mental kerygma is in general by no means represented as specifically apostolic (e.g. in I Cor. 15:1 ff.), yet in Gal. 1:17 ff. Paul thinks that he can guarantee his independence of *men* by proving his independence of *apostles*. Paul, otherwise so modest, emphatically sets himself forth as an apostolic example. Paul expects an early Parousia, but this *temporal* expectation does not determine his concept of the apostle.

In addition there are certain technical terms which appearently have been taken over with the apostolate itself, for example, expressions for the appearing of Christ (*vide* p. 25); further, the concepts μίμησις, ἐξουσία, μυστήριον; the figure of the New Testament prophet also belongs here.

Occasionally double traditions are found, arousing the impression that a new, genuinely Pauline form of an idea has been set alongside one that has been taken over and has proved inadequate. Thus in one instance Paul appeals, for the sake of his apostolic rights, to the ἀποκάλυψις Χριστοῦ, another time to the success of his words, a third time with some hesitation to the σημεῖα τοῦ ἀποστόλου. On one occasion he accounts for his apostolic sufferings by saying that he is comforted so that he in turn may give comfort; while another time he does it by pointing to the greater brilliance with which the message of the gospel shines forth against the background of the weakness of the messenger.

All this necessarily leads us to pose the question as to the origin of the primitive Christian apostolate. It is obvious that the analysis of this apostolic office which we have given so far in the course of our investigation forms the precondition for answering this question. We intend now to show that careful observation will find that this analysis already contains the answer.

PART TWO
The Primitive Christian Apostolate

First, however, we must interrupt the course of our investigation. We have presented Paul's concept of the apostle. But does the Pauline concept of the apostle correspond to the concept of the apostolic in the early time of the church in general? Is Paul really a normal exponent of the primitive Christian apostolate, or is he perhaps an exceptional one? Can one speak simply of a primitive Christian apostolate at all? And, if not, which other concepts of what "apostolic" means are found in earliest Christianity? Clearly an answer to this question essentially determines any further progress of this investigation.

I

G. Sass ([1], p. 113) speaks of the "individuality and uniqueness of Paul's eschatological-prophetic consciousness of his office." "There is only *one* apostle who in a unique sense, by God himself and by Christ, is determined to be an apostle, and that is Paul himself. . . . There are many apostles of Christ, but only one eschatological apostle to the peoples, to whom all other apostles are only helpers in his work. . . . Thus the concept of apostle is nothing but a form which is filled by Paul with a content wholly different from that in the case of the other apostles" (*ibid.*, p. 141). "Though he knows a number of other apostles and recognizes their significance, still his missionary praxis and his religious conviction exclude the possibility that there could be even a single other apostle besides himself with the same tasks and authorizations from God as he himself possessed" (*ibid.*, p. 131).

Are these assertions correct? They rest upon a comparison of the Pauline apostolate with that of the other apostles. But do the other apostles provide a basis for this comparison? What, after all, do we know about them? Certainly the apostolate of Paul cannot be brought into agreement with the self-interpretation of the Twelve.[1] But were the twelve disciples of Jesus regarded in primitive Christianity as apostles in the technical sense of this word?

One can form a judgment as to the particular nature of the Pauline apostolate only when one sees Paul in relationship to the apostles of *his* time. One must then above all else make inquiry of Paul himself. But the result of this inquiry is that Paul places himself wholly within the one unified context of the primitive Christian apostolate.[2] At no point does he withdraw himself from the circle of the other apostles. When he speaks in I Cor. 9:5 of the λοιποὶ ἀπόστολοι, he and Barnabas together with them clearly form the host of *all* the apostles. The fact that he explicitly makes the point that he and Barnabas had voluntarily renounced the right of all apostles to be supported by the congregations shows how little he distinguished himself from all the others in other matters. When he asks in I Cor. 9:1, "Am I not an apostle?" the implication is "like the others." On one occasion he calls himself the "least of the apostles" (I. Cor. 15:9), but with this modest self-designation he placed himself precisely within the apostolic circle. He is indeed the most zealous of all the apostles, in whom the grace of God was especially effective; in addition, he is certainly also the most successful of all. However, he does not claim to be *more* than the others, but only the one in their midst who has been especially favored: εἴτε οὖν ἐγὼ εἴτε ἐκεῖνοι (I Cor. 15:11). It is true that he (along with other apostle colleagues) by special commission is the apostle to the Gentiles, just as Peter is the most eminent apostle to the circumcision, but together with Peter he stands in the one apostolic circle, and he no more withdraws from the circle because of the relative particularity of his commission than does Peter.

Thus Paul himself gives us every reason to regard him throughout as a typical representative of the primitive Christian apostolate. One may call him its "classical representative" [3] and emphasize his special zeal and success. One has no right, however, against Paul's own conviction, to detach him from the larger circle of the apostles. Paul himself in any case felt himself to be totally bound up together with that circle.

All the more does the concisely framed and distinctively filled concept of the ἀπόστολος Χριστοῦ forbid the assumption that at the time of Paul there was as yet no fixed image of the apostle at all (thus D. Georgi, *op. cit.*,

---

[1] On the basis of this awareness, also K. H. Rengstorf ([1], pp. 441-42) discusses "the special nature of Paul's position among the other apostles of Jesus," wherein by "the other apostles" are meant the twelve disciples of Jesus. But unfortunately we do not learn on which side all the rest of the apostles stand.

[2] Cf. H. v. Campenhausen [1], pp. 110 ff.

[3] K. H. Rengstorf [1], p. 437.

pp. 39 ff.; similarly D. Lührmann, *op. cit.*, pp. 93 ff.), a thesis which of course would make our investigation superfluous. Georgi's thesis already runs aground on the fact that Paul has in view a closed circle of apostles which has experienced no further expansion since his call of almost twenty years earlier (I Cor. 15:9). And must not the charisma of the apostle be just as functionally intended as the charismata which are enumerated along with it (I Cor. 12:28 ff. *et passim*)? The conflict over the apostolate in Corinth is explained only if two well-defined concepts of the apostle collided, and people are not, as Georgi thinks, being reproached only for inability in a missionary ministry. D. Lührmann (*op. cit.*, pp. 93 ff.) thinks moreover that the Corinthian counterapostles are missionaries *like* Paul, who therefore cannot dispute their title: a strange assertion in view of II Cor. 11:13 ff., where Paul calls the Corinthian apostles "false apostles" and "servants of Satan" who *falsely* represent themselves to be apostles of Christ.

II

Now however the question arises as to whether one may speak at all of *one* apostolic circle in primitive Christianity. It has generally become customary to distinguish between a narrower and a wider circle of apostles.[4] It is beyond question that this distinction would have to be affirmed in Paul's writings if it existed in early Christianity.

Two passages in Paul, II Cor. 8:23 and Phil. 2:25, point to such a distinction between a wider and a narrower apostolic circle. On his last journey to Achaia from Macedonia, Paul sent Titus to Corinth in matters of the collection. With Titus traveled two companions whom the Macedonian congregations had chosen for this purpose as fellow workers for the collection and for protection of Paul against spiteful accusations (II Cor. 12:16). These two brethren, whose names are lacking in our text, are described as ἀπόστολοι ἐκκλησιῶν (II Cor. 8:23). Epaphroditus, who brought the Philippians' gift of money to Corinth for the personal needs of Paul (Phil. 2:25; 4:18), is also called ἀπόστολος. As ὑμῶν δὲ ἀπόστολος he is likewise an ἀπόστολος ἐκκλησιῶν.

It is obvious that one cannot connect these congregational apostles with the apostolate of Paul.[5] The designation "your apostle" or "apostles of the churches" is manifestly intended to distinguish these messengers from the

---

[4] Cf. M. Barth, *op. cit.*, n. 275, and the literature cited there; P. Althaus in NTD, VIII (7th ed., 1955), p. 5; O. Linton, *op. cit.*, pp. 76 ff.; finally L. Cerfaux, "Pour l'histoire du titre Apostolos dans le Nouveau Testament" (RechdeSciRel, XLVIII (1960), pp. 76-92); C. F. D. Moule, *op. cit.*, pp. 156-57.

[5] This is already forbidden by the completely different functions of the two apostolates and by the fact that *here* Christ calls to a lifelong ministry, and *there* the community calls to a temporary one.

apostles as ἀπόστολοι Χριστοῦ.[6] But one should not speak here of a "wider" concept of the apostle. Such usage leads to the mistaken idea that the ἀπόστολοι ἐκκλησιῶν had a commission which is related to that of the actual apostles. In truth the ἀπόστολοι ἐκκλησιῶν as apostles have nothing to do with the ἀπόστολοι Χριστοῦ,[7] and Paul can call these fellow workers in the service of the ministry "apostles" only because it does not even enter his mind that one could give them and their service the description of "apostolic." One would do well in connection with Phil. 2:25 and II Cor. 8:23 (as well as John 13:16 [8] and possibly Luke 11:49 and Mark 6:30) to speak of a general use of the word "apostle" in contrast to the technical application[9] which alone concerns us in our investigation. The two afore-mentioned passages therefore are to be excluded from our investigation.

III

But with these two points, basically quite obvious ones, only the preliminary questions are clarified. The distinction between a wider and a narrower circle of apostles is not connected, for the most part, with a difference between the apostles in a technical sense of this word and the others who were sent out; it is more correctly seen in the fact that frequently a group of ἀπόστολοι κατ' ἐξοχήν is set off from a wider circle of primitive Christian missionaries who are called apostles. This narrower group of apostles embraces then, ordinarily, the twelve disciples, in some cases with the addition of Paul [10] and sometimes James as well.[11] How the boundary runs between the apostles in the wider and those in the narrower sense is often not clear,[12] and the technical outlines of the two groups remain

[6] Thus, contrary to the view of D. Georgi (op. cit., p. 43), Paul is employing sharply different concepts. G. Schille (op. cit., pp. 13 ff.) regards the "Christ apostolate" as an original creation of Paul who therewith has "deepened" the earlier community apostolate. But the specific features of the Pauline Christ apostolate are explained neither from the community apostolate nor from Pauline theology. Our analysis, rather, has shown that Paul found already existing a Christ apostolate in the technical sense; he is the last but by no means the first apostle of Christ (I Cor. 15:8)! Hence Schille must, e.g., deny that such a specific feature as the calling by the resurrected One was constitutive for the Christ apostolate.

[7] K. H. Rengstorf ([1], p. 422) describes these congregational apostles as "religious figures." The propriety or impropriety of such a designation is like that of calling an ecclesiastical jurist a spiritual leader.

[8] See p. 97, n. 5.

[9] Thus also H. v. Campenhausen [1], p. 103; C. F. D. Moule, op. cit., p. 156.

[10] Cf. in K. H. Rengstorf [1], pp. 422-23; K. Holl [1], p. 924.

[11] Cf. A. Wikenhauser, op. cit., col. 554.

[12] J. Héring (op. cit.) can even distinguish four different circles of primitive Christian apostles.

even more obscure.[13] One hesitates to place, without further ado, the so-called original apostles in Jerusalem, i.e. the twelve disciples, in the same category with apostles like Junias and Andronicus (Rom. 16:7).

Over against this we must utter a word of caution, that Paul never expressly acknowledges that he is acquainted with a double technical usage of ἀπόστολος. If one nevertheless intends to presuppose such in Paul, he must prove that in certain passages where Paul speaks of ἀπόστολοι he cannot mean πάντες οἱ ἀπόστολοι, but only a special group within the entire circle of the apostles.

Whom does Paul number with certainty among the apostles?

First of all, himself; there can be no doubt of this.

Further, Junias and Andronicus. In Rom. 16:7 Paul writes: ἀσπάσαθε Ἀνδρόνικον καὶ Ἰουνιᾶν τοὺς συγγενεῖς μου καὶ συναιχμαλώτους μου, οἵτινές εἰσιν ἐπίσημοι ἐν τοῖς ἀποστόλοις, οἳ καὶ πρὸ ἐμοῦ γέγοναν ἐν Χριστῷ. J. B. Lightfoot [14] has already established that ἐπίσημοι ἐν τοῖς ἀποστόλοις does not mean "regarded by the apostles" but rather "regarded as apostles." In spite of occasional contrary assertions,[15] this translation, which is the only natural one, is generally preferred down to the present. It is found also in the Greek fathers.[16] Thus Junias and Andronicus are apostles. Since Paul calls them συγγενεῖς μου, they may have been Jews. Because Rom. 16 in my judgment was addressed to Ephesus,[17] we have to look for them at the time of the epistle in Ephesus, where they probably had been in prison with Paul. That they must have been ἐν Χριστῷ before Paul is concluded also from I Cor. 15:8, where Paul calls himself the last of the apostles; and for Paul, calling and conversion admittedly occurred together (*vide* pp. 30-31). The two non-Jewish names indicate that we have to do here with Hellenistic Jews like Paul. That they received the title of ἀπόστολος as "emissaries of the primitive community," as E. Lohse ([1], p. 267) argues, is not indicated by any evidence. At any rate, one could venture such an assertion only if, as is not the case, we had evidence of the use of ἀπόστολοι in the technical sense as emissaries of the primitive community. The two are rather simply apostles.

Further, Peter certainly qualifies as an apostle. This is evident from Gal.

[13] H. J. Schoeps, *Paulus* (1959), p. 65, considers the apostolate of the twelve original and has it based upon eyewitness testimony. Paul then places *in opposition to* this apostolate of the twelve the further charismatic apostolate, whose numerous representatives are called by the exalted Lord.

[14] *Op. cit.*, p. 96, n. 1.

[15] B. Weiss, Th. Zahn (see O. Michel on Rom. 16:7); such contrary assertions apparently seek to oppose the expansion of the apostolic circle.

[16] See J. B. Lightfoot, *op. cit.*, p. 96, n. 1.

[17] See the commentaries on Rom. 16.

1:18-19. Paul reports on his visit in Jerusalem with Peter and then states: ἕτερον δὲ τῶν ἀποστόλων οὐκ εἶδον. Gal. 2:8 also presupposes that Peter, like Paul, was an apostle: ὁ γὰρ ἐνεργήσας Πέτρῳ εἰς ἀποστολήν. That the claim of Peter to membership in the apostolic circle was not very secure, however, will be shown in our further investigation. Finally, Barnabas may have been an apostle.[18] To be sure, Paul does not explicitly give to him the name of apostle. However, in I Cor. 9:6 Paul names him alone among his fellow workers, because he also renounced his right to support by the congregations. Now Titus also refrained from claiming this right (II Cor. 12:18), and with respect to the Corinthians one would have expected a mention of him or of Timothy. The reason that Barnabas instead is named must be that as an apostle he deserves the preferential place of such a mention.

This is confirmed by Gal. 2:9. Together with Barnabas and Titus, Paul has traveled to Jerusalem to the so-called apostolic council, in order to carry the point of the freedom of the Gentile mission (Gal. 2:1). In Gal. 2:9 the result of these efforts is reported: δεξιὰς ἔδωκαν ἐμοὶ καὶ Βαρναβᾷ κοινωνίας, ἵνα ἡμεῖς εἰς τὰ ἔθνη, αὐτοὶ δὲ εἰς τὴν περιτομήν. Paul and Barnabas as equal partners receive the assurance that they carry forward their missionary work in fellowship with the congregation at Jerusalem, but Titus is not mentioned. The reason is that Barnabas, in contrast with Titus, is an apostle.

Finally, this point is confirmed by Acts 14:4, 14. According to Acts 13:1 ff., Paul and Barnabas were sent out by the congregation at Antoch—a quite reliable historical note.[19] In the subsequent report of their common labors in Iconium and Lystra they are twice called apostles. Since even Paul himself is never elsewhere in Acts called an apostle, one must assume that Luke is dependent upon an early source[20] in which Barnabas was counted among the apostles.

These testimonies suffice to call for agreement with J. B. Lightfoot, who declares: "The apostleship of Barnabas is beyond question" (op. cit., p. 96).

---

[18] Clem. Alex. Strom. II, 6.31; in 7:35 he is called an apostle and numbered among the seventy disciples; cf. Strom. II, 20.116; V, 10.63.

[19] This does not conflict with the fact that Paul knew himself to have been called and sent by Christ. For Paul does not first become an apostle through being sent out by Antioch, but the Antiochian community sends out the apostle Paul on the mission. But that at the beginning of his activity Paul had scorned any connection with the older congregations is not to be assumed. During the fourteen years of his work in Syria and Cilicia, in which he did not go to Jerusalem (Gal. 1:21 ff.), hardly any community other than that of Antioch, in which he dwelt even at the time of the encounter portrayed in Gal. 2:11 ff., can have been the point of departure for his journeys.

[20] See pp. 247 ff.

Wellhausen[21] even calls it "utterly ridiculous to deny the title of apostle to Barnabas." [22]

Whether one can trust all the reports in the book of Acts about Barnabas is uncertain. According to Acts 4:36 he came from Cyprus. He was thus a Hellenistic Jewish Christian. It is also uncertain whether he resided in Jerusalem. The field which he sold could have been situated anywhere in the world. Possibly, however, Barnabas had connections with the congregation in Jerusalem, as Acts 4:36; 9:27; and 11:22 intend to show, but certainly closer and incontestable ones with that of Antioch, as emerges from Acts 11:22, 25, 30; 12:25; 13:1 ff., and so on (*vide* pp. 90-91).

That already exhausts the list of undisputed representatives of the apostolate. Still contested is the question as to whether James, the brother of Jesus, served as an apostle. J. B. Lightfoot considered it certain that he did.[23] Today the majority of scholars are of the contrary opinion.[24] The passages in question, it is true, hardly yield a clear meaning. In I Cor. 15:7 James is not named an apostle. That he belonged to the πάντες ἀπόστολοι mentioned in the same verse, as J. B. Lightfoot (*op. cit.*, p. 95, n. 4) and K. Holl ([1], p. 927) assert, is not indicated by Paul himself and is, as will appear later, a mistaken assumption. Just as little is he counted among the apostles in I Cor. 9:5; for if the brothers of the Lord had been apostles, Paul would not have been able to introduce them separately, joined to the λοιποὶ ἀπόστολοι with a καί. In Gal. 2:9, likewise, James is not called an apostle, but if he, ahead of Peter and along with John, as εἰς τὴν περιτομήν, is set over against the two apostles εἰς τὰ ἔθνη, Paul and Barnabas, nothing could actually hinder his being called an apostle also, since the resurrected One certainly had appeared to him (I Cor. 15:7).

The decisive passage, Gal. 1:19, appears to be incurably ambiguous. The sentence ἕτερον δὲ τῶν ἀποστόλων οὐκ εἶδον, εἰ μὴ ᾽Ιάκωβον τὸν ἀδελφὸν τοῦ κυρίου can be translated either as "Besides Peter I saw no apostle; I saw only James," or as "Besides Peter, among the apostles I saw only James." In either case, Paul unnecessarily expressed himself in such a complicated way as to be incomprehensible. If he intended to say that besides Peter he saw only James among the apostles, one cannot understand why he first says

---

[21] NGG (1907), p. 5.

[22] Thus also e.g., W. G. Kümmel, *op. cit.*, p. 45, n. 13; K. H. Rengstorf [2], p. 21, n. 57; Lietzmann on I Cor. 9:6; J. Munck [1], p. 101; on the contrary, H. v. Campenhausen [1], p. 106, n. 7.

[23] *Op. cit.*, p. 95, n. 4; K. Holl [1], pp. 925 ff.; Lietzmann in HNT, X on Gal. 1:19; E. Bammel, *op. cit.*, p. 417; undecided is K. H. Rengstorf [1], p. 422, n. 93; p. 431.

[24] Th. Zahn and H. Schlier, *op. cit.*, on Gal. 1:19; H. v. Campenhausen [1], p. 106, n. 7; W. G. Kümmel, *op. cit.*, p. 45, n. 13; E. Lohse [1], p. 265, n. 25; J. Munck [1], p. 107; [2], pp. 92-93; W. Seufert, *op. cit.*, p. 45.

plainly, "Besides Peter I saw none of the apostles." [25] But if he intended to say that of the apostles he had seen only Peter, then why did he add on "except James, the brother of the Lord"? The εἰ μή introduces an apposition to ἕτερον δὲ τῶν ἀποστόλων, but is not connected with εἶδον in such a way as to say that other than Peter, Paul did not see anyone at all in Jerusalem except James. However, that James is named by Paul because he was the only one of the "recognized ones" in Jerusalem besides Peter to be seen by Paul,[26] not only is not indicated by Paul, but does not fit into the intention of the sequence of thought in Gal. 1–2. Paul wishes to see preserved the independence of his *apostleship* and its message, in which he still could be dependent only upon other *apostles*.[27] The mention of James alongside Paul makes sense only if he qualified, or at least could qualify, as an apostle.

The result, then, remains equivocal, so that we can only conclude that this lack of clarity was intentional with Paul. If one recognizes this, then the passages becomes clear. Paul says: Besides Peter, I saw none other of the apostles, except James. εἰ μή, then, is to be translated in the usual sense: "if not," or "except." [28] Paul limits the assertion that he has seen no apostle besides Peter, by leaving room for the possibility that one could, if need be, count James among the apostles—something he was not himself accustomed to doing—whom he had also seen.

It is understandable that James did not qualify in principle as an apostle; for according to all that we know of him, his work consisted in leading the congregation in Jerusalem, not in a missionary activity. Since, on the other hand, he had seen the resurrected Lord (I Cor. 15:7) and certainly did not remain completely without any missionary activity (cf. Gal. 2:9, 12; I Cor. 9:5), there was no basic reservation forbidding one to count him among the circle of apostles. That such a count is not the original one[29] is not without significance for the question as to where and in what personal sphere the apostolate is at home.

Finally, there exists the possibility that Silvanus also was an apostle.[30]

---

[25] Th. Zahn, *in loc.*: "It would be incomprehensible why Paul would have denied so emphatically that other than Peter he had seen even a second apostle, if he felt compelled in the same breath yet to name a second apostle whom he likewise had seen at the same time."

[26] This is the opinion of Th. Zahn (*in loc.*), according to whom "the reader must thus generalize the object of οὐκ εἶδον."

[27] Indeed only the apostles are direct recipients of the revelation and therefore authorized mediators of the gospel. For this mediatorial function which is so decisive for Paul in Gal. 1 there are no other "recognized ones" than just the apostles themselves.

[28] Cf., e.g., II Cor. 13:5; I Cor. 14:5; 15:2; I Tim. 5:19.

[29] Hegesippus (in Eus., CH II, 23.4) does *not* count James as one of the apostles.

[30] Cf. A. M. Farrer, "The Ministry in the New Testament," in *The Apostolic Ministry* (London, 1947), p. 130; E. Meyer, *op. cit.*, I, 265; A. v. Harnack [1], I, 321; E. v. Dobschütz, *Thessalonicherbriefe* (1909), p. 7.

Paul had taken him along on the second missionary journey as a substitute for the apostle Barnabas. He mentions him, alongside himself, in the salutations of the two Thessalonian epistles, indeed, along with Timothy, but *before* him. Silvanus is named in the same company in II Cor. 1:19. In these two passages there was no necessity to name him as apostle, even if he was one. The frequent and commendatory (Acts 15:22, 32) mention of him in Acts 15–18, as well as I Peter 5:12, shows that he possessed a good reputation in early Christianity. It is not surprising that the book of Acts does not call him an apostle, since for the author of Acts only the twelve disciples qualified as apostles.[31] Besides the fact that Silvanus appears as a substitute for Barnabas and apparently performs apostolic service until we lose sight of him after Acts 18:5, I Thess. 2:7 could argue for the point of view that he was counted among the apostles.

From I Thess. 2:1 onward, Paul reminds the Thessalonians of the time of the first preaching among them. In doing this he speaks in the plural. This could be, as it often is with Paul, a literary plural, with which he then would be indicating only himself.[32] But he could just as well include his fellow workers, in particular Silvanus (cf. Acts 17:4, 10), who joined with him in sending I Thessalonians. P. Schmiedel[33] is probably essentially correct in saying: "He evidently intends to include them in the plural, even if perhaps more as a matter of *honoris causa;* and they, in spite of the plural, retreat more and more into the background of his thinking, as the things he says apply more and more only to him." In any case, an unconditional decision can hardly be made in a particular instance[34]; yet one may suppose that in the portrayal of his missionary work (I Thess. 2:1 ff.), Paul does not leave his fellow worker of the time, Silvanus, wholly unconsidered.[35] Then, however, Silvanus also is intended[36] in I Thess. 2:7 with the designation ὡς Χριστοῦ ἀπόστολοι, for which I Thess. 2:4 has already prepared the way.[37]

If this is correct—a completely unambiguous decision is not possible—it is of interest that Silvanus was a Hellenistic Jew who, besides his grecized Hebrew name Silas, bears the Latin name Silvanus, which Paul uses exclusively.[38] He can have possessed Roman citizenship, as did Paul, if Acts 16:37 can be trusted. He has ostensibly close connection with Jerusalem

[31] On the exception in Acts 14:4, 14, see pp. 248-49.
[32] Cf. E. Lohse [1], p. 268, n. 31; E. Haupt, *op. cit.,* p. 111.
[33] In the *Handkommentar* on I Thess. 3:5.
[34] One should observe that the singular is found only in 2:18, 3:5, and 5:27.
[35] Timothy, who at the time of the mission in Thessalonica had been associated with Paul only for a short time, hardly deserves here such consideration.
[36] *Contra,* e.g., H. v. Campenhausen [1], p. 106, n. 7.
[37] "We are found as counted worthy of God to be entrusted with the gospel."
[38] See pp. 89-90.

and the (Hellenistic) Christian community there (Acts 15:22), without, however, being bound to Jerusalem in any wise (Acts 15:40-41).

With relatively great certainty, then, the following qualify as apostles[39]: Andronicus, Junias, Barnabas, Silvanus, and Peter.[40] In the case of Peter the opinion of Paul is unsettled (*vide infra*); and he *himself* would prefer not to count James among the apostles.

IV

Some readers will be surprised that so far we have not spoken of the twelve (or eleven) disciples of Jesus. It is generally accepted as self-evident that they were apostles.[41] To be sure, for Paul and earliest Christianity, nothing is less self-evident than the apostleship of the so-called original apostles.[42] Peter is the only one out of their circle whom Paul expressly calls apostle, and even for him this title is not original, as will be shown. Paul however not only never *names* the other men of the circle of the twelve as apostles; for him they are not apostles. The proof of this assertion in the following will at the same time decide the question as to whether there was a broader and a narrower concept of the apostle.

1. First of all, the following systematic consideration of K. Holl is to be taken up: "In contrast to the view current among us, which very early appeared in the legends, we must enunciate the fact that according to the primitive Christian view *the apostle* did not have the task of going out into the world, but rather of staying in Jerusalem" ([1], p. 934). This assertion is incontestable.[43] Its correctness is shown in Acts 8:1, Gal. 2:9, and Matt. 19:28 (or Luke 22:28-30), among other passages. The early tradition knows

---

[39] One should not infer from I Cor. 4:9 that Apollos bore the title of apostle: ὁ θεὸς ἡμᾶς τοὺς ἀποστόλους ἐσχάτους ἀπέδειξεν. By "ἡμᾶς τοὺς ἀποστόλους" are meant all the apostles together, as whose representative Paul is regarded, but not Paul and Apollos. In I Clem. 47.4 Apollos is explicitly distinguished from the apostles.

[40] The opinion of J. L. Leuba (*op. cit.*, pp. 52-53): "It is in fact philologically impossible to name with certainty other apostles than Peter, the twelve and Paul," is thus too skeptical with regard to individual representatives of the apostolic circle, but of course at the same time too optimistic with regard to the twelve, as is now to be shown.

[41] "It is evident that not only in the later tradition throughout, . . . but also in Paul himself, by 'the apostles' is understood only the closed circle of the twelve" (E. Meyer, *op. cit.*, III, 255); thus more recently, and with emphasis, J. L. Leuba, *op. cit.*, pp. 52-89.

[42] "Originally precisely these hardly served as a group as apostles, but rather as 'the twelve.' They only later became apostles and finally the only apostles" (H. v. Campenhausen [2], p. 15).

[43] "Even if not much of their (*sc.*, the twelve) missionary activity, apart from Peter's, is reported, still they doubtless regarded this as their chief task" (A. Wikenhauser, *op. cit.*, col. 553). This assertion not only cannot be documented but is contradicted by everything known to us. Whether, after the disintegration of the circle of the twelve, others of its members in addition to Peter left Jerusalem or Galilee—this is a question in itself (see pp. 259-60).

nothing of mission trips of the twelve disciples.[44] At the time of Gal. 2:7-8 Peter is an express exception.[45] K. Holl has only neglected, in his sentence cited above, to set "apostle" in quotation marks. That is to say, he is of the strange opinion that these "pillars" in Jerusalem, who hold their position in the city so steadfastly and valiantly, were called "apostles," or "sent ones." But to assume this is as absurd as if one were to conclude from the word "prisoners" that the people so designated were free men, or as if one explained that the ambassador of a state is called ambassador because he must stay at the seat of his own government. If the members of the circle of the twelve bear the name of apostle, they must also have performed the ministry of the apostle.[46] But if the constitutive mark of the circle of the twelve was not the missionary activity of its members[47]—and everything that we know about them supports this, in spite of the mission activity of a single one of the twelve—then the twelve as such were not apostles.[48]

2. To this we must add a second basic consideration. If one is justified in speaking of an apostolate of the twelve, then the closed circle of the twelve must have existed for a somewhat extended period of time, at least; and if Paul, who speaks of the contemporary ἀπόστολοι, means thereby the twelve so-called original apostles, this circle must have been for him a very familiar entity, one extending down to his time.[49]

Neither of these, however, is the case. As regards the circle of the δώδεκα, generally, in my opinion it does not reach at all back into the time before the resurrection.[50] To show this *in extenso* would go beyond the

[44] This fact may be a deposit of a later tradition which claimed to know that the δώδεκα were first to remain for twelve years in Jerusalem: Kerygma Petri in Clem. Alex. Strom. VI, 5.43; cf. A. v. Harnack [1], I, 45, n. 1; J. Wagenmann, *op. cit.*, p. 15; Apollonius in Eus., CH V, 18; Ps.-Clem. Rec. 1.43; 9.29.

[45] See K. Holl, *op. cit.*, p. 934; H. v. Campenhausen [2], p. 16; E. Lohse [1], p. 265.

[46] If one proceeds from the Jewish concept of the *Schaliach* (*vide infra*, pp. 103 ff.), one could perhaps avoid this conclusion (cf. H. v. Campenhausen [1], p. 106, n. 1). But the Greek word ἀπόστολος—whether it is a translation of *Schaliach* or not—never existed without the conception of a *missio*.

[47] Cf. also H. v. Campenhausen [1], p. 106, who speaks of the so-called twelve apostles, "who—except for Peter—to our knowledge did not conduct any mission, but rather, it seems, saw their calling to consist in not departing from Jerusalem." Of course whether the twelve ever or at least originally were to be sought in Jerusalem and not rather in Galilee is a problem in itself, which here may be left aside.

[48] E. Haupt, *op. cit.*, p. 109: "In the first period, according to all that we know, the twelve, but above all, Peter and John, were firmly stationed in Jerusalem. Thus a name which in the first place belonged to them without being contested cannot designate a characteristic which at that time was not at all under discussion among them."

[49] F. Kattenbusch (*op. cit.*, p. 341), by the way, rightly points out that Jesus must have known himself to be the Messiah if he gathered around himself twelve disciples as eschatological rulers.

[50] Most recently P. Vielhauer has emphatically represented this conviction in the *Festschrift* for G. Dehn (pp. 62 ff.). G. Klein (*op. cit.*, pp. 34 ff.) joins him in this. Cf.

limits of this work. Therefore only a few indications will be given here.

In Mark, for example, who has μαθηταί over forty times—and that is the old designation for the *whole* body of disciples in the early congregations—δώδεκα is found only ten times,[51] and these ten passages belong collectively to the more recent traditions of Mark's Gospel![52] This shows that the twelve did not originally belong in the Jesus traditions. One might respond to this by pointing to the figure of the traitor Judas, who certainly was one of the twelve and as one of the twelve already before the resurrection had left the circle of the δώδεκα. It would be unthinkable, one might say, that anyone should have added the compromising figure of the traitor to the circle of the first disciples, if Judas did not originally belong to it.[53] Indeed! Judas Iscariot is one of the twelve and is a traitor. But he did not originally belong in the passion narratives. The traditions about him may still today be easily separated from the Gospels, and no exegete has yet been able satisfactorily to explain wherein his betrayal actually consisted. Further, since the old tradition speaks of an appearance of Jesus before the twelve,[54] Judas must have been present at this appearance (I Cor. 15:5). His "betrayal" then comes in the time of the early church. Judas, the witness to the resurrection, was then, an apostate, who betrayed Jesus through his apostasy, and as such possibly had caused damage to the primitive community through denunciation to the authorities. When the existence of the twelve was projected back into the life of Jesus, Judas and his betrayal found a place in the passion narratives.[55]

If the twelve had been the carefully chosen companions of Jesus on his

---

further Wellhausen, *Einleitung*, pp. 138 ff.; R. Schütz, *op. cit.*, pp. 68 ff., and the discussion in O. Linton, *op. cit.*, pp. 72-73.

[51] Cf. G. Sass [1], p. 133.

[52] Cf., e.g., Maurice Goguel [1], p. 335; P. Vielhauer in *Gnomon*, XXVI (1954), 462; Béda Rigaux in *Der historische Jesus und der kerygmatische Christus* (ed. H. Ristow and K. Matthiae, 1960), pp. 470 ff.

[53] For example E. Lohse [1], pp. 262-63; W. G. Kümmel, *op. cit.*, p. 30, who adduces additional but little convincing arguments; H. Mosbech [1], p. 186; E. Meyer, *op. cit.*, I, 296-97. In the *Festschrift* for Günther Dehn (1957), pp. 62 ff., P. Vielhauer discusses this argument and, although by an entirely different route, comes to the conclusion that the membership of the traitor Judas in the circle of the twelve is no proof of the pre-Easter existence of that circle. Cf. also G. Klein, *op. cit.*, p. 36. E. Barnikol, *Das Leben Jesu der Heilsgeschichte* (1958), pp. 330 ff., reports on earlier efforts to eliminate the figure of Judas from the passion narrative.

[54] A careless form of expression—twelve instead of eleven—may perhaps be presumed elsewhere, but not in an official confession of the primitive community which preserved the key witnesses to the resurrection. Cf. G. Klein, *op. cit.*, n. 138. *Contra*, e.g., H. v. Campenhausen in SAH (1958), II, p. 17. Correctly P. Vielhauer, *op. cit.*, p. 63.

[55] In the passion narrative since the earliest time the concept of παραδίδωμι is found, and indeed with the meaning of "hand over" or something similar (cf. I Cor. 11:23), which formed a satisfactory point of contact for the taking over of the Judas tradition.

journeys, they would not have been able so completely to disappear in the history of the young church, as in fact they did. One can only agree with K. H. Rengstorf [56] "that there is no passage in the NT which makes it plain that the twelve played any special role either in Jerusalem or later on." They have their significance as witnesses of the resurrection. With this, our knowledge about them as a closed circle is exhausted.[57] What the book of Acts claims to know about them—selection of Matthias, Acts 1:15-26; further, their appearance, Acts 2:14, 6:2—is legend.[58] Even Paul mentions the twelve only in the formula taken over from the primitive community as witnesses of the resurrection (I Cor. 15:5). Otherwise he does not know them.[59]

Thus, under the impact of Jesus' appearing before Peter (I Cor. 15:5) a circle of Jesus' followers, who saw in the resurrection of Jesus the advent of the general resurrection of the dead (I Cor. 15:20), will have gathered together. The twelve formed the core of this group as the representatives of the eschatological community of salvation. A resurrection vision was shared with them. Very soon, then[60]—probably with the slackening of the eschatological expectation upon which it lived—this circle of the twelve must have fallen apart [61]; at the latest after the death of James the son of Zebedee, and perhaps already after the "betrayal" of Judas,[62] it was scattered.[63] The primitive community accommodated itself to the new situation, began with the (Jewish) mission, and had men at its head who indeed in part, like Peter and John (and his brother James), had belonged to the circle of the twelve, but who gained the leading positions not as members

[56] TDNT, II, 326.

[57] Not even the limited activity which R. Bultmann ([1], I, 58) concedes to them can be exegetically justified: "Their practical work was evidently as proclaimers of the word both within the Congregation and outside, and on missionary journeys they seem to have left Jerusalem either temporarily or (like Peter) permanently."

[58] The account of the later choice of Matthias may, of course, go back to early traditions which told of a filling out of the circle of the twelve after Judas' apostasy. In other respects, in the book of Acts the twelve "apostles" lead a shadowy existence. Only the figures of Peter, John, and James have authentic contours. Not very convincing is P. H. Menoud, "Les additions au groupe des douze apôtres, d'après le livre des Actes," RHPhR, XXXVII (1957), 71-80, who thinks that the significance of the twelve was still current at the time of the writing of the book of Acts.

[59] Cf. G. Sass [1], p. 97.

[60] The fact that the lists of names of the twelve differ somewhat argues for this (Mark 3:16 ff.; Matt. 10:2 ff.; Luke 6:14 ff.; Acts 1:13). This would hardly be conceivable in case of a long continuance of this circle.

[61] Thus it happens that the majority of the twelve have for us "no face and no history" (H. v. Campenhausen [2], p. 16).

[62] At that time, that is to say, if the election of Matthias has no historical background.

[63] Cf. E. Lohse [1], p. 265.

of this circle but on the ground of their achievement, and who later could be supplanted by the Lord's brother, James.[64]

The reason that, in spite of this situation, the recollection of the twelve is so well preserved in the primitive church lies in the fact that they as representatives of the new salvation community experienced the appearance of the resurrected One, in which the church actually was founded. This appearance, in spite of all the other contradictions of the resurrection reports, forms the central point of the reports, in the Synoptics as well as in John, and not least in the primitive-church tradition taken up into I Cor. 15:5.[65]

If one visualizes this state of affairs, it is inconceivable that the δώδεκα ever could have been apostles in the early times of the church. Neither can Paul, who correctly judges their position throughout, have given them the title of "apostle."

3. For many readers, the picture of the circle of the twelve drawn here may be too critically conceived. In view of the difficulty that there are no generally recognized principles for the evaluation of the Synoptic tradition, one will further have to reckon with the fact that a large number of studies would relate the circle of the twelve to the life of Jesus. The backward projection from a later period into the time before the resurrection, as asserted here, occurred so early that one can view the δώδεκα as growing from the beginning onward together with the traditions about the historical Jesus. That, however, one cannot *in any case* speak of a connection between the historical Jesus and twelve *apostles* becomes clear when one asks whether these twelve disciples—whether they found themselves together before or after the resurrection—served from the beginning onward as apostles. This question can only be answered with a clear "No." [66]

A look into the concordance suffices as demonstration of this. In the Gospels, ἀπόστολος is found in the technical sense in John not at all, in Mark and Matthew at most one time each,[67] and in Luke thirty-one times—five times in the Gospel [68] and twenty-six in the book of Acts.[69]

---

[64] The reasons for this supplanting still are unexplained. The existence of the primitive community in Jerusalem rested upon its conservative attitude with reference to the law. Apparently the especially conservative stance of James in the course of the increasingly vigorous disputes between Jews and Jewish Christians in Jerusalem of itself led him to the head of the primitive community in the holy city, and tended to push aside more liberal people like Peter, though this does not mean that there must have existed serious tensions within the community itself. The change in leadership was of a tactical sort.

[65] Cf. H. v. Campenhausen [2], pp. 17-18.

[66] *Contra*, e.g., P. Wernle [1], p. 83. On the whole matter, cf. the discussion in O. Linton, *op. cit.*, pp. 73 ff.

[67] On Mark 3:14, see below.

[68] In addition, the variously interpreted passage of Luke 11:49 (see p. 97).

[69] In addition, a variant reading: Acts 5:34.

John is a different story. One will not *have* to assume that the title of apostle for the twelve was wholly unknown to him, although that is not ruled out. That he should intentionally refrain from giving the disciples this title, however, would be entirely impossible if they actually had been the "original apostles" who bore this title from the very beginning. We must come back to John in the further course of this investigation.

The Synoptic writers show a clear line of development. Luke names the twelve as apostles without any restriction. The difference in the frequency of the appearance of ἀπόστολος in the Gospel and in Acts rests upon the fact that in his first book Luke was more closely tied to his sources. And these sources knew nothing of the title for the twelve. The fact that Mark and Matthew have the title once each does not argue against this point. In Matt. 10:2 the listing of the names of the twelve is introduced with the remark: τῶν δὲ δώδεκα ἀποστόλων τὰ ὀνόματά ἐστιν ταῦτα. But the Sinai-Syriac has in place of ἀποστόλων the otherwise customary μαθητῶν, and not a few researchers hold this Syriac reading to be the original one.[70]

The words οὓς καὶ ἀποστόλους ὠνόμασεν in Mark 3:14 have later slipped in from Luke 6:13, as the tradition shows and as the exegetes fairly unanimously agree. On the other hand, in Mark 6:30, ἀπόστολοι is clearly attested; when the disciples returned to Jesus after he had sent them out, they were called "apostles." But H. v. Campenhausen rightly points out ([1], p. 105) that in this passage no one would suspect the Christian office designation if the Lucan usage of the term were not so well-known to us. For this reason he assumes[71] that in this unparalleled appearance in Mark the word is not employed in the technical sense at all, but is meant simply to signify "messengers."

The single occurrence of ἀπόστολος in Mark and in Matthew can hardly be explained with absolute clarity. But if one compares the foregone conclusion of later times, that the twelve simply were "the apostles," with the silence of older sources, even those who seem unable to come to any clarity about Mark 6:30 and Matt. 10:2 must conclude that the title apostle was transferred later to the twelve.[72] In any case, the assertion that it may "be taken as certain" that the name of apostle was used by Jesus with reference to the twelve needs no refutation.[73]

[70] See H. v. Campenhausen [1], p. 104, n. 6; A. Merx, *Die vier kanonischen Evangelien nach ihrem ältesten bekannten Texte*, II/1 (Berlin, 1902), p. 156; W. Bauer, ZwTh, LIV (1912), 339 ff.; *contra* F. Haase, *op. cit.*, pp. 15 ff., who treats the question in detail. Cf. also A. v. Harnack [1], I, 320.

[71] Thus also E. Lohse [1], p. 262; H. Mosbech [1], p. 176.

[72] Thus, e.g., R. Schütz, *op. cit.*, pp. 67-68; A. Fridrichsen, *op. cit.*, n. 12.

[73] Thus K. H. Rengstorf [1], p. 429, who depends here upon a rather venturesome exegesis of the Lucan (!) passages alone. This exegesis has rightly been criticized by G. Klein (*op. cit.*, pp. 28 ff.).

4. I Cor. 15:5 ff.

If Mark and Matthew did not know the twelve as apostles, then it is not right to expect that Paul would have known twelve apostles,[74] all the less since already for him the circle of the twelve was no longer a tangible entity. But a glance into the literature will reveal the remarkable fact that it is almost taken for granted that at least Paul counted the twelve among the ἀπόστολοι. The strongest impression in this respect has been made by the argument which Karl Holl has set forth in the context of his interpretation of I Cor. 15:7 in his well-known essay on the idea of the church in Paul. For this reason I Cor. 15:5 ff. demands a more thorough discussion.

In Corinth, certain people contest the resurrection. Against them Paul intends to prove that Jesus himself, as the ἀπαρχὴ τῶν κεκοιμημένων (I Cor. 15:20), has arisen. Thus he is interested in the fullest possible list of witnesses. It is not the appearances of the resurrected One as such that concern him in the verses I Cor. 15:5-7, but the persons to whom the resurrected One has appeared. Paul is able to adduce the following witnesses:

(1) ὤφθη Κηφᾷ,

(2) εἶτα τοῖς δώδεκα·

(3) ἔπειτα ὤφθη ἐπάνω πεντακοσίοις ἀδελφοῖς ἐφάπαξ, ἐξ ὧν οἱ πλείονες μένουσιν ἕως ἄρτι. . . . ·

(4) ἔπειτα ὤφθη Ἰακώβῳ,

(5) εἶτα τοῖς ἀποστόλοις πᾶσιν·

(6) ἔσχατον δὲ πάντων ὡσπερεὶ τῷ ἐκτρώματι ὤφθη κἀμοί. Ἐγὼ γάρ εἰμι ὁ ἐλάχιστος τῶν ἀποστόλων, ὃς οὐκ εἰμὶ ἱκανὸς καλεῖσθαι ἀπόστολος, διότι ἐδίωξα τὴν ἐκκλησίαν τοῦ θεοῦ.

First of all, it is not to be contested that this enumeration is intended to be chronological.[75] Whether Paul perhaps has made a mistake in the order of his list is another question. But if he begins chronologically with Peter and goes on to the twelve, and, also chronologically, concludes with himself as the ἔσχατος πάντων,[76] one cannot well suppose that in the other three parts of the list the (ἔπ)ειτα is all at once to be taken simply as enumerative.[77]

---

[74] Cf. P. Schubert in *Neutestamentliche Studien für Rudolf Bultmann* (1954), p. 168, n. 11; M. Goguel [1], p. 218.

[75] This is done, e.g., by F. Kattenbusch, *op. cit.*, p. 330; G. Sass [1], p. 97; and W. Michaelis, *op. cit.*, pp. 23 ff., at times in the interest of their exposition. On the contrary, and correctly, H. v. Campenhausen in SAH (1958), II, p. 11.

[76] G. Sass [1], p. 97, n. 266) indeed thinks that "ἔσχατος is to be understood religiously, not temporally," but this unfounded assertion requires no refutation.

[77] Cf. W. G. Kümmel in Lietzmann, HNT, IX, p. 77, l. 17; *ibid.*, *op. cit.*, p. 5; E. Bammel, *op. cit.*, p. 406, n. 23, otherwise p. 414.

The first two parts of the enumeration belong to a formula of the primitive community, which Paul cites beginning at vs. 3. This has been so often demonstrated [78] that it suffices here simply to mention the fact. Attempts to carry the formula beyond vs. 5[79] or to end it with ὤφθη[80] will hardly find general acceptance. Whether Paul also in vss. 6 and 7 takes over fixed traditions is a question which we do not need specifically to investigate. In recent times it has frequently been supposed [81] that parts (4) and (5) compete with (1) and (2). As a pupil of Lohmeyer, G. Sass thinks that (1)+(2) belongs to Galilee, and (4)+(5) to Jerusalem; on the other hand, E. Bammel (op. cit., pp. 416 ff.) would place both formulas in Jerusalem and understands (4)+(5) as a counter formulation to (1)+(2), developed in conflicts between Peter and James. According to this view, then, Paul is supposed either intentionally or clumsily to have bound the two formulas together and to have completed them with (3) and (6). Under this presupposition, naturally an original chronological order of the six parts is no longer to be maintained.

But I do not consider correct the thesis of Lohmeyer about the two primitive communities, nor am I able to persuade myself that Peter and James were rivals in Jerusalem. In the first place, I do not believe that one could have attempted in the earliest times to set James up as the first witness of the resurrection in place of Peter. In I Cor. 15:6-7 itself, however, there appears no clue for the assertion that here a rival tradition to vs. 5 is employed. These verses rather exclude any such assumption.[82]

This is shown when we now pose the decisive question as to who then the ἀπόστολοι πάντες actually are. One should reasonably take these words just as they stand, so that by "all the apostles" are meant: Andronicus, Junias, Barnabas, Paul, and whoever else belongs to the acknowledged circle

---

[78] Cf., e.g., F. Kattenbusch, op. cit., p. 330; G. Sass [1], p. 97; J. Jeremias, The Eucharistic Words of Jesus, pp. 101 ff.; A. v. Harnack in SAB (1922), Phil.-hist. Klasse, pp. 62-80; W. G. Kümmel, op. cit., p. 3, and the literature which he cites on p. 44, n. 9.

[79] J. Weiss in loc.

[80] E. Bammel, op. cit., pp. 401 ff., whose thesis nevertheless is still worthy of consideration. He refers to the fact that the formula of the primitive community is constructed in a truly parallel form only if there is only a ὅτι ὤφθη to correspond to the ὅτι ἐτάφη. Of course one should not overestimate such an argument based upon linguistic parallelism in prose texts and confessional formulas. Nevertheless it is possible that originally the formula did not go beyond this element. But Paul had certainly found it already including the whole of vs. 5.

[81] Thus A. v. Harnack in SAB (1922), Phil.-hist. Klasse, pp. 62-80, esp. pp. 65 ff.; P. Winter, "I Corinthians 15:3b-7," Novum Testamentum, II (1957), 142-50; E. Stauffer, Jesus (1957), pp. 112-13; U. Wilckens, Die Missionsreden der Apostelgeschichte (1961), pp. 73 ff. Contra, H. v. Campenhausen, Der Ablauf der Osterereignisse, SAH (1958), II, 8, n. 4; 10, n. 12.

[82] Further counterarguments in W. G. Kümmel, op. cit., pp. 4-5.

of the apostles, handed down to us by name in only a few representatives.[83] Yet one finds this reasonable version only rarely among the exegetes. Karl Holl could still say that it has been the "generally dominant view since Lightfoot" (op. cit., p. 924); but E. Bammel (op. cit., p. 405) thinks now: "The ἀπόστολοι πάντες are according to the thesis of Holl which is, to be sure, problematical but generally accepted,[84] the twelve and James." Not until in W. G. Kümmel [85] do we find again the only illuminating interpretation, that πάντες ἀπόστολοι embraces a circle which included "in any case according to the view of Paul all the ἀπόστολοι without exception at that time." [86] I cannot quite understand how W. G. Kümmel intends the "at that time" to be understood—at that time when the appearance occurred; or at that time when Paul was describing this appearance. Only the latter is correct. Paul's reference to "all the apostles" must include all who then were and had been apostles. This is, further, made certain by the fact that Paul does not without good reason refrain from quoting any kind of witnesses to the resurrection. All the apostles, not just a few, can give a testimony to the resurrection.[87] Between "all the apostles" and Paul as the last witness of the resurrection, no other apostles, as capable of bearing this witness as were the others, can have remained unnamed.[88] But K. Holl ([1], p. 924) declares that this explanation is "simply impossible." The reasons which he and others[89] bring forward in support of such an assertion demand some consideration.

They say that "all the apostles" cannot be taken literally, for Paul, who himself also is an apostle, certainly does not count himself among these ἀπόστολοι πάντες; he mentions the manifestation which he experiences

[83] Eusebius (CH I, 12.5) already understood the passage thus.

[84] This is probably somewhat exaggerated. Even when they do not actually take the "πάντες" seriously, numerous students in the present have the circle of ἀπόστολοι πάντες extend beyond the twelve and James; cf., e.g., A. Wikenhauser, op. cit., col. 554. A. v. Harnack (op. cit., n. 89) makes the equation ἀπόστολοι πάντες = οἱ δώδεκα! Cf. also P. Winter, op. cit., n. 89; E. L. Allen in NTS, III (1957), 349.

[85] Op. cit., p. 7. H. Grass, Ostergeschehen und Osterberichte (1956), pp. 103-4, understands by the ἀπόστολοι πάντες the Jerusalem "circle of leaders" from a later period, which no longer coincides with the twelve who were called in Galilee. A. Fridrichsen (op. cit., n. 12) writes: "These 'Apostles' must have been the messengers chosen by James to carry the message of the risen Christ out to the disciples of Jesus in all parts of Palestine. Before starting they had a collective revelation."

[86] Cf. E. L. Allen, "The Lost Kerygma," NTS, III, 349.

[87] Yet on the other hand it is of no interest to Paul, who wishes to introduce as many witnesses as possible, whether individual witnesses had witnessed more than one appearance. This would not lend any support to his proof. For this reason itself it is unlikely that οἱ ἀπόστολοι πάντες were the twelve and James, for they all had already been named as witnesses, and it is doubtful whether the twelve and James are even to be counted among "all the apostles."

[88] Cf. E. Bammel, op. cit., p. 403; H. v. Campenhausen in SAH, II (1958), p. 20.

[89] E.g., E. Meyer, op. cit., III, 255 ff.

after this, as the sixth part of the enumeration. Now it is by no means so certain that Paul did not count himself among the ἀπόστολοι πάντες. When he continues: ἔσχατον δὲ πάντων ὡσπερεὶ τῷ ἐκτρώματι ὤφθη κἀμοί, it should be asked whether one must not complete this assertion thus: ἔσχατον δὲ πάντων ἀποστόλων—that is, as the last of these afore-mentioned ἀπόστολοι πάντες, to me also was an appearance of the resurrected One given. Usually, to be sure, one assumes that Paul names himself as the last, not of the apostles, but of the whole series of witnesses from Peter onward. I hold this to be correct.[90] Does the apostle Paul, then, not belong to τοῖς ἀποστόλοις πᾶσιν? Indeed; for he himself declares that he is not worthy to be called an apostle. This is, to be sure, said rhetorically; but since Paul has already spoken of all the apostles, to whom he himself belongs, he actually would now have to break off the enumeration. On the other hand, however, he naturally did not wish to neglect setting forth his —the writer of the epistle and the apostle of the Corinthians—own status as witness.[91] He therefore had to set himself apart from τοῖς ἀποστόλοις πᾶσιν, and this he does in I Cor. 15:9-10.[92] Any other reason which would lessen his authority is not involved in a situation where he unconditionally demands authority as a witness. Indeed he then again extols his authority in vs. 10. The perception of the exegetes that Paul still could not well have counted himself among τοῖς ἀποστόλοις πᾶσιν, if he thereafter specifically mentions himself, is, then, correct; only they have not considered the fact that Paul already had the same feeling and for this reason formally, but really only for the sake of form, set himself apart from the other apostles.

But, objects K. Holl, "how is one to conceive of the Lord's having appeared to them (sc., all the apostles) together? Were they gathered at a certain place at the same time, so that Christ could have appeared to them together?" Now it is quite certain that they were never gathered at one place so that the Lord could have appeared to them ἐφάπαξ. But who says that one should picture here a public appearance before all the apostles? Paul at any rate says nothing of that.[93] In the case of the five hundred brethren, on the other hand, he says expressly that Christ appeared to them

[90] Thus also G. Klein, op. cit., pp. 43-44, n. 179.
[91] Also to enumerate the other apostles singly was not of equal interest to him; besides, Paul certainly would not have been able to do so, just as he was not able to list the five hundred brethren singly.
[92] G. Klein (op. cit., p. 42, n. 174) infers incorrectly from this argument that I would actually have Paul include himself in the πάντες of vs. 7. The chronological sequence from vs. 7b to vs. 8, which Klein (ibid.) misses in the above interpretation, is explicitly set forth in vs. 9.
[93] Of course E. Meyer (op. cit., III, 258) disagrees; for him the only thing considered is that "here clearly a single mass appearance is involved."

ἐφάπαξ. If it were to be taken for granted that all the appearances named by Paul happened "at once," then the ἐφάπαξ would be superfluous. The fact that Paul adds it shows rather that the contrary is taken for granted. Indeed Christ appeared to the five hundred brethren all together, but for the rest, all the apostles, like Paul and James, were individually called.[94] The only calling of an apostle of which we know any particulars, namely that of Paul, shows this very distinctly. But why the εἶτα τοῖς ἀποστόλοις πᾶσιν cannot be separated into individual experiences, as K. Holl (*op. cit.*, p. 925)[95] asserts, is incomprehensible. A comparison with εἶτα τοῖς δώδεκα is out of place, for this phrase, which certainly presupposes a general appearance, still stems from the firmly fixed tradition which Paul had before him. Paul himself definitely makes a distinction between a mass manifestation before the five hundred brethren on the one hand and the following individual manifestations before James, all the apostles, and finally before himself.[96] Paul certainly never got off on the erroneous idea[97] that anyone could have conceived of the callings of the various apostles as taking place during a manifestation to a massed group.[98]

In other words, Paul wishes to provide as complete a list of witnesses as possible. Hence he speaks expressly of *all* the apostles (vs. 7b), which includes, after all, his own witness as that of the last and least of all the apostles. However, he understandably does not wish to refrain from setting himself forth especially as a witness to the resurrection of Jesus. After vs. 7b, however, this is possible only by Paul's formally setting himself apart from "all the apostles," which he therefore does in vss. 9-10 in a way, typical of him, that glorifies the grace of God. No one in Corinth could infer from vss. 8 ff. that Paul really intended to renounce his apostolic rights; of that there can be no question.[99] Precisely as the least of the apostles, who

[94] Cf. H. Mosbech [1], p. 190.

[95] Cf. H. Lietzmann in HNT on I Cor. 15:6.

[96] Thus also E. v. Dobschütz, *Ostern und Pfingsten* (1903), p. 35.

[97] Since the manifestation first and foremost established the apostolate, but by no means all the witnesses to the resurrection became apostles, one would have to assume that in an assembly of the community the Lord appeared to the Christians present, among them Peter, Barnabas, Silvanus, Andronicus, Junias, etc., and these all henceforth knew themselves to be apostles (and accordingly now all go forth as apostles), but that with them the apostolic circle was closed. This seems to me to be an utterly nonsensical conception. And how Paul could then get the idea of pushing his way into this circle as a unique missionary and of claiming the title of apostle remains all the more inconceivable.

[98] G. Klein's requirement (*op. cit.*, p. 43) that Paul would have had to add, in a free formulation, a καθεξῆς in vs. 7 to the ἐφάπαξ of vs. 6 is therefore unreasonable. If asked how many children my wife has borne, I do not reply, "Five, one after another."

[99] Of course one can ask with E. Güttgemanns (*op. cit.*, p. 87) why Paul does not simply say that he is the last of the apostles mentioned in vs. 7. But apart from the fact that the Pauline manner of expression does admit of this interpretation, one must

actually does not deserve this title, he is the unique apostle to the Gentiles.

Verses 8 ff., thus, contrary to the contention of G. Klein (*op. cit.*, p. 40), lie precisely in the train of thought of vss. 1-11, in which Paul's concern is to adduce as abundant and convincing an array of witnesses as possible. Hence one may by no means ascribe to vss. 8-10 the character of an excursus, as Klein does.[100]

Karl Holl asks further: "But then was a revelation of Christ something so ordinary, something in a certain manner to be expected according to a rule, that it could be presupposed for every minor missionary?" Surely not, for not every minor missionary was called an apostle. It may be proper to say of the missionaries generally that they formed "a formless, constantly growing group" (K. Holl, *op. cit.*, p. 924), but this is not true when we are speaking of the apostles. The apostles were only those missionaries who were called by the resurrected One himself. And these alone are meant by Paul, naturally, by the words οἱ ἀπόστολοι πάντες.

Finally, K. Holl objects, Paul could not have so abased himself, in comparison with *all* the apostles, as is done in vs. 9[101]; for he could not place them all with himself on the same level. Certainly not: In vs. 10 Paul

answer that Paul apparently intended to represent himself as definitively last of *all* the witnesses, whereby the significance of his testimony and his gospel, as Marcion in a certain way correctly sensed, is heavily underscored.

[100] E. Güttgemanns proposes an opinionated exegesis of I Cor. 15:7-11 ([1], pp. 88 ff.). According to him, the Corinthian Gnostics made the charge against Paul that he was an ἔκτρωμα, i.e. an outsider, who was the only one in the church who disputed the identity between Christ and the Christians and instead of this set forth a difference between Christ and the Christians. Paul takes a stand against this charge in I Cor. 15:1-11 by asserting that he in no way stands at the beginning of a christological heresy but at the end of a proclamation which comes out of the primitive community, and thus within the community of all those who make the proclamation.

Thereby, however, 15:1-11 is isolated from the context of I Cor. 15, in which it is not the "christological distance" but the resurrection of Jesus that is under discussion. Now one cannot at all deny that in I Cor. 15:1-11 Paul wishes to offer a proof by witnesses of the resurrection and does not seize just any theologoumenon as evidence of the commonality of the primitive Christian proclamation. Also the charge that with his christological kerygma Paul stands in an isolated position in Christianity as distinguished from the Gnostics is so utterly and for every Christian obviously fantastic that with it the Gnostics would only have been able to undermine their own trustworthiness and authority. And would they actually have labeled the Pauline preaching as untraditional in order to be able to claim tradition for themselves? Do they understand themselves instead of an "abortion" to be a healthy offspring of tradition? This is utterly alien to the Gnostic pneumatics!

Unsatisfactory and lacking any attempt at an exegetical explanation of the problem is the comment of G. Blum (*op. cit.*, pp. 26-27, n. 15): "Naturally the relation between vs. 7 and vss. 8-9 is difficult. Paul appears not to include himself among the ἀπόστολοι πάντες. This however emphasizes the special character of his apostolate and the conclusion of apostolic callings."

[101] Thus also E. Lohse [1], p. 270.

says to what extent he actually does not place them on the same level with himself. That, however, he had to "abase" himself before them was shown above. What could have hindered him in this? The reasons with which he does it in vs. 9, moreover, do not concern his apostolic office at all fundamentally,[102] so that one cannot properly speak of an abasement as *apostle* in the strict sense; the reasons in themselves are nevertheless thoroughly real and convincing.

If then οἱ ἀπόστολοι πάντες actually means "all the apostles," the concept in this passage excludes James and Peter, for it is not to be assumed that the two of them were, in the opinion of Paul, accounted worthy of a second manifestation, a special manifestation as apostles. Especially in the case of James this is inconceivable; the manifestation to him is listed immediately before that to the apostles for precisely the reason that Paul does not count him among the apostles. Rather, after all the others, as last in the list, Paul mentions the apostles, and he can do this without thinking of Peter or James. Accordingly, Peter is, as will become still clearer in a moment, a παρείσακτος ἀδελφός within the apostolic circle, and James is apparently not even this with certainty (*vide* pp. 64-65).

Furthermore, Paul is convinced that no more apostles have been called subsequent to his call. He is the ἔσχατος of all apostles. One should not call into question this clear affirmation. Paul himself, at any rate, has not heard of any calling of an apostle that has taken place in the more than twenty years that have passed since his Damascus-road experience.[103]

Thus I Cor. 15:7 gives us no occasion to suppose that Paul had a dual concept of the apostle. The ἀπόστολοι πάντες are actually all the apostles; and that the twelve should have belonged in that company[104] is not indicated by anything,[105] and there is nothing to make it likely.[106] On the contrary, it is ruled out by the fact that Peter himself is not reckoned among the apostles in I Cor. 15:7.[107]

[102] Paul did not in fact persecute the church as an *apostle*. Rather, he glories in the grace of God, who called the persecutor (vs. 9) to be so successful an apostle (vs. 10).

[103] Thus correctly H. v. Campenhausen, *Der Ablauf der Ostereignisse*, SAH (1958), II, 19-20.

[104] "The appearance before 'all the apostles' certainly also included the twelve" (W. G. Kümmel, *op. cit.*, p. 8).

[105] Cf. G. Sass [2], p. 236.

[106] "He probably implies that James and the Twelve all belong to the larger group of Apostles . . ." (K. Lake, *op. cit.*, p. 55).

[107] Even G. Klein (*op. cit.*, pp. 38-43) comes to the conclusion that I Cor. 15:7 says nothing for the apostolicity of the twelve. His attempt to demonstrate the words "τοῖς ἀποστόλοις πᾶσιν" in the midst of the other Pauline phrases as a traditional formulation is incomprehensible to me as to its intention and not convincing in its prosecution.

On the difficulties which Klein thereby creates for his own thesis of the non-Palestinian origin of the apostolate of the twelve, see below, p. 81, n. 113.

I Cor. 9:5

Here Paul writes: μὴ οὐκ ἔχομεν ἐξουσίαν ἀδελφὴν γυναῖκα περιάγειν, ὡς καὶ οἱ λοιποὶ ἀπόστολοι καὶ οἱ ἀδελφοὶ τοῦ κυρίου καὶ Κηφᾶς. The problem of this sentence for the exegetes lies not so much in the question as to what circle the λοιποὶ ἀπόστολοι form, but in the other, as to whether the brothers of the Lord are here counted among the apostles or not. In the interpretation of this passage one usually proceeds from the assumption that Cephas obviously is an apostle, thus is already included in the λοιποὶ ἀπόστολοι, and only because of his importance is named in particular. Then however it is only consistent when Lietzmann, in his *Handbuch* at this passage,[108] asserts that likewise "the brothers of the Lord are counted among the apostles"; for the second and the third καί must surely have the same significance! [109] Now, however, one rightly has a number of reservations about including the brothers of Jesus in the apostolic circle, and the majority of exegetes therefore decide for the quite illogical solution that indeed Peter is to be counted among the λοιποὶ ἀπόστολοι, but not the Lord's brothers. The explanations for this understanding of the passage are correspondingly tortuous,[110] and the conclusion is quite often uncertain.[111]

This whole difficulty arises out of the false presupposition that in I Cor. 9:5 Paul counts Peter among the apostles. If one leaves aside this presupposition, the clear meaning of the verse at once presents itself. Paul enumerates three groups of missionaries: the apostles, the brothers of the Lord, and Peter as an individual and as representative of the twelve. Thus the brothers of the Lord, among whom James is counted, do not qualify as apostles. That appears also from our interpretation of I Cor. 15:7, where James is explicitly distinguished from the apostles. Since he is there mentioned as the only one of the Lord's brothers, the other siblings of the Lord may not have had any manifestation, unless they were among the five hundred brethren. However, because James had encountered the risen Lord, the title of apostle, insofar as he is a missionary, cannot be denied him altogether, as Gal. 1:19 shows (*vide* pp. 64-65). But basically he, like his brothers, does not belong to the circle of apostles.[112]

---

[108] Thus also J. Weiss in the Meyer *Kommentar, in loc.*; J. B. Lightfoot, *op. cit.*, p. 95, n. 4; de Wette, *in loc.*; G. Sass [1], p. 102.

[109] Thus correctly K. v. Hofmann *in loc.* The emphatic καί for example in Mark 16:7.

[110] "Since the casual reference to the already mentioned class of the apostles is hardly conceivable before Κηφᾶς, Paul here probably does not count the ἀδελφοὶ τοῦ κυρίου among the apostles" (P. W. Schmiedel in the *Handkommentar zum NT, in loc.*).

[111] "The question of the inclusion of the brothers of Jesus in the circle of the apostles must therefore remain an open one" (W. G. Kümmel, *op. cit.*, p. 45, n. 13).

[112] The missionary activity of James and his brothers can hardly have gone beyond the boundaries of Palestine. In the older tradition we meet James only in Jerusalem itself.

Now the same holds true for Peter. In I Cor. 9:5, as in I Cor. 15:5-7, Paul does not count him among the ἀπόστολοι πάντες.[113] This assertion is derived, at any rate, from the only interpretation of the verse which is not forced. Peter did not *originally* belong to the circle of the apostles. On the other hand, for Paul there was far less an occasion in the case of Peter than in the case of James to deny him the title of apostle. For not only had Peter seen the Lord,[114] but further, in contrast with James, he was in his later time an outspoken professional missionary, whose activity among the Jews of the Diaspora was hardly less wide-ranging than was the activity of Paul among the Gentiles. Therefore it is not surprising that in Gal. 1:19 and 2:8, Paul calls the counterpart of his person, Peter, an apostle.[115] The fact that this designation in the case of Peter is not original is less important for the estimate of Peter, who apparently never claimed this title for himself, than for the answering of the question as to where the apostolate is native.

Now if we ask who, then, the λοιποὶ ἀπόστολοι are, the answer is self-evident: the other apostles besides Paul and Barnabas, in other words, Andronicus and Junias, perhaps Silvanus, and further the unknown number of other missionaries who before Paul knew themselves to be called by the resurrected Christ to the apostolic ministry. That the twelve disciples did not belong to this number should now be quite clear. Since Peter is reckoned

[113] Thus also G. Klein, *op. cit.*, who of course thinks that at the time of I Cor. 9:5 Peter was *no longer* an apostle. This explanation, however, runs aground on the fact that in 9:5 Peter is described precisely as a missionary.

Klein discusses this problem more in detail in his essay, "Galater 2, 6-9 und die Geschichte der Jerusalemer Urgemeinde" (ZThK, LVII (1960), pp. 275-95, esp. pp. 293 ff.). His objections to my statements above go astray since he takes the "originally" in a temporal sense, although it is meant in an essential sense (see further below, pp. 94-95). That Peter was an apostle *at the beginning*, but later, at the high point of his missionary activity, was no longer one (thus Klein) would be impossible to assume even if Klein could account for the origin of the title of apostle for Peter in his "pre-missionary" time. Yet he rightly does not attempt this impossible task.

He also apparently does not see how much the assumption of a Palestinian apostolate of the primitive Christian period burdens his correct thesis that the apostolate of the twelve ultimately goes back to the Pauline concept of the apostle; for this correct thesis must become questionable at the moment one is compelled to incorporate a pre-Pauline apostolic circle in Jerusalem into the development of the concept of apostle.

[114] A special "call" in addition to or during the manifestation was not requisite for any of the apostles, as we saw above (pp. 30-31).

[115] E. Lohse ([1], p. 269, n. 33) among others states that Peter first received the title of apostle through Paul. Over against this, G. Klein (*op. cit.*, p. 55) insists that one must first explain "how Paul, in a situation where the decisive issue was the unmediated nature of his own apostleship, could get the idea of making the legitimation of his apostleship more difficult through an arbitrary elevation of the Jerusalem authorities to the rank of apostles." Now *"arbitrary* elevation" is not what is involved here. Paul gives the *title* of apostle only to those in Jerusalem who according to their authority were long since apostles: Peter and, on occasion, James. But their authority like his own was not established by the *title!*

by Paul, with reservations, among the apostles and that only at a time when the circle of the δώδεκα had long since ceased to exist, the slightest possibility of an original existence of twelve apostles is excluded.

Gal. 1:17 ff.

This is the last passage to be considered in this connection.[116] After his conversion Paul did not immediately go εἰς Ἱεροσόλυμα πρὸς τοὺς πρὸ ἐμοῦ ἀποστόλους. It was three years later when he first went to Jerusalem, and during his fourteen days' stay there he saw only Peter among the apostles (ἕτερον δὲ τῶν ἀποστόλων οὐκ εἶδον). That these apostles mentioned in Gal. 1:17 and 19 are the twelve is, the less Paul himself will allow this, all the more positively asserted by the exegetes. To most exegetes this is so self-evident that they neglect to make any special reference to it. Even those who consider this to be needed nevertheless refrain from offering any proof of their assertion.[117]

But why then are the apostles of Gal. 1:17, 19 suddenly supposed to have been the twelve[118] or to have included the twelve?[119] The πρὸ ἐμοῦ ἀπόστολοι are *those* members of the apostolic circle whom Paul can presuppose as present in Jerusalem.[120] And since elsewhere he does not count the δώδεκα among the apostles, he quite certainly does not count them in that company in Gal. 1:17, 19.[121] When Paul was in Jerusalem for the first time after his conversion, the fixed circle of the twelve may in fact already have ceased to exist; otherwise Paul would hardly have been able to pass over them so completely in his epistles as he actually did. Paul no longer encountered the δώδεκα. Should they, however, against all likelihood, still have existed, then they cannot be identified with the apostles of Gal. 1:17, 19 for the very reason that these apostles (except Peter) were all absent from Jerusalem. This is clear from the fact that during the fourteen days of his visit in the Jerusalem congregation, which certainly was still not very large, Paul saw none of them,[122] for to suppose that Peter kept Paul hidden from the

---

[116] "It is the one text where one is tempted to take 'apostles' as the twelve earliest disciples" (J. Munck [1], p. 106).

[117] "He counts among these apostles not only certainly the twelve (Gal. 1:17, 19) but also . . ." (W. G. Kümmel, *op. cit.*, p. 5). A. v. Harnack ([1], I, 323), to be sure, does not wish to rule out all doubt.

[118] If, as we saw (see pp. 64-65), in Gal. 1:19 the title of apostle is not strictly withheld from James, the apostles of Gal. 1:17, 19 clearly cannot be *limited* to the twelve.

[119] Cf. G. Sass [2], p. 236.

[120] "It is more probably the wider meaning of 'apostle' that we have here" (J. Munck [1], p. 107; cf. [2], p. 213). "He does not mean οἱ δώδεκα" (A. Fridrichsen, *op. cit.*, n. 12).

[121] Thus correctly G. Klein, *op. cit.*, pp. 44 ff.

[122] "Probably because of their absence": thus de Wette unreflectingly but correctly glosses vs. 19. Still more unequivocally K. H. Rengstorf, *op. cit.*, p. 431: at the time to

apostles or that the apostles wanted to know nothing of Paul would be absurd. That the apostles were absent from Jerusalem is, on the other hand, obvious. Their field of activity certainly was not primarily in Jerusalem. The twelve, on the other hand, whose task was not "to go out into the world, but rather to remain in Jerusalem" (K. Holl [1], p. 934), there to await the Parousia, certainly never all went out on a missionary journey while just Peter stayed at home.

Who the Jerusalem apostles in particular were is naturally very difficult to determine. The question is essentially bound up with another problem. The charge against Paul speaks of his dependence upon men *in general*. This naturally can only have meant "dependence upon *Christians*," but just on Christians, not on a special category of Christians.

If Paul wishes to refute this charge historically—and this is precisely what he intends in Gal. 1–2—then he must actually demonstrate that he has not received his gospel from other Christians. He apparently was quite conscious of this fundamental necessity; for he begins his apology with the words: εὐθέως οὐ προσανεθέμην σαρκὶ καὶ αἵματι (Gal. 1:16). Naturally a defense that totally denies dependence upon men is practically not feasible on this basis, for Paul did not become a hermit. Therefore he continues by showing his independence of the *special* human authorities in the church. What were for Paul decisive authorities? The answer is clear: the Jerusalem Christians; for he continues: οὐδὲ ἀνῆλθον εἰς Ἱεροσόλυμα (Gal. 1:17); further: ἔπειτα μετὰ τρία ἔτη ἀνῆλθον εἰς Ἱεροσόλυμα (Gal. 1:18); and then ἔπειτα διὰ δεκατεσσάρων ἐτῶν πάλιν ἀνέβην εἰς Ἱεροσόλυμα (Gal. 2:1); and finally, with his presentation of the confrontation in Antioch Paul intends to show his independence of the *Jerusalem* authorities, as vs. 12 in particular shows.

This observation is fruitful for understanding the relationship of Paul and his circle to those in Jerusalem and therefore for the question of authority in the early church in general. If there was a human authority in the church under discussion, this authority could only be Jerusalem, and even Paul and the apostles in general could not wholly avoid this authority. This is not surprising, and it is confirmed by other observations. The apostles known to us are, without exception, Jewish Christians. This is true of Paul and Barnabas, of Andronicus and Junias, of Silvanus, of Peter (and of James) (*vide* pp. 89 ff.). Thus already in their Jewish time they possessed a special connection with the authority of and the authorities in Jerusalem, and after their conversion they changed only the holders of this authority. Further, as

which Gal. 1:18 ff. refers, "there were no ἀπόστολοι in Jerusalem except Peter." Unfortunately he draws the conclusion that the twelve were diligently engaged in mission work.

Paul himself shows by his regular trips to Jerusalem and as the book of Acts indicates about Barnabas and Silvanus, they never denied at least the moral authority of Jerusalem (cf. Gal. 2:11-13!). In the beginning Jerusalem certainly served as the place of the Parousia (*vide* K. Holl [1], p. 933). Jerusalem is the place of origin of the gospel (cf. Rom. 15:19). In this connection the problem bound up with the collection for Jerusalem might appropriately be mentioned: Paul engages himself to collect at the same moment in which his apostleship gains recognition in Jerusalem (Gal. 2:10).[123] Karl Holl ([1], pp. 939 ff.) may be right in sensing that for the authorities in Jerusalem this collection signified more than a free-will service of love. They saw in it "a just tribute which is levied upon the Gentile Christians by the mother congregation" ([1], p. 940).[124] That Paul himself viewed the collection only as a service of love and did not think of recognizing any *legal* authority of the Jerusalem congregation needs, to be sure, no question. But even the apostle Paul always considered Jerusalem as headquarters of the church in a *moral* sense.

All this suffices to explain the fact that Paul refutes the general accusation of his opponents as it is found in Gal. 1:1, 11-12—that he is dependent upon *men*—simply by declaring his independence of *Jerusalem* (Gal. 1:17, 18 ff.; 2:1 ff., 12). To be sure, one might well consider the possibility that the accusation made against him included the *explicit assertion* that he was dependent upon Jerusalem.[125] Since the Jewish-Christian Gnosticism of the Syrian-Antiochian region had never stood in connection with Jerusalem,[126] and the Hellenistic Christianity (including that of Paul) resident in the same geographical region could hardly deny this connection, the anti-Pauline charge of dependence upon men cannot have meant, in the last analysis, anything but dependence upon Jerusalem. Even if Paul should have heard no more than that he received his gospel from *men*, still a motif of *traditional* apologetics of Hellenistic Christianity may have come to light here, when against this accusation he asserts his (relative) independence of Jerusalem and of the apostles there as the direct recipients of the gospel.

The particular character of the authorities in Jerusalem apparently

---

[123] This problem is treated in detail by G. Sass [1], pp. 113 ff.

[124] K. Holl ([1], p. 940) rightly refers to the collection for Jerusalem described in Acts 11:27 f., which presents an exact parallel to the collection of Paul.

[125] Thus, e.g., J. Munck [2], p. 9; E. Haenchen, *Die Apostelgeschichte* (12th ed., 1959), pp. 79-80.

[126] The origin of this Jewish-Christian Gnosticism lies in the heretical Jewish Christ-Gnosticism of the pre-Christian era (see pp. 173 ff.). The Jewish-Christian Gnosticism thus brought along the rejection of the Jewish authorities of Jerusalem from its pre-Christian roots.

changed in the course of time.[127] At the time of the conversion of Paul the authorities were, for him, the apostles; and three years later this has not changed, though Peter is named among them specifically. Apparently there is still a widespread lack of a legally structured authority. Fourteen years later the picture looks quite different. The δοκοῦντες in Jerusalem are now a collegium of three, the στῦλοι, namely James, Peter, and John, listed in an order which is not accidental. We recognize in this development a part of the change from an authority that is charismatic to one that is more legal in character.[128]

Of interest to us is only the charismatic authority of the apostles in the early period. The apostles are the direct recipients of the gospel. For the time of his conversion Paul apparently can or will imagine no other binding ecclesiastical authority, to which which *he* could be indebted for the gospel, than the *apostolic,* that is to say, than the authority of such Christians who *like himself* were sent forth by the exalted Christ to proclaim the gospel (regardless of whether the Christians concerned bore the title of "apostle" as a self-designation or not). In view of his own apostolic self-awareness, of course, this is surprising only for one who does not note that the so-called historical Jesus and the relationship with him lie wholly outside Paul's theo-

---

[127] Here I go along with G. Klein, who to be sure only inadequately estimates the fact (*op. cit.*, p. 48) that "Paul apparently could picture such ἄνθρωποι upon whom his opponents could make him seem dependent . . . as different personalities and groups, according to the situation."

[128] In his interesting essay (mentioned on p. 81, n. 113) which sharply focuses on the problems, G. Klein seeks to solve the various difficulties which emerge in Gal. 2:1-10 with the thesis that at the time of the "apostolic council," the δοκοῦντες did not have any standing, but only Peter did. In Gal. 2, Paul is supposed to have introduced the circumstances of his present time into the past of which he is reporting!

In view of Paul's account in Gal. 2, this thesis is, of course, utterly arbitrary. Moreover, it already runs aground on the fact that where Paul bases his apology upon history, he could not afford a historical inaccuracy of such measure as Klein's thesis presupposes, one which could be ascertained by every reader at any time and which would have destroyed his entire apology. In other words, the three στῦλοι must have had standing in the person of these three *at that time,* as Paul reports. Hence it is not accidental that Paul also travels to Jerusalem with two companions. Perhaps this hypothesis could be discussed—it is certain that Peter's charismatic authority is older than the legal authority of the δοκοῦντες in Jerusalem—if Klein could explain a reason for Paul's incorrect portrayal of the historical reality. But he is not in a position to do this.

In addition, there is the fact that the hypothesis does not at all accomplish what it is supposed to. It is first of all supposed to make vs. 6 comprehensible, which according to the hypothesis says: "Those who *today* have standing—the fact that *at that time* they still had no such standing is unimportant for me; God does not judge according to the outward appearance of man—I say, those who *today* have standing *at that time* imposed no requirements on me." It is obvious that such a statement, which of course no one will dispute with Paul, is meaningless and as an apology is absurd. Further, "οἱ δοκοῦντες" in vs. 6 can only be taken as it is in vss. 2 and 9, thus: those who had standing *at that time.*

logical circle of vision. In addition one will have to consider that for the sake of proving his independence Paul was anxious to keep as small as possible the circle of possible authorities in Jerusalem upon whom he, the apostle, could be dependent. Thus, in view of the fact that the Galatian adversaries hold apostolic authority in high esteem, he skillfully restricts it to the apostles, although elsewhere (e.g., I Cor. 15:1 ff.) he in no way characterizes the fundamental kerygma as *specifically* apostolic and, indeed, in 1:22 ff. again stresses his independence of the Christians in Judea in general. Therefore, there is no reason at all to suppose that Paul was concretely charged with dependence upon *the apostles*.

Just as little does Paul's presentation presuppose that the apostles were to be found only, or only preeminently, in Jerusalem.[129] In any case, when he journeyed to Jerusalem three years later, there was no apostle other than Peter in the city (*vide supra*). For Paul that serves as evidence of his independence, although there were apostles elsewhere; but the authority primarily disclaimed by Paul is just that of *Jerusalem*,[130] and as the authorities considered binding for Paul he names the apostles, for the reasons given. Finally, it is a completely open question whether the *concept* of the apostle was already in use in *Jerusalem* at the time of Paul's conversion. Everything argues for the view that this *title* was first applied by Paul in Gal. 1-2 to the members of the Jerusalem community who merited it (*vide* p. 81, n. 115; *vide infra*, p. 94) because Paul could thereby fix a narrowly limited circle of Jerusalem authorities and prove his independence of the ecclesiastical authorities before him. Gal. 1 is nevertheless the only passage in which Paul presupposes apostles in Jerusalem or gives the title of apostle to Christians resident in Jerusalem—Peter and James—while elsewhere he plainly dis-

---

[129] "In any case it is strange that Paul would have had to go to Jerusalem in order to meet apostles" (G. Sass [1], p. 104). *Contra* K. Holl ([1], p. 934), who thinks that "if one is determined to find them [the apostles], one finds them of course in Jerusalem." G. Klein (*op. cit.*, p. 45), strangely enough, agrees with this. How should Paul be able to expect to find *the* apostles, not one of whom, so far as we know, came from Palestine and whose function was the mission, precisely in Jerusalem!

[130] G. Klein (*op. cit.*, pp. 45-46) does not consider this when he bases his interpretation of Gal. 1:15 ff. on the assertion: "If for Paul the idea of a trip to Jerusalem implies without further indication (17) the other idea of an encounter with the apostles there, then a traveling activity of these apostles can hardly have been the normal thing. . . ." In n. 191 he calls the thesis of the traveling activity of the apostles simply "fantastic"! Such a short-circuiting then of course leaves no other choice than to capitulate before the text: "Why Paul, on his first visit to Jerusalem, met none other of the apostles than Peter remains a question to which at present no certain answer appears possible" (*op. cit.*, p. 46). Addressed to the statements of Paul also is the statement of B. Gerhardsson (*op. cit.*, p. 119) that in Gal. 1:17 Paul presupposes that at least the leading apostles were always present in Jerusalem. He does not tell us which apostles and how many of them Paul hopes to find in Jerusalem. From his words we can deduce only the obvious fact that the authorities in Jerusalem who were binding for him were *apostolic* authorities.

tinguishes Peter and James, as he does the twelve, from the apostles (I Cor. 9:5; 15:1 ff.). If the title of apostle had been established in Jerusalem early or even originally, Paul could not have wavered, as he does, in the use of the title for Peter and James. Also the fact that the *certainly* proved apostles are without exception Hellenistic Jewish Christians (see below) argues decisively against an early apostolate established in Jerusalem. It should be considered also that according to I Cor. 15:7 *all* the apostles were called only after the appearance of the resurrected One before the five hundred brethren. But this appearance does not belong to the first period of the community; the community must already have been relatively large, and the appearance before the five hundred brethren was no longer accepted in the old confessions of faith. But then the title of apostle in Jerusalem cannot have been very old, let alone foundational.

This is further confirmed by W. Kramer's previously mentioned proof (*op. cit.*, pp. 51 ff.) that even the Hellenistic Jewish Christian kerygma was not coupled with the concept and the conception of the apostle; for then all the less can Palestinian Jewish Christianity have been familiar with this title. Since the Synoptic tradition has its setting in the life of the community, the absence of the concept of the apostle in Q, Mark, and Matthew also testifies that it was still foreign to the Hellenistic Jewish Christian community.

Thus the apologetic necessity of limiting the circle of the Jerusalem authorities as much as possible may have led in Gal. 1:17 ff. to the unique transferral, not occurring anywhere else in Paul's works, of the title of apostle to Jerusalem. Therefore to make Gal. 1:17 ff. the basic passage for the representation of the early Christian concept of the apostle, as is still being done on a wide scale, must be misleading. Peter is the only one of whom we can say with certainty that he belonged to the apostles in Jerusalem. Beyond this, however, it is not entirely ruled out that besides him still other members of the former circle of the twelve (or other resurrection witnesses of the primitive community) fulfilled in Paul's judgment the conditions which qualified one for the apostolate and for this reason were present in his mind in Gal. 1:17 ff.; perhaps Philip (*vide* p. 260) or John (p. 260). To be sure, Paul does *not* call the στῦλοι, Peter, James, and John, whom he visited during the "apostolic council," apostles. Therefore they had not *all* earned this title. On the apostleship of James, see pp. 64-65. In any case, the number of the apostles in Jerusalem cannot have been large.[131]

---

[131] Against my interpretation of Gal. 1:17 ff., J. Roloff objects: "(1) How can Paul expect to find *the* apostles in Jerusalem when on the other hand he must know that they are constantly on the move? (2) How can a special teaching authority be attributed to the *apostles* when they were nothing more than charismatic itinerant missionaries?" (*op.*

V

Now to summarize. The question which concerns us is whether Paul distinguished between a wider and a narrower circle of apostles. The latter would focus upon the circle of the twelve, perhaps completed by James or by Paul himself. We have seen that Paul is not aware of any group of twelve "apostles" at all,[132] indeed, that at his time there was not yet a group of twelve "apostles," a conclusion confirmed by the Synoptists, who did not take over the apostolic designation for the disciples until long after Paul.[133] Thus Paul knows only of a single apostolic circle,[134] which means that early Christianity possessed only one apostolate.[135]

In the first part of this work we have attempted to determine the nature

---

cit., p. 59.) But have I not said plainly that in my opinion Paul by no means hoped to find *the* apostles in Jerusalem? And does it not clearly emerge in Part One of this work that in my opinion the apostles are not only some kind of charismatic itinerant missionaries?

According to Roloff, the twelve are "without question" to be reckoned among the apostles in Gal. 1:17 ff. because at the time of Paul's visit to Jerusalem they certainly will have been among the men who were decisively influential there. But this is a mere postulate which moreover proceeds from the erroneous view that the men in Jerusalem who were authoritative for Paul must have been witnesses of the historical Jesus; here as elsewhere Roloff inadmissibly throws together the Pauline concept of the apostle and the Lucan image of the apostle. The logical conclusion from this short-circuited argument is that already a few years after Jesus' death the twelve served as apostles in Jerusalem. A presentation of the early Christian apostolate built upon this untenable basis must necessarily go astray.

[132]After what has been said, it seems hardly necessary to point out that naturally also in I Cor. 12:28 (God has set in the church first apostles) the reference is not to the twelve, as K. Holl (*op. cit.*, p. 941) still thinks. "In fact, Paul never calls the Twelve 'Apostles' " (A. Fridrichsen, *op. cit.*, n. 12). This testimony of the sources cannot be nullified by general reflections, for example by the consideration that in any case it would have been very obvious for the twelve to be understood in the primitive community as *scheluchim*, i.e., as people authorized by Jesus, "who were commissioned by the departing one with the leadership of the community" (E. Schweizer, TLZ (1962), col. 840). There is no evidence for the view; the sources contradict it. E. Schweizer appeals to Matt. 19:28, where, however, the concept *Schaliach* does not appear and where moreover, as the Lucan wording of the logion makes clear, the thought may originally have been not especially of the twelve but of the community in general. Schweizer then also must speak of a "relatively unstressed designation of the twelve," which Paul is supposed nevertheless to have adopted and combined with the conception of the world mission, whereby in the strict sense he became the actual creator of the apostolate. But Paul in no way understands himself to be the creator of the apostolate, but rather as the last of the apostles; thus he found *his* concept of the apostle in essence already existent when he was called.

[133] Cf. G. Sass [2], p. 236: "Before Paul and at the time of Paul . . . the group of the twelve did not qualify as apostles."

[134] Thus also, emphatically, H. Mosbech [1], pp. 180-81.

[135] H. Mosbech [1], pp. 180-81, in his discussion with K. Holl, also points out that it is hardly conceivable that the title ἀπόστολος could have been given to the ordinary missionaries if it had originally been the exclusive title of the δώδεκα, and that then later the original limitation became effective again.

of the apostolate of Paul. By doing so, we have determined the nature of the primitive Christian apostolate, for Paul basically incorporated himself in the larger apostolic circle (*vide* pp. 58-59). All exceptions to this rule would have to be explicitly demonstrated.

Our subsequent investigations will throw some light upon the external form of this circle. If one excepts Peter, who in fact did not originally belong to the group of apostles, a quite unitary picture emerges.

All the apostles known to us by name were *Jewish Christians*. This is clear from Phil. 3:5 (Paul); Rom. 16:7 (Andronicus and Junias); Acts 4:36-37 and Gal. 2:1 ff. (Barnabas); and Acts 15:22 (Silvanus). From this, one may conclude that the entire apostolic circle was composed, without exception, of those who were Jews by birth. For at the time of the conversion of Paul, who was the last of them, there certainly had not been a Gentile mission long enough for converted Gentiles to have entered the apostolic circle.

At the same time, however, in the case of all the apostles we are dealing with Greek-speaking Jews of the Diaspora. This needs no further proof insofar as Paul is concerned.

According to the trustworthy statement in Acts 4:36, the family of Barnabas came from Cyprus; his surname[136] Barnabas means Bar-Nebo, a theophoric pagan name.[137]

Andronicus bears a favorite ancient Greek name; the name Junias is not found elsewhere but can hardly be anything other than the hellenized short form of the current Latin Junianus.[138] The two apostles who bear these names lived in Ephesus in the Greek-speaking community[139] and as fellow prisoners of Paul (Rom. 16:7) were for a time also his fellow workers in the Gentile mission. Thus they too were Hellenistic Jews.

Silas is an Aramaic name which is frequently encountered among Jews and Syrians.[140] Silvanus, as Paul calls Silas in his epistles, is indeed a Latin name, but it is not the latinized form of Silas;[141] rather, "here is one of the many cases in which a Jew bore, in addition to his Jewish name, a Greek or a Roman name which had a similar sound." [142] Silas-Silvanus corresponds to

---

[136] Ἰωσὴφ δὲ ὁ ἐπικληθεὶς Βαρναβᾶς (Acts 4:36).

[137] See E. Haenchen, *op. cit., in loc.*

[138] See the commentaries.

[139] I have no doubt that Rom. 16 is a letter of recommendation for Phoebe to Ephesus.

[140] Cf. Th. Zahn, *Einleitung*, I, 22; E. Haenchen, *op. cit.* on Acts 15:22.

[141] Thus E. Haenchen, *op. cit.*

[142] Th. Zahn, *Einleitung*, I, 22. On these problems of the giving of more than one name, cf. G. A. Harrer in HThR (XXXIII, 1940), 19-34, and also E. Haenchen, *op. cit.,*

Saul-Paul, to Jesus-Justus (Col. 4:11), and to Joseph-Justus (Acts 1:23). Thus Silvanus also, no less than Paul and Barnabas, is a Hellenistic and, as fellow apostle with Paul, doubtless a Greek-speaking Jew. A similar assumption is proper concerning the λοιποὶ ἀπόστολοι.

As a matter of course it is unlikely that this circle of Hellenistic Jews was native to Jerusalem. A tie to the Jerusalem authorities and the connection with the primitive community there, in whatever form, is beyond question; but until the expulsion of the Hellenistic part of the community from Jerusalem (Acts 8:1), they would have felt themselves less bound to the later στῦλοι and their more or less "Judaistic" following than to the Hellenistic community in Jerusalem.[143] The subsequent ties with the "Judaists" who were gaining influence then did not continue without some strain, as is shown by the dispute carried on with those of Jerusalem by Paul as representative of all the apostles to the Gentiles. But this connection with Jerusalem does not mean that the apostolate also stemmed from Jerusalem.

Rather, the native country of the apostolic circle appears to lie precisely in that area in which Paul begins his work as an apostle: τὰ κλίματα τῆς Συρίας καὶ τῆς Κιλικίας (Gal. 1:21), and thus to have reached from Damascus to Tarsus, with Antioch as a middle point.[144] All evidences point in this direction. In this territory lay the home, the place of conversion, and the region of first activity of Paul, who placed great stress upon the fact that in the first fifteen years of his apostolate he was in Jerusalem only one time, for fourteen days, and that during this period he had not spent any time in Judea (Gal. 1:17–2:1).[145] Barnabas likewise belongs to this area.[146] The

---

on Acts 13:9; cf. E. Dobschütz, *Thessalonicherbriefe*, Meyer's *Kommentar*, X (7th ed., 1909), p. 7; W. Hartke, "Die Sammlung und die ältesten Ausgaben der Paulusbriefe," Diss. (Bonn, 1917), p. 22.

[143] We must free ourselves of the notion that besides the "Judaistic" congregation in Jerusalem there could have been no other authority there. There could certainly have been Hellenists among the δώδεκα. The majority of the twelve bear Greek or grecized names! But also apart from these, there were Hellenists among the witnesses to the resurrection, at least of course the apostles, but certainly also some of the five hundred brethren (I Cor. 15:6). In the earliest period the authority of the community in Jerusalem may have been based only upon such witnesses, for the idea that a personal acquaintance with the historical Jesus is required for such authority is still unknown to Paul. Also, the development into an explicit *Judaismus* must have begun relatively late. The old Jerusalem primitive community was not Judaistic. Peter, e.g., was never a Judaist.

[144] The unity and particularity of the Syrian-Cilician region along with Antioch at the time of early Christianity is attested, e.g., by Acts 15:23, 41.

[145] E. Haenchen, *op. cit.*, pp. 256 ff., has again correctly shown that Paul was not staying in Jerusalem as an accessory to the murderers at the time of Stephen's murder. Similarly, the remark in Acts 22:3 that Paul had studied with Gamaliel in Jerusalem may be unhistorical (cf. E. Haenchen, *op. cit.*, pp. 559-60; R. Bultmann, RGG [2nd ed.],

more reliable assertions of the book of Acts place him in Antioch; he brought
Paul there (Acts 11:25-26); together with Paul he was sent by the Antiochian congregation with a collection to Jerusalem (Acts 11:27 ff.), and
was sent out from Antioch on a missionary journey (Acts 13:1 ff.). That
the "Jerusalem" Barnabas introduced the recently converted Paul to the
distrustful apostles (Acts 9:27) is, on the other hand, as unhistorical [147]
as his inspection trip to the newly established congregation in Antioch
(Acts 11:22 ff.). This is Luke's device for transplanting the "Jerusalem"
Barnabas from Jerusalem to Antioch, which he then never left again.[148]
Possibly the Cypriot Barnabas belonged to the ἄνδρες Κύπριοι (Acts 11:
20), who founded the congregation in Antioch.[149] That he earlier had
belonged to the circle of Stephen[150] does not necessarily follow; for the
mission is certainly not the result but the cause of the persecution of the
Hellenistic part of the congregation in Jerusalem (*vide infra*), so that the
note in Acts 11:19 does not indicate the real state of things. In Gal. 2:1,
9, and 13, it is equally clear that Barnabas is an Antiochian and that he
is a non-Jerusalemite.[151] One must seek the home of Andronicus and Junias,
the fellow prisoners of Paul and therefore also associates in his mission
territory, in Antioch and its environs, the beginning point of the Pauline

---

IV, 1020-21). And a persecution of the Christians in Judea by Paul is ruled out by Gal.
1:22 (Acts 8:1 ff.; 9:1-2).

[146] Κύπριος τῷ γένει means the national (not racial) origin of Barnabas and does not
presuppose that Barnabas himself was born in Cyprus, and even less that he lived there
(cf. Acts 18:2, 24).

[147] Cf. E. Haenchen, *op. cit.*, pp. 289-90. In the first place, Paul did not even go to
Jerusalem after his conversion, as he expressly assures us in Gal. 1:17. On his first trip
there three years later, however, he was certainly no longer feared. In the second place,
it is not comprehensible why the truth about Paul should have been known just to
Barnabas in Jerusalem.

[148] In Acts 4:36-37, Luke apparently implies that Barnabas was originally resident in
Jerusalem. Thus on account of his later activity in Antioch, Luke had to relocate him
there in some manner. Now of course it is by no means necessary to conclude from Acts
4:36-37 that Barnabas was a member of the Jerusalem community when he placed the
proceeds from his field at the disposal of the Jerusalem community. E. Haenchen (*op. cit.*,
p. 195) has correctly noted that in Barnabas' conduct in this matter we have an unusual
occasion and not an ordinary case. I am inclined to regard this case like the other payments
from the scattered communities to Jerusalem (Acts 11:30; Gal. 2:10), which were not
presented *by* Jerusalemites but *to* Jerusalemites.

[149] See E. Haenchen, *op. cit.*, p. 322.

[150] E. Haenchen, *op. cit.*, p. 322 concerning Acts 11:19.

[151] E. Schwartz's conjecture (NGG [1907], p. 282, n. 1) that Barnabas originally was
in the text of the earlier material which Luke used in Acts 13:1 ff. is appropriate and
well grounded. Then it would be completely clear that it is only Luke who misplaces
Barnabas by setting him in the Jerusalem context. The basis of Schwartz's conjecture is
the thesis that the impossible Lucan interpretation of the name Barnabas as "son of
consolation" (Acts 4:36) rests upon the erroneous use of a note that concerned Manaen
(=Menachem, the comforter, Acts 13:1).

mission. Silas, finally, joins Paul in Antioch on the so-called second missionary journey (Acts 15:40). This is a clear and trustworthy statement but difficult to harmonize with the report, Acts 15:22, 27, and 32, that Silas was sent from Jerusalem with the "apostolic decree" to Antioch and, before the departure of Paul, returned again to Jerusalem. The Western text corrects this mistake in the account by means of the addition of vs. 34, which cannot be harmonized with vs. 33: "But it pleased Silas to remain there." However, "in vss. 22, 27, and 32, Luke told of Silas only in order to prepare the reader for his participation in the Pauline missionary work," [152] but not for the purpose of handing down dependable historical notes. The composition of the "apostolic decree" at the so-called apostolic council simply runs aground on Gal. 2:6; no manner of apologetic cunning can salvage it. Along with this, however, the remark that Silas had brought this "decree" to Antioch in the company of Paul also becomes untenable. Silas, too, is reliably shown only in Antioch.

With all due respect which the apostles have toward the congregation in Jerusalem, and with all the recognition at least of the moral authority of the city of Zion, they nevertheless do not become Jerusalemites. They are Hellenistic Jews who live in and around Antioch, the actual missionary center of primitive Christianity; there, and later from there, they perform their ministry. Normally one does not encounter them in Jerusalem (Gal. 1:18 ff.; *vide* p. 86).

Even those who place the origin of the primitive Christian apostolate in Jerusalem at least make room for Antioch to have a significant place in the development of the concept of apostleship. K. H. Rengstorf, for example ([1], p. 435), considers it likely that in Antioch the Greek word ἀπόστολος came into use from the Aramaic שליחא, which is supposed to have designated the apostle in the primitive community (*vide* pp. 98 ff.). On the other hand H. Mosbech, who rightly holds that the δώδεκα were not original apostles, correctly transfers the *origin* of the apostolate to Antioch ([1], p. 188). Kirsopp Lake (*op. cit.*, p. 50) and F. Kattenbusch (*op. cit.*, p. 339, n. 1) do likewise.

It is noteworthy that the apostolic ministry was very early, in any case even before the conversion of Paul,[153] a ministry in the non-law-observing Gentile mission. The book of Acts shows this when it transfers the first Gentile mission to Antioch (Acts 11:20-21) and asserts that this mission

---

[152] E. Haenchen, *op. cit.*, *in loc.*

[153] Paul himself never claims to have been the *first* missionary to the Gentiles; cf. A. v. Harnack [1], I, 75. Indeed, even in his Jewish period he had never persecuted the "Judaists," who were tolerated even in Jerusalem, but the non-law-observing Christians of Jewish origin.

resulted from the work of members of the exiled community of Stephen. That the Gentile mission began in Antioch is certainly correct.[154] That it did not begin until after the martyrdom of Stephen, I hold to be incorrect. Why had the Hellenists been driven out of Jerusalem, while the Judaists could remain there in peace? What then was the actual core of the bloody strife between the Hellenistic Jews (Acts 6:9) and the Jewish Christians? [155] According to the account in Acts, Stephen had made blasphemous speeches against the law and the temple. But the destruction of the temple in the last times is an idea of late Jewish apocalyptic which is not at all heretical,[156] and people had been allowed to discuss the law;[157] even the "Judaists" had discussed it without being harmed. The reason for the uprising against the Jewish Christians can only have been what later, too, determined the conflicts between Jews and Christians and even the disagreements within the primitive community itself: the question of the non-law-observing mission.[158] And in this question the circle around Stephen must already have shared the later conviction of Paul.[159] Thus there was already before the outcries against the Hellenistic Jewish Christians of Jerusalem a Christian mission which refused to demand circumcision and which thereby in principle severed Christianity from its association with Judaism. The Jewish protest in this connection then may have been directed less against the *Gentile* mission, against which, from the Jewish side, one could hardly bring forward a serious argument, than against the emancipation also of the *Jewish* Christians from the compulsion of the law—an emancipation which was almost inevitably bound up with this mission—and against the non-law-observing *Jewish* mission as a consequence of the non-law-observing Gentile mission.

[154] The reliable note in Acts 11:25 says that the name "Christians" first appeared in Antioch. This is probably evidence for the fact that it was first in Antioch, the third largest city of the Roman Empire, that the Christian community clearly distinguished itself from the Jews; cf. A. v. Harnack [1], I, 53-54.

[155] On this question, the otherwise splendid study of E. Haenchen on the Stephen tradition in his commentary (*op. cit.*, p. 226) breaks down.

[156] See R. Bultmann, *Das Evangelium des Johannes*, p. 88, n. 7. Cf. G. Friedrich, "Messianische Hohepriestererwartung in den Synoptikern," in ZThK (1956), pp. 289 ff. For example, the Essenes were able even in Judea to polemicize against the *prevailing* temple cult without being arrested by the Jewish authorities for doing so.

[157] Cf. A. v. Harnack [1], I. 50. Even of the Jesus of the Synoptics it is true that "his critical interpretation of the law, in spite of its radicality, likewise stands within the scribal discussion of it" (R. Bultmann [1], I, 34-35).

[158] This also explains that the persecution originated with Hellenistic Jews, esp. with those from Asia and Cilicia, where the Christian mission may in the meantime have begun. If the reasons given by Luke for the persecution of the Hellenists had been determinative, then one still has to reckon with the fact that instead of Hellenistic Jews the higher Jewish authorities would have intervened.

[159] G. Klein represented the same view in his thorough discussion of E. Haenchen's commentary on Acts in ZKG (1957), p. 368. Cf. now my book *Paul and James*, pp. 16 ff.

I am not inclined to assume that the impetus to such a mission arose out of the Hellenistic primitive community in Jerusalem itself. The book of Acts is quite correct when it places the beginning and origin of this revolutionary innovation in Antioch. But the Hellenistic "board of control" in Jerusalem must, in opposition to the Judaistic part of the primitive community, have approved of this proceeding and, at least theologically, supported it. To Luke, then, who no longer wishes to see through the state of things or at least does not see through it, this support [160] appears in the form of "speeches against this holy place and the law" (Acts 6:13).

According to Acts 11:20 the first missionaries to the Gentiles were ἄνδρες Κύπριοι καὶ Κυρηναῖοι. Some of them are mentioned by name in the reliable list in Acts 13:1: Barnabas, Simeon with the surname Niger, Lucius from Cyrenaica, Manaen, who had grown up with Herod Antipas, and Saul. None of them belonged to the seven "deacons," who had had to withdraw from Jerusalem! According to the tradition employed in Acts 13:1 they are all instead native to their Syrian-Cilician area of activity. As to Barnabas and Saul, this has already been established on the basis of the more precise tradition preserved concerning them. A σύντροφος of Herod will have to be sought in Antioch rather than in Jerusalem. And to suppose Jerusalem as an intermediate station for the Cyrenians Lucius and Simeon,[161] now living in Antioch, is not very likely. If the designation "prophets and teachers" (Acts 13:1) for these people stems from Luke's source, it, too, points not to Jerusalem but rather in the Syrian direction.

The Gentile mission is thus an independent undertaking of the Antiochian Christians.[162] It began in the same area where the apostolate is native, and where Paul, as well as the Hellenists exiled from Jerusalem, already found it. When in Acts 11:19 ff. Luke attempts to present the matter as if it were the Jerusalemites who also first undertook the Gentile mission, this simply corresponds to his tendency to make the "original apostles" the responsible agents of the total development of the primitive church.

This last point now makes it decisively clear why Peter and all the more James were not originally counted among the apostles, but why Paul

---

[160] Did Nicolaus, the proselyte from Antioch, form the bridge from Antioch to the Hellenists in Jerusalem? His person cannot have been insignificant among the seven; he is the only one of the seven whose origin is remembered and handed down in the tradition. Further, one cannot completely ignore that the Gnostic sect of the Nicolaitans (Rev. 2:6, 15)—whether justly or unjustly—appealed to *him,* as early traditions assert (see Bo Reicke, *Glauben und Leben der Urgemeinde,* p. 121, n. 10).

[161] Simeon's surname "Niger" may refer to North Africa. Cf. E. Haenchen, *op. cit.,* p. 316. *Contra* Th. Zahn, *Einleitung,* II, 257-58. To identify him with the Simon of Cyrene of the passion narrative (F. Spitta, *Die Apostelgeschichte,* p. 134) is a conjecture not to be rejected out of hand, but nothing more than a conjecture.

[162] On the spiritual origins of this revolutionary activity, see below, pp. 201 ff.

leaves Peter out of consideration when in I Cor. 9:5 and 15:7 he speaks of the apostles as a whole. This is due not only to the fact that he entered his missionary service[163] relatively late.[164] But Peter had no *actual* connection with the primitive Christian apostolic circle. He belonged to Jerusalem and not to Antioch; he was not a Hellenistic Jew and would hardly have spoken Greek originally; he was never active in the Gentile mission. Only in view of his activity in the Jewish mission can Paul concede to him, whose "revelation of Jesus Christ" is indeed well established, the professional designation of an apostle.[165] This was all the more possible because, in the meantime, Paul through his unique activity had become outstanding among the apostles and, further, because the ecumenical Jewish mission of Peter grew to a position uniquely comparable to the worldwide prosecution of the Gentile mission of the apostle Paul (Gal. 2:8).[166]

Thus the ἀπόστολοι, down to the time of Paul, form a relatively closed group of missionaries, obviously localized and, thanks to Paul, easily comprehended as to its nature. On the basis of this knowledge, we may now attempt to answer the question which was posed at the end of Part I of our study, concerning the source and origin of this apostolate. For it has already been ascertained that the primitive Christian concept of the apostle is not an original creation of primitive Christianity.

---

[163] At least it is not true for Peter as it was for Paul, that the experience of conversion and that of calling to be a missionary are identical.

[164] The—relatively late—organized missionary activity of the Jewish-Christian primitive community in Jerusalem within the Diaspora certainly was set in motion only by the success of the mission to the Gentiles which went out from Antioch. Thus Antioch is the home of the Christian world mission in general.

[165] Thus, correctly, E. Lohse [1], p. 269: "Paul understands the apostolic office of Peter from the perspective of his own office," and: "It [*sc.,* the missionary office of Peter] may have been described as an apostolic office first by Paul." Cf. also G. Schulze-Kadelbach in ThLZ (1956), col. 7, n. 35; A. Fridrichsen, *op. cit.,* n. 12. *Contra* G. Klein, *op. cit.,* pp. 54-55.

[166] Of course we must reckon with the possibility that, besides Peter and James, also other witnesses to the resurrection of the Jerusalem community earned the title of "apostle" because of their missionary activity, without our knowing anything of them. For that matter, such people could have been among the apostles mentioned in Gal. 1:17.

PART THREE
The Origin of the Primitive Christian Apostolate

I

The evidence for the non-Christian use of ἀπόστολος has been, since J. B. Lightfoot, so often and so thoroughly investigated, so completely collected, and so frequently published,[1] that we can summarize our views in this section of the third part of our work quite briefly.

1. In the secular Greek idiom, ἀπόστολος is a technical word belonging to the language of seafarers. Originally an adjective (Plat. Ep. VII, 346a: ἐν τοῖς ἀποστόλοις πλοίοις πλεῖν), τὸ ἀπόστολον simply designates the *ship* (Pseudo-Hdt., Vita Hom. 19). ὁ ἀπόστολος is then the *sending out of a fleet* (Lys. Or. 19. 21; Demosth. Or. 18. 107) or the *naval expedition* itself (Demosth. Or. 18. 80; cf. 3. 5).[2] Finally, the *company of colonists* (Dion. Hal. Ant. Rom. IX, 59) or even the *commander of a naval expedition* is similarly named (Hesychius: ἀπόστολος· στρατηγὸς κατὰ πλοῦν πεμπό-μενος; cf. *Anecdota Graeca,* ed. Bekker 217. 26). One may also compare the definition in Suidas: ἀπόστολος ὁ ἐκπεμπόμενος μετὰ στρατιᾶς καὶ παρασκευῆς εἰς πόλεμον.

In the papyri the abstraction of the concept is still further pursued. Here one meets ἀπόστολος in the sense of a *bill of lading* or a delivery paper (P. Oxy. IX, 1197. 13; other passages in Preisigke, Wört., I, 95 and W. Bauer [2]), and one time even as a *travel permit* (BGU, V, 64).

That this usage has nothing to do with the technical application of ἀπόσ-

[1] K. H. Rengstorf [1], pp. 407 ff.; H. Lietzmann, HNT on Rom. 1:1; H. Mosbech [1], pp. 166 ff.; W. Bauer [2]; W. Seufert, *op. cit.,* pp. 6 ff.; G. Sass [1], pp. 11-12; J. B. Lightfoot, *op. cit.,* pp. 92 ff.

[2] Posidonius, see W. Bauer [2]. The officials responsible for the sending out are called ἀποστολεῖς; see in Pauly-Wissowa, II, 1, col. 182.

τολος in primitive Christianity is generally acknowledged, and this is rightly asserted by K. Rengstorf ([1], pp. 407-8).

2. However, there are also some passages in which ἀπόστολος is used more generally and even in the personal sense of "one who is sent." Lightfoot has referred to Herodotus I. 21: ὁ μὲν δὴ ἀπόστολος ἐς τὴν Μίλητον ἦν. In Herodotus V. 38 it is said of Aristagoras: αὐτὸς ἐς Λακεδαίμονα τριήρεϊ ἀπόστολος ἐγίνετο, a passage which appears to build a bridge between the technical usage of ἀπόστολος in the context of seafaring and the general employment of the word. The same may hold true of the occurrence in Josephus (Ant. XVII. 300), where ἀπόστολος describes the *sending*[3] *of messengers* to Rome, who of necessity had to travel by ship. The word ἀπόστολος also signifies "embassy" in Ant. I. 146, where it appears as an alternate reading alongside ἀποδασμός. The word occurs once in the LXX, in I Kings 14:6, where the prophet presents himself to the wife of Jeroboam with the words: ἐγώ εἰμι ἀπόστολος πρός σε σκληρός. Here ἀπόστολος undoubtedly signifies "one sent." [4] Symmachus also has the word once, again in connection with seafaring: He translates Isa. 18.2 using ἀπόστολος for ציר, while the LXX has ὅμηρον. The expression designates the Ethiopian emissaries who also visited Jerusalem. To this category also belong the passages in the New Testament in which ἀπόστολος is used in a nontechnical sense: John 13:16[5]; Phil. 2:25 and II Cor. 8:23 [6]; and perhaps Luke 11:49 [7] and Mark 6:30.[8]

None of these passages shows a technical usage of the word ἀπόστολος which could have been a prefiguring of the primitive Christian concept of apostle. Both Hellenism and Hellenistic Judaism, then, appear to be eliminated as sources of the New Testament apostolate.

It is, however, noteworthy that the word ἀπόστολος=emissary was

[3] Harnack translates it as personal and lets Varus, the head of the Jewish embassy to Rome, be called ἀπόστολος. So also K. Lake *op. cit.*, p. 46. However, this is incorrect.

[4] The passage is lacking in Codex Vaticanus, so that the possibility of a later emergence must remain open (cf. A. Ehrhardt, *op. cit.*, p. 17).

[5] This passage is the only one in John in which the word ἀπόστολος appears. Perhaps what is involved here is the repetition of a Jewish formula (thus Rengstorf [1], p. 421). But the rabbinical *terminus technicus* for an emissary, שליח, does not occur in the only rabbinical parallel (Gn r 78 on 32:26) which Rengstorf can cite (see A. Ehrhardt, *op. cit.*, pp. 18-19). Consequently, it is by no means certain that ἀπόστολος in John 13:16 is a simple translation of שליח. An even more general language usage may be present.

[6] See p. 60.

[7] With near certainty this passage comes from a Jewish book of wisdom and had already been taken over by Luke's source. If, as is not ruled out, the word ἀπόστολοι in Luke 11:49, which Matthew does not have, was not inserted by Luke in view of the Christian (twelve) apostles, then we would have here a relatively early witness for the pre-Christian use of ἀπόστολος in a general personal sense (cf. H. v. Campenhausen [1], p. 102; E. Haupt, *op. cit.*, pp. 107-8; G. Klein, *op. cit.*, p. 33).

[8] See p. 72.

nevertheless understandable to Greek ears. This is shown also in the passages from the second century which H. v. Campenhausen ([1], p. 100; cf. *ibid.*, p. 109, n. 3) cited in support of this assertion. The vocabulary of the Koine is, moreover, richer and more comprehensive than our sources would indicate. If Herodotus and Josephus, LXX and Symmachus, Paul and John and the Jewish apocalypticists (Luke 11:49) at least occasionally employed ἀπόσ-τολος in the general sense as "messenger" and were convinced that the Greek reader would understand the word, then the technical use in the New Testament to mean the same thing cannot have been "an innovation to Greek ears," as K. H. Rengstorf ([1], p. 408) thinks.

II

Nevertheless, we do not find a prototype for the New Testament apostolate among the ἀπόστολοι of the entire body of pagan literature in the Greek language. We must therefore turn our attention to contemporary Judaism,[9] where we find the figure of the שליח,[10] to which Lightfoot (*op. cit.*, p. 93) has already referred and which today is acknowledged in many circles as the immediate prototype of the primitive Christian apostle.

Rengstorf speaks of the "later Jewish institution of the שליח" ([1], p. 414), but we must not let this expression conceal the fact that the institutional character of the activity of the שלוחים is often hardly discernible at all. This explains why significantly different exemplifications of the שליח can be referred to by the individual investigators. Further, adequate attention is not always given to the question whether in the illustrative passage cited with reference to שליח this concept is actually used in a technical sense, for only in such a case does it come into consideration as prototype for the New Testament concept of apostle. Finally, one must be more than ordinarily cautious about classifying messengers or embassies in Judaism as belonging to the institution of the שליח when the term itself is lacking. The sending out of messengers of one sort or another was quite commonplace, and only in exceptional cases was it institutionally arranged. If one keeps this in mind, then with the sources at hand and by use of the quite extensive literature about the שליח, one can form a relatively clear picture of this late Jewish emissary.

1. A special exemplification of the *Schaliach,* to which Harnack ([1], I, 327 ff.) turned his attention, is represented by those of the apostles whom

---

[9] That our attention must be turned quite generally to the Orient is shown by the simple fact that the Oriental languages have their own equivalent to ἀπόστολος, while in Latin "apostolus" appears as a foreign word.

[10] "This is the usual form. In the plur. and with suffixes, שלוח is used (Str.-B., III, 2); שליחא is the corresponding Aram." (Rengstorf [1], p. 414, n. 50).

the Palestinian patriarchate used to send forth. The sources for this are following:

Eusebius on Isa. 18:1-2 [11]: "We found in the writings of the ancients[12] how the priests and elders of the Jewish people who lived in Jerusalem wrote letters and sent them to all the people of all Jewry and calumniated the doctrine of Christ." The bearers of these letters were then called ἀπόστολοι αὐτῶν, and it goes on to say: ἀποστόλους δὲ εἰσέτι καὶ νῦν ἔθος ἐστὶν Ἰουδαίοις ὀνομάζειν τοὺς ἐγκύκλια γράμματα παρὰ τῶν ἀρχόντων αὐτῶν ἐπικομιζομένους. While Eusebius does not describe more precisely the task of the contemporary Jewish apostles, since he says nothing to us about the content of the letters, we learn something more definite in Epiph. Haer. 30. 4. Epiphanius tells of a certain Joseph from Tiberias who belonged to a group of Jewish dignitaries, who are described in the following fashion: εἰσὶ δὲ οὗτοι μετὰ τὸν πατριάρχην ἀπόστολοι καλούμενοι, προσεδρεύουσι δὲ τῷ πατριάρχῃ καὶ σὺν αὐτῷ πολλάκις καὶ ἐν νυκτὶ καὶ ἐν ἡμέρᾳ συνεχῶς διάγουσι διὰ τὸ συμβουλεύειν καὶ ἀναφέρειν αὐτῷ τὰ κατὰ τὸν νόμον.[13] In 30. 11, then, we hear how Joseph had received the blessed activity τῆς ἀποστολῆς, and thereupon was sent with the corresponding pieces of writing to Cilicia, in order to bring the tithes and the first fruits from the Jews of each city to Jerusalem. In addition to collecting, he concerned himself, in apostolic capacity, with the internal conditions in the congregations, replaced heads of synagogues and elders, and so on. This agrees with the passage in Codex Theodosianus XVI, 8. 14: "Superstitionis indignae est, ut archisynagogi sive presbyteri Judaeorum vel quos ipsi *apostolos* vocant, qui ad exigendum aurum atque argentum a patriarcha certo tempore diriguntur," etc. Further, the context of Jul. Ep. 25 shows that Julian was thinking of the financial side of the apostolic activity of the Jewish messengers when he alluded to τὴν λεγομένην παρ' ὑμῖν ἀποστολήν. Hieronymus (on Gal. 1:1) reports only: "Usque hodie a patriarchis Judaeorum apostolos mitti solent," but his expressions are important, because he gives "Slias" as designation of these apostles,[14] and this is the latinized שליחא (cf. Rengstorf [1], p. 414, n. 52).

---

[11] This is the passage in which ἀπόστολος occurs in Symmachus. It reads (following Kautzsch): "Woe to the land of whirring wings, and to the people of might and conquest, who sent envoys (LXX ὅμηρα, Symmachus ἀπόστολοι) over the water upon the Nile and in vessels of papyrus! Go, you swift messengers (ἄγγελοι) to the nation tall and smooth. . . ." Eusebius connects the ἀπόστολοι to the false Jewish apostles, and the ἄγγελοι to the Christian apostles.

[12] This source and its reliability are unknown to us. In spite of assertions to the contrary (see Lietzmann on Rom. 1:2), it is by no means certain that it already contained the concept of ἀπόστολος. It is possible that Justin is this source (see below).

[13] Cf. Procopius on Isa. 18:2 (MSG LXXXVII, 253).

[14] "Apostolus autem, hoc est missus, Hebraeorum proprie vocabulum est, quod Slias

These passages are clear and, in their decisive points, unequivocal. There were Jewish apostles who were sent out by the Jerusalem patriarchate, whose most important task it was to take up the offerings for the central authorities, but who were at the same time authorized to attend to the supervisory powers of Jerusalem.[15] It is, of course, incorrect to connect with this institution the references in Just. Dial. 17.1 and 108.2-3 (cf. 117.3) to the sending out of Jewish countermissionaries, and then wherever possible also to refer to Acts 28:21; 9:1-2; 22:4-5; and 26:10.[16] In all these passages one does not encounter the term "apostle" at all. Justin is dependent upon Acts or its tradition[17]; Eusebius, in turn, in the first part of the expressions cited above ("in the writings of the ancients"), upon Justin; and the presentation of Justin and of Acts itself is unhistorical.[18] That Jewish slanders contributed much to the persecution of the Christians and that Jews participated in the persecution is indeed true[19]; but that official emissaries from Jerusalem had to enlighten the Diaspora as to the threat from the Christians at a time when the stream of pilgrims to the temple was not diminishing is just as improbable as the supposition that the Jews in Rome at the time of Acts 28:21 had still heard nothing of Paul. Thus we actually know nothing about "apostles" engaged in combating the Christians.

But can the above-mentioned apostolate of the central authorities have been the prototype of the primitive Christian apostolate? That is ruled out because before A.D. 70 it did not exist, at least not in this form. H. Vogelstein has pointed this out ([1], 1905, and again in [2], 1925),[20] and if I see it correctly, he has generally carried his point.[21] Only after the destruction of the temple, when there was a diminishing of the stream of pilgrims to Jerusalem, which up till then had supported by its gifts the Jewish teaching program in the holy city,[22] the Jewish authorities found

---

quoque sonat, cui a mittendo missi nomen impositum est. . . . Aiunt Hebraei inter ipsos quoque prophetas et sanctos viros esse quosdam, qui et prophetae et apostoli sint, alios vero, qui tantum prophetae. . . ."

[15] Of course in the rabbinical texts these emissaries always bear names other than "Schaliach" (cf. F. Gavin, op. cit., p. 255).

[16] A. v. Harnack [1], I, 327-28; texts in [1], I, 57, n. 4; H. Vogelstein [1]; H. Lietzmann, excursus on Rom. 1:2; K. H. Rengstorf [1], 417-18.

[17] Dial. 108. 2 also rests upon Matt. 27:63 and 28:13.

[18] E. Haenchen, op. cit., on Acts 9:2.

[19] A. v. Harnack [1], I, 57 ff.

[20] "As financial agents we find the apostles of the central authorities only after the destruction of the temple" ([1], p. 438).

[21] Cf. K. H. Rengstorf [1], p. 418; H. v. Campenhausen [1], p. 99; while F. Gavin, op. cit., goes back into the Persian period with the institution we are discussing, Graetz (Geschichte der Juden [4th ed.], IV, 279 ff.) places it first in the third century under Gamaliel IV or Judah II (cf. K. Lake, op. cit., p. 49).

[22] K. H. Rengstorf [1], p. 417; H. Vogelstein [1], pp. 437 ff.

it necessary on their own initiative to ask the Diaspora for love offerings.[23] These eventually became the so-called patriarchal tribute, which was collected by the empowered apostles.[24] It is only obvious and self-explanatory that these apostles, on their visits, attended to the former supervisory functions of the patriarchate.[25] They were, in view of their significance, as a rule ordained rabbis.[26] But since before the year 70 [27] a need for such an apostolate did not exist and therefore this institution naturally is not recorded so early,[28] this apostolate is ruled out as a source for the New Testament concept of the apostle.[29] It is therefore superfluous to examine the inner criteria on the basis of which a relation of the two institutions would

[23] Cf. j Pes. IV, 31b, 61, and on the entire problem, Str.-B., III, 316 ff.

[24] In j Hor. 48a, this task is mentioned without the title שליחא.

[25] In j Chag. 76c, 31 ff., such tasks are committed to three rabbis; the term שליחא is lacking.

[26] K. H. Rengstorf [1], p. 417; H. Vogelstein [1], p. 443; that they were commissioned for their mission by the laying on of hands is a conception which has appeared since A. v. Harnack ([1], I, 328), if not earlier (cf. in K. H. Rengstorf [1], p. 417; G. Sass [1], p. 19), but which rests only upon a mistaken interpretation of Justin's Dial. 108. 2. There χειροτονήσαντες simply implies "to select," not "to lay hands upon" (cf. A. Ehrhardt, op. cit., p. 16; E. Lohse [2], p. 63), Cf. J. Jeremias in ZNW, XLVIII (1957), 129.

[27] It has recently been asserted with good reasoning that the sacrificial cult in Jerusalem was again taken up after the destruction of the temple and continued until the year 132 (K. W. Clark, "Worship in the Jerusalem Temple After A.D. 70," in NTS, VI [1960], 269 ff.). If this is correct, then, for the origin of the apostolate discussed above, one would have to go on down to the Bar Cochba uprising. Nothing stands in the way of this.

[28] To be sure H. Vogelstein attempts in his essays to date the institution of the שלוחים as apostles of the central authorities in Jerusalem for various purposes back in the early post-exilic period, and K. H. Rengstorf even thinks that it is "probably older still" (op. cit., 414), but I regard these attempts as unjustified. The collection of money by the Jewish apostles is obviously not an activity which was attached to their office after A.D. 70 (thus H. Vogelstein [1], pp. 437-38), but the task with which their ministry stands or falls. They are "just financial officials" (A. v. Harnack [1], I, 330)! So long as the pilgrims from all over the world yearly streamed into Jerusalem, the Jewish authorities there did not find it necessary regularly to send out emissaries on year-long journeys. The problems that arose were settled on the spot in Jerusalem. It is naturally to be assumed that occasionally and for special occasions, particularly in Palestine itself, envoys of the Sanhedrin were sent to individual local sanhedrins. But the sending forth of (mostly epistolary) emissaries is one thing, and an institutional apostolate of the Jerusalem central authorities is something else. This latter may not be inferred from II Chron. 17:7 ff., nor from II Chron. 19:5; 30:1; 34:8-9; Esth. 9:20, 30, or II Macc. 1:1–2:19 (H. Vogelstein [1], pp. 435 ff.), and all the less from I Kings 14:6. Cf. G. Sass [1], p. 15. Likewise all the references to the Persian government (Ezra 7:14) with its circumstances wholly different from those in Israel prove nothing for the situation in Jerusalem at the time of Christ's birth, even if—and this cannot be proved—the community coming out of the exile should have temporarily followed the Persian order (H. Vogelstein [1], pp. 429 ff.; F. Gavin, op. cit., pp. 251 ff.). One cannot even point to the rabbis who were to carry through the new arrangement of the calendar in the Diaspora, following the corresponding decision of the Sanhedrin (H. Vogelstein [1], p. 436; cf. K. H. Rengstorf [1], p. 416), since they belong to the time after 70 and usually are not called "Schaliach" (Jeb. 16:7; T Meg. 2:5).

[29] Thus also H. Monnier, op. cit.

be set forth as possible, probable, or, as would actually be the case, impossible.

2. The ἀπόστολοι ἐκκλησιῶν, who before the destruction of the temple brought the temple tax from the Diaspora to Jerusalem, are often suggested as another, special exemplification of the institution of the שליח.[30] Unfortunately, however, we are lacking any Jewish documentation to the effect that the transmission of this temple tax took place in the context of a *Schaliach* institution. One may wish to point to II Cor. 8:23, where Paul speaks of the two Macedonian brethren who cooperated in the gathering of a collection and the bringing of it to Jerusalem, as ἀπόστολοι ἐκκλησιῶν; by this he is supposed to be joining himself to the corresponding Jewish arrangement.[31] This is possible, but by no means certain. Epaphroditus for instance is also called ἀπόστολος, when the congregation at Philippi sends him with a gift of money to Paul (Phil. 2:25), and for such a sending there certainly can have been no Jewish institution to serve as a direct prototype. These emissaries of the congregation must indeed have enjoyed a great degree of confidence on the part of those who sent them, but as simple bearers of a gift of money they were in no wise bearers of a special authority and power; with the assignment of such authority, however, the office of the *Schaliach* stands or falls (*vide infra*).

Philo does not even call the bearers of the temple tax ἀπόστολοι, but rather ἱεροπομποί (Philo, Leg. Gaj. 216, par. 578).[32] Thus we are still uncertain about all this: the existence of the technical expression שליחא for the bearers of the temple tax before the year 70; the translation of this term in the territory of Hellenistic language as ἀπόστολος[33]; and the taking over of this usage in the case of sending money within primitive Christianity. It is at least equally probable that in Phil. 2:25 and II Cor. 8:23 Paul simply took up the common Greek use of ἀπόστολος, which is testified to, although quite infrequently.[34] This would then best explain the fact that the Gentile Christian congregations in Macedonia understood the expression.

If, however, Paul had been dependent, in the two above-mentioned passages, upon an institutional prototype, then this prototype would be distinguished from his own concept of the apostle. For Paul can casually call the three brethren from Macedonia apostles only because he has no idea that one could confuse these ἀπόστολοι ἐκκλησιῶν with the ἀπόστολοι Χριστοῦ

[30] G. Sass [1], p. 24.

[31] G. Sass [1], pp. 104 ff.; K. H. Rengstorf [1], p. 422; H. Vogelstein [1], pp. 438 ff.; K. Holl [1], p. 930, n. 1; A. Ehrhardt, *op. cit.*, pp. 18-19.

[32] Cf. Philo., Spec. Leg. I, 77; cf. K. Lake, *op. cit.*, p. 49. Jos. Ant. XVIII, 9.1; Str.-B., I, 760 ff.

[33] However, cf. Str.-B., III, 316.

[34] Perhaps one should also remember that in late Judaism occasionally consignments of gifts in general were described as ἀποστολαί; see the preceding note.

or even posit any commonality between them. Thus for Paul the two forms of the apostolate have nothing to do with each other. If the institution of the congregational apostles goes back to a Jewish institution, then this institution is ruled out as prototype for the *technical* use of ἀπόστολος in primitive Christianity.

But even apart from this train of thought, it is true that only by an acrobatic sleight-of-hand can one place side-by-side the Christian apostle, who was called by Christ to missionary service and sent into the world, and the—hypothetical—Jewish congregational apostolate, which was familiar with emissaries who were sent by many to Jerusalem in order to deliver tax money. Apart from the fact of their being sent, the two figures have nothing in common.

3. Thus there remains the general Jewish legal institution of the *Schaliach* as possible source of the primitive Christian apostolate. Following the lead of S. Krauss and H. Vogelstein, it is above all the achievement of Billerbeck to have investigated the nature of this institution and to have collected numerous passages in evidence. K. H. Rengstorf ([1]) has carried this investigation forward in an excellent way.

The juristic concept שליח is determined not so much by the original meaning of the word, that of "being sent,"[35] but rather by the fact that the sent one is authorized for the performance of some task. Thus *Schaliach* is a fixed term of juristic technical language and designates a person who acts authoritatively for another, without regard to the personality of the emissary or of the one who commissions him, and also without regard to the commission itself. The correct translation of שליח,[35a] therefore, is not "one sent," but rather "one commissioned," "representative," or "authorized deputy" (Rengstorf [1], p. 418).

The *Schaliach* is an officeholder, and he is this quite independently of the content of the commission; the only decisive thing is that he acts in place and on the authority of the one who does the sending.[36] He is best characterized by the legal dictum often cited in the rabbinical writings: "The messenger of a man is as the man himself." [37] Rengstorf may be correct ([1], p. 416) when he traces the legal foundation of this office of a represen-

---

[35] Thus, e.g., the leader in prayer in the synagogue is the *Schaliach* of his congregation (Ber. 5. 5), and the high priest is the plenipotentiary of the priesthood or of the entire community of the people (Joma 1. 5; cf. Rengstorf [1], p. 416). Often the "plenipotentiary" remains at home while the one in whose stead he serves is away. The conception of being sent forth is completely lost.

[35a] Cf. also IV Ezra 1:104 (Violet, III, 14.2 ff.).

[36] Rengstorf [1], p. 415.

[37] שלוחו של אדם כמותו (Ber. 5. 5; cf. Men. 93b; M. Ex. 12. 6; Qid. 41b; B. M. 96a; Chag. 10b; Ned. 72b; Nazir 12b; b B. Q. 113b; j Chag. I, 76d. 1; j Ned. X, 42b. 16).

tative back to the Semitic messenger law which we also encounter in the Old Testament: The honor which is due to the Lord is to be rendered to his representative.[38]

The office of the *Schaliach* is an office for a time. It vanishes when the commission is fulfilled for which the authority was extended. There was no *Schaliach* with a life-term appointment.[39]

The authorization thus was sometimes made for a quite specific commission to which the *Schaliach* was bound. Misuse of the office was possible; hence the selection of the representative required special caution, or else the content of the commission had to be specified in writing by means of a covering letter (j. Chag. 76d. 3-4). If the *Schaliach* went beyond his authority, his decisions were invalid.[40]

The authorization could be given by an individual, but it might also come from a group such as, for example, the Sanhedrin or the local congregation. Thus a man might arrange his betrothal with a woman through a *Schaliach* (Qid. 2.1; T. Qid. 4.2; T. Jeb. 4.4; Qid. 41a-b), or be divorced from a wife (Git. 4.1; 3.6; Qid. 41a). Through such a one he might arrange a purchase (T. Jeb. 4.4) or have the Passover lamb slaughtered (Pes. 8.2). A court of law could engage a *Schaliach* to execute its decisions (Git. 3.6; B. Q. 9.5; Joma 1.5); the Sanhedrin could send out authorized persons to arrange the calendar or to announce the fixing of the time of the new moon (R. H. 1.3, 4; 2.2)[41]; the congregation and the priesthood authorized the high priest (Joma 1.5),[42] and the congregation authorized the one to lead in prayers (Ber. 5.5).[42a]

We are still within the legal context when Moses is called a *Schaliach* of God because he has the water flow from the rock (b. B. M. 86b), and when Elijah, Elisha, and Ezekiel are called *Schaliach* on account of other miracles such as raising the dead, which are reserved to God alone (Midr. Ps. 78 § 5; cf. b. Taan 2a; b. Sanh. 113a); all these are acting in these cases as men commissioned by God.[43] In a similar sense the priest, when he presents the sacrifice, serves as one "authorized by the Merciful" (B. Kid. 23b; Joma 19a-b; Ned. 35b).

---

[38] Cf. I Sam. 25:40-41; II Sam. 10:1 ff.; b B. Q. 113b (the commissioned servant of the king resembles the king himself); SNu, CIII on 12:9. This derivation is actually much more probable than Vogelstein's recourse to the situation in the Persian government (see above, n. 28).

[39] Cf. Vogelstein [1], p. 429.

[40] Ter. IV, 4; cf. Lohse [1], p. 261; Rengstorf [1], p. 415.

[41] Cf. Vogelstein [1], p. 436.

[42] F. Gavin, *op. cit.*, p. 253.

[42a] On this, see also Str.-B., IV, 1, 149 ff.

[43] "In the background there may even be a tendency to clear the four of any violation of the divine prerogatives by showing them to be instruments" (Rengstorf [1], p. 419).

But on the other hand, Jewish missionaries do not function as שלוחים. In fact, the Judaism of the New Testament time knew no more of a regular authorized mission by professional missionaries than did the primitive church in Jerusalem[44]; yet the missionary achievements of the Jews which were traceable to private initiative were not inconsiderable.[45] Still, nowhere in the range of expressions about the missionary activity and missionary accomplishments of the Jews do we encounter the concept of *Schaliach*.

Nor do the Old Testament prophets function as שלוחים, although the term שלח is encountered as a technical expression in the accounts of their calling. Still this is not surprising in view of what the *Schaliach* represents. The "commissioned" are people "who, sent out by the authorities with a specific mandate, receive for the duration of this mandate certain official powers which they require for the fulfillment of their commission, *but which do not otherwise belong to them*" (H. Vogelstein [1], p. 429). It is clear that missionaries, like prophets, in the exercise of their ministry do not represent a strange office; but they unfold precisely their most thoroughly innate activity for which God has already prepared them in their mothers' wombs (Jer. 1:5; cf. Gal. 1:15). The designation of *Schaliach* for them thus would be utterly mistaken.[46]

In view of the last presentation of the late Jewish legal institution of the *Schaliach,* E. Lohse ([1], p. 260, n. 7) declares: "After Rengstorf has comprehensively made full use of the preliminary work of Krauss, Vogelstein, and Billerbeck, the Jewish origin of the concept of apostle may no longer be placed in doubt." Nevertheless this doubt has not been silenced, and I should like, in opposition to Lohse, to assert that the late Jewish legal institution of the *Schaliach* has not even the least to do with the primitive Christian apostolate. The fact that in both cases the same title is employed still cannot suffice to derive the one institution from the other. A close actual relationship would have to be established, and this is simply completely lacking.

This is shown already by the fact that missionaries and prophets are never called *Schaliach* by the Jews. Primitive Christianity, however, cannot have bound up with the Jewish concept of *Schaliach* any other representation than that of contemporary Judaism. If missionaries and prophets are not called *Schaliach* because such a commissioned person takes on an alien

[44] "We know absolutely nothing about any official sending forth of missionaries by the Jewish authorities" (J. Jeremias, *Jesus' Promise to the Nations* [1958], p. 16). Cf. also H. Gressmann [2], pp. 169 ff., esp. pp. 177 ff.; C. Clemen, *op. cit.,* p. 228.

[45] Rengstorf [1], p. 418; J. Jeremias, *op. cit.;* H. J. Schoeps, *Paulus* (1959), pp. 233 ff., 17-18.

[46] Cf. Rengstorf [1], p. 420.

function as a deputy, and only for a time, then for the same reason the apostolate of the earliest Christianity cannot be derived from the institution of the שלוחים.

The authorization of the *Schaliach* is of a formal kind; he is the holder of an office, "while the task as such is of no significance for the quality as שליח" (Rengstorf [1], p. 415). His message is to be accepted for the sake of his authorization. Precisely the opposite characterizes the apostolate; all authority lies in the message itself (*vide* pp. 33 ff.; 40 ff.).[47]

The apostolate has a purely religious character; the meaning of the *Schaliach* lies altogether within the realm of the juristic.[48]

The apostle is always a missionary; the *Schaliach*, never.[49]

The apostolate is an eschatological phenomenon all the way through; an eschatological character does not belong to the institution of the *Schaliach*, not even by way of suggestion.

The *Schaliach* always has a commission that is limited in time[50]; the apostle always has a life-long calling.

There is nothing at all which is common to the two figures; for even though the name still suggests it, the *Schaliach* is no longer one sent. He is rather, whether sent or not, a "commissioned one." The apostle, on the other hand, is "one sent forth," in the unabbreviated basic sense of the word. "We know of no apostle who was not at the same time a missionary" (H. v. Campenhausen [2], p. 23).[51]

If one wished to derive the figure of the present-day missionary to the heathen from the diplomatic position of the "ambassador," one could do this with a greater intrinsic correctness than he could trace the "apostle" back to the *Schaliach;* for "ambassador" and "missionary" are at least related by the characteristic of their sending forth, even if in other respects they have nothing to do with each other.

Now one expects, of course, that those investigators who derive the

---

[47] This naturally does not rule out his knowing himself to be called.

[48] Rengstorf [1], pp. 414-15. That in Judaism even the realm of law was sacrally determined naturally is not questioned. But from this, one may not derive the assertion that the religious phenomena also always bear a juridical character (*contra* B. Gerhardsson, *op. cit.,* p. 108). The primitive Christian apostolate as we come to know it in Paul can in no wise be grasped with the juridical categories of the *Schaliach* institution.

[49] Cf. A. Ehrhardt, *op. cit.,* p. 19.

[50] Cf. E. Lohse [2], p. 62; G. Sass [1], p. 19.

[51] Thus there exists neither a material nor a formal kinship between "Schaliach" and "apostle"; therefore one cannot cling to the derivation of the Christian apostolate from the late Jewish legal institution of the *Schaliach* with the argument that what is involved is in fact "not the appropriation of a content but rather of a formal category" (G. Blum, *op. cit.,* p. 24, n. 5). Precisely the formal characteristics of a *temporary legal commission* are lacking in the primitive Christian apostolate.

primitive Christian concept of the apostle from the late Jewish figure of the *Schaliach* will attempt to draw parallels in detail. In this expectation, however, one finds himself constantly disappointed. Rengstorf correctly writes concerning Paul: "He is the only apostle who is to some extent known to us in his apostolic position; the others leave us no direct information concerning the manner of their apostolate" ([1], p. 437). Now one would suppose that with reference to this, the only tangible representative of the primitive Christian apostolate, the statement would be substantiated that this apostolate goes back to the legal institution of the *Schaliach,* which Rengstorf has so thoroughly investigated. But in the entire exposition about the ἀπόστολος Παῦλος, I find only one single reference—to me an unintelligible one—to the *Schaliach!* [52] Instead of this, Rengstorf speaks very explicitly of the connection of the apostolic consciousness of Paul with the consciousness of having been sent of the Old Testament prophets and particularly of Jeremiah ([1], pp. 439 ff.). To be sure, it certainly admits of discussion whether the primitive Christian apostolate as represented by Paul is dependent upon the self-consciousness and the consciousness of having been sent on the part of the prophets.[53] But the more parallels one draws between the apostles and the Old Testament prophets, the less probable becomes the dependence of the Christian concept of the apostle upon the late Jewish institution of the *Schaliach;* for Rengstorf himself has correctly declared ([1], p. 420) that the prophet and the *Schaliach* are not related figures. In the fact that he compares Paul only with the Old Testament prophets and not at all with the שלוחים, and apparently cannot compare

---

[52] "The special nature of Paul's position among the other apostles of Jesus cannot be separated from his recovery of the prophetic sense of calling in the predominant position of the concept of God. It is not originally determined by this, but by his calling to be a messenger in the sense of the Jewish שליח institution, as in the case of the other ἀπόστολοι. If this aspect and basis of his office came to be more strongly accentuated by Paul, one of the main contributory factors was the fact that opponents challenged his equality of status and dignity with the other apostles" (Rengstorf [1], p. 441). What does this mean? Is the special nature of Paul's position among the other apostles of Jesus originally not determined by the prophetic sense of calling but by his calling in the sense of the שליח institution as in the case of the other "apostles"? But the *special nature* or particularity cannot rest upon the *general nature* or universality of the call! Or conversely, is the recovery of the prophetic sense of calling supposed to spring, not from the special position of Paul but from the *Schaliach* institution? But this cannot be what Rengstorf means, for he himself rightly denies any connection between *Schaliach* and prophets ([1], p. 420).

[53] We have already established (pp. 55-56) that it is not possible to understand the primitive Christian apostolate in terms of the Old Testament prophetic office, although it is not to be denied that they have certain things in common. Since no one to my knowledge has asserted that the apostolic office is simply a revival of Old Testament prophetism, it is unnecessary to set forth the independence of the two of one another in any more detail than has already been done.

him with the latter, Rengstorf himself becomes an unwilling witness to the fact that *Schaliach* and apostle have nothing to do with each other.

Two secondary traits, upon which Rengstorf thinks he is able to establish a commonality between *Schaliach* and apostle, rest squarely upon an error. Rengstorf thinks that he is able to assign to the שלוחים a "religious as well as an official character," because the "commissioned ones" were set apart for their service by the laying on of hands ([1], p. 417). But there is no documentation for this, as has already been shown (*vide supra*, p. 101, n. 26).

It is just as little in accordance with the facts to say that the "commissioned ones" were sent out "usually two or more together" ([1], p. 417; so also E. Lohse [1], p. 262), as it appears in fact to have been the case with the Christian apostles. For this assertion there is only one single, very late (ninth century?) bit of evidence: the inscription on the tombstone of a Jewish girl in Venosa, which mentions "duo apostuli et duo rebbites" who delivered the burial oration (H. Vogelstein [1]; A. v. Harnack [1], I, 330, n. 1). On the other hand, A. Ehrhardt (*op. cit.*, p. 16) rightly declares: "The Rabbinic sources, on the other hand, make it quite clear that no sending out in pairs was contemplated." B. B. 8*b* (at least two men are to disburse the money to the poor[54]; cf. II Cor. 8:23) is not actually a parallel; it would be better to compare Ber. 63*a*. The number "two" in that inscription may be an accident; in any case it is not the deposit of a fixed rule of the *Schaliach* institution.

In fact, Rengstorf can venture to set the investigation of the *Schaliach* as preliminary to the treatment of the Pauline concept of the apostle only because he inserts, between these two investigations, two stages in the development of the concept. First, Jesus himself, during his lifetime, had already sent out שלוחים; second, as the resurrected One he had renewed this apostolate from his days on earth. Rengstorf is able to describe the sending forth in Jesus' lifetime in some contexts in the categories of the *Schaliach* institution; and in the case of the post-Easter apostolate of the former disciples there are still some suggestions which may be employed in the same way, whereas the Pauline concept of the apostle has been completely cut loose from any ties with its Jewish prototype. The difficulty here is that, in actuality, these two stages in which the concept of apostle in Christianity is supposed to have been so greatly altered do not exist, as our investigation has demonstrated in Part Two. I can only continue to be amazed at the unabashed certainty with which Rengstorf holds the reports

---

[54] This principle was a fixed rule in late Judaism; Str.-B., II, 643, 4 A *c-e.*

of the Synoptists and of the book of Acts to be historically unassailable and is able to bracket the real historical problematic out of his considerations.[55]

To be sure, the question of the sending forth of the disciples of Jesus before and after Easter may be answered in various ways. Even those who hold it to be historical cannot do away with the fact that the only primitive Christian concept of the apostle which is moderately recognizable to us, namely the Pauline one, has nothing to do with the *Schaliach*.

In this connection, still other observations must be made. If the concept of apostle is derived from the *Schaliach*, all the marks of the essence of the New Testament apostolate, which we have established in the first part of this work, remain unexplained: The primitive Christian apostle is a missionary; he is not called of men; the calling coincides with a manifestation of the resurrected One, as does the reception of the message with the authorization; the apostle proves his authority by means of the results of his mission or by "signs of an apostle," while he cannot prove his calling at all; the apostle summons people to "imitation" of himself; he does not feel rushed, nor will he work where the gospel has already been proclaimed; he refrains from claiming the rightful maintenance by the congregations; suffering belongs to his calling; he proclaims "secrets"; in his ministry he stands in close relation to the New Testament prophet; and so on. The duplicated traditions, the manifold gaps in the concept of the apostle, and the *termini technici* which belong to the New Testament apostolate, to which we have already referred on pp. 56-57, do not become understandable in the context of the *Schaliach*. How can one then reasonably speak of a "derivation!"

Also unexplained is the translation of שליח in the Greek-speaking territory with ἀπόστολος. To be sure, one does not need to be as skeptical as Rengstorf, who characterizes the use of ἀπόστολος in the sense of "messenger" as "an innovation to Greek ears." [56] But as the Greek equivalent for שליח, ἄγγελος[57] or πρεσβευτής[58] would have lain much nearer at hand than

---

[55] Cf. now the choice destruction of Rengstorf's exegeses by G. Klein, *op. cit.*, pp. 28 ff.

[56] *Op. cit.*, p. 408; see p. 98; also E. Schweizer, *op. cit.*, p. 206, § 25a, and H. Mosbech [1], p. 167. Mosbech draws this conclusion from several considerations, among them the fact that ἀπόστολος is not translated into Latin but appears as "apostolus." But this probably is not due to the fact that ἀπόστολος is an unusual Greek word, but rather that ἀπόστολος as a restricted technical term had made such an impression on the Christian consciousness that it could not very well be duplicated with the broad "legatus." Tertullian (de praescr. haer. 20. 4) must explain to his readers: ". . . apostoli (quos haec appellatio 'missos' interpretatur). . . ."

[57] Thus, e.g., in the Jewish writing προσευχὴ Ἰωσήφ (see in E. Schürer, *A History of the Jewish People*, Div. II, Vol. III, 128), where Jacob says: ἄγγελος θεοῦ εἰμὶ ἐγὼ καὶ πνεῦμα ἀρχικόν. From the language usage to which we are accustomed we would expect ἀπόστολος. Cf. also n. 11.

[58] Thus e.g. Act. Thom. 10 for Jesus instead of ἀπόστολος.

the uncommon ἀπόστολος,[59] especially for one who had an εὐαγγέλιον to proclaim. The choice of the word ἀπόστολος remains rare if it is to be a Christian or a Jewish[60] translation of שליח.[61]

Besides, if the apostle is the Christian expression of the *Schaliach*, the missionaries altogether would be expected to be called apostles. Apostle, however, is the name only of the representatives of that quite particular missionary position whom we have come to know in the first two parts of our work and who among all the missionaries of early Christianity, numerically speaking, may have played a very limited role.

In summary: If there were any two "sent ones" who had nothing to do with each other, they would have been the Christian apostle and the Jewish *Schaliach*.[62] I am firmly convinced of this, even without the concurrence, in most recent times,[63] of numerous scholars.[64]

[59] Thus also H. Mosbech [1], p. 187.

[60] Cf. K. Lake, *op. cit.*, p. 49.

[61] What Rengstorf offers ([1], p. 435) by way of explanation of this "particularly strange" fact contains only the admission of inability to explain anything.

Not to be rejected out of hand, by the way, is the view of A. Ehrhardt, *op. cit.*, pp. 18 ff., "that the term 'apostolos' was earlier than the term 'shaliach.'" At any rate our sources allow this conclusion rather than the opposite one, although in view of the state of the sources a definitive judgment would not be justified.

[62] B. Gerhardsson (*op. cit.*, pp. 107 ff.) therefore wishes to explain the primitive Christian apostolate in terms of the conception of the "messenger of God." It is a mistake, he thinks, to give attention one-sidedly to the term *Schaliach* instead of proceeding phenomenologically (p. 110). But the more evidence Gerhardsson adduces for the figure of the "messenger of God"—he rightly seeks it above all in the image of the Jewish prophet—the clearer it becomes that this does not get us to the root of the primitive Christian apostolate; for the prophets and related divine messengers are *not* as such called *Schaliach*. But one cannot explain the origin of the conception of the apostle if one brackets out the *concept* of the apostle.

[63] Of course such an objection is not *only* of recent date. E. Haupt, *op. cit.*, pp. 106-7, already rejects the derivation of the ecclesiastical apostolic office from the *Schaliach*, with sufficient reasons.

[64] The derivation from *Schaliach* appears not to satisfy A. Fridrichsen (*op. cit.*, pp. 5-6) for various reasons (cf. H. Mosbech [1], p. 182).

Negatively inclined also is A. Ehrhardt (*op. cit.*, pp. 18 ff.), who of course is influenced in part by the fact that the *Schaliach* yields nothing for the apostolic succession, which is Ehrhardt's special interest. Further, see G. Sass [1], p. 24; H. Mosbech [1], pp. 187-88; E. Käsemann [1], p. 51; K. Holl [1], p. 930, n. 1; J. Munck [1], p. 100; "Far too much importance has for some time been attached to these Jewish apostles"; A. Wikenhauser, *op. cit.*, col. 555; G. Klein, *op. cit.*, pp. 26 ff. In *Verkündigung und Forschung* (1953-55), p. 163, E. Käsemann writes: "I would not deny certain influences. Nevertheless they are not constitutive, because the Jewish institution, as distinguished from the apostolate, has a specific legal character, and conversely, the eschatological horizon of the apostolate is decisive." E. Pax (*op. cit.*, p. 206) objects to a connection as far as *content* is concerned, but of course holds, though inconsistently, that a terminological connection is possible. Cf. also the discussion in O. Linton, *op. cit.*, pp. 83-84; E. Schweizer, *op. cit.*, p. 202, § 24i.

III

If genuine Judaism is ruled out as a source for the primitive Christian concept of the apostle, then we must turn our attention to the Hellenistic world, even though here the *concept* ἀπόστολος cannot give use further help, as has already been established (*vide supra*, pp. 96 ff.). The question is whether there is not at least an *institution* to be found which could be compared with the primitive Christian apostolate. This question is to be answered in the affirmative. Rengstorf can serve here as an unequivocal witness: "We can at least say that the Cynic-Stoic sage in his role as κατάσκοπος is the figure of the period which we can set in closest proximity to the apostle" ([1], p. 411). One can all the more readily agree with this opinion since it is generally recognized "that the earliest Christian mission can only be considered in the context of the intensive propaganda activity which was carried on at that time by the Oriental cults, by the most diverse philosophical currents, by Sophists, magicians, miracle workers and wandering preachers" (K. Deissner, *op. cit.*, p. 781).

Epictetus' *Dissertations* are the preeminent source for this figure, and in addition to these it is not rewarding to consider other sources.[65] The splendid presentation which the Cynic-Stoic "apostle" has received at the hands of Rengstorf ([1]) and Deissner (*op. cit.*, pp. 782 ff.) makes it possible for me to summarize quite briefly.

The genuine Cynic is ἄγγελος (III, 1. 37; 22. 23, 69), ἀπὸ τοῦ Διὸς ἀπέσταλται πρὸς τοὺς ἀνθρώπους (III, 22. 23; 22. 56, 59; I, 24. 6), in order to show them where good and evil is (III, 22. 23). At the same time he is "sent forth" to teach by his own example and to summon to discipleship (III, 22. 46-47); he is a παράδειγμα ἀπὸ τοῦ θεοῦ ἀπέσταλται (IV, 8. 31). He is "sent" from God to Gyara or into prison in order to present himself as a μάρτυς of true freedom to other men (III, 24. 113). He must suffer in poverty, in humiliation, in sickness, in order to make his witness effective in such a situation (III, 24. 113). In such a service it is all the same to him whether he is subject to good or evil reports; he keeps his gaze set unalterably upon God (III, 24. 114) and strives not to give offense to any man (III, 22. 93; IV, 8. 32).

Instead of ἄγγελος he can also be called κῆρυξ (III, 21. 13; 22. 69), for

---

[65] These are in fact available and are able to give the impression of the diversity of religious emissaries in Hellenism; but none of the other accounts leads to such proximity to the New Testament apostolate as the presentation which is given to the Cynic-Stoic sages in Epictetus. For literature on the Hellenistic itinerant preachers in general, one may consult H. Gressmann [2]; E. Norden [1], pp. 373 ff.; 381; K. Holl [2]; P. Wendland, *op. cit.*; Pauly-Wissowa, XII, 14; E. v. Dobschütz [1], pp. 2 ff.; R. Reitzenstein, *op. cit.*, pp. 25 ff.; C. Clemen, *op. cit.*, pp. 230 ff.; G. P. Wetter, *op. cit.*

he must announce that freedom and peace which God has had proclaimed through reason (III, 13. 12; IV, 5. 24; 6. 23). Not every man is suited for this office, but only the one whom God has found worthy for it (III, 22. 66; IV, 8. 32). God himself must call the ἄγγελος (III, 21. 18; 22. 2). He is also called κατάσκοπος (I, 24. 6-10; III, 22. 24, 69), for in all life situations he must discern what is friend and what is enemy to man, in order then to report how one can live in genuine freedom (III, 22. 2-25). His task is further τοὺς ἄλλους ἐπισκοπεῖν (III, 22. 72), what they do, how they live, what troubles them, wherein they neglect their obligations (III, 22. 77, 97). He labors untiringly for men, and for their sake spends sleepless nights (III, 22. 94-95).

As a living and perfect example of a quiet life the Cynic sage can ask: οὐκ εἰμὶ ἐλεύθερος (III, 22. 48) and can assert that everyone who may see him will think that he is seeing a βασιλεὺς καὶ δεσπότης (III, 22. 49). With great courage (θαρρεῖν) and candor (παρρησία) he speaks to men, for their affairs are matters of most intense concern to him (III, 22. 96-97). He conceals nothing from them (III, 22. 16). There is no higher office than his (III, 22. 85), which is royal and bears the scepter (III, 21. 19; 22. 63, 79). He has accepted all men as his children and is father to all of them (III, 22. 81). He interests himself in the Athenians, the Corinthians, the Romans; indeed he concerns himself with all men in the very same way (III, 22. 84).

As a king before men he is at the same time a ὑπηρέτης (III, 22. 82, 95; 24. 98, 113) or διάκονος (III, 22. 63; 24. 65; 26. 28; IV, 7. 20) of Zeus; he makes God's will his own (IV, 7. 20). He is *voluntarily* obedient to God (IV, 3. 9) and he serves the one who has sent him (III, 22. 56); as God's friend he willingly obeys him (IV, 3. 9). He, the coregent of God, subjects himself to the divine government (III, 24. 65). He, the father to all men, himself recognizes Zeus as his father (III, 22. 82). Therefore he speaks nothing other than that which God puts in his mind (III, 1. 36).

Deissner is certainly not too incautious when, on the basis of such a presentation, he comments: "Quite apart from the terminological connections (cf. in particular κῆρυξ, κηρύσσω, ἀπαγγέλλω, ἀποστέλλω, μάρτυς, ἄγγελος), one cannot mistake definite similarities to the primitive Christian consciousness of mission. In those passages where κατάσκοπος and ἐπισκοπεῖν appear, a consciousness of responsibility toward all men becomes obvious which corresponds to the compulsion of the Christian missionary" (cf. ὀφειλέτης, Rom. 1:14) (*op. cit.*, p. 786). Much of what characterizes the Cynic sage according to our brief sketch above we find again in the case of the primitive Christian apostle.

Both[66] are religious figures; both are sent from God (Gal. 1:1); both stand in unconditional service to man (Rom. 1:14); both are to teach by their example (I Cor. 1:16) and to avoid every offense (II Cor. 6:3); for both suffering belongs to their calling and serves to make effective their witness (II Cor. 4:10); both have a message to proclaim that comes from God (II Cor. 4:5); both must be found ἱκανός by God and must have been called by God himself (II Cor. 3:5); both are free (I Cor. 9:1) and wish to make others free (Gal. 5:13); both speak with great candor (II Cor. 3:12-13) and conceal nothing (II Cor. 4:1-2); both are called "father" of other men (I Cor. 4:15; Gal. 4:19); both make no distinction among men (Gal. 3:28); both are God's servants (II Cor. 11:23); both voluntarily obey their Lord (I Cor. 9:16 ff.); both speak nothing of themselves (Rom. 15:18); and so on.

If intelligent researchers have long since ceased to cherish any doubt that one cannot isolate the Christian apostle from the other religious emissaries of Hellenism, then the comparison offered above can show that among all the missionaries brought into consideration hitherto, the Cynic κατάσκοπος shows the most extensive relationship with the primitive Christian apostolate.[67] But does that mean that we have here a direct or even an indirect dependence? In view of individual expressions in Paul's presentation of his office and in view of definite formulations, it may be said with certainty that they stem from the Cynic-Stoic diatribe,[68] whether through a direct or an indirect[69] appropriation. But with equally great certainty one may affirm that the primitive Christian apostolate is just as little a further development of the κατάσκοπος as the latter is a development out of the former. The differences are too great for this, and the relationship is often only of a formal kind.

The self-consciousness of the κατάσκοπος, whose human, rational achievement finally determines his service and his worth,[70] stands in exact opposition to the self-consciousness of Paul, who through God's grace is what he is. The Cynic sage is in no respect an eschatological figure. To be sure, he is to do nothing without God, but it is basically he himself who explores God's will with his reason. His self-consciousness does not allow for his authority to be questioned. He suffers so that suffering he may display his existence to others as an example, while the apostle suffers

---

[66] The corresponding passages from Epictetus' *Diss.* are not repeated.

[67] Cf. G. P. Wetter, *op. cit.*, p. 27.

[68] Cf. also Bultmann, *Der Stil der paulinischen Predigt und die kynisch-stoische Diatribe*, 1910.

[69] Cf. H. Thyen, *Der Stil der jüdisch-hellenistischen Homilie* (1955), p. 63.

[70] Rengstorf [1], p. 412.

so that in the annihilation of his own being the power of a message not his own may shine forth. Neither the concept of mystery nor the figure of the prophet is encountered in the vicinity of the κατάσκοπος. The emergence of the technical expression ἀπόστολος remains unexplained on the basis of the κατάσκοπος, even if occasionally ἀποστέλλειν appears; ὅρασις, ἀποκάλυψις, and similar terms do not appear in his context.

With all the affinity which certainly connects the two figures, the milieu out of which the concept of apostle stems, by comparison with the rationally determined nature of the Cynic sage in Epictetus, seems strange and almost mystical. In spite of the connections which are undoubtedly present, a derivation of one from the other is ruled out. All the common points rest upon the fact that "apostolos" and "katascopos" are figures of a time and a world which were determined by a religious syncretism which is hardly imaginable today, a syncretism which no philosophy or theology could escape. The insight that even the primitive Christian concept of the apostle is native to precisely this syncretistic world and not to orthodox Judaism may be claimed as a certain, though quite modest, result of this last section of our investigation.

IV

But beyond this, does the search for the immediate prototype of the New Testament concept of the apostle remain fruitless? Are we lacking in the sources which alone could lead us further? Or is such searching pointless because the primitive Christian apostolate is an original creation, perhaps within and as a result of the afore-mentioned syncretism?

Mosbech, who very discerningly acknowledges the impossibility of a derivation of the ἀπόστολος from the *Schaliach,* conceives of this original creation ([1], pp. 187-88) in the following manner: The first Christian missionaries, for the most part "occasional workers" in the missionary field, were called εὐαγγελισταί or something else. Later, however, in Antioch some missionaries wished to provide their services with enhanced authority, namely, as sent from a congregation, preferably that of Jerusalem, or from God himself. Thus a distinction developed between the occasional missionary and the missionary by vocation. This distinction caused them to be on the lookout for an appropriate designation for the chief official evangelists. Because ἄγγελος was too generally taken, and besides that it was already a *terminus technicus* for the heavenly emissaries, they chose as a new linguistic creation the word ἀπόστολος, an expression which quickly came to prevail and spread.

All this is quite fanciful and at best explains the linguistic expression

114

ἀπόστολος[71]; it in no way demonstrates the figure and the nature of the primitive Christian apostolate as a new creation, indeed, it makes it not even conceivable (*vide* pp. 56-57).

It is one of the remarkable characteristics of the New Testament research of the past decades that the attention of the researchers has not been drawn to that figure who not only actually presents the precise counterpart of the primitive Christian apostle, and who not only (like the Christian apostle) is native to the Syrian setting, but who indeed employed the title "apostle" as a self-designation with great emphasis: the Gnostic apostle. To be sure, we possess only a very few sources of Gnosticism from its earliest times, which are contemporaneous with the original ecclesiastical apostolate. The extant primitive Christian sources, however, which we owe to the conflict with Gnosticism, permit us to gain a knowledge of the Gnostic apostolate with hardly less clarity than we have concerning the primitive Christian apostolate.[72]

It is certainly advisable at this point to establish some points of information. The actual function of the Gnostic apostle is his activity as redeemer. Redemption is the central concern of the Gnostic religion. An investigation of the Gnostic thought concerning redemption will thus necessarily take the Gnostic apostle into consideration, and indeed will treat of his most essential function. In the following, in view of the redeemer-apostle, we will inquire after the types of the Gnostic conception of redemption.

1. The fundamental constitutive importance of the fact of redemption for the Gnostic religion is matched by the lack of importance of the figure

[71] In comparison with this, then, Rengstorf's explanation would be the lesser evil: "Perhaps the word first began to be used in this way in Antioch, being originally applied to the missionary expedition as such, then to its individual members, and finally, . . . as a recognized translation of שׁלּיחַ" ([1], p. 435).

[72] In the following I presuppose the existence of Gnostic communities for the early period of Christianity—just as ancient, then, as the Judaistic and Hellenistic communities. Without labeling the contesting of this presupposition as unscientific, I think I may claim for its champions at least the same scientific seriousness as for its opponents.

I can clarify the problem with an example. The reminiscences in the Pauline literature of Gnostic language and of the mythological thought world of Gnosticism are evident. In the 1930's, A. Loisy attempted to explain this fact by a radical division of Pauline epistolary literature into original and later pieces. Anyone who cannot take this course attempts, down to our own day, to make Gnosticism comprehensible as a product of the decay of Paulinism. Against this is raised the irrefutable objection that the Gnostic terminology in Paul cannot have first created the Gnostic myth, but presupposes it! What else then remains but to admit Gnosticism into the very beginnings of Christianity? But then one must also reckon with Gnostic communities, for a mythological religion of redemption like Gnosticism can have existed at all only in such communities. Cf. further Bultmann, *Theology of the New Testament*, I, § 15; E. Käsemann in ZThK, LIV (1957), p. 19; *Die Gnosis in Korinth* (first ed.), pp. 247 ff.; "Die Häretiker in Galatien," in *Paulus und die Gnostiker*, pp. 44-45.

of the redeemer. "The souls can find their way to conversion either through Gnosis which blazes up within them, or through the doctrine of salvation which is proclaimed to them by the anointed One, either in a Christian-colored system or a directly Christian one. The latter feature, however, is altogether nonessential for Gnosticism." [73] This judgment applies also to the mythological Gnosis of Gnosticism's early times. Gnosis is not interested in a redeemer, least of all in a particular redeemer figure, but only in redemption itself. Consequently we have numerous testimonies which tell of a redeemer-less Gnosis. Although this form of the Gnostic system of redemption hardly concerns us in the context of our question, some of these testimonies may be introduced here.

Irenaeus tells (I, 25. 1) of the Carpocratians' view that the spirit of Jesus had preserved the recollection of the pure which it had seen in the company of the "unbegotten Father" before its fall into the world. By the power of this recollection this spirit could find its way upward and be freed from the world creators. Every spirit which has the same powers can follow the same way. Thus it is not surprising that the followers of Carpocrates according to Irenaeus place the apostles and even themselves on the same level with Jesus; for "their souls had been in the same circles, had received the same power and returned there, and had also scorned the creator of the world." Indeed, "si quis autem plus quam ille contempserit ea quae sunt hic, posse meliorem quam illum esse." It is clear that for these Gnostics Jesus did not possess any sort of redemptive function. He has been taken over by a redeemer-less Gnosis only as an example of the Gnostic existence in general.

"Further, according to the little that we know of him, Cerinthus appears to have stood very close to Carpocrates." [74]

Especially in Jewish Gnosticism apparently a redeemer was often unknown. That may be connected, among other things, with the fact that the orthodox Jewish tradition was oriented wholly to the coming Messiah, while for Gnosticism in general only a redeemer figure of the past is logically conceivable. Therefore the adherents to this belief liked to trace the transmitted Gnosis back to Adam. In connection with him we are not, in our present context, interested in the surprising glorification which is bestowed

---

[73] W. Schultz, *Documente der Gnosis* (Jena, 1910), p. xiii. Cf. M. Dibelius, "Die Isisweihe bei Apuleius und verwandte Initiationsriten" in *Botschaft und Geschichte*, II (1956), 69: "If, further, the figure of the redeemer is still lacking in some Christian-Gnostic sects . . . ." C. Colpe in RGG, 3rd ed., II, cols. 1650-51. G. Kretschmar, *ibid.*, col. 1657. W. Bousset, *Hauptprobleme der Gnosis*, p. 321: "It is curious that in some of these sects, like the Ophites of Celsus-Origen, the Nicolaitan Gnostics with the obscene cults, the Archontics, and so on, the figure of the redeemer still is not at all present."

[74] W. Bousset, *Hauptprobleme der Gnosis*, p. 327.

upon him as a consequence of his identification with the primal man in numerous gnosticizing late Jewish and early Christian writings, but rather in his frequent characterization as "prophet," as which he has foretold the future to the coming generations.[75]

Instructive at this point is the gnosticizing Book of Adam, an edition of which Kautzsch has published.[76] Adam, who was worshiped by all the heavenly creatures but was expelled by God (= the fall of primal man), before his death or his withdrawal into Paradise gives to his offspring (Seth!) the "knowledge" concerning the "secrets" of his origin which he remembers, and of his future, which God "reveals" to him in a "withdrawal" or through the eating of the tree of "knowledge." [77] This knowledge is to be transmitted to the coming generations[78]; yet for Gnosticism the whole of humanity is taken up into the fate of Adam-primal man.

The Syrian *Book of the Cave of Treasures*,[79] in its present form a Christian writing, abounds in ancient Jewish and Jewish-Gnostic traditions. In 5. 13 it says that God has revealed to Adam the entire future. On his deathbed Adam passes on this revelation: "My son Seth! Give heed to what I command you today! On your deathbed you are to pass on the command to Enos and Enos to Kenan and Kenan to Mahalaleel! This word is to be continued in all generations" (6. 9-10). The secrets of Adam come by way of Noah down to the generations of the end time. The content of the tradition which is thus transmitted is, gnostically formulated, the unity of the universal man Adam with Christ (6. 18 ff.). Of interest to us is only the fact that this knowledge is transmitted from the primal man onward. For this a redeemer figure is not required.

The same is true of the "Testament of Adam" (Riessler, pp. 1084 ff.). Adam gives the knowledge which he received in Paradise (3. 4) to his son Seth, who wrote it down and concealed it until the time of Christ (3. 20-21).[80]

Epiphanius mentions (26. 2. 6) a Gospel of Eve, of which he also hands down to us a fragment. This Gospel may have contained the original revelation which Eve received by eating of the tree of knowledge or by way of instruction from the serpent.[81] Thus the Gnosis is known from the beginning onward and without the mediation of a special redeemer.

---

[75] Passages and literature in H. J. Schoeps, *Aus frühchristlicher Zeit* (1950), pp. 7 ff.; E. Käsemann [1], p. 128; see also n. 85.

[76] Kautzsch, *Apokryphen und Pseudepigraphen des Alten Testaments* (1900), pp. 512 ff.

[77] Vita 25–29 = Kautzsch, p. 516.

[78] Apok. Mos. 3 = Kautzsch, p. 515; Vita 44 = Kautzsch, p. 520.

[79] Riessler, *Altjüdisches Schrifttum*, pp. 942 ff.

[80] Cf. W. Staerk, *Soter*, II, 33.

[81] Hennecke-Schneemelcher-Wilson, *New Testament Apocrypha*, II, 241 ff.

Jewish "sorcerers" then also call upon God in the person of Adam for liberation from the darkness of the world, or praise him because of the completed heavenly journey; yet a redeemer figure does not thereby enter the picture.[82]

With good reason Anz[83] surmises that in certain Gnostic circles it was also asserted that Marduk as primal man in the primordial time had mediated the redeeming Gnosis to man.

Concerning the Ophites, Irenaeus relates (I, 30. 7) that according to their doctrine Adam-primal man and Eve ate of the tree in Paradise: "Then they recognized the heavenly power and turned away from their creators." Here also, then, Gnosis is achieved without the involvement of a redeemer, even in the primordial time. Thus Jesus, who is not omitted from this Ophite system, is nevertheless superfluous and certainly not even original to the system.[84]

The figure of the "true prophet" in the Pseudo-Clementine literature has frequently been discussed in recent times.[85] Without going into this discussion, we may establish the following: This true prophet is identical with Adam.[86] It is his task to make known the Gnosis (Hom. XI, 19. 1 ff.). Henceforth, however, this Adam is encountered as the true prophet in many different figures, even in Jesus, until he comes to (heavenly) rest (Hom. III, 20. 2). Indeed, he is actually present in every man, in order to kindle the light of knowledge (Rec. I, 52; VIII, 59-62). Strecker is correct in his assertion: "The task of the true prophet corresponds to the activity of the redeemer in the Gnostic systems." [87] But it is to be observed that the "prophet," at least in his basic character, does not at all present a redeemer figure sent from heaven, but is rather the fallen primal man himself, whose "knowing," in whatever man it is awakened, rests upon recollection. The change in the figure of the "prophet" is no other than that of souls generally who, proceeding forth from Adam, the "treasure-house of souls," wander from body to body[88] until they come to heavenly rest. Thus also

---

[82] Cf. E. Peterson, "Die Befreiung Adams aus der ἀνάγκη, in *Frühkirche, Judentum und Gnosis* (1959), pp. 107 ff. Cf. also G. Widengren [3], pp. 23-24, 63.

[83] *Zur Frage nach dem Ursprung des Gnostizismus* (1897), pp. 94 ff.

[84] W. Bousset, *Hauptprobleme*, pp. 264-65.

[85] G. Strecker, *Das Judenchristentum in den Pseudoclementinen*, TU, LXX (1958), 145-53; H. J. Schoeps, *Theologie und Geschichte des Judenchristentums* (1949), pp. 98-116; *ibid., Urgemeinde, Judenchristentum, Gnosis* (1956), pp. 50-54; W. Staerk, *Soter*, II, 98-112.

[86] H. J. Schoeps, *Theologie und Geschichte des Judenchristentums*, p. 100; G. Strecker, *op. cit.*, pp. 147-48.

[87] *Op. cit.*, p. 151.

[88] Cf. Lidzbarski, *Johannesbuch*, 83. 18 ff., where John appears as a manifestation of Adam.

the knowledge is nothing other than that which is brought from the beginning, often forgotten, and again and again revived or reawakened.

The same meaning underlies Hippolytus' report of the teaching of Elchasai: "Concerning Christ he says that he was a man like all others; that he is not now born of a virgin for the first time, but also earlier, that he has been and will be born again and again, has been and will be present, changing from place to place and from body to body. . . ." [89] "They do not acknowledge *one* Christ, but say that there was one in the heavens who on many occasions has entered into many different bodies, and most recently into Jesus, . . . that he continues to enter into other bodies and to reveal himself from time to time in many." [90] Obviously "Christ" is here only a designation for the fallen primal man, and *as such* he lives in men, not as an actual redeemer figure.[91]

In the same vein, Epiphanius reports that the Christ of the Elchasaites is identical with Adam (*Haer.*, 53. 1-2). But then the Gnosis must have been handed down from the time of the first Adam and must often have been revealed in many of his members.

Many fragments of the Mandaean literature are lacking in any reference to a redeemer figure. Here we are dealing primarily with poems from the third book of the Left Part of the *Ginza*. The emphasis rests upon the ascent of the soul, which redeems itself:

> The soul loosed the chain,
> It broke the bonds.
> It laid aside the corporeal cloak,
> Then turned 'round, saw him, and trembled.[92]

Then the soul flies hence, until it comes to the house of life; no redeemer is required as helper. The saving way has been at hand since primitive times:

> May peace and salvation attend the way,
> Which Adam rightly has blazed;
> May peace and salvation attend the way,
> On which the soul is raised.[93]

In the twentieth fragment of this book the soul tells of its fate: It has come into the corporeal body through Adam. The soul apparently has known

[89] Hipp. 9. 14.

[90] Hipp. 10. 29; cf. Epiph. Haer. 30. 3. 5; 53. 1. 8.

[91] On the equation primal man = Christ, see my *Die Gnosis in Korinth*, first ed., pp. 82-134, and below, pp. 173 ff.

[92] Lidzbarski, *Ginza*, 514. 1 ff.

[93] *Ibid.*, 513. 28-31.

this from time immemorial; no redeemer brought this Gnosis to it. Only "when its measure and its number was fulfilled" comes one who releases it, and who leads it upward.[94]

Or further, one may compare the interesting fifty-first fragment:

> My soul in me longed after life,
> Within me knowledge began to blossom forth.
> My soul within me longed after life,
> My way led to the place of life.
> I fled and thither drew,
> Until I came to the house of life.[95]

Here again the redemption comes about without a redeemer.

In this connection we may also refer to the numerous passages of the Mandaean writings in which the simple anonymous "Word" performs the service of redemption; for example:

> You were raised up and fortified
> By the word of truth which has come to you.
> The word of truth has come to the good,
> The truthful word to the believers.
> To the place where life is complete
> Your souls are called and invited.[96]

In the Odes of Solomon it is explicitly said of this "Word":

And it never falls, but it stands and stands, and does not know its descent nor its way.[97]

Thus it already has always been known.

In the Odes of Solomon it is frequently God himself who in a thoroughly Old Testament manner rescues him who prays, without a redeemer entering into the process. Cf. for example Ode 15:

> As the sun is a joy for those who long for their day,
> So is my joy the Lord.
> For he is my sun
> And his rays have allowed me to stand,
> And his light has driven away all darkness from before my face.
> From him I have received my eyes,
> And I have seen his holy day.
> I have received ears,
> And I have heard his truth.

[94] *Ibid.*, 544.
[95] *Ibid.*, 578 ff.
[96] *Ibid.*, 529. 5 ff.
[97] Od. Sol. 12. 6.

I have been given the thought of knowledge,
And I have been gladdened by him.
I have left the way of error,
And I have fled to him and have received redemption from him
    abundantly.
And according to his gift he has given to me,
And according to the greatness of his beauty he has made me.
Through his name I have put on incorruptibility,
And through his goodness I have put off corruptibility.
Death has passed away before my face,
And the underworld has vanished through my word.
And life without death has flourished in the land of the Lord
And has has been made known to his believers
And has been given without reservation to all those who build
    upon him.
Hallelujah! [98]

This is Gnosis in the clothing of Old Testament language. Cf. further Ode
25:

I have escaped from my bonds
And have fled to thee, my God.
For thou wast the right hand of redemption
And my helper.
. . .
And I was clothed with the garment of thy spirit
And I put off from me the garments of flesh (= the body). [99]

Ode Sol. 26 reads like an express polemic against any special redeemer
figure:

Or who is it who rests upon the Most High,
Who could speak from his mouth?
Who is able to declare the wonder of the Lord?
For the one who declares will pass away,
And the one who is declared will ever remain.
For it is enough to have knowledge and (therein) to find rest.

These citations may suffice to establish the above-proposed assertion,
that Gnosis is not oriented to the figure of a redeemer. [100] Nevertheless we
are used to thinking about redemption through a Gnostic redeemer in
accustomed terms. Quite rightly so! Still, one will do well sharply to
distinguish the different types of the Gnostic redeemer figure. Two chief

---

[98] Following the translation of Walter Bauer in *Kleine Texte,* LXIV, 31-32.

[99] *Ibid.,* p. 53; cf. Od. Sol. 10; 12; 18; 21; 37; 40.

[100] This is true, moreover, of Jewish eschatology; cf. P. Vielhauer, *Gottesreich und
Menschensohn, Festschrift für Günther Dehn* (1957), pp. 71, 76.

types are to be kept in mind: on the one side, the redeemer sent from heaven, and on the other side, the earthly being who fetches the Gnosis from heaven.[101]

For the purpose of preliminary orientation to this distinction we may, with M. Dibelius,[102] set over against each other two basic expressions. John 3:11-13: "Truly, truly, I say to you, we speak what we know and testify what we have been, and you do not accept our testimony. If I tell you of earthly things and you do not believe me, how will you then believe if I tell you of heavenly things? And no one has ascended to heaven except the one who has descended from heaven, the Son of Man." This means for John that only the heavenly ones themselves can bring a message from the heavenly One. Alongside this should stand Corp. Herm. X, 25: "For no one of the heavenly gods will come to the earth, since he would be leaving the region of heaven; but the man ascends to heaven and surveys it and knows what its height is, and what its depth, and comes to know all the rest precisely and—what is the greatest of all—he comes into the heights without leaving the earth! Of such greatness is his ecstasy." This means that the earthly ones themselves fetch the redemptive message from the heavenly world.[103]

We next direct our attention to the first type of the redeemer.

2. This type is far from forming a unity within itself. The figure of the heavenly redeemer is encountered in various forms, and a closer examination shows that the form most commonly known to us, namely the figure of the heavenly being that has come into flesh, is very rare and not at all characteristic of the whole group.

a) To be sure the redemption frequently comes from above, but an actual redeemer as a heavenly being comes not at all or only barely into view. The only important thing is that *a call* is sounded from outside the world [104]:

> *A call* comes
> And is more instructive than all calls.
> *An address* comes
> And is more instructive than all addresses.[105]

[101] G. P. Wetter (*op. cit.*, p. 47) speaks "of the fully concretely and realistically interpreted Son of God who, flying from heaven or borne by his angels, has come to earth" and of the "almost spiritualistically psychologically interpreted Gnostic who in ecstasy, in a vision, becomes God and is raised to Heaven."

[102] *Botschaft und Geschichte*, II, 78.

[103] E. Pax (*op. cit.*, p. 80) characterizes the total thought of the Corp. Herm. in the sense of the last quotation with the words: "It is not ἐπιφάνεια that is sought for, but θέα."

[104] See H. Jonas, *Gnosis und spätantiker Geist*, I (2nd ed., 1954), 120 ff.

[105] Lidzbarski, *Ginza*, p. 91.

> An Uthra calls from without
> And instructs Adam, the man.[106]

Even in this last word we have to do not with the person of the speaker but rather with his speech, which can sound forth equally well from any other messenger who may be chosen or from Manda d'Hayya:

> It is the call of Manda d'Hayya,
> Who stands at the boundary of the worlds.
> He stands at the boundary of the worlds
> And calls to his chosen ones.
> He says: . . . .[107]

The situation is similar when, as is often the case, Manda d'Hayya does not appear in personal form at all but rather as the original γνῶσις, whose name he bears:

> A call resounded over the whole earth,
> The brilliance subsided in every city.
> Manda d'Hayya revealed himself to all the children of men
> And redeemed them from the darkness to the light,
> from the shadows to the light of life.[108]

All the circumstances of this revelation are irrelevant.[109]

The one sent can also come into this world simply as "Word" from the beyond:

> I am a word, a son of words,
> Who have come hither in the name of Jawar.[110]

This word says:

From the building of Jerusalem until the age of Mohammed the Arab, I tarried among my disciples. I selected some from among them and had these ascend to the place of light.[111]

The frequently recurring formula,

> Life is highly esteemed and is victorious,
> And victorious is the man who has attained it,[112]

[106] Ibid., p. 387; cf. Lidzbarski, Johannesbuch, p. 225. 5.
[107] Lidzbarski, Ginza, p. 397.
[108] Ibid., p. 182; cf. pp. 179, 253, 322 ff., 345, 353 ff., 371, 388-89.
[109] Cf. further ibid., pp. 253. 3 ff.; 256. 11 ff.
[110] Ibid., p. 295.
[111] Ibid., p. 300.9 ff.; cf. pp. 295 ff.
[112] E.g., ibid., p. 360. 9-10.

does not at all require a specific coming of a specific man, but simply the coming of the Gnosis.

The Book of John of the Mandaeans begins:

> At the gate of the worlds stands Kusta
> Who speaks inquiringly to the world.

Here Kusta is the totality of the Mandaean community, which inquires after the origin of man and the universe. If Ptahil or, in chap. 2, Jokasar gives the answer to this question, then the person of one speaking from the Beyond to this world—the redeemer—remains without significance.[113]

From the Manichaean drama of redemption I cite the following from the cosmogony according to Theodore bar Khonai [114]:

Then the living spirit called with his voice, and the voice of the living spirit became like a sharp sword and (he) unveiled his form to the primal man. And he said to him:

> Blessed be thou, Good in the midst of evil ones,
> Light in the midst of darkness,
> (God), who dwells in the midst of the beasts of wrath,
> Which do not know your honor.
> Then the primal man answered him and said:
> Come with blessing, bringing the cargo of peace and blessing,
> And he said to him further:
> How goes it with our fathers,
> The sons of light in their city?
> And the Call said to him: It goes well with them.
> And Call and Response led each other and ascended to the
> Mother of Life and to the living spirit.

Here, as in the following Mandaean fragment, the redeemer remains standing at the border of the world; only his call penetrates from the beyond into the earthly darkness:

> The elect one makes his proclamation hither from beyond
> And illumines the sons of Adam.

[113] This way of receiving redemption occurs also in the Deluge tradition of the Ethiopic Book of Enoch, esp. in chaps. 65 ff. and 106-7: "And in those days Noah saw the earth that it had sunk down and its destruction was nigh. And he arose from thence and went to the ends of the earth, and cried aloud to his grandfather Enoch: And Noah said three times with an embittered voice: Hear me, hear me, hear me" (65.1 ff., R. H. Charles's translation). In this tradition Enoch is a celestial being who dwells among the angels (106. 7). H. L. Jansen (Die Henochgestalt [Oslo, 1939]) suspects the figure of the Babylonian Ea-Oannes as a prototype behind this type of the heavenly redeemer (op. cit., pp. 13 ff.).

[114] Cf. Reitzenstein-Schaeder, Studien zum antiken Synkretismus, Anhang I, 342 ff.; H. Jonas, Gnosis, I, 301 ff.

> He illumines the sons of Adam,
> These simple ones, who have gained no knowledge.
> He says to them: . . . .[115]

The call can also come in the form of a letter:

> And (they) wrote to me a letter,
> And every mighty one put his name thereupon.
>
> . . .
>
> It flew like an eagle,
> The king of all fowls.
> It flew and alighted beside me
> And became simply a Word.
> At its call and its loud rustling
> I was aroused and I arose from my sleep.
> I picked it up and kissed it,
> And I began to read it;
> And thus, as it was engraved on my heart,
> Were the words of my letter written.[116]

In the Mandaean literature the redeeming revelation was often put in the mouth of an anonymous messenger. He is presented thus:

> I am the messenger of the light
> Whom the Great One has sent into this world.
> I am the true messenger,
> In whom is no falsehood.[117]

Still we learn nothing as to the name, the appearing, or the time of the messenger. As a person he is totally uninteresting. Only the words which are put in his mouth are interesting, and these words may, considered in terms of the history of tradition, be older than the messenger in whose mouth they are found.

Anonymous also are the addresses in the Book of John of the Mandaeans, chaps. 42-51.[118] Even the "fisher of souls" in chaps. 36-39 is such an anonymous redeemer. The number of anonymous songs in the Mandaean literature supposedly was originally much greater than today.

Hymns in which the Gnosis itself simply speaks are not infrequently found in the Odes of Solomon, e.g., 8; 9; 22; and 23:

---

[115] Lidzbarski, *Ginza*, p. 391. 23-27.

[116] From the Song of the Pearl of the Syrian Acts of Thomas; German translation by A. Adam, *Die Psalmen des Thomas*, BZNW, XXIV (1959), 51-52.

[117] Lidzbarski, *Ginza*, p. 58.

[118] Cf. Chap. 13.

> And recognize my knowledge, you who in truth recognize
> me.[119]
> And his thought was like a letter,
> And his will came hither from the heights.
> And he was sent like an arrow from the bow,
> Which is sped on its way with force.[120]

Not least of all, we must in this connection refer to the speeches in the Gospel according to John. That they go back to a literary source I regard as already proved.[121] But even an "oral" source must have had a "Sitz im Leben." What Revealer speaks in the source? Apparently an anonymous figure, concerning whom one may not inquire as to the time and place of his appearing; all the names which this Revealer bears[122] are pictorial ones which portray his significance. The Revealer is in truth the Gnosis itself,[123] no historical figure and no historicized mythological being. The theological anti-Gnostic achievement of John consists precisely in the fact that he has this redeemer come in Jesus Christ in the flesh. This gives us an insight into a development which we have already observed in the Mandaean writings and will have occasion to note still more frequently: An originally anonymous word of redemption is placed only later in the mouth of a mythologically or historically characterized redeemer figure. At the beginning of Gnosticism stands no redeemer myth, but rather the redeeming Gnosis as such.

The hypostatized Wisdom of late Jewish literature[124] is likewise such an anonymous heavenly redeemer figure. It says:

> I came forth from the mouth of the Most High,
> And covered the earth as a mist.
> I dwelt in high places,
> And my throne is in the pillar of the cloud.
> Alone I compassed the circuit of heaven,
> And walked in the depth of the abyss.
> In the waves of the sea, and in all the earth,
> And in every people and nation, I got a possession.
> . . .
> He created me from the beginning before the world,
> And to the end I shall not fail.

[119] Od. Sol. 8.12.

[120] Od. Sol. 23.5-6.

[121] In this connection, besides Bultmann's commentary on John, see H. Becker, *Die Reden des Johannesevangelium*, FRLANT NF L, 1956.

[122] Light, son, vine, life, way, good shepherd, and so on.

[123] Hence Bultmann rightly compares the revelational discourses of the source which he has tried to reconstruct with the Od. Sol. (*Johannesevangelium*, p. 4, n. 5 *et passim*), while Becker makes the comparison with the Mandaean writings (*op. cit.*, pp. 123 ff.).

[124] Cf. U. Wilckens, *Weisheit und Torheit*, BhTh, XXVI (1959), 160-97.

. . .
Come unto me, ye that are desirous of me,
And be ye filled with my produce.
. . .
They that eat me shall yet be hungry for me;
And they that drink me shall yet be thirsting for me.[125]
The Lord created me at the beginning of his work,
  the first of his acts of old.
Ages ago I was set up,
  at the first, before the beginning of the earth.
. . .
And now, my sons, listen to me:
  Happy are those who keep my ways.
Hear instruction and be wise,
  and do not neglect it.
Happy is the man who listens to me,
  watching daily at my gates,
  waiting beside my doors.
For he who finds me finds life
  and obtains favor from the Lord;
But he who misses me injures himself;
  all who hate me love death.[126]

This calls for comparison with the Logos in the *source* of the prologue to John's Gospel [127]:

In the beginning was the Word
And the Word was with God,
And the Word was God;
He was in the beginning with God.
All things were made by him,
And without him was nothing made.
That which was made in him was life,
And the life was the light of men
And the light shines into the darkness. . . . (John 1:1-5.)

b) If one asks in what manner in the Mandaean writings the one sent achieves certain historical or, rather, concrete-mythological configurations and thus emerges from his anonymous intangibility, the answer is quite clear: The redeemer has been sent to the earth in the *primeval age*. This mythological determination of time dominates the major part of the Mandaean literature, especially the Right Part of the *Ginza*.[128] We call this

---

[125] Sir. 24:3-6, 9, 19, 21 (RV).
[126] Proverbs 8:22-23, 32-36 (RSV); cf. 1:20-33.
[127] Cf. also the fragment in the Eth. En. 42. 1-3.
[128] Cf. W. Bousset, *Hauptprobleme*, p. 274; K. Rudolph, *op. cit.*, pp. 149-50.

exemplification of the redeemer the primordial messenger. He has his counterpart *inter alia* in the angelic figures of the Jewish apocalyptic, which were sent to the patriarchs in order to proclaim to them what was imminent (cf., e.g., Eth. Enoch 10. 1). Anz[129] refers to the original revelation which occurs through Marduk in the Babylonian religion and writes: "This implies then that in the original Gnosticism the saving revelation was thought to come not at the end but at the beginning of time. Thus indeed the Mandaeans teach a primordial revelation with explicit rejection of the revelation brought about through Jesus . . ." (*op. cit.*, p. 95).

The names of the primordial messengers of the Mandaean tradition correspond to a considerable extent with those of the early biblical history, yet the latter itself appears not to have been used directly.[130] The dramatic encounters between the powers of light and those of darkness are always enacted in the primordial time, often even before the creation of the world or of man, as e.g. in the first fragment of the fifth book of the Right *Ginza*.[131] The imparting of the redeeming Gnosis through one sent from the heavenly world however is often bound up with the creation of the world which then follows the encounters. In the extensive third book of the Right *Ginza* the history of the original creation and of the creation of the world is first told. In chap. 100 (Lidzbarski, *Ginza*, p. 107) Ptahil conceives the plan to form Adam. This is accomplished after many difficulties. Still before Eve is formed, Manda d'Hayya appears to Adam in bodily form, in order to impart to him the truth, through which he can come to know himself and can keep himself free from the power of the evil ones:

> I sat down beside him and instructed him concerning that
> Which life had entrusted to me.
> I preached to him with a sublime voice,
> Which was sublime and more illuminating than all the world,
> I preached to him with gentle voice
> And awakened his heart out of sleep.
> I spoke to him in the discourse of the Uthras
> And taught him my wisdom.
> Out of my wisdom I taught him and said to him,
> That he should arouse himself and worship and praise the
>   powerful [life].
> He should praise the lofty place,
> The place in which the good dwell.

[129] *Ursprung des Gnostizismus*, TU, XV (1897), 93 ff.
[130] Cf. Lidzbarski, *Ginza*, p. VII.
[131] *Ibid.*, pp. 149 ff.

He should praise Adakas-Ziwa,
The Father, from whom he came hither.[132]

This instruction is successful:

As I sat there and instructed him,
He arose, and honored and praised the powerful.
He praised his Father Adakas-Ziwa,
The Mana, by whom he had been formed.[133]

After the formation of Eve the instruction by Manda d'Hayya is continued.[134]

Many other fragments reflect such a revelation of the messenger to the first men:

My Lord called and commissioned me, the true messenger, and said: Go, call with your voice to Adam, to his wife Hawwa, and to all his kindred. With a lofty voice call to them and instruct them concerning every thing. Instruct them concerning the high king of light, whose power is far-reaching and great, beyond all limits and number. Instruct them concerning the worlds of light, the eternal. Speak with him, that his heart may be illumined, and instruct him, that his mind may be illumined. Show yourself gracious to him and keep him company, you and the two angels who are with you. Teach knowledge to Adam, Hawwa his wife, and all his kindred. Say to them that the evil ones and Satan, the unworthy, are not to lead them astray.[135]

It is not always Adam who is the recipient of the first revelation. In many passages, Eve-Hawwa, Abel-Hibil, Seth-Sitil,[136] or Enosh-Anos appear as those figures of the primeval time to whom or in whose time the Gnosis is first imparted [137]:

These words Manda d'Hayya directed to Sitil (Lidzbarski, *Ginza*, p. 260. 9).
Then Manda d'Hayya said to me: Little Enosh, do not be afraid of me (Lidzbarski, *Ginza*, p. 264. 20-21).
When Hibil was the protector of the age, I (Jokabar-Kusta) was the emissary before him (Lidzbarski, *Ginza*, p. 319. 5-6).
Go, speak to Hawwa, and cause her heart to rest upon its support (Lidzbarski, *Ginza*, p. 439. 7-8).

[132] *Ibid.*, p. 112.24-37.
[133] *Ibid.*, pp. 112.38–113.2.
[134] *Ibid.*, pp. 119, 141.
[135] *Ibid.*, p. 16.5-15; cf. pp. 34 ff., 220 ff., 387; Lidzbarski, *Johannesbuch*, p. 66.
[136] Seth plays an esp. large role in Gnosticism, as is evident from many other examples. On Seth, cf. E. Preuschen, *Die apokryphen gnostischen Adamschriften, Sonderdruck aus Festgruss für B. Stade* (Giessen, 1900); W. Staerk, *Soter*, II, 41-42; G. Widengren [3], p. 47; Epiphanius, Haer. 39.9.
[137] Cf. K. Rudolph, *op. cit.*, pp. 162 ff.

In chaps. 14–17 of the Book of John of the Mandaeans, Sum bar Nu (=Shem, Noah's son) is the recipient of the revelation which an anonymous "emissary from the heights" brings.

This always implies that the Gnosis is known from primeval times onward.[138] This alone is important, and not any special form of the redeemer myth. The apostle who descends as teacher of Gnosis is one of the numerous heavenly figures who battle with the planetary deities in the Mandaean primordial history. He is described according to their prototype, if they do not refrain altogether from portraying or indeed only mentioning his descent.

Thus the first men received the Gnosis by the hand of a heavenly messenger; they passed it on to the living generations:

> Adam, the head of the whole race, said:
> I am Adam,
> Hibil-Ziwa was a helper to me.
> Hibil was a helper to me
> And redeemed me out of the world,
> From the anxiety of the seven stars
> Which they let loose against the souls.
> . . .
> I call to you and declare to you,
> You souls, who bear witness to life,
> Stand firm in this world,
> Until your measure is full.
> To you I say and declare,
> You souls, who dwell in a perishable house:
> If you depart from your bodies,
> What decision will you give to the great Life? [139]

Manda d'Hayya gave the teaching to "Hibil, Sitil, and Anos, and Hibil, Sitil, and Anos gave it to those who love their names." [140] In other words, the original revelation was valid for all coming generations:

I instruct you, my disciples, you chosen ones, perfect and believing, you who are to live in that age (of Moses).[141] Further, I proclaim to you, you Nasoreans, who in this world are, originate, and are to be born. . . .[142]

---

[138] This explains such Gnostic sect names as Sethians, Melchizedekians, Adamites, Noachites, Cainites, etc.

[139] Lidzbarski, *Ginza*, pp. 404.19-25; 405.21-28; cf. pp. 246.16 ff.; 248.10 ff.

[140] *Ibid.*, p. 223.18 ff.

[141] *Ibid.*, p. 43.16 ff.

[142] *Ibid.*, p. 45.20 ff.

'l'hus also:

> Adam heard and believed—
> Blessing to the one who after you hears and believes.
> Adam received Kusta—
> Blessing to the one who after you receives Kusta.
> Full of hope, Adam looked up and ascended—
> Blessing to the one who after you ascends.[143]

Sometimes the address of the apostle appears to have in mind Adam not as the first man, but rather as "all men"; thus for example in the interesting second fragment of the first book of the Left *Ginza* (Lidzbarski, *Ginza*, pp. 429 ff.).

The Manichaean system also is familiar with the revelation of the primeval envoy to Adam, and indeed *Jesus* is sent in the primeval time to Adam:

The luminous Jesus drew near to the unconscious Adam; he awakened him out of the sleep of death, so that he might be freed from many spirits. And as a man who is just and who finds a man possessed of a frightful demon and through his power calms him down—such a one Adam resembled, when that friend found him sunken in deep slumber, awakened him, bestirred him, shook him, drove from him the demon that leads astray and imprisoned the powerful female Archon away from him. Then Adam examined himself and discovered who he was. He (Jesus) showed to him both himself and the Father in the heights. . . .[144]

Since in spite of a warning Adam approaches Eve, the propagation and scattering of the seed of light begins; and all this in its turn makes possible rather than demands (as in Mandaean literature) the appearance of later emissaries down to Mani himself.

Among the manuscripts from Nag Hammadi, in Codex II a writing is found which at the end bears the title: "The Nature of the Archons." [145] This writing stems from the circle of those Gnostics of whom Irenaeus tells in I, 29-30 under the heading of Barbelo-Gnosis, the Ophites and the Sethians. Adam and Eve receive the Gnosis from the mouth of the serpent: "But the spiritual came in the serpent, the teacher; and it taught him with the words . . . (col. 665).

Norea, the wife of Seth, who in our writing plays the role of the actual recipient of revelation, receives in response to her call a visit from

---

[143] Lidzbarski, *Johannesbuch*, p. 57.17 ff.

[144] Reitzenstein-Schaeder, *Studien zum antiken Synkretismus*, pp. 346-47; Jonas, *Gnosis*, I, 134; 310-11.

[145] H. M. Schenke has translated it into German: ThLZ (1958), cols. 661 ff.

an angel who comes from Heaven and introduces himself: "I am Eleth, Wisdom, the great angel, the one who stands before the Holy Spirit. I was sent forth to speak with you and to save you out of the hand of these lawless ones. And I will instruct you concerning that which is yours" (col. 667). The instruction that follows is the content of the book; once again the instruction is brought about by a primeval apostle.

In the system of Baruch-Gnosticism of the Gnostic Justin, Baruch is sent into Paradise: "When the Father Elohim saw this, he sent Baruch, the third of his angels, to lend help to the spirit which is in men. So Baruch went and placed himself among the angels of Edem, that is, in the middle of Paradise, and proclaimed to man . . ." (Hipp. 5. 26). That this redemption should fail is, in view of the secondary Christian character of the system before us, unavoidable; room must remain for the redeeming activity of Christ. The structure of the primeval mission, however, is still easy to recognize.

c) We turn now to the figure of the *historical envoy*, i.e., of that envoy who appears in the figure of a specific historical man. In Christian Gnosticism Jesus Christ is this historical emissary. Because Christian Gnosticism is the most familiar to us, it is understandable that the historical emissary often is taken as the normal type of the Gnostic apostle in general. This is by no means the case. On the contrary, the historical emissary actually stands in contradiction to the overall outlook of Gnosticism. In Gnosticism everything is aimed at the idea of freeing the pneuma from the power of the flesh. In view of this it is a paradoxical conception that the very redeemer himself is tainted with the flesh, in order to fulfill the redemption. Bousset properly writes,[146] "that the Gnostic systems were not at all able to assimilate to themselves the complete and true figure of the redeemer Jesus, that they actually have no room at all for his historical appearance." Gnostic thinking corresponds rather to the sentence previously cited from Corp. Herm. X, 25: "None of the heavenly gods will come to the earth." In the *Ginza* (Lidzbarski, *Ginza*, p. 43. 29 ff.) the "first emissary" explicitly criticizes the false emissaries, who indeed are called emissaries but have originated in the "bodies of women." One may compare also the following passage from the Manichaean Psalms of Thomas:

> It is not possible that the sovereign light
> Should go forth to the land of the demons of darkness.
> Again it is not possible that the sweet aroma
> Should be spread abroad in the land of a stench.

[146] *Hauptprobleme*, p. 238.

It is not possible that the image of the living man
Should come to the abode of the beasts.
The light is supposed to come to the light,
The sweet aroma is to come to the sweet aroma,
The image of the living man is to come
To the living land, from which it has gone forth.
The light is to return to its place,
The darkness is to fall and not to rise again.[147]

For this reason the call of redemption so often sounds forth from the "outer rim of the world," [148] issues from primeval beginnings, or comes in the form of a letter.

How basically un-Gnostic the figure of a historical redeemer is becomes apparent in the attempts of Christian Gnosticism to de-historicize Christ. This is done in a most thorough-going manner by Docetism, which has Christ appearing only in a make-believe body.[149] If one does not deny the fleshly reality of Jesus, then this fleshly Jesus is set in radical opposition to the heavenly Christ.[150] If in later Christian Gnosticism one must, for the sake of the name "Christian," renounce such an unbiblical dualism, then one seeks, in tortuous and complicated speculation about the person and work of the redeemer, to explain the connection between *pneuma* and *sarx* in the heavenly emissary.[151]

In view of this, it is only with difficulty that one can imagine the figure of the historical emissary having originated in Gnosticism itself. Alien influences must have been at work. But even in Judaism one does not encounter the figure of a heavenly being which has entered into a historical man. Thus one is naturally led to suspect Christian influences[152]; for the earliest historical emissary witnessed to in Gnosticism is Jesus

[147] Following A. Adam, *Die Psalmen des Thomas*, p. 14, vss. 24-29.

[148] Lidzbarksi, *Ginza*, pp. 387, 397; *Johannesbuch*, p. 4.

[149] Gnosticism here makes use of a motif widely employed in the history of religions, according to which the god disguises himself so that he can be perceived by human eyes, or so that he is not recognized by the demons as god; cf. Bultmann, *Das Evangelium des Johannes*, p. 39, n. 1; H. Windisch in *Ergänzungsband* of HNT on Barn. 5.10.

[150] Thus already I Cor. 12:3; I John 2:22; 4:1 ff.; Iren. I, 24.4.

[151] Cf. e.g., W. Foerster, "Die Grundzüge der ptolemäischen Gnosis," in NTS, VI (1959/60), 28 ff.

[152] With respect to the figure of the *historical* emissary, one may concur with G. Quispel ("Der gnostische Anthropos und die jüdische Tradition," *Eranos-Jahrbuch* XXII [1953], 195-234), who writes (p. 224): "And finally, Gnosticism, so far as we have come to know it up to the present, did not have a redeemer figure; it is incorrect to picture the Anthropos, Adam, Poimandres, as a redeemer. Even if perhaps there was a pre-Christian Gnosis, still there was never a pre-Christian Gnostic redeemer." But one may not, with Quispel, use this concession (which is limited to the historical redeemer) as evidence for the independence of the Gnostic thought-world from the Iranian system of religion.

Christ.[153] The Christ hymn in Phil. 2:6-11 already shows the connection of the historical figure of Jesus of Nazareth with the Gnostic presentation of the descent of the primal man. Either Christ was first fitted out in Gnostic circles with the traits of the primal man or primal emissary, or the significance of the person of Jesus was first expressed in the forms of the Gnostic myth within the ecclesiastical communities. John shows in a fully developed way how the latter was possible, and already in pre-Christian times, in fact, representations of the primal man had influenced Jewish theology in the figure of the (coming) Son of man-Messiah.[154] Exact data are hard to come by; still the beginnings of the reciprocal influence of ecclesiastical and Gnostic representations of the redeemer must be very early, as the Christ hymn in Philippians, I Cor. 2:7-8, and the Pauline Christology in general show.

For the detailed portrayal of the figure of this historical emissary one may refer to John's Gospel, even though the emphasis upon the fleshly existence of Jesus testifies to the anti-Gnostic interest. In addition, some other examples may be cited.

And I heard the words of the Most High, the Father of my Lord, as he said . . . to my Lord Christ: Go and descend through all the heavens and descend to the firmament and to this world. . . . And after two months of days, when Joseph was in his house and Mary his wife, the two alone, then it happened that while she was alone, Mary suddenly looked up with her eyes and saw a little child, and she

---

[153] The judgment of Bultmann (*Das Evangelium des Johannes*, p. 10): "However, the idea of the incarnation of the redeemer did not somehow penetrate Gnosticism from Christianity, but is originally Gnostic," appears to me accordingly to need correcting. The redeemer myth is undoubtedly Gnostic, but the special form of the myth which speaks of the incarnation of the redeemer in a concrete historical person is not proved in the pre-Christian era, not even in the documentation cited by Bultmann, p. 10, n. 5. Cf. A. Adam, *Die Psalmen des Thomas*, pp. 81-82; K. Rudolph, *op. cit.*, pp. 169-70.

Because of their significance I quote here the sentences of W. Brandt (*Mandäische Religion*, pp. 191-92) which W. Bousset (*Hauptprobleme*, p. 273) repeated: "The great distinction between the Gnostic and the Mandaean writing consists in the fact that in the latter the Christian doctrine of redemption completely disappears. In its place there appears here the primeval revelation, through which man is informed of his belonging to the world of the first life and the religious exercises, which are appropriate and which maintain this connection, are communicated to him . . . . The divergent Gnostic treatment (is) determined by the simple fact that to the Gnostic the Christian gospel was a given fact." "The transposition of the decisive struggle against hell from the beginning of creation to the end of time therefore appeared required; and the giving of the law through Moses or, where one omitted this, the revelation first given through Christ, stood in the way of the primeval revelation. For this reason the Mandaean usage must qualify as more ancient than the Christian-Gnostic one."

[154] "There can be no doubt that the syncretistic apocalypticism of Judaism stands under the influence of Gnostic mythology" (Bultmann, *Das Evangelium des Johannes*, p. 12). This opinion is brilliantly confirmed in the study by J. Jervell, *Imago Dei*, FRLANT NF, LVIII, 1960.

was astonished. And when the astonishment had gone away, her womb became as it had been before she was pregnant. . . . And when he was grown, he did great signs and wonders in the land of Israel and in Jerusalem. . . . In Jerusalem itself I saw how they crucified him on the tree. . . . And I saw forthwith how he sat down at the right hand of that great majesty.[155]

While I came from the Father of the universe, while I passed over to the heavens, . . . I was in the heavens . . . while I possessed the measure of the wisdom of the Father who has sent me. . . . At that time I appeared to Mary and spoke with her and her heart received me, she believed and laughed, and I, the Word, entered into her and became flesh.[156]

> He lived a divine existence
> But did not cherish the honor,
> The exaltation of divine Being;
> He surrendered honor and exaltation
> To exchange them for a wretched existence,
> Became like man in form
> And like man in appearance.
> Obedient unto death,
> To death on the cross,
> He chose renunciation.
> Therefore God has exalted him to the highest honor
> And has bestowed on him the name above all names.[157]

> Send me, Father,
> That I may descend with the seals,
> Make my way through all the Aeons,
> Open all secrets,
> Show the forms of the gods
> And deliver the mystery of the holy way,
> Which is called Gnosis.[158]

The Word of God is his Son, as we have said earlier. And he is called "angel" and "messenger." For he himself tells how much one must acknowledge, and he is sent to proclaim what he has experienced, as even the Lord himself said to us: Whoever hears me hears the one who has sent me.[159]

Consider how Jesus, the Son of Mary, said: O, you children of Israel! Truly, I am God's messenger for you.[160]

When (Jesus) became flesh, in order to descend into the realm of man's vision, then in his knowledge they were set free from ignorance, and came out of death into life. . . . This happened when men came to know him.[161]

---

[155] Asc. Jes. 10.7-8; 11.7 ff., 18, 20, 32.
[156] Ep. Ap. 13-14.
[157] Phil. 2.6-11 following the translation of M. Dibelius in HNT XI, 3rd ed., 1937.
[158] Hipp. 5.10.
[159] Justin, Apol. 63.4-5.
[160] Koran, 61st Sura; following E. Norden, *Agnostos Theos* (4th ed., 1956), p. 191.
[161] Iren. I, 15.2 (Marcosians).

Thus (Jesus) went forth and descended to his sister and to the scattered light. Now when the lower Sophia recognized that her brother intended to descend to her, she proclaimed through John his coming, prepared the baptism of repentance, and prepared Jesus beforehand, so that upon his arrival Christ might find a pure vessel and that through Jaldabaoth, her son, the woman might be proclaimed by Christ. Now he descended through the seven heavens, became like their sons, and gradually emptied them of their power. All the scattered light flowed together to him, and when Christ then came into this world, he first knew his sister Sophia, and they both rejoiced trembling, and this they explain in terms of bridegroom and bride. Jesus was more righteous, purer, and wiser than all men, and he was born of a virgin through God's doing. United with the Sophia, Christ descended upon him—and thus Jesus became the Christ.[162]

In the polemic against Christ in the Mandaean writings is found the following characterization:

He says to you: I am the one who has his origin from God. That deceiver says: I am the Son of God, whom my Father has sent hither. He says to you: I am the first emissary, I am Hibil-Ziwa, who has come forth from the heights above.[163]

From among the Odes of Solomon, in many respects enigmatic, we should refer to those Odes in which the Gnosis which comes from above plainly bears the traits of the Christian revealer: Od. Sol. 7; 19; 31; 41; and 42. For example:

> For he is a helper to me to the Lord.
> In his graciousness he allowed me to acknowledge him,
> For his friendliness made his greatness lowly.
> He became like me, so that I could comprehend him,
> As to similarity, he appeared like me, so that I could put him on.
> And I was not afraid when I saw him,
> Because he is my grace.[164]

Here we need only to be reminded of the numerous Gnostic writings which are based upon the secret communications of the (risen) Christ.

In this connection belongs, of course, also the designation ἀπόστολος for Jesus, as it appears in Heb. 3:1 [165]; Justin Apol. I, 12. 9; 63. 5, 10, and 14,[166] as well as the verb ἀποστέλλειν, for example in the Gospel of John[167] and in the Acts of Thomas.[168] Even in Islam the title "emissary"

---

[162] Iren. I, 30.12 (Ophites).
[163] Lidzbarski, Ginza, p. 47.30 ff.; cf. pp. 29.17 ff.; 49.8 ff.
[164] Od. Sol. 7.3-5.
[165] Cf. E. Käsemann [1], pp. 95 ff.; O. Michel, Der Brief an die Hebräer (1949), pp. 94 ff.
[166] Cf. the quotation from the Presbyter in Eus., CH VI, 14.4; cf. I, 13.20.
[167] Cf. Bultmann, Das Evangelium des Johannes, p. 30, n. 2. Curiously, John does not have (or no longer has?) the noun ἀπόστολος. The reasons for this can only be

for Jesus is preserved.[169]

Christ[170] is not the only historical figure who was united with the Gnostic myth and thus made into an "emissary." Simon Magus should be mentioned in particular.[171]

Doubtless Simon was originally a Gnostic, far from any Christian influence. In his own self-estimate, he was an apostle, though to be sure, as we shall see, not of the type of historical emissary here being discussed. The later tradition first made him into such, perhaps in an antithesis to Christ. The account of Irenaeus (I, 23 = Hipp. 6. 19-20) has him coming down from heaven in order to free Helena, who is the personification, drawn from the sagas, of the Pneuma which is imprisoned within the world.[172] He appeared as a man, without actually being one (Iren. I, 23. 2). In the "Martyrdom of Peter and Paul," chap. 15, Simon says to Nero: "Hear, good king, I am the Son of God, who has descended hither out of heaven." [173]

As in the case of Simon, in certain Gnostic sects people such as Menander, Elchasai,[174] Dositheus,[175] and Cerinthus[176] may have been honored as "historical emissaries" without having raised such a claim for themselves.

John the Baptist has also been honored as such a preexistent redeemer.[177]

---

surmised (see p. 191). G. P. Wetter, however, rightly asserts (op. cit., p. 49): "The phrase ὃν ἀπέστειλεν ὁ θεός is actually used as a kind of proper name" (3:34; 5:30; 5:38; 6:29; 17:3).

[168] Act. Thom. 10; 48; 122; 156; cf. Iren. I, 23.5; Ep. Ap. 19; Eus. CH III, 26.1.

[169] See in E. Norden, Agnostos Theos (4th ed., 1956), p. 191; cf. K. H. Rengstorf [1], p. 444, n. 229; G. W. Widengren [3], p. 9.

[170] Cf. further the following from a Coptic magical text (according to V. Stegemann, Die Gestalt Christi in den koptischen Zaubertexten (1934), p. 21): "Jao, Jao, Christ Pantocrator, who was born in the bosom of the Father, until for us he was born as perfect man by the angels and archangels and they sent him down to us upon the earth . . . . I adjure thee today . . . ."

[171] One may hardly refer here to those few remarks in the Mandaean writings in which the light emissary appeared in a milieu that was at least by intimation historical: Lidzbarski, Ginza, p. 29. 32 ff.; 47.40 ff.; 181.27; 336 ff.; ibid., Johannesbuch, chaps. 54; 76. These are quite late fragments whose historical references are supplied from various traditions. The light emissary himself is never identified with a historical figure.

In addition, K. Rudolph (op. cit., pp. 90-91; cf. p. 102) recognizes the strangeness of these fragments within the Mandaean literature and suspects, probably with good reason, Christian influences. The connections between this emissary and the figure of John the Baptist will be discussed later.

[172] Cf. E. Haenchen, "Gab es eine vorchristliche Gnosis?" in ZThK, XLIX (1952), 316-49. Cf. Justin Dial. 120; Apol. 26.1-3.

[173] Lipsius-Bonnet, I, 132; cf. Epiph. Haer. 21.1-2.

[174] Epiph. Haer. 19.4.

[175] Origen, Cels. I, 57 = Koetschau, I, 108.25; Ps.-Cl. Rec. II, 8-9; 11.

[176] Eus., CH III, 28.

[177] See Bultmann, Das Evangelium des Johannes, p. 4, n. 7; G. P. Wetter, op. cit., pp. 76-77.

Mani, who, as is known, gave himself out to be an apostle of God, was seen by the Manichaeans as the one God come down from heaven,[178] which he himself had not at all asserted (vide infra): "Mari (Mani) came from the Gods, the God of brilliant fame, . . . God has come, the pure, the good, from the Paradise of light. . . ."[179] "An apostle came from the Paradise of light, with a worthy name, the Illustrious, God, Mari Mani."[180]

As we have already said, the figure of the historical redeemer is not found in the witnesses of pre-Christian times,[181] yet older Gnostic systems are historicized under the influence of the Christian representation of the redeemer. Thus in the later Sethians, Christ is equated with the primeval redeemer Seth; Seth has thus appeared anew in Christ.[182] Examples of this precedure are not rare. [183]

d) A redeemer of a special kind is the so-called "deliverer" or "helper" in the Mandaean literature[184]:

Thereunto the First Great Life called, commissioned, equipped and sent the deliverer Saurel—Qmamir-Ziwar, who delivers the spirits and souls out of the body and leads them forth. He is called "death" in the world, but those who know call him Kusta. Everyone who commits an offence to escape death heaps up before himself sixty-six offences. For he is called, he is commissioned, he is sent forth. He accepts no bribes, receives no gifts, and barters no man for another.[185]

In this text the "deliverer" is explicitly identified with death. He is the helper who is expected at the end of life, when "the measure is full" [186];

---

[178] G. P. Wetter, op. cit., pp. 15-16.

[179] Müller, Manichäische Fragmente, AAB (1904), No. 64, p. 92.

[180] Ibid., p. 44.

[181] One may hardly see in Melchizedek such a historical redeemer. This curious figure from Gen. 14 unquestionably played a significant role in Jewish Gnosticism, but he still serves here as a figure of the primeval period and as such is identified with Shem and even with Adam (Epiph. Haer. 55.6; Riessler, p. 969; Str.-B., IV, 1, 453, n. 2; W. Staerk, Soter, II, 46 ff.; 92). His eschatological function as priest corresponds to his significance in the primeval period. He appears only relatively late as a celestial angelic being. Citations and literature most recently in O. Michel, Der Brief an die Hebräer (1949), pp. 159-60; O. Cullmann, The Christology of the New Testament (rev. ed.), pp. 85-86; G. Widengren [2], p. 50; E. Käsemann [1], pp. 129 ff.

[182] Cf. Epiph. Haer. 39.1.3 = Holl. II, 72.11 ff.; Ps.-Tert. Haer. 2.

[183] In a Coptic magical text (in A. Kopp, Ausgewählte koptische Zaubertexte (Brussels, 1930), II, No. 72) is found an appeal to the "only begotten son, whose true name is Seth—Seth, the living Christ." Cf. R. Wünsch, Sethianische Verfluchungstafeln, pp. 112, 116.

[184] Cf. K. Rudolph, op. cit., pp. 159 ff.

[185] Lidzbarski, Ginza, p. 424.29 ff.

[186] Ibid., pp. 51.18 ff.; 571.25; 585.27.

When the Great Life heard this,
It sent an envoy of light.
The Great One said to Hibil-Ziwa:
Good Uthra of beloved name!
Redeem Adam out of darkness
And bring him up hither.
I clothed myself with brilliance from my place
And came forth from my position.
I brought Adam out of the world of the evil
And led him past every hateful visage.
I darkened the light of the evil ones
And demolished all their guard-houses.
. . .
And to him they said:
You have borne the soul hither, you have brought it here,
And you were a helper to it.[187]

The names of the helpers vary; often they are nameless; frequently several helpers appear:

The soul sits there;
Perhaps an escort will come.
Perhaps an escort will come,
And I will go with them in their company.
The soul looks up and sees
That the escort of the Good is approaching.
Brilliance precedes them,
Light follows them.
. . .
If it please you, my good brothers,
Take me with you in your company.[188]

The soul which thus prays already possesses Gnosis[189] and now hopes for the helpers at the hour of death, the helpers which will lead it through the world of the evil ones. Frequently, it is true, the helper first of all shares the Gnosis with the erring soul:

As I stood in my place,
I was anxious and my soul was anxious.
I said to myself that I had no high helper,
No man as guardian.
While I still stood there in my place,

---

[187] *Ibid.*, pp. 530.8-19; 531.40 ff.; cf. pp. 547.1 ff.; 564.8 ff.; 569.13 ff.; 570-71; 572.33 ff.; 190 ff.

[188] *Ibid.*, pp. 540.36–541.4, 11-12; cf. p. 590.14 ff.

[189] "When will the exalted man come, who has let me hear his voice" (*ibid.*, p. 593.2-3).

> The Great Life heard me and did not condemn me.
> He sent to me a high helper.
> . . .
> He instructed me about glorification,
> Until I forgot the persecution of Tibil.
> He said:
> O gentle Uthra!
> You have not come to this place by the will of the Great (Life).
> . . .
> Now, gentle Uthra,
> Stand up, ascend to the house of your family.
> . . .
> He demolished their guardhouses
> And led him with splendor out of the world.[190]

It is clear that this helper figure is expected as *coming*. Its actual task is not the mediation of Gnosis, but rather the providing of help for the poor soul,[191] which is terrified at the guardhouses of the demons; a task which elsewhere in Gnosticism is performed by the powerful secret words which are communicated to the soul.

In the Pistis Sophia, this task is entrusted to Melchizedek:

Because . . . Melchizedek is the emissary of all lights which are purified in the archons, while he leads them into the light-treasure. . . .[192]

In Od. Sol. 38, the hypostatized Truth itself is this helper:

> I ascended to the light of truth as upon a chariot,
> And the Truth guided me and led me.
> And it let me step over chasms and gorges,
> And it saved me from hidden reefs and billows.
> And it became to me a harbor of deliverance
> And laid me in the arms of life without death.
> And it went with me and made rest for me and did not abandon
> me, that I should go astray,
> Because it was and is the Truth.
> . . .
> And I became wise, so that I did not fall into the hands of those
> who lead astray,
> And I congratulated myself on the fact that the Truth went with
> me.[193]

---

[190] *Ibid.*, pp. 328.25-31; 328.39–329.3; 329.34-35; 330.23-24; cf. pp. 550-51.

[191] Cf. Herm. Vis. 5.2: Ἀπεστάλην ὑπὸ τοῦ σεμνοτάτου ἀγγέλου, ἵνα μετὰ σοῦ οἰκήσω τὰς λοιπὰς ἡμέρας τῆς ζωῆς σου.

[192] Pist. Soph., GCS, XLV (13, 1959), 237.5 ff.; cf. pp. 21.4 ff.; 22.6 ff.; 218.17 ff. Melchizedek is called παραλήμπτωρ.

[193] Od. Sol. 38.1-4, 15.

The conception that, at its death, the soul is borne to heaven by helpers is common also to late Judaism.[194]

It is clear that the figure of the "helper" within the Gnostic pattern of thought on redemption considered here can be called "redeemer" only with some limitations; but it is equally clear that the structure of the "helper" as "one sent" is that of the here considered heavenly emissary in general; for the—not originally Gnostic—figure of the "helper" appears in the Mandaean documents just as "one sent."

e) We have seen that occasionally the "helper" first communicates the Gnosis to the soul to whom he is sent, before he leads the knowing soul out of the body and out of the world. If we consider only the first activity of the "helper," we encounter therein the heavenly emissary in a new form, which we will call the "mystical" emissary. This one is sent as a heavenly being to the individual man, in order to enlighten him as to his heavenly nature and to stand by him, as helper, during his earthly life. He is not contaminated with evil matter. Either he draws the man, who then is an ecstatic person, to instruction in the heavenly world, or he betakes himself to the man and appears to him in a vision. But never does this emissary become a historical person.

In the Mandaean writings we frequently encounter this mystical envoy in the twenty-eight unified fragments of the second book of the Left *Ginza.* Only one of the fragments is here cited:

> I am a Mana of the great life,
> I am a Mana of the mighty life,
> I am a Mana of the great life.
> Who has cast me into the sorrow of the world?
> Into the sorrow of the world, who has cast me,
> Who has misplaced me in the evil darkness?
> . . .
> While the Mana stands there and seeks to be enlightened,
> There comes a man, his helper:
> You are not a part of the sorrow, that you should ponder thereupon,
> You are not a part of the darkness, which would make an end of you.
> . . .
> You are a part of the brightness,
> Which is without disturbance.
> You are a part of the throng of light,
> In which there is no darkness, which would make an end of you.
> You will win, Mana,
> And your own figure will illumine you.
> Your mind will firmly support you,

---

[194] Riessler, pp. 134 ff.; 161 ff.

And your heart will be a helper and master builder for you.
Persevere in the world and dwell in it,
Until we reach you.
When we reach you,
We will betake ourselves hither and come to you.
We will betake ourselves hither and come to you,
Then we will take you away from here and raise you up to your
treasure-house.[195]

Bultmann[196] supposes that the Paraclete of John's Gospel goes back to the Gnostic prototype of such a redeemer figure, as it is represented by the "mystical emissary." This is quite possible, for undoubtedly the "Paraclete" also shows the structure of the "mystical emissary":

But when he comes, who is the spirit of truth, he will guide you into all truth. For he will not speak what is his own, but will say what he hears. . . .[197]

The already mentioned Baruch Gnosticism of the Gnostic Justin pictures the redeeming Baruch in the characteristics of the "mystical emissary." As such he comes to the people in Paradise, then to Moses, to the prophets, to Heracles, and finally to Jesus:

Finally in the days of King Herod, again sent by Elohim, Baruch came to Nazareth and found Jesus, the son of Joseph and Mary, while he, twelve years old, was keeping sheep. He proclaimed to him all that had happened since the beginning, of Edem, of Elohim and what happened thereafter, and said to him: All the prophets before you allowed themselves to be led astray. Now Jesus, Son of man, strive to let yourself not be led astray, but proclaim this word to men and communicate to them the message concerning the Father and the Good and ascend to the Good and sit down there with Elohim, the Father of us all. . . .[198]

With the Baruch Gnosis has often been compared, properly, that teaching of Mani according to which the Light-Jesus, who as original revealer revealed the Gnosis to Adam, later on often appeared to Buddha, Zarathustra, the historical Jesus, and finally to Mani himself, this time as the "living Paraclete":

In the years of Ardaschir, the king of Persia, I was drawn up and I grew up and arrived at a certain time. In that certain year of the reign of Ardaschir the "living Paraclete" came down to me and spoke to me. He revealed to me the hidden mystery which was concealed from the worlds and the generations. . . .[199]

---

[195] Lidzbarski, *Ginza*, pp. 457.27-32; 458.12-15, 20-33.
[196] *Das Evangelium des Johannes*, pp. 437-41. By way of supplement to this, cf. S. Schulz, *Untersuchungen zur Menschensohn-Christologie im Johannesevangelium* (1957), pp. 151 ff.
[197] John 16:13-14.
[198] Hipp. 5.26.
[199] Schmidt-Polotsky, *Ein Mani-Fund in Ägypten*, SAB (1933), Heft 1, pp. 53-54.

In the Pseudo-Clementine Rec. I, 33, the "true prophet" appears in the form of an angel-like mystical emissary, in order to enlighten Abraham concerning everything divine.[200]

If one describes the character of Jewish wisdom as a *personal hypostasis*, then this figure connected with the Gnosis must also be mentioned here. Cf. the passages already cited on pp. 126-27 with the following:

> And with thee is the wisdom, who knows thy works
> And who was present when thou didst make the world,
> And who knows what is well-pleasing in thy sight,
> And what is right according to thy commandments.
> Send it forth from the holy heaven
> And from the throne of thy splendor send it,
> So that it may stand beside me in my work
> And I may recognize what is well-pleasing to thee.[201]

I will penetrate all the lower regions of the earth and will visit all those who sleep and will illumine all who hope in the Lord.[202]

Further, in this connection belongs also the hypostatized Logos who, proceeding from God, leads men to the knowledge of God. It is well known what central significance this Logos possesses in the religious speculation of Philo. Of this Logos it is said, for example:

He is . . . the ambassador of the sovereign to his subjects. He rejoices in this honored position, and, proud of it, he explicitly declares: "And I stood between God and you . . ." (Deut. 5:5). For like a herald I bring to the creatures the message of peace of the one who has determined to end wars, of the God who constantly stands guard over peace.[203]

Frequently the instruction by the "mystical emissary" is combined with an ecstasy of the mystic. Thus especially in the Hermetica, although ecstasy is not essential in them[204]:

It happened once that, when I had begun to reflect upon the things that are, and my thoughts had been caught up on high, and when my bodily senses had been put under restraint, like those who are weighed down by sleep resulting from overeating or bodily fatigue, I seemed to see an immense figure of boundless size

[200] Cf. H. J. Schoeps, *Aus frühchristlicher Zeit*, pp. 25, 32.

[201] Wisd. Sol. 9:9-10.

[202] Addition to Sir. 24:32; see in Kautzsch, *in loc.*

[203] Rer. div. Her. 205-6.

[204] Cf. Cornutus, theologia graeca; "Hermes serves as the *Logos* whom the gods have *sent* to us from heaven."

who was calling me by name and saying to me, "What do you wish to hear and to behold, and, by your thought, to learn and know?" "Who are you?" I said. "I am Poimandres," said he, "the Mind of the Sovereignty. I know what you wish, and I am with you everywhere." "I wish," I said, "to learn the things that are, and to understand their nature, and to know God; how I wish to hear this!" He replied, "Keep in your mind the things you wish to learn, and I will teach you."

When he had said this his aspect changed. Everything was opened to me in a moment, and I beheld a boundless vision.[205]

The instruction of the mystic begins with the ecstatic vision which is presented at this point.

One may compare with this the parallels from the Shepherd of Hermas:

I fell asleep while I was walking. And a spirit took me and carried me through a desert, through which no man could walk. . . . But while I was praying, the heavens were opened and I saw. . . .[206]

From the Hermetic writings I refer further to the φύλαξ πνευμάτων which leads the alchemist Zosimus on his way through the world of the evil ones, where he is changed into the perfect Pneuma,[207] and to Hermes as mystagogue of Thoth in Corp. Herm. 13.

The gnosticizing *Vita Adae* says:

And Adam said to Seth: Listen, my son, I wish to tell you what I have heard and seen. After we were driven out of Paradise, your mother and I, there came to me, while we were praying, the archangel Michael, sent from God. I saw a chariot like the wind, with wheels of fire, and I was caught up into the Paradise of righteousness. And I saw the Lord sitting there. . . . Then I went thence, and Michael with me, and he brought me again to the place from which he had snatched me up. Listen, my son Seth, to still other secrets of the future which were revealed to me, which I, when I ate of the tree of knowledge, came to know and comprehend, which will happen in this age.[208]

In the "Apocryphon of John" Jesus also appears as "mystical emissary" after his ascension:

I turned away from the sanctuary to the mountain, to a lonely place, and with great sorrow in my heart I thought: How then was the redeemer appointed and why. . . . As soon as I had thought this, the heavens were opened, . . . I was afraid and fell down. And lo! there appeared to me a child. . . . He said to me, . . . I am the one who is always with you. . . . Now I have come in order to reveal to you what is, what has happened, and what is to happen.[209]

[205] Corp. Herm. 1.1-4.
[206] Herm. Vis. I, 1.3-4; cf. Vis. V.
[207] See in Reitzenstein, *op. cit.*, pp. 312-13.
[208] Vita Adae 25; 29 (Kautzsch, p. 516).
[209] See Hennecke-Schneemelcher-Wilson, *New Testament Apocrypha,* I, 321-22.

In the sixth book of the Right *Ginza*—according to Lidzbarski an ancient fragment—there comes an Uthra Din-Mlikh, in order to take the "wise scribe" Dinanukht from his books and out of his body. He carries Dinanukht past the guardhouses of the evil ones to the threshold of the world of light. There Dinanukht says:

I saw death, I saw life. I saw the darkness, I saw the light. I saw falsehood, I saw the truth. I saw destruction, I saw building-up. I saw the blow, I saw the healing. I saw this exalted man, who is older and was there earlier than the builder of heaven and earth.[210]

He is then sent back to the earth by the Uthra in order to proclaim what he has seen.

Often cited is the Asc. Jes. 7:2-9:

I saw a lofty angel, and he was not like the splendor of the angels which I was otherwise accustomed to seeing, but he possessed great splendor and honor, so that I cannot describe the splendor of this angel. And when he had taken me by the hand, I ascended; and I said to him: Who are you, and what is your name, and where are you leading me? For the power had been given to me to converse with him. And he said to me: When I have led you upwards by degrees and have shown you the face to which I have been sent, then you will recognize who I am; but my name you will not learn, for you must return once again to this your body. But you will see the place to which I am bearing you upward; for I have been sent for this purpose. And I rejoiced that he conversed with me in friendly fashion. And he said to me: Do you rejoice because I converse with you in friendly fashion? And he said further: But you will see one who is greater than I, how he will talk with you in a friendly and gentle way; and you will even see his father, who is greater; for to this purpose I have been sent from the seventh heaven, in order to bring light to you in all this. And we ascended to the firmament.[211]

The Gnosticism of this fragment speaks most clearly out of the body-soul dualism which is presupposed for this writing.

The (in part strongly gnosticizing) parallels from primitive Christian and especially from late Jewish literature are innumerable, both those in which the heavenly messenger only visits the earthly recipient of the revelation[212]:

When I had spoken these words, the angel was sent to me who already in the night just past had come to me. He said to me: Listen to me, and I will teach you; pay attention to my word, and I will speak further with you,[213]

---

[210] Lidzbarski, *Ginza*, p. 210.27-31.

[211] See Hennecke-Schneemelcher-Wilson, *New Testament Apocrypha*, II, 652-53.

[212] Luke 1:26 ff.; Rev. 1:1 ff.; IV Ezra 4:1 ff., 52; 6:33; 7:1 ff.; 8:62; 10:29 ff.; Eth. En. 65.5 ff.; Riessler, pp. 514 ff.

[213] IV Ezra 5:31 ff.

and those in which the messenger helps the recipient on the heavenly journey[214]:

> Then comes to me the angel
> Whom he had sent to me
>
> . . .
>
> and says:
> Abraham, stand up!
> Friend of God, who is fond of you!
> No longer let yourself be gripped by human anxiety!
> I am sent to you, in order to strengthen you.
>
> . . .
>
> Then we ascended as if upon many winds,
> To Heaven, which was established yonder above the firmament.[215]

Then follows the vision of God.

f) The variety of figures in which the heavenly envoy can appear shows that only the being sent as such, i.e., the redemption itself, is of significance, and not the specific "how" of the embassy. In view of this it is not surprising that the account of the sending of the emissary occurs also in the form of a fable. The "Hymn of the Pearl" in the Acts of Thomas is the best known and finest documentation of this.[216] The third of the Manichaean Psalms of Thomas shows similar fable motifs:

> The ship, whose bow is the brilliance of light:
> The strands of light are upon it.
> Its sailors are in the ray,
> Its crew is clothed with the brilliance of light,
> They who have brought the treasure of the mighty one, which is on
>   the ship;
> It is great beyond measure or counting.
> It is loaded with the wealth of the living ones,
> Which never can be counted.
> I have not been able to establish where the son of the evil one caught
>   sight of it;
> He hired plunderers and sent them forth.
> The plunderers overran the ship,
> They captured it in the middle of the sea.

---

[214] Ezek. 8:3; Rev. 17:1 ff.; Riessler, pp. 40 ff.; 126 ff.; 156-57; 168 ff.; 234 ff.; 452 ff.; 1097 ff.; 1142 ff.

[215] Apoc. Abr. 10.5-8 (Riessler, p. 21); 15.5 (*ibid.*, p. 25).

[216] Most recently in A. Adam, *Die Psalmen des Thomas*, pp. 48 ff. In the form of legend the redemption drama also appears in the story of Barlaam and Josaphat. Barlaam as redeemer enters into the palace in disguise, in order to redeem the prince Josaphat. He succeeds in doing this. (The text is in the translation of L. Burchard in the Theatiner-Verlag, Munich, n.d., esp. pp. 116-17.) The Acts of Thomas also, e.g., are filled with many such legendary motifs.

. . .

But then the news came to the mighty one,
That a stormy wave had reached his ship;
That his sailors were wounded,
The ones entrusted with his treasure were in danger.
He called a messenger,
A part of life, namely reason;
He called a messenger,
Sent him to the ship:
Go to the place where the storm has seized the ship;
Take the ship and bring it here.

. . .

Then the Son of light and of the riches
Immediately armed and girded himself;
He armed himself and girded his loins,
Sprang forth and came to the ship.
He healed the sailors,
Helped his believing ones.

. . .

He fortified the ship and gave it a guard-rail,
He took it as a gift upward to the mighty one.
He took it as a gift upward to the mighty one,
Brought it upward into the land of light.
The ship sprouted palm branches;
Its sailors came to their home.[217]

Here any possibility of concretely picturing the actual process of redemption is lacking. But Gnosticism can dispense with that. For it, the sending of the redeeming emissary is always an act in the past, which has its significance only in the fact that the Gnosis at one time sent is handed down to the present.

In all the foregoing texts I have refrained from stressing especially the term "apostle," which repeatedly occurs. For this much is clear: Whatever particular form of the heavenly messenger one may take, none of them comes into consideration as the direct prototype of the church's apostolate. To be sure it is evident that each of these apostles has a prominent eschatological significance and to this extent—in contrast with the Jewish *Schaliach*—suggests a prototype of the church's apostle. But the church's apostle does not bear the marks of a *heavenly* emissary, not even by way of a hint, even if he appears with absolute heavenly authority. Only an earthly figure can be the prototype of the church's apostle, a figure which indeed *as such*—formally, at any rate—must possess

[217] Ps. 3.1-6, 16-20, 29-31, 37-39 = A. Adam, pp. 6 ff.

the same eschatological significance and heavenly authority as belongs to the heavenly emissary.[218]

We will soon become acquainted with such a figure, when we turn now to the other chief type of the Gnostic redeemer which we have already basically characterized: the earthly envoy who gains redemption in heaven; for, to repeat,

No one of the heavenly gods will come to the earth, since he would be leaving the region of heaven; but the man ascends to heaven and surveys it and knows what its height is, and what its depth, and comes to know all the rest precisely and—what is the greatest of all—he comes into the heights without leaving the earth! Of such greatness is his ecstasy.[219]

3. The messenger of this type is himself a man and a recipient of the Gnosis; he is a messenger when he receives the Gnosis with the commission to pass it on to other men.

a) First of all we must explore the texts cited to discover who of the recipients of revelation receives the Gnosis from the current heavenly emissary not for his "personal needs" but rather in order to pass it on to other men. We begin with Poimandres as a most impressive example. Poimandres communicates to the mystic all the mysteries, and climaxes the transmission of the Gnosis with the words:

This is the good aim of those who have achieved the Gnosis, to be deified.

Then Poimandres continues:

What further do you wish? When you have assimilated all this, should you not be a guide to those who are worthy, so that the human race may *be saved* by God *through you?* While he said this to me, Poimandres communicated to me the powers. But I thanked and praised the Father of the Universe and was sent forth by him, equipped with powers and instructed concerning the nature of all things and concerning the great vision; and I began to teach men the beauty of piety and of the Gnosis: O people, earth-born men, you who have surrendered yourselves to drunk-

---

[218] In order to avoid misunderstanding, it should be stated here that I regard the above-portrayed individual formulations of the celestial emissary throughout as *pre-Christian*. An exception is provided only by the special figure of the "historical emissary," which appears to me, for the reasons given, to be originally Christian. Only when one overlooks the difference in the Gnostic conception of the apostle and assumes that one may describe only the "historical emissary" in the specific sense as redeemer can one reach the conclusion that there was not a redeemer in pre-Christian Gnosis. Thus most recently J. Jervell in *Imago Dei*, FRLANT NF, LVIII, e.g., pp. 134, 137, 145, 147, 211, where he inadmissibly enlarges the correct insight that Gnosis did not require a redeemer figure.

[219] Corp. Herm. 10.25.

enness and sleep and ignorance of God, be sober, end your drunkenness, you who are shackled by insensate sleep.[220]

This, then, is the manner in which the *mystic* speaks, who in the following is identified with Poimandres[221] and to whom "all power is given."[222] He himself is the actual redeemer[223] and emissary.[224]

In the same manner, in the Baruch Gnosticism of Justin, Jesus is the emissary, for Baruch speaks to him, the earthly son of Joseph and Mary:

Proclaim this word to men and communicate to them the message concerning the Father and concerning the Good.[225]

Jesus promises to do it and goes forth and preaches. In contrast to his predecessors, Moses, the prophets, and Heracles, he does not allow himself to be led astray out of Eden.

Mani himself had understood himself to be an apostle in this sense, even though later on he was honored as a "historical emissary." We note once again his autobiographical (?) portrayal of his call:

In that certain year of the reign of Ardaschir the "living Paraclete" came down to me and spoke to me. He revealed to me the hidden mystery which was concealed from the worlds and the generations . . . . He taught me the mystery of the tree of knowledge from which Adam ate, whereby his eyes were opened, the mystery of the apostles who are sent into the world.[226]

In the same sense—not as the explanation of a "historical emissary" —the following sentence from Mani's Saburakan is to be understood:

Then this present revelation descended and this present prophecy resulted in the present and most recent age through me, Mani, the apostle of the true God, in the land of Babel.[227]

---

[220] *Ibid.*, 1.26-27.

[221] *Ibid.*, 1.30.

[222] *Ibid.*, 1.32.

[223] The *Shepherd of Hermas* is also suggested here as a parallel. In Vis. V, 5, e.g., the revealer explains: ἀπεστάλην γάρ, φησίν, ἵνα ἃ εἶδες πρότερον πάντα σοι πάλιν δείξω, αὐτὰ τὰ κεφάλαια τὰ ὄντα ἡμῖν σύμφορα. Then Hermas writes down the commandments and parables of the Shepherd and begins to proclaim: "If now you hear them and keep them and walk in them and do them with a pure heart, then you will receive from the Lord what he has promised to you . . ." (Vis. V, 7).

[224] Cf. H. Becker, *op. cit.*, p. 20; U. Wilckens, *Weisheit und Torheit*, p. 59, who is struck by the affinity of this process of redemption with the New Testament understanding of the apostle.

[225] Hipp. 5.26.

[226] Schmidt-Polotsky, *Ein Mani-Fund in Ägypten*, SAB (1933), Heft 1, pp. 53-54.

[227] Preserved in Al-Biruni's chronology; cited following G. P. Wetter, *op. cit.*, p. 16; cf. G. Widengren [2], p. 59.

As apostle of the "living Paraclete," who is identical with the primal revealer Light Jesus, Mani is able to call himself, in his letters, "apostle of Jesus Christ"; for the most part he is called "apostle of God." [228]

Here one should also refer to the primeval figures already considered, Adam, Seth, Norea, Methusaleh, Melchizedek, and others, who in fact are occasionally sent to posterity with the message received from the heavenly emissary, and to this extent as emissaries themselves were participants in the work of redemption[229]:

Then the fellowship (with the Life) was shared with the spirits and souls of the men of proved righteousness, those who themselves were understanding and who produced understanding among those who dwell in this world, which is full of disappointment and illusion. Adam, who had instructed and warned Hibil, said: Hail to the one who stands firm in this warning of Hibil, Sitil, and Anos.[230]

The Gnostic, who has received Gnosis from the heavenly emissary, himself becomes an emissary, who has Gnosis to communicate.

In the Mandaean writings, in supposedly late fragments,[231] appears John the Baptist. He is not a heavenly figure:

Further, there was born in that age a child, whose name was called Johana, the son of the aged father Zakhria.[232]

Up to his twenty-second year he is instructed upon the mountain Parwan by Anos-Uthra,[233] and receives direction by heavenly epistles.[234] For forty-two years, then, he baptizes in the Jordan, until Manda d'Hayya takes him out of his body.[235]

According to chap. 12 of the Book of John of the Mandaeans, the "Good Shepherd" receives from *without* the call of an Uthra, and therewith the commission to become a redeemer-shepherd. Apparently he had been living in the world below from primal beginnings on, and there was awakened by the call of the heavenly emissary and thus himself became an emissary.

Dinanukht,[236] after his heavenly journey, receives from the "mystical messenger" Din-Mlikh the commission:

---

[228] G. P. Wetter, *op. cit.*, p. 15; E. Rose, *op. cit.*, pp. 30 ff.
[229] See pp. 127 ff.
[230] Lidzbarski, *Ginza*, p. 246.16-21.
[231] Cf. now K. Rudolph, *op. cit.*, pp. 66 ff.
[232] Lidzbarski, *Ginza*, p. 51.5-6.
[233] Lidzbarski, *Johannesbuch*, chaps. 18-33.
[234] *Ibid.*, pp. 95.7 ff.; 107.24 ff.; 110.13 ff.
[235] Lidzbarski, *Ginza*, pp. 190 ff.
[236] On this interesting figure, cf. G. Widengren [2], pp. 62 ff.

Go into the world of the evil ones, to the place which exists completely outside the royal realm. Go, burn your books in the fire and sink your book of memory in the water. Go into the world, utter the call of life and instruct disciples for sixty years and sixty months. [237]

After initial resistance he lets himself be sent and burns his books:

He went forth to this world, uttered the call of life and instructed disciples for sixty years, sixty months, and sixty days.[238]

Of a Mana, to whom his "helper" brings the Gnosis, it is said:

When the Mana heard this,
He no longer brooded in evil
And he made the plans of the perishable come to nought.
He called with a loud voice
And begot the luminous offspring.[239]

He is bearer and bringer of Gnosis:

Illumine and enlighten, Mana.[240]

In this connection we should refer especially to the disciples of Jesus in the Gnostic and gnosticizing Gospels:

As the Father has sent me, so send I you.[241]

But now (John), lift up your face and come, hear and receive what I will say to you today, so that you in turn may proclaim it to those who are like-minded with you, who are of the kind that do not waver, of the perfect man, and to those who are in a position to grasp it.[242]

The Pist. Soph. describes the relationship of the heavenly Jesus to his earthly disciples in the following words of Jesus to his apostles:

Now rejoice and be jubilant, for when I set out for the world, I brought along with me, from the first, twelve powers, as I said to you from the first, which I had taken from the twelve redeemers of the light-treasure according to the commandment of the first mystery. These now I thrust into the womb of your mother. . . .

[237] Lidzbarski, *Ginza*, p. 211.3-7.
[238] *Ibid.*, p. 212.2-4.
[239] *Ibid.*, p. 460.15-19.
[240] *Ibid.*, p. 455.23.
[241] John 20:21; cf. 17:18.
[242] Apocryphon of John; see Hennecke-Schneemelcher-Wilson, I, 322; cf. pp. 336-37; 343-44.

For these powers were given to you ahead of the whole world, because you are the ones who will save the whole world.[243]

Rejoice now and be jubilant, for you are favored above all men who are upon the earth, because you are the ones who will save the whole world.[244]

It is God himself who as redeemer has opened the mouth of the singer of the beautiful Ode Sol. 10, so that he becomes God's envoy:

> Through his word the Lord has controlled my mouth,
> And by his light he has opened my heart.
> And in me he has caused to dwell his imperishable life
> And has given to me to speak of the fruit of his salvation,
> To convert the souls of those who wish to come to him,
> And to lead captive noble captives to freedom.
> I have become strong and powerful and have taken the world captive;
> And this happened to me to the praise of the Most High and of God my Father.
> And the peoples who were scattered have been gathered togther,
> And I was not stained by sins of my own commission.
> Because they have adhered to me in the heights,
> The traces of light have been placed upon their hearts,
> And they have entered into my life and have been redeemed,
> And they have become my people for all eternity. Hallelujah![245]

Compare Ode Sol. 12, in which the *Word* is praised:

> And the Most High gave it to his worlds,
> To the interpreters of his beauty
> And to proclaimers of his splendor
> And to preachers of his plan
> And to envoys of his thought
> And to teachers of his works.[246]

Most impressive is Ode Sol. 17. First of all the later emissary portrays how he himself was redeemed by God:

> But I have been crowned by my God,
> And my crown is a living one.
> I have been justified by my Lord,
> But my redemption is imperishable.
> I have been freed from idleness

---

[243] Pist. Soph. 7 = Schmidt-Till, p. 7.1 ff.
[244] Pist. Soph. 8 = Schmidt-Till, p. 9.35 ff.; cf. 46 = 53.1 ff.; 96 = 148; 110 = 181.12 ff.
[245] Od. Sol. 10.1-6.
[246] Od. Sol. 12.4; cf. 12.1-3.

> And I am not condemned.
> My fetters have been broken by him,
> I have received the face and figure of a new person
> And I changed into it and was redeemed.

Everyone is astounded at him:

> And all who saw me were amazed,
> And I appeared to them as a stranger.

But God

> exalted to the height of truth my powers of knowledge.

Then the redeemed one himself becomes a redeemer:

> And from that time on he opened to me the way of his steps,
> And I opened the doors which were closed,
> And I smote the iron bars.
> But my own iron began to glow and melted before me.
> And nothing proved to be closed to me,
> Because I had become the one who opens all things.
> And I went to all those who were mine, who were locked up, to free them,
> So that I should leave no one bound or binding.
> And I gave my knowledge without grudging
> And my intercession full of love.
> And I sowed in the hearts my fruits
> And transformed them through me.
> And they received my blessing and became alive,
> And they gathered themselves together to me and were redeemed.
> For they have become members of me, and I their head.[247]

As David Friedrich Strauss[248] recognized and E. Norden[249] has called to attention again, the same soteriological system lies in the background of Jes. Sir. 51. The praying one sought the saving wisdom:

> While I was still young, before I wandered in an alien realm,
> I honestly sought for wisdom.
> In my prayer I begged for it
> And to the end I will seek it out.

Through God's help he found it:

> It blossomed like a ripening grape;
> Then my heart rejoiced over it.

[247] Cf. further Od. Sol. 22; on this, see G. Bornkamm, *op. cit.*, pp. 31-32.
[248] ZwTh, VI (1863), 92.
[249] [2], pp. 280 ff.

> My foot trod on a level path;
> From my youth onward I followed its traces. . . .
> My inward self was stirred to seek after it;
> Therefore I have taken possession of it as a worthy possession.

Then the one thus redeemed himself becomes a redeemer:

> Abide with me, you untutored ones,
> And tarry in the house of tutoring!
> How long yet will you remain in want of it,
> And your souls heartily thirst after it?
> I opened my mouth and spoke with it:
> Get for yourselves wisdom, which is obtainable without money!
> Bow your necks beneath its yoke,
> And let your soul accept instruction!
> It is near to the one who desires to have it,
> And whoever yields himself to it will find it.[250]

Perhaps here one may allude to the *original* meaning of Matt. 11:27-28 [251]:

Everything has been given to me by Father, and no man knows the Son except the Father, and no man knows the Father except the Son and those to whom the Son wills to reveal him. Come to me, all. . . .

To be sure, in this "Johannine" passage the preexistence of the Son could already be presupposed, and in the source of Matthew he could have already been the one heavenly emissary.

As a Jewish counterpart [252] to this form of the earthly envoy, Moses may be compared as an example:

> Or what did it hurt Moses,
> That he lived only 120 years?

---

[250] 51.13 ff., 21, 23-26.

[251] Cf. E. Norden [2], pp. 292-93.

[252] Here one naturally can refer to the whole of the prophetic self-consciousness, particularly to specifically soteriological prophecy, e.g., in Deutero-Isaiah: πνεῦμα κυρίου ἐπ' ἐμέ, οὗ εἵνεκεν ἔχρισέν με· εὐαγγελίσασθαι πτωχοῖς ἀπέσταλκέν με (Isa. 61:1). Hence Origen, among others, can also give to individual prophets the title of apostle (cf. G. Widengren [3], p. 76). Approximately in the middle between this Old Testament conception and the specifically Gnostic usage of the same schema stands the figure (of the Teacher of Righteousness?) who speaks in the hymns of Qumran: "Thou hast made me . . . a foundation of truth and understanding for those whose way is straight; . . . thou has made me a banner for the elect of righteousness and an interpreter of (perfect) knowledge of the marvellous mysteries, to examine men as to the truth . . ." (I QH II 9-10; 13-14; cf. Dupont-Sommer, *Die essenischen Schriften vom Toten Meer* (1960), pp. 223-24; cf. *ibid.*, pp. 390-ff.).

For this reason
Because he was subject to his creator,
He brought to the sons of Jacob the law,
Kindled a light for the tribe of Israel.[253]

Between Judaism and Gnosticism stands Philo.[254] For him there served as recipients of the divine revelation the tribal fathers and especially Moses,[255] the great revealer, who, instructed by the Logos, were to lead men from ἄγνοια to ἐπιστήμη.[256]

Mohammed also may be named as an example of such a type of redeemer.[257]

The examples cited hitherto are related to such earthly emissaries as were sent forth by a heavenly emissary or from God himself. In this doubling of the emissaries the decisive role is played always by the heavenly apostle, who first sets in motion the activity of the earthly apostle.

b) In the following examples the activity of the heavenly emissary is less prominent or is lacking. A single distinguished man himself brings the message from the heavenly world and passes it on. This type of the earthly emissary is best known to us from the Enoch literature.[258] I begin therefore with citations from the Enoch writings, even though in these writings, in spite of many gnosticizing traits,[259] we are not dealing with Gnostic literature:

I saw in my sleep what I now, with human tongue and with the breath of my mouth, will tell, which the Great One has bestowed on men, so that they should speak therewith and understand it with their hearts (En. 14:2).

The following manifestation appeared to me in the vision: Behold, clouds invited me in the vision, and a mist lifted me up; I was borne on the course of the stars and the lightning, and the winds gave me wings in the vision and lifted me up. They bore me up into heaven (En. 14:8-9).

---

[253] Apoc. Bar. (syr.) 17.4 = Riessler, p. 65; cf. IV Ezra 12:35 ff.; 14:18 ff.; further in W. Bousset, *Die Himmelsreise der Seele*, Nachdruck, WBG (1960), pp. 20-21.

[254] But cf. also, e.g., Test. Levi 2 ff.; G. Widengren [2], pp. 35-36.

[255] Cf. G. P. Wetter, *op. cit.*, pp. 34-35. In this connection Philo is acquainted with the verb ἀποστέλλειν as a *terminus technicus:* Migr. Abr. 22; cf. K. H. Rengstorf [1], pp. 399, 402-3; W. Staerk, *Soter*, II, 50 ff.

[256] Cf. Antonie Wlosok, *Laktanz und die philosophische Gnosis*, Diss. (Heidelberg, 1957 [typescript]), pp. 47 ff.

[257] Cf. the Ferman Sb 7240.4-5: οὐκ ἔστιν θεὸς εἰ μὴ ὁ θεὸς μόνος. Μααμετ ἀπόστολος θεοῦ.

[258] Insofar as Enoch appears as a celestial being, he does not concern us here. On Enoch, see esp. E. Sjöberg, *Der Menschensohn im äthiopischen Henochbuch* (Lund, 1946); E. Peterson, *Frühkirche, Judentum und Gnosis* (1959), p. 48; G. Widengren [2], pp. 36 ff.

[259] Cf. U. Wilckens, *Weisheit und Torheit*, pp. 190-97; M. Friedländer, *Die religiösen Bewegungen innerhalb des Judentums im Zeitalter Jesu* (1905), pp. 180 ff.

In those days a cloud and a whirlwind picked me up from the earth and set me down at the end of the heavens. Here I saw . . . (En. 39:3-4).

Thereafter I saw all the secrets of the heavens, how the (future) kingdom is divided. . . . There I saw. . . . There my eyes beheld . . . (En. 41:1-2, *et passim*).

In those days the angel Uriel answered me and said to me: Behold, I have shown to you, O Enoch, everything, and have unveiled everything to you, so that therewith you might see (En. 80:1).

The late, so-called Hebrew Book of Enoch reports:

Then said R. Jismael: As I went up into the heights, in order to be able to view the chariot-works, I went first through six palaces, room by room, and as I came to the gate of the seventh palace, I stood in prayer before the Lord, praised be he. . . . Then Metatron set me before the throne of the glory of God, in order to look upon the chariot-works.[260]

Enoch is sent with the knowledge he has received to men:

Hear, you fathers, and give heed, you who come after them, to the sacred words. It would be better to tell (them only) to the fathers; but we intend not to withhold the true wisdom even from those who come after them (En. 37:2-3).

My son Methuselah, preserve the books from your father's hand, and hand (them) on to the (coming) generations of the world. To you, to your son, and to your future sons I have handed over wisdom, in order that they may hand it on to their children (and) to the generations forever, this wisdom which goes beyond your thoughts (En. 82:1-2).

And now, my son Methuselah, call to me all your brothers and gather to me all the sons of your mother, for the Word calls me, and the spirit has been poured out upon me, to show you all that will befall you forever (En. 91:1).

And now, my son Methuselah, I have shown you all things, and the law of every star of the heavens has (now) been completely (portrayed) (En. 79:1).

One may compare further:

> The spirit of the Lord lifted me up
> And led me to the southern parts of the world.
> There I saw. . . .[261]

The book of the seer reproduces the revelation which was viewed.

---

[260] A. Jellinek, *Bet Ha-Midrasch,* V (1873), 170; following K. Schubert, *Die Religion des nachbiblischen Judentums* (1955), p. 90.

[261] Book of Elijah 1.4 = Riessler, p. 234; cf. further Test. Abr. 8 ff. = Riessler, pp. 1097-98; Test. Isaac 6 ff. = Riessler, pp. 1142 ff.; Test. Lev. 1 ff. = Riessler, pp. 1159 ff.

In the Slavonic Book of Enoch we read:

> Then the Lord called me
> And placed me on his left,
> Near to Gabriel.
> I prayed to the Lord.
> He said to me:
> Enoch! you have seen all things,
> The abiding and the transient
> And the things fulfilled through me;
> I show them to you before they receive form.
> Go down upon the earth
> and say to your sons
> Everything which I told you,
> And all that you have seen
> From the lowest heaven right up to my throne! [262]

Enoch does as he is commanded and is praised by men on account of his heavenly pilgrimage:

> For the Lord has chosen you
> And has made you the redeemer of our sins. [263]

From the Old Testament, we may refer only to Ezek. 1-2 [264]; from the New Testament, to Rev. 1:9 ff.; 4:1-2. [265]

This type of the earthly redeemer occurs hardly at all in actual Gnosticism, in which, interestingly enough, Enoch likewise plays no significant role. Strongly gnosticizing, however, is the portrayal of ecstasy in Test. Job 48-50:

> And so then the one who is called Hemera arose,
> And girded herself,
> Just as the Father said.
> And she received another heart,
> So that she thought no more at all upon earthly things.
> She spoke in the language of the angels
> And sent, in angelic fashion,
> A song upward to God.
> And these songs which she sang
> The Spirit had imprinted upon her cloak. [266]

---

[262] Slav. En. 24.1-2; 33.6b.

[263] Slav. En. 64.4. On Enoch, cf. further G. Widengren [3], pp. 141-42.

[264] Cf. G. Widengren [2], pp. 31 ff.

[265] According to texts of the Zoroastrian religion, Zarathustra also receives his apostolate in a visit with Ormuzd: "Zarathustra in the company of Vohu Manah departs in ecstacy to confer with Ahura Mazdah" (G. Widengren [1], p. 71).

[266] Test. Job 48 = Riessler, p. 1132.

In addition, I can only refer to Ode Sol. 36 (cf. Ode Sol. 38):

> I found rest with the spirit of the Lord,
> And he raised me up to the heights.
> And he set me upon my feet in the heights of the Lord
> Before his perfection and his splendor,
> While I praised (him) with the preparation of his songs.
> He (sc. the spirit) bore me before the face of the Lord;
> And while I was a man,
> I was called the shining one, the son of God,
> Because I was praised among those praised
> And was great among the Great Ones.
> For, as the greatness of the Most High is, so has he
>   made me,
> And, as his renewing is, he has renewed me.
> And he has anointed me with his perfection,
> And I became one of his close attendants.
> And my mouth was opened like a cloud that yields the dew,
> And my heart overflowed, an overflow of righteousness.
> And it was my being near in salvation,
> And I was firmly established in the spirit of lordship.
> Hallelujah!

But here, too, the spirit still plays a significant role as heavenly "mystical emissary."

Further we can refer to the first fragment of the twelfth book of the Right *Ginza,* a fragment which is unique in form:

I am the great Anos, the son of the great Sitil, the son of the great Adam, the son of the mighty king of splendor, the son of the place of light, the son of the leaves of all knowing. My feet brought me up to this place. I am sitting in the place of rich brilliance. I reflect and speak, I view and see this world, the heaven and the earth, the sun, the moon and the stars of the ascending and descending of the heaven, the light in which I stand, and the power in which they stand. By whose power do they stand there, by whose light do they shine? I opened my eyes and raised my brows, then I beheld and saw. . . .[267] When I beheld that being of light, my body shook and trembled, and my feet were unsteady. I dropped and fell prostrate before him. There stood an angel of light before him, who took me by the right side, pushed me before him and said to me: Come, great Anos, son of the great Sitil, the son of the great Adam, son of the mighty king of the house of splendor, son of the place of light, son of the leaves of all knowing, come; I wish to reveal to you concerning the great life.[268]

The absence of this type of redeemer in Gnosticism is not accidental. For the Gnostic it is quite conceivable that one or another of men should

---

[267] Lidzbarski, *Ginza,* p. 269.9-18.
[268] *Ibid.,* p. 270.4-11.

be commissioned by the heavenly emissary in a special way for the dissemination of the Gnosis and thus himself becomes an emissary. It is not conceivable, however, that one of the pneumatics should be *more* in a position than are the others to achieve the heavenly Gnosis in ecstatic rapture.[269] Whatever the one pneumatic is capable, by virtue of the inner Pneuma-Self, of achieving, the others are *in principle* capable of the same. Thus if in Gnosticism the type of earthly emissary appears at all as one who is this emissary on the basis of his ecstatic experience, then he can only appear in the form of a *number* of such ecstatic apostles. In this form, however—we call it the plural apostolate—the Gnostic apostle frequently appears. The proof of this which now follows will be held to more explicit references than was the case in the previously cited collections of texts; for we now encounter directly the prototype of the primitive Christian apostolate.

c) We have already concerned ourselves with Simon Magus, who appears in one stream of tradition as "historical emissary." In addition to this, there is in Hipp. 6.9 ff. a wholly different tradition. Hippolytus cites a writing ascribed to Simon, the μεγάλη ἀπόφασις. The Gnostic system contained in this writing is of a truly classical simplicity: The root of the universe is an eternal power, which can be described as fire. As the eternal root of all being it is called ἑστώς. Out of this power proceed matter and Pneuma, and in the mixing of these two substances the "Great Power" presently lives as στάς. Because of its pneumatic nature, however, the στάς carries in itself the power of returning to the light of the ἑστώς. In the realization of this possibility the στάς is at the same time the στησόμενος. Thus the root of the universe which loses itself in the world and finds itself again there is called ὁ ἑστώς, στάς, στησόμενος.[270] Thanks to the Gnosis which the μεγάλη ἀπόφασις communicates to him, the pneumatic, as a part of this one eternal power, as στάς, has the ability to conceive of himself as στησόμενος. What is presented thus in 6.9-17 in varying conceptuality appears finally in 6.18, the last chapter devoted by Hippolytus to the "Great Proclamation," under the use of the terms (important also for the Simon-Helena legend) *Nous* and *Epinoia*, as the

---

[269] Thus Enoch: "Up till now such wisdom was never bestowed by the Lord of the Spirits as I received according to my understanding and according to the good will of the Lord of the Spirits, from whom the lot of eternal life was allotted to me" (Eth. En. 37.4). This role of Enoch, fixed in late Judaism, as the ecstatic One κατ' ἐξοχήν made his figure unusable for Gnosticism.

[270] On this formula, see E. Haenchen, "Gab es eine vorchristliche Gnosis?" in ZThK, XLIX (1952), 316-49, esp. 330-31. According to Hipp. 6.17, the "Great Power" once stood in the heights as ἑστώς, is now found below as στάς, and will someday again stand above as στησόμενος.

159

designations of the heavenly and the earthly parts of the "Great Power."

This system of the "Great Proclamation" does not inquire into the problem which is so decisive for all later Gnosticism, as to how matter could have developed and how the eternal power could have been mixed with it. The "Great Proclamation" knows nothing at all of a genuine dualism. In this fact its system shows itself as belonging to the Jewish-Gnostic milieu. Further, the μεγάλη ἀπόφασις is lacking any redeemer figure, insofar as one means by this a heavenly emissary. Simon himself seems not to appear in the system, and he apparently serves only as the author of the revelation writing.

In Iren. I. 23 the system of the "Great Proclamation" is reworked. The development of the lower world is reflected upon, the capturing of the Ennoia is described, and Simon is introduced as the redeemer who comes from heaven. The Gnostic myth of the fall and redemption of the primal man or of the Dynamis appears in the legendary form of the story of Simon and Helena, as Justin (Apol. I. 26:1 ff.) knew it.

This legendarily historicized form of the myth is undoubtedly not original. However the development within Simonianism may have gone as to particulars, the system of the "Great Proclamation" is the oldest handed down under the name of Simon,[271] and is by no means (as, e.g., A. Hilgenfeld [272] thinks), "only a product of later Simonianism." The historicizing identification of Nous and Epinoia as Simon and Helena is just such a sign of advanced development as is the increasing speculation, to be observed in all the Gnostic systems, concerning the emergence of darkness and the fall of the light. It is further to be observed that the system of the "Great Proclamation" still shows no Christian influences. This speaks for its antiquity, since the reports about the Simonians refer to definite Christian influences, e.g., the figure of the historical redeemer.[273] Above all else, however, the system of the μεγάλη ἀπόφασις shows itself to be the original, even if its formulation in this writing should be late, in the fact that in it Simon does not appear as the redeemer. To be sure, E. Haenchen[274] thinks, "The historical figure of Simon has disappeared; now he is only the revealer of the Ἀπόφασις." But the order of things, that the one who is proclaimed becomes the proclaimer, would be without

[271] Cf. W. Schultz, *Dokumente der Gnosis* (1910), pp. 130 ff.

[272] *Die Ketzergeschichte des Urchristentums* (Leipzig, 1884), p. 181.

[273] See p. 137.

[274] ZThK, XLIX (1952), 349. I cannot agree with Haenchen's opinion that the system of the "Great Proclamation" presents a "philosophical Gnosis." Certain philosophical influences upon language and conception are still only one part of the environment of an unbroken myth which also occurs in similar form elsewhere in mythological Gnosis. Cf. also J. Jervell, *Imago Dei*, p. 132, n. 50, *et passim*.

parallel. In the case of Simon, as everywhere else, the reverse is to be assumed.[275]

To be sure, the distance from Simon as author of the *Apophasis* to him as the heavenly apostle of later Simonianism is not very great. According to the "Great Proclamation" every pneumatic participates in the ἑστώς, στάς, στησόμενος. This, in fact, the "root of the universe," has indeed entered into τὸν ἄνθρωπον τοῦτον τὸν ἐξ αἱμάτων γεγενημένον,[276] and now lives in the pneumatics: Ἐν δὲ τούτοις ἅπασιν ἐμμέμικται καὶ κέκραται, ὡς ἔφην, ἡ μεγάλη δύναμις ἡ ἀπέραντος, ὁ ἑστώς.[277] Naturally Simon also is a part of this "great power," and when he proclaims his Gnosis, he does it as the one who himself also is ὁ ἑστώς, στάς, στησόμενος. As such he is not distinguished from the other pneumatics, who all together are parts of the μεγάλη δύναμις, but this fact does not signify any depreciation of the self-evaluation of Simon. Together with all the other pneumatics he is the root of the universe, true Being, since indeed the ἑστώς like the στησόμενος are nothing other than the sum of the many parts of the στάς.

When Simon speaks, he speaks in the authority of the great power itself, which he is, in his own divine authority. Therefore he speaks only the language of the heavenly revealer: Ὑμῖν οὖν λέγω ἃ λέγω καὶ γράφω ἃ γράφω.[278] Thus speaks the one who as redeemer is his own authority. Expressions such as the following, ascribed to Simon, may then correspond to his own self-interpretation: τοὺς πιστεύοντάς μοι μακαρίους ποιήσω, εἰς δὲ τούτους τοὺς ἀρνησαμένους με τὴν ὀργήν μου ἐνδείξομαι (Mart. Petr. et Paul. 49 = Lipsius-Bonnet I, 160. 15 ff.); "ego sum filius stans in aeternum, et credentes mihi similiter stare in perpetuum faciam" (Ps. Cl. Rec. III, 47).

Now it is to be noted that already in the earliest report which we have of Simon, that of Acts 8:10, his title is ἡ μεγάλη δύναμις.[279] As we have seen, this title also appears in the "Great Proclamation" and is another designation for ὁ ἑστώς, στάς, στησόμενος. Thus later Simon is frequently called simply "The Standing One." [280] Other titles say the same thing:

[275] It is significant also that the very ancient Naassene sermon has as its basis the same redeemer-less system as the "Great Proclamation," even though the concepts vary. Thus what is called in the "Great Proclamation" ὁ ἑστώς, στάς, στησόμενος, e.g., is here (Hipp. 5, 7) called τὴν τῶν γεγονότων καὶ γινομένων καὶ ἐσομένων . . . φύσιν, ἥνπερ φησὶ τὴν ἐντὸς ἀνθρώπου βασίλειαν οὐρανῶν ζητουμένην.

[276] Hipp. 6. 9 = Wendland, 136.19-20.

[277] Hipp. 6. 13 = Wendland, 139.9 ff.

[278] Word-for-word quotation from the "Great Proclamation" in Hipp. 6. 18. Cf. with it John 3:11: ὃ οἴδαμεν λαλοῦμεν καὶ ὃ ἑωράκαμεν μαρτυροῦμεν (cf. 8:42 ff.).

[279] Cf. Ps.-Cl. Hom. II, 22; Orig. Cels. 5.62; 6.11; Hipp. 6. 19; Iren. I, 23.1; Epiph. Haer. 21.1.

[280] Ps.-Cl. Rec. III, 46-47; Hom. II, 22; Clem. Alex. Strom. II, 11.52; Mart. Petr. 2 = Lipsius-Bonnet I, 80.37.

God,[281] Son of God,[282] Christ,[283] Father, [284] Holy Spirit,[285] Lord.[286] Whether all these titles, or which of them, were self-designations of Simon can no longer be determined.[287] It is certain, however, that he made the claim to what is common to all these titles, namely, to be part of the "root of the universe."[288] Only, in order not to misunderstand Simon, one may not interpret these titles in the sense of the Gnostic or the Christian myth of the *one* emissary. In the original Simonian Gnosticism all these titles designate the "Great Power" which seeks and finds itself in the world[289] and thus redeems itself and leads upward[290]; and it is only natural that the "Great Proclamation" is not speaking of the particular descent of a redeemer. As redeemer, Simon has been upon the earth with the στάς and as a part of it for a long time. Naturally there are other parts of this power, and these other pneumatics can also be active as redeemers, just as Simon is. They certainly were in the circle around Simon, whom the later tradition, in representing him as a heavenly emissary, first made into the *one* redeemer, still without being able to erase the fact that he was one among many who appeared with the same claim.

Thus Justin begins his report on Simon with the words: "After the ascension of Christ the demons caused certain men to appear who made themselves to be gods."[291] Alongside Simon he mentions by name Menander,[292] who is said to have been a pupil of Simon. Another pupil or companion of Simon mentioned by name was Cleobius.[293] Hippolytus speaks

---

[281] Ps.-Cl. Hom. II, 22; Rec. II, 9; III, 63; Iren. I, 23; Just. Apol. I, 26.1; here on Matt. 24:5; Just. Dial. 120.

[282] Hipp. 6. 19; Iren. I, 23.1; Mart. Petr. et Paul. 15; Epiph. Haer. 21.1.

[283] Ps.-Cl. Hom. II, 22; Hipp. 6. 20; Ps.-Cl. Hom. XVI, 16; R. Eisler (*Jesus Basileus* . . . I, 133; II, 708) offers the conjecture that the disturbances which led to the expulsion of the Jews from Rome by Claudius and which, according to Suetonius (Vita Claudii 25), went back to the instigation of a certain Chrestus/Christus, had been instigated by Simon.

[284] Hipp. 6. 19; Epiph. Haer. 21.1.

[285] Hipp. 6. 19; Iren. I, 23.1.

[286] Hipp. 6. 20.

[287] Hippolytus (6. 19) thinks that Simon had himself called "by whatever name people wished to call him." This may be an accurate observation.

[288] Thus also E. Haenchen, ZThK, XLIX (1952), 348.

[289] Hipp. 6. 17.3-4.

[290] We should be glad to know whether the title "Christus," as it occurs for Simon and Dositheus (see below) was original. If so, this would be an indication that already in pre-Christian Jewish Gnosis "Christus" occurred as a title for the "primal man." That this was in fact the case will be shown later on.

[291] Apol. I, 26.1; cf. 56.1.

[292] Cf. Iren. I, 23.5.

[293] Hegesippus in Eus., CH IV, 22.5; Ap. Const. VI, 8; 16; Apocryphal Epistle of the Corinthians to Paul, vs. 2; cf. A. Hilgenfeld, *op. cit.*, pp. 185-86, n. 270.

in general of pupils of Simon who "under another name venture similar things" (*6.7*; cf. *6.19-20*). Again, Simon himself appears as pupil of Dositheus.[294] Along with Simon, Hippolytus introduces the Libyan Apsethos, who allegedly had sent out parrots which could say "Apsethos is God." [295] In Ep. Ap. 1, Simon and Cerinthus appear as a pair of false teachers.

It is clear that all these figures alongside Simon made the same claims as did he.[296] Cf. further Ps. Tert. Haer. 1-2: "quomodo se Simon dixerat, hoc se Menander esse dicebat." [297] "And after the times of Jesus also the Samaritan Dositheus wished to persuade the Samaritans that he was the Christ who had been promised by Moses." [298]

If Simon, according to his self-interpretation, had been the *one* emissary, then his "teachers" and "pupils" must have competed with him in such a fashion that the claim of the one excluded the claim of the other. The opposite is actually the case, as all the passages cited show. Even according to his self-interpretation Simon shared with many others the claim to be the "great power." Every pneumatic could appear basically in the same way and could gather himself up in all parts of the στάς to form the στησόμενος, and thus redeem himself.

Since Simon and the movement which is connected with him are, according to all extant accounts, native to the Samaritan region, we may here refer also to John 8:48, where the Jews bring up against Jesus the charge: Σαμαρίτης εἶ σύ. This charge follows (according to Bultmann's reconstruction of the text) the words of Jesus in John 7:28-29: κἀμὲ οἴδατε καὶ οἴδατε πόθεν εἰμί· καὶ ἀπ' ἐμαυτοῦ οὐκ ἐλήλυθα, ἀλλ' ἔστιν ἀληθινὸς ὁ πέμψας με, ὃν ὑμεῖς οὐκ οἴδατε· ἐγὼ οἶδα αὐτόν, ὅτι παρ' αὐτοῦ εἰμι κἀκεῖνός με ἀπέστειλεν. Thus such a claim was nothing extraordinary among the Samaritans.[299] People regarded Jesus also as one of the *many* Samaritans who spoke thus. The Jesus of John's Gospel naturally wishes to be the *one* emissary, but the Samaritans would have none of that, as precisely the polemic of John shows (*vide* p. 190).

We should like to know in what way these redeemers, according to their own declaration, wish us to understand that they came to the knowledge

---

[294] Ap. Const. VI, 8; Ps.-Cl. Hom. II, 24; G. Widengren [2], pp. 48 ff.

[295] Hipp. 6. 7-8.

[296] "In any case we have to do with . . . savior figures who, with the exclusion of other authorities, represent their person and their doctrine as obligatory for the believers" (E. Fascher, *Prophetes*, p. 193).

[297] Cf. Philaster Haer. 30; Epiph. Haer. 22.1; Eus., CH III, 26.1.

[298] Orig. Cels. I, 57 = Koetschau I, 108.25; cf. VI, 11 = II, 81.17.

[299] Cf. E. Norden [2], pp. 189-90. In the context of the present text of the Gospel, the charge of the Jews follows a speech of Jesus which to Jewish ears could identify him as a redeemer in the sense of Simon.

of the Gnosis transmitted by them. Has it remained in their memory from the heavenly world, to which they once belonged as ἑστώς? We learn of almost all these figures that they are supposed to have been active as *magicians*. It is well known that Simon bore the fixed surname "Magus." [300] "His pupils now μαγείας ἐπιτελοῦσι καὶ ἐπαοιδάς." [301] Menander also "ad summum magiae pervenit." [302] We will encounter in other Gnostics of this sort such a characteristic, which will make it plain that the many-sided concept "magician" is simply a derogatory designation for the ecstatic. [303] Even among the Simonians the label "magician" may have referred above all else to the fact that as Gnostics they were entrusted with the technique of ecstasy. Then however it will have been preeminently the ecstasy and the possibility of the "heavenly journey" [304] which is bound up with it, to which all these Gnostic preachers around Simon, and he himself, owed not only the Gnosis of all Being, but also the capability of demonstrating such Gnosis *ad oculos* of their hearers. [305] For the ecstasy signifies nothing other than the fact that the soul, the νοῦς, the ἔσω ἄνθρωπος, or whatever the Pneuma-Self is called, temporarily leaves the body. The totality of the Pneuma-Self however is that figure which Simon calls the "Great Power" and which in the study of Gnosticism appears generally as primal man; and the ecstatic "magic" shows in fact the power of the Pneuma, which *vincat angelos, qui mundum fecerunt* (Iren. I, 23. 4).

Certainly not all pneumatics have appeared in a missionary role, as did Simon and his companions, even when they, as disciples of the afore-named, in like manner participated in the "Great Power" which has been mixed with the material world. The missionary élan and impetus of an individual among these Gnostics, however, cannot have rested upon an eminent *being*. It is only the expression of a function which, as one may suppose, will have stood in connection with a special gift for the ecstatic technique, which in the nature of things was not suited to every Gnostic in equal measure, but was nevertheless significant for the success of the mission.

In this connection it is interesting, and for our purposes important,

---

[300] Hipp. 6. 7, 19; Acts 8:9; Iren. I, 23.1; cf. Ps.-Cl. Hom. II, 22.3.

[301] Hipp. 6. 20.

[302] Iren. I, 23.5; cf. Just. Apol. I, 26.2, 4; 56:1; Eus., CH III, 26.1 ff.

[303] Cf. H. Lietzmann, "Gnosis und Magie," in *Kleine Schriften* I, TU, LXVII, 84 ff.

[304] The ability to do this is explicitly ascribed to Simon in Mart. Petr. 2 = Lipsius-Bonnet, I, 80.35; Mart. Petr. et Paul. 30 = 144.8 ff.; cf. 162.2; 164.10; 209.14 ff. Cf. also Ps.-Cl. Rec. II, 61-62.

[305] "Simon dixit: Audi, Caesar Nero, ut scias istos falsos esse et me de caelis missum: crastina die ad caelos vadam . . ." (Mart. Petr. et Paul. 49 = Lipsius-Bonnet, I, 160.13 ff.).

that occasionally among these people the term ἀπόστολος also appears.[306] In Eus., CH III, 26. 1, Menander is called ὁ σωτὴρ ἄνωθεν ἀπεσταλμένος.[307] According to Apost. Const. VI, 8, the devil has undertaken ἀποστεῖλαι ὀπίσω ἡμῶν (the true apostles) ψευδαποστόλους εἰς βεβήλωσιν τοῦ λόγου; Cleobius and Simon are named as such false apostles specifically and as pupils of Dositheus. In Ep. Ap. 1, Simon and Cerinthus are presented as "lying apostles." In a fragment from the dialogue of Gaius (ca. 200) with Proclus, preserved by Eusebius (CH III, 28. 2), it is said of Cerinthus alone: "Cerinthus gives us false reports of miracles in the form of ἀποκαλύψεις, as if they were written by a great ἀπόστολος, reports which allegedly have been given to him by angels." In any case, this passage makes it possible for us to see how one has to represent the reception of Gnosis through the many apostles. But perhaps one may also further conclude from it that Cerinthus also, who probably is rightly placed in actual connection with Simon, claimed the title of apostle. Here we must refer in particular to Ps. Cl. Hom. XI, 35. While Peter is giving a warning about the Gnostic Simon, he explains: ὁ ἀποστείλας ἡμᾶς κύριος ἡμῶν καὶ προφήτης ὑφηγήσατο ἡμῖν ὡς ὁ πονηρὸς . . . ἐκ τῶν αὐτοῦ ἐπηκόων ἐπηγγέλλετο πρὸς ἀπάτην ἀποστόλους πέμψαι· διὸ πρὸ πάντων μέμνησθε μηδένα δέχεσθαι ἀπόστολον ἢ διδάσκαλον ἢ προφήτην μὴ πρότερον . . . . This remark also, which does not stem from any traditional word of Jesus, presupposes the knowledge that Gnostics of Simon's kind gave themselves out to be apostles.[308]

We summarize: Simon Magus appeared with the claim to be a manifestation of the "Great Power" which had been mixed with matter, but

---

[306] On the relation of the titles ἀπόστολος and ἑστώς, cf. G. Widengren [3], p. 79; [2], pp. 49 ff.

[307] The ἄνωθεν is an *interpretamentum* of Eusebius; cf. Iren. I, 23. 5: ". . . qui missus sit ab invisibilibus, salvatorem pro salute hominum." The frequency of this claim also comes from the fact that such a manner of speaking had also penetrated Roman antiquity; cf. E. Norden, *Die Geburt des Kindes*, pp. 48 ff. On Menander, see further G. Widengren [3], pp. 63-64; [2], p. 49.

[308] It is of course certain that behind the Simon of the "Kerygmata Petrou," which are the basis of the Pseudo-Clementine writings, the apostle Paul is concealed (see G. Strecker, *Das Judenchristentum in den Pseudoclementinen*, TU, LXX (1958), 187 ff.). Was the polemic originally directed only against Paul and did the author of the basic writing only insert Simon into the anti-Pauline parts of the "Kerygmata Petrou" (thus G. Strecker, *op. cit.*, p. 154, n. 1; pp. 187 ff.)? Then it would still be strange that the anti-Pauline polemic appears so exactly tailored also to Simon, whom it fits in fact just as well as it does Paul (rejection of the law, appeal to "revelations," apostolic claim). Thus it may rather involve a polemic which from the first was tailored to Simon-Paul, which placed Paul on the side of the Gnostic arch-heretic and therefore envisioned Gnostic features in Pauline theology, above all his apostolic consciousness. But then this also means that the author of the "Kerygmata Petrou" has been struck by an essential affinity of the Gnostic and the Pauline concepts of the apostle.

now, in all the pneumatics, is being gathered out of the world to the στησόμενος. All pneumatics are participants in the same "Great Power," and are members of the κοινωνία τοῦ πνεύματος. Individuals among them, for whom the title "apostle" was apparently also used, perform in a special way the work of "gathering," in that they seek out the other pneumatics and inform them of their origin. This seeking and finding, as also the "being found," is essentially of an ecstatic nature. Only later was Simon honored by Gnosticism as redeemer κατ᾽ ἐξοχήν and as specially commissioned heavenly emissary. This is a quite natural development, which can be observed here and there in and outside Gnosticism.

For a long time already[309] it has been customary to compare the famous portrayal of the Gnostic prophet by Celsus with the apostle figures of the Simonian Gnosticism.[310] According to the allegations of Celsus, these preachers, appearing in ever-increasing numbers, used to bring their religious propaganda before the public eye with the following words: "᾽Εγὼ ὁ θεός εἰμι ἢ θεοῦ παῖς ἢ πνεῦμα θεῖον. ἥκω δέ. For the world is already about to collapse, and you, o men, will be lost because of your unrighteousness. But I will save you, and you will see me come again with heavenly might. Blessed is the one who honors me now! But upon all others I will send the eternal fire, upon cities and upon the country, and men who do not confess their sins will do penance in vain and will groan. But those who steadfastly obey me I will protect." After this speech they continued their proclamation with a demonstration, which according to the portrayal of Celsus can only have consisted in ecstatic speaking in tongues.

Here we find again all the essential characteristics of the redeemer type now under investigation.

The people call themselves God, Son of God, divine Pneuma. This is clearly a selection of titles patterned, probably by Celsus, after the Christian Trinity, which certainly could be enlarged by the names which one encounters among the Simonians. In addition, Celsus calls them prophets; their activity consists in προφητεύειν. This also is a fitting designation, which we will often meet among such people. In view of the close connection between the titles "prophet" and "apostle," [311] it may be supposed that they also bore or could have borne the latter designation. The divine predicates make it clear that these people appeared as redeemers,[312] a fact of which their speech itself leaves no doubt.

---

[309] Cf., e.g., G. P. Wetter, *op. cit.*, pp. 4 ff.
[310] Orig. Cels. VII, 8-9.
[311] See pp. 212-13.
[312] Cf. further Orig. Cels. I, 57; V, 62.

Further, it is clear that they appeared as such redeemers in great numbers without competing with one another: "There are many, he (Celsus) says, who, though they do not have the calling or the name, at every opportunity with great readiness prophesy in the temples or outside the temples. Some go into the cities, others to the armies, call the people together, and act as if they were inspired by God." [313] The one "god" allows the other "god" to make his divine claims. But this can only mean that these prophets all wish to appear as *part* of God or of the Pneuma which is imprisoned in the world and is liberating itself. Otherwise the manner of their appearing would not be understandable. The *one* heavenly emissary must speak in a quite different fashion, as for example John 10:7-8 shows.

How far the speech of these prophets actually reproduces their own words, or how far it has been assimilated by Celsus, for understandable polemical reasons, to the words of the biblical Christ, cannot be said. The *Gnostic* content of the speech, in any case, is that to the "hylics" the collapse of things is proclaimed,[314] and, on the other hand, that to the Gnostics the return to the heavenly home is promised, a return which the preacher likewise claims for himself.

The ecstasy which follows the speech ἐν νοῖ obviously is supposed to demonstrate to the hearers the truth of the Gnosis which has been recited; for the ἄγνωστα καὶ πάροιστρα καὶ πάντη ἄδηλα, ὧν τὸ μὲν γνῶμα οὐδεὶς ἂν ἔχων νοῦν εὑρεῖν δύναιτο is nothing other than the ἀγγελικὴ φωνή[315] of the Pneuma-God, who in the ecstasy is released from the fetters of the body. Perhaps it is in *this* sense that the preceding promise is to be understood: καὶ ὄψεσθέ με αὖθις μετ᾽ οὐρανίου δυνάμεως ἐπανιόντα = you will yet see me ascend with heavenly power. Whatever the pneumatic proclaims by way of Gnosis, it is the Gnosis of that which he ecstatically enacts. It is therefore clear that this pneumatic does not repeat the words of another redeemer, another emissary, another god, but is himself all this in his own authority.

Finally, we recall further that these prophets of Celsus appear in Phoenicia and Palestine, i.e., in the very same region in which Simon was at home and in which also Paul became a Christian and an apostle. Therefore it is not surprising that there are polemics against such people even in the Talmud: "When a man says: 'I am God,' he lies. 'I am the Son of man,' he will regret it. 'I ascend up to heaven,' he will not achieve it" (j Taan 65b).

[313] Orig. Cels. VII, 8.

[314] Cf. as the doctrine of the Valentinians, Iren. I, 7.1: when the Pneuma is saved, "the fire that is hidden in the world will break out, blaze up, destroy all matter, and at the same time along with it be extinguished and return to nothingness."

[315] See p. 157.

G. P. Wetter[316] has already seen that this passage is not specially directed against Jesus Christ.

From the Simonians and the prophets of Celsus we turn now to the Valentinians. They form a quite widely variegated school with many chief teachers, among whom, in addition to Valentinus himself, the most famous are Theodotus, Ptolemaeus, Secundus, Marcus, and Heracleon. The striking and, in Gnosticism, unusual fact, that Valentinus has many pupils, is not accidental but, as in the case of the Simonians, is grounded in the peculiarity of the portrayal of the redeemer, as we shall presently see.

In the reports of the church fathers, Jonas[317] counts no less than seven accounts of the development of the Pleroma which deserve to be called Valentinian even though in places they sharply diverge from one another. It may be that no one of these systems is Valentinus' own.

The explicitness of all these reports in portraying the events within and outside the Pleroma which lead to the emergence of matter and finally to the creation of man is matched by the sparseness of what is said about the event of redemption. It is, of course, clear just what redemption is: "The mere knowledge of the inexpressible Greatness is complete redemption. For while through ignorance both failure and passion developed, through Gnosis the whole set of circumstances emerging as a result of ignorance will be dissolved." [318] But one learns little about the "how" of this redemption, and the little which we do learn is varied and contradictory. "So many interpreters, so many redemptions," is Irenaeus' complaint (I, 21. 1) with respect to the Valentinian doctrine of redemption.

Now to be sure Christ and Jesus, as different figures—Hipp. 6. 36. 7 in fact enumerates three Christs of Valentinus—play a significant role in the different systems; not, however, in the redemption of man, but long before the creation of the world, in the development of the Pleroma. Thus the Valentinians had no place for Christ as the "historical redeemer." The third Christ of Valentinus according to Hippolytus is, of course, the Christian redeemer. His descent, however, is only incidentally mentioned, and there can be no question that the figure of the historical emissary Christ in the Valentinian systems is a purely external borrowed figure, in whom this system itself is indeed not at all interested. Bousset[319] writes: "We now see altogether clearly that the redeemer myth in the Valentinian system originally has nothing to do with the idea of the redemption by

---

[316] Op. cit., pp. 17, 85; cf. Die Gnosis in Korinth, pp. 47-48.
[317] Gnosis, I, p. 362.
[318] Iren. I, 21.4.
[319] Hauptprobleme, p. 269.

Jesus." This judgment is correct, even if Bousset's reconstruction of a primitive myth of the Valentinians, in which the marriage of Soter and Sophia is told as a foreshadowing of the fate of the believers, should prove untenable. According to Iren. I, 6. 1 Christ appears to have come to earth in order to save the "psychics" who belong to the church, not the pneumatics, who "in any case are saved." [320]

But if the figure of a heavenly redeemer is essentially alien to Valentinian Gnosticism, the question arises: Who then in this system actually sets the process of redemption in motion? The answer can only be: Valentinus and his pupils themselves.

Hippolytus (6. 42) reliably reports on a vision which Valentinus is supposed to have received, in which he had seen the *Logos* in the figure of a child, as he learned upon questioning the child. To the report of this vision Valentinus has attached a "tragic myth," and upon this rests the heresy which he began. This account creates the impression that visionary experiences or ecstatic heavenly journeys form the basis of the Valentinian Gnosis.[321] In Hipp. 6. 37 we have pictured another vision of Valentinus. Valentinus finds himself in the Pleroma and views from *above* the world, beginning with the realm of the pure spirit all the way down to matter.[322] Thus he gains the Gnosis for himself and proclaims it: He is the redeemer.

The so-called *Evangelium Veritatis* from the Coptic finds of Nag Hammadi concludes with the words: "The rest may know in their places that it is not fitting for me, having been in the place of rest, to say any more." The writing does indeed belong to a late Valentinianism, but its author also has gained his Gnosis from "above."

A very old [323] Valentinian writing, a part of which Epiphanius has preserved, begins: παρὰ φρονίμοις, παρὰ δὲ ψυχικοῖς, παρὰ δὲ σαρκικοῖς, παρὰ δὲ κοσμικοῖς, παρὰ δὲ τῷ Μεγέθει. νοῦς ἀκατάργητος τοῖς ἀκαταργήτοις χαίρειν. Ἀνονομάστων ἐγὼ καὶ ἀρρήτων καὶ ὑπερουρανίων μνείαν ποιοῦμαι μυστηρίων πρὸς ὑμᾶς, οὔτε ἀρχαῖς οὔτε ἐξουσίαις οὔτε ὑποταγεῖς οὔτε πάσῃ συγχύσει περινοηθῆναι δυναμένων, μόνῃ δὲ τῇ τοῦ Ἀτρέπτου Ἐννοίᾳ πεφανερωμένων. ὅτε . . . (Haer. 31. 5-6). Only the *redeemer* himself speaks thus, whether it be Valentinus or one of his pupils.

"Incorruptible mind greets the incorruptible ones"—the identity of the

---

[320] Iren. I, 6.2; cf. W. Foerster, "Die Grundzüge der ptolemäischen Gnosis," in NTS, VI (1959-60), p. 30.

[321] "The ultimate source of the Gnosis of Valentinus appears to have been a mystical vision" (H. Leisegang, *Die Gnosis* (4th ed., 1955), p. 282).

[322] *Ibid.*, p. 283.

[323] See K. Holl, *Epiphanius*, GCS, XXV, I, 390, n.; cf. A. J. Visser, "Der Lehrbrief der Valentinianer," *VigChr* (1958), pp. 27 ff.

redeemer with the redeemed ones and the being of all as *one* essence cannot be more clearly expressed. This *one* essence, however, can only be the fallen light-being which now is gathering itself together again, which in the fragment cited is called *Ennoia*—in Simon, *Epinoia* (Hipp. 6. 18).

If Valentinus' self-interpretation as just presented is rightly seen, it only logically follows that he does not stand alone in his claim. In fact we see him, like Simon, surrounded by "pupils," and these pupils of his imitate him: ὁ δὲ Μάρκος μιμούμενος τὸν διδάσκαλον καὶ αὐτὸς ἀναπλάσσει ὅραμα . . . (Hipp. 6. 42).[324] And the system of Marcus which is pictured in detail by Hippolytus, again without an explicit redeemer myth, goes back to an ἀποκάλυψις, according to Hipp. 6. 42,[325] which had never happened before Marcus to either a god or a man. Here, there does not appear an inadmissible competition between Marcus and Valentinus, for Valentinus intends as redeemer to awaken in the other person the sleeping Pneuma and thus to assist him to the ecstatic freeing of the self from the *sarx*. The redemption then has only achieved its goal when the personal identity of redeemer and redeemed is demonstrated in the practical accomplishment of ecstasy. This, again, gives to the one thus redeemed the possibility of serving himself as redeemer. The original redeemer is multiplied in the redeemed ones, and thus the entire person of the *Ennoia* is collected from its scattered location in many bodies and is brought again to the unity of the original heavenly figure.[326] That Christ can play no role as redeemer if Marcus receives the Gnosis immediately through an ἀποκάλυψις is obvious.

Even in the polemical distortion in which Irenaeus tells of this (I, 13. 3; cf. I, 15. 6),[327] we can see how Marcus also again leads his "hearers" into ecstasy. He says: "I will tell you of my grace, for the Father of the Universe ever beholds your angel before his face. But the place of your greatness is in me; therefore we must become *one*. First receive grace from me and through me. Prepare yourself as does a bride who awaits her bridegroom, so that you may become what I am, and I what you are. Let the seed of light be settled in your bridal chamber. Receive from me

[324] On Marcus, see E. Fascher, *Prophetes*, pp. 197-98; G. P. Wetter, *op. cit.*, pp. 8, 74 ff.

[325] Cf. 6. 45; Epiph. Haer. 34.4; Iren. I, 14.1, 4.

[326] This process is described in the alphabetical symbolism of the Marcosians as follows: "Each of them, though being only a part of the whole, contains its own sound for the whole and does not cease to sound until he has arrived at the last sign of the last letter in a single utterance. But then, it is said, there follows the restoration of the whole when all comes to the one letter and gives forth one and the same sound, and the 'Amen' which we utter together is supposed to be an image of this sound" (Hipp. 6. 42).

[327] The Marcosians rightly objected to the distortion of their actual position: Hipp. 6. 42.

your bridegroom, make a place for him and take your place in him. Behold, grace has descended upon you; open your mouth and prophesy."

According to Hipp. 6. 41 these proceedings among others are connected with φωνῇ ἀρρήτῳ, i.e., originally with speaking in tongues. That in such a connection Marcus is called "magician" (Hipp. 6.39; Iren. I, 13. 1 et passim) is obvious.[328]

Irenaeus continues: "Through such words she is excited and confused; the expectation of prophesying inflames her soul, her heart beats more strongly than usual, and she attempts to stammer something; but what she says is all empty, idle, impious stuff, since it is by an empty spirit that she has been thus heated. . . . But from then on she considers herself to be a prophetess and praises Marcus for having given to her of his grace . . . ."

Thus the glory of redemption is owed to Marcus, and the redeemed woman on her part emerges also as a redemptrix. She is called a prophetess, which reminds us of the prophets of Celsus who were called "God," and like these prophets she speaks publicly in an ecstatic speaking in tongues.[329]

Marcus himself also serves as a prophet (Iren. I, 13. 3), and in the meetings of the Marcosians, according to Iren. I, 13. 4, it is decided by lot whose task it is on this occasion to προφητεύειν. Marcus calls himself also τὴν μεγίστην ἀπὸ τῶν ἀοράτων καὶ ἀκατονομάστων τόπων . . . δύναμιν, which corresponds to the Simonian ἡ μεγάλη δύναμις.[330] Here as there this expression does not designate the one emissary, but rather the whole of the "power" which "from the invisible and unnameable places" has descended into matter and is scattered there. Thus then Marcus also says to his pupils that they can sin against the flesh without peril[331] διὰ τὸ εἶναι τῆς τελείας δυνάμεως καὶ κατέχειν τῆς ἀνεννοήτου ἐξουσίας (Hipp. 6. 41). Actually many others imitated Marcus in this respect. Like the prophets of Celsus, they wander about as itinerant preachers. They "represent themselves as the perfect; no man could equal them in the greatness of their knowledge, not even Paul, Peter, or any of the other

---

[328] Cf. also Iren. I, 25.3, where it is reported of the Carpocratians, whose conception of the redeemer resembles the Valentinian and who demonstrate their definite apostolic self-consciousness in that they equate themselves with Jesus: "Artes enim magicas operantur . . . dicentes se potestatem habere ad dominandum iam principibus et fabricatoribus huius mundi." Cf. Exc. ex Theod. 24.

[329] She speaks specifically "ληρώδη καὶ τὰ τυχόντα πάντα κενῶς καὶ τολμηρῶς." "Thus we can see what προφητεύειν and prophet actually signify: it stands for ἐν πνεύματι λαλεῖν and is expressed in enthusiastic ecstatic phenomena" (G. P. Wetter, op. cit., p. 74).

[330] Hipp. 6. 39; cf. Iren. I, 13.1. According to Iren. I, 14.1, he is also the σιγή and is called ὁ μονογενής. Thus like the Simonians and the prophets of Celsus, he can bear every divine title. "He is not man, but God or Son of God" (G. P. Wetter, op. cit., p. 76).

[331] Marcus is charged, hardly without reason, with sexual libertinism: Iren. I, 13.3, 5.

apostles; they knew more than anyone else, and they alone had imbibed the great and inexpressible Gnosis; they stood in the heights above all power." And this "position in the heights above all power" which they have and share—it is the position as μεγάλη δύναμις—is the "redemption" (Iren. I, 13. 6). Irenaeus obviously knows these wandering preachers from his own observation in Asia and in the Rhone territory (I, 13. 5; 13. 7).

At their ascent to heaven they are supposed to say: "Ἐγὼ υἱὸς ἀπὸ πατρός, from the Father who was before, but Son in the one who is . . . . I have come to behold what is alien and what is my own, . . . it comes from the one who was before, and I come into my own possession, from which I have gone out" (Iren. I, 21. 5). Thus speaks the ἑστώς, στάς, στησόμενος!

The polemically distorted account of the appearance of Marcus in the strophes about a "divine patriarch and herald of the truth" in Iren. I, 15. 6 finally allows us once more to note how Marcus interpreted himself as divine power, intended to lead men through doctrine and spiritual deeds on the way of salvation, and performed this ministry as a traveling preacher:

Εἰδωλοποιὲ Μάρκε καὶ τερατοσκόπε,
Ἀστρολογικῆς ἔμπειρε καὶ μαγικῆς τέχνης,
Δι' ὧν κρατύνεις τῆς πλάνης τὰ διδάγματα,
Σημεῖα δεικνὺς τοῖς ὑπό σου πλανωμένοις,
Ἀποστατικῆς δυνάμεως ἐγχειρήματα,
Ἃ σοι χορηγεῖ σὸς πατὴρ Σατᾶν ἀεί,
Δι' ἀγγελικῆς δυνάμεως Ἀζαζὴλ ποιεῖν,
Ἔχων σε πρόδρομον ἀντιθέου πανουργίας.

Here we pause for a moment. We have become acquainted with a new and quite precisely recognizable type of the Gnostic redeemer. He is indeed an essentially heavenly figure and therefore can bear all the predicates of divinity, but he is not sent from heaven. He belongs to the earthly parts of the light-being which had fallen into matter in primordial times. This explains that this type of Gnostic redeemer apparently never appears alone, as we saw in b) (pp. 155 ff.), but always in company with people who make the same claim; for in principle every pneumatic is in a position also to make his appearance as missionary prophet. Naturally it is not to be assumed that every one of them did so.

This redeemer receives his Gnosis through ecstatic revelations. The production of such ecstasies and of the prophetic speaking in tongues, scornfully called "magic" by the church's heresy fighters, belongs essentially to his missionary service. A heavenly redeemer is not necessary to these ecstatics. They receive the Gnosis by virtue of their belonging to the heavenly world, and their preaching bears witness, not of an alien redeemer, but of their own selves.

An encounter of the *one* heavenly emissary with the earthly redeemer takes place where, as we have seen in a) (pp. 148 ff.), the heavenly envoy commissions one particular individual man with the task of disseminating the Gnosis. The last-considered type of earthly redeemer, however, needs no such commission. He acts in the authority of his own divinity, he preaches a self-won knowledge. This earthly redeemer *competes* with the heavenly emissary (*vide* pp. 189 ff.).

We have already found some traces that suggest that the title ἀπόστολος also belonged to the self-designations of these figures.[332] This title was for a long time, and has remained, a technical expression for the *one* heavenly emissary, the *one* divine redeemer, without, however, the suggestion that the idea of "being sent" should always be dominant. As such a *terminus technicus* for the redeemer, it, like other titles (Great Power, God, Christ, Prophet, etc.), could also be claimed by the many earthly redeemers without any further ado.

To be sure, we should keep in mind that these many redeemers wandered about as missionaries; this title of "apostle" could have been a simple designation of function, which *as such* did not pertain to all the pneumatics but only to the traveling missionaries. Supposedly the latter was *determinative* for the type of apostle-redeemer here being investigated; still the designation ἀπόστολος offers itself as a functional designation precisely on account of the divine claim which lies within it. Perhaps this question will admit of a more precise answer if we look for further documentation for the figure of the Gnostic redeemer which interests us here, and indeed for such documentation in which the title ἀπόστολος appears.

We turn first to the Corinthian epistles. I have earlier sought to characterize the opponents of Paul in Corinth.[333] They are Gnostics of that type which here interests us.

Their self-interpretation expressed itself in the formula: ἐγώ εἰμι Χριστοῦ

---

[332] This title is attested for the Valentinians by Origen, according to whom (in Joh. II, 8 = Preuschen 70-71) Heracleon justified an arbitrary exegesis with the conviction ἀξιοῦντα ὁμοίως προφήταις ἢ ἀποστόλοις τοῖς μετ᾽ ἐξουσίας καὶ ἀνυπευθύνως καταλείπουσι τοῖς καθ᾽ αὑτοὺς καὶ μεθ᾽ αὑτοὺς σωτήρια γράμματα. On this, W. Foerster (*Von Valentin zu Heracleon*, BZNW, VII [1928], 4) remarks, probably correctly: "Accordingly there are in the sect of Heracleon prophets and apostles who have left behind them the written words, and what they uttered was said with authority and was not subject to any accounting."

[333] *Die Gnosis in Korinth*, FRLANT NF, XLVIII, 2nd ed., 1965.

(I Cor. 1:12; II Cor. 10:7). This typically Gnostic *ego-eimi* formula in the mouth of the Gnostic is not to be understood historically, but rather mythologically. Here is expressed a belonging to Christ which is not a matter of faith—as it is with Paul who takes over this formula from Gnosticism and makes it useful for his own thought—but rather a matter of being.[334] The ἐγώ εἰμι Χριστοῦ thus corresponds to the ἐγώ εἰμι ὁ ἑστώς, στάς, στησόμενος of Simon, to the ἐγὼ θεός εἰμι of the prophets of Celsus, to the ἐγὼ υἱὸς ἀπὸ πατρός of the Marcosians (Iren. I, 21. 5), and to the numerous corresponding formulas in Gnosticism. Χριστός is the designation, not of the heavenly emissary who takes up residence in Jesus, but of that heavenly being which is scattered among all men and is otherwise known as God, Great Power, Ennoia, Primal Man, Pneuma, and so on.

In view of the multiple influences of Judaism and Gnosticism, no one should be surprised that this figure can also bear the name "Christ," the designation of the Jewish redeemer or lord of the end time. Already among the Simonians we have encountered the designation "anointed" for the Gnostics of Simon's kind. According to Epiph. Haer. 26. 9, certain Gnostics after the attainment of their redemption say: ἐγώ εἰμι ὁ Χριστός. It is not accidental that these are precisely those Jewish-Gnostic Elchasaites of whom Hippolytus (10. 29; cf. 9. 14) reports that they did not acknowledge *one* Christ. To be sure Christ is supposed to have been *one* in the realm above, but this *one* is now scattered in many bodies and shows himself from time to time in many. Thus here "Christ" is the name of Primal Man. The Pauline terminology of definite Gnostic origin identifies Christ and the church in manifold fashion and has the Christians "in Christ" or Christ in the Christians. Above all, the equation of Primal Man = Messiah, as it is already present in the book of Daniel and is self-evident in the Gospels in the form son of Man = Christ, shows that quite early "Christ" was a designation of that Gnostic primal figure which is scattered about in matter, which speaks forth from all the many redeemers just considered.[335] All this originally has nothing to do with the figure of the Christian Christ,

---

[334] *Ibid.*, pp. 182 ff.

[335] I have gone into this equation in detail in the above-mentioned work (2nd ed., 1965), pp. 32-80. Much documentation is also given there. The title of Christ was transferred to the figure of the self-redeeming primal man. The possibility for such a transferral was simply given by the fact that "primal man" like "Messiah" had eschatological significance. The Messiah had *only* such a meaning, but the primal man was in fact to be assembled by all the efforts at redemption into the wholeness of the "new man" from the condition of being scattered in matter; he is, as the Simonians put it, the eschatological στησόμενος. This connection certainly sufficed for the pre-Christian Jewish Gnosis to place alongside innumerable other titles also that of the "anointed one" for the Gnostic central figure of the self-redeeming "primal man."

and the formula ἐγώ εἰμι Χριστοῦ therefore does not permit us at all to see Christians in its representatives. In the latter we are dealing, rather, with Gnostics who stand close to Judaism.

The genitive form Χριστοῦ correctly indicates that each of these Gnostics is not the Christ in general, but rather a *part* of the Christ–Primal Man. It is therefore to be understood like the genitives in Hipp. 6. 41, where Marcus tells his pupils that they can, at will, sin διὰ τὸ εἶναι τῆς τελείας δυνάμεως καὶ κατέχειν τῆς ἀνεννοήτου ἐξουσίας. This genitive occurs also in the Pauline formula οἱ τοῦ Χριστοῦ (I Cor. 15:23), which is intended in the original Gnostic sense as pertaining to the very being itself.

Perhaps Paul had known the particular form of the Christ myth in Corinth and is indignantly rejecting this myth: μεμέρισται ὁ Χριστός. Perhaps however "Christ" in this question is also Paul's designation for the community as in I Cor. 12:12. This equation of Christ = Community, surprising in Paul, is likewise to be understood only as terminological borrowing in just that Gnosticism for which all pneumatics are parts of the Christ.

Just as for the prophets of Celsus (ἐγὼ ὁ θεός εἰμι ἢ θεοῦ παῖς ἢ πνεῦμα θεῖον), God, Son of God, and Pneuma are identical, so also for the Corinthian Gnostics, Pneuma apparently can appear in place of Christ: I Cor. 7:40 (cf. II Cor. 10:7); 12:1; II Cor. 11:4.[336] This again means, however, that Christ is not at all represented as an individual figure, but is the heavenly being which as Pneuma is found in all the pneumatics.

That the Corinthian Gnostics actually speak of Christ in this sense is shown by the fact that they do not recognize any heavenly redeemer figure. In any case, in the polemic of Paul the heretical Christology appears only as anthropology; we hear nothing whatsoever of a special redeemer figure,[337] and the church's Jesus, including his cross, is explicitly cursed (I Cor. 12:1-3; 1:18–2:5; II Cor. 11:4).[338]

The Gnostics are themselves redeemers. For this, Paul has found a fitting formulation: they preach themselves (II Cor. 4:5).[339] Precisely the same is true of all the figures of this type of Gnostic redeemer. Therefore, alongside the proclamation of Gnosis which is bound up with it (I Cor. 1:18–

---

[336] *Die Gnosis in Korinth*, pp. 157-68.

[337] U. Wilckens, *Weisheit und Torheit* (1959), has not convinced me that the σοφία proclaimed by the Gnostics (I Cor. 2:1 ff.) was a personal redeemer figure. This thesis unnecessarily complicates a simple state of affairs and with altogether too weak a reason. It is not by chance that U. Wilckens eliminates as a gloss the double reference to the ἐγώ εἰμι Χριστοῦ of the Corinthian Gnostics. Cf. *Die Gnosis in Korinth*, pp. 130-32.

[338] *Die Gnosis in Korinth*, pp. 117-33.

[339] *Ibid.*, pp. 173-74.

2:5 ff.; 3:18; 8:1; 13:8 ff.; II Cor. 11:4 ff.),[340] their actual task is the ecstatic demonstration (II Cor. 5:11-15)[341] of the Christ who speaks in them (II Cor. 13:3, 5),[342] i.e., of their Pneuma-Self: speaking in tongues (I Cor. 12–14)[343]; ὀπτασίαι and ἀποκαλύψεις (II Cor. 12:1-10).[344] Paul is scorned because he preaches only prosaically (II Cor. 5:11-15), and does not proclaim himself, but rather Christ Jesus as Lord (II Cor. 4:5).

The self-evaluation of the Corinthian Gnostics which is connected with such apotheosis is pictured by Paul exactly as it appears in Irenaeus I, 13. 6, for example, with reference to the Marcosians: I Cor. 4:7 ff., 10.[345]

If one further observes that these people appear *to many* with such lofty claims (*vide infra*) and that they all purport to be τοῦ Χριστοῦ in the sense described, then it becomes clear from the foregoing summary presentation that in them we have to do with Gnostics of that type which we encountered in the Simonians, in the prophets of Celsus, and in Valentinus and his imitators. Since they are Jews (II Cor. 11:22), they may have been native to the same region in which we also meet the Simonians about the same time and, later on, the prophets of Celsus.

Now Paul delivers, in certain passages of I Cor. and in large parts of II Cor., an extended apology on behalf of his apostolic office. In addition to all the discussion about the content of the Christian kerygma, the opponents of Paul in Corinth attempt to undermine his authority by contesting his rights as an apostle. They take the position that only the one who first can show that he is a regular apostle has the right to proclaim the "Christian" message; the nonapostolic message, on the other hand, deserves no notice.

They appear to have made some impression with this argument; for Paul attempts with equally great zeal as with unmistakable displeasure (II Cor. 11:1, 16-17; 12:1, 11) to present evidence that he actually is an apostle. We have already (pp. 32 ff.) examined the arguments which he adduces for this.

The whole discussion, especially that in II Cor., becomes understandable only if the apostolic authority of Paul is doubted by another apostolic authority. In Corinth, in opposition to Paul they are not contesting the necessity of apostolic authority for the correct proclamation; they rather affirm it with great emphasis. It is only that Paul, so the charge goes,

[340] *Ibid.*, pp. 133 ff.
[341] *Ibid.*, pp. 177 ff.
[342] *Ibid.*, pp. 182 ff.
[343] *Ibid.*, pp. 161 ff.
[344] *Ibid.*, pp. 197 ff.
[345] *Ibid.*, pp. 169 ff.

has no right to call himself an apostle (I Cor. 9:1). But these people must then have laid claim to this right *themselves,* for they expect that the Corinthians will accept the new teaching (II Cor. 11:4), and according to the opinion of the false teachers in Corinth the true message can only be an *apostolic* message.

That they are *apostles* who appear in Corinth in opposition to Paul would then be certain, even if Paul did not inform us that his opponents had called themselves apostles. But now he makes abundantly clear beyond doubt that people making the same claim to apostleship which he makes are working against him in Corinth. To be sure, he does not recognize them as apostles any more than they recognize him, and he scornfully calls them, for this reason, ὑπερλίαν ἀπόστολοι (II Cor. 11:5; 12:11), or, quite sharply, ψευδαπόστολοι, . . . μετασχηματιζόμενοι εἰς ἀποστόλους Χριστοῦ (II Cor. 11:13); but these designations[346] leave no doubt at all that the missionaries thus labeled have appeared in Corinth as ἀπόστολοι.

The Tübingen school of F. C. Baur took these apostles of course to be Judaists. This resulted in a labyrinth of difficulties. The "superlative apostles" are surely active in Corinth; they personally are disturbing the congregation. This much is indisputably clear from II Cor. 11:4-5. One cannot pull these two verses apart[347]; the people who come to Corinth to proclaim "another gospel" are the "superlative apostles" themselves, and not their envoys. The supposition that in these ὑπερλίαν ἀπόστολοι the so-called "original apostles" have come personally to Corinth is today probably nowhere any longer advocated.[348] This is simply ruled out. If one nevertheless wishes to cling to the equation, "superlative apostles = original apostles,"[349] he must not view the Corinthian agitators as identical with the superlative apostles. But that is, as we have just demonstrated, equally impossible.[350] Thus it remains true that in Corinth Paul is dealing with apostles who are not the "original apostles."

In view of this state of things one may see that these servants of Satan were apostles in the broader sense of this word. They are said to be ἀπόσ-τολοι "in the broader sense occasionally acknowledged even by Paul, a sense which embraces all the missionaries of primitive Christianity who work

---

[346] R. Reitzenstein, *op. cit.,* p. 368, asserts against all reason that the "superlative apostles" (II Cor. 11:5; 12:11) and the "false apostles" (II Cor. 11:13) are not identical. Against this, and correctly, H. Lietzmann in HNT on II Cor. 11:13.

[347] E. Käsemann has recently done this ([2], pp. 41-42); against this, esp. Bultmann, *Exegetische Probleme des Zweiten Korintherbriefes* (1947), pp. 20 ff.

[348] P. Schmiedel (in the *Handkommentar,* p. 63) briefly summarized sufficient reasons against this assumption.

[349] Thus finally R. Reitzenstein, *op. cit.,* pp. 366 ff.; E. Käsemann [2], pp. 45 ff.

[350] See H. Windisch in Meyer's *Kommentar* on II Cor., p. 330; P. Schmiedel in the *Handkommentar,* p. 63; W. G. Kümmel in HNT, IX (4th ed.), on p. 146, l. 12.

independently but were sent out by congregations." [351] But apart from the error to which H. Windisch falls victim in this quotation, in his acceptance of a double concept of apostle in Paul, the whole discussion about apostleship in the Corinthian epistles is understandable only from the standpoint of recognizing that the false teachers *compete* as apostles with the apostle Paul. Nowhere is it to be noted that they appealed to any other earthly authority than themselves. Only with them, therefore, must Paul compare himself, in order to prove that he is not inferior to *them* (II Cor. 11:5). They wish *themselves* to be apostles of Christ (II Cor. 11:13); with *them* Paul compares himself as διάκονος Χριστοῦ (II Cor. 11:23); he has the same revelations as they have and for this reason is not inferior to *them* (II Cor. 12:11); like *them* Paul has produced the σημεῖα τοῦ ἀποστόλου; he has withheld from the congregation nothing which *they themselves* could give to it (II Cor. 12:13). In short, in Corinth two equivalent claims stand over against each other. As apostles of Christ, the Corinthian false teachers contest the apostolic right and message of Paul; as an apostle of Christ Paul calls the apostolic claim and teaching of his opponents demonic. Behind Paul, as also behind his opponents, as the only immediate authority of the apostle, stands Christ himself (II Cor. 10:7).[352]

Judaistic apostles of Christ other than the "original apostles" [353] are, however, nowhere reported to us, and they can all the less have existed since indeed the designation of the "original apostles" as ἀπόστολοι is an already canonical anachronism. Therefore the modern exegetes, insofar as they together with almost all the earlier expositors hold the "superlative apostles" to have been the Judaists, refrain from explaining their origin.[354] This is certainly an advance beyond the untenable historical combinations of the Tübingen school and its followers. But a mere refraining from an explanation can never suffice.

If one notes that Paul delivers his apology on behalf of his apostolic office in almost every part of his correspondence with the Corinthian congregation, there can hardly be any doubt that the Gnostic opponents and the "superlative apostles" are identical, indeed in the Corinthian epistles there is only *one* line of battle.

[351] H. Windisch in Meyer's *Kommentar*, p. 330; P. Schmiedel in the *Handkommentar*, p. 63; H. Lietzmann in HNT on II Cor. 11:5.

[352] It is pointless to argue whether the Corinthian false apostles legitimately (thus F. C. Baur) or illegitimately (thus G. Heinrici) depended upon Jerusalem authorities, and which authorities these were, the "pillars" or the "false brethren" of Gal. 2:4. They depended solely upon their own authority "in Christ."

[353] If one may at all call these people Judaists!

[354] H. Windisch in Meyer's *Kommentar*, pp. 330-31; Lietzmann in HNT on II Cor. 11:4 ff.; W. G. Kümmel, *ibid.*, p. 146, l. 12 at the end; K. H. Rengstorf [1], p. 445.

The self-interpretation which stands behind the apostolic claim of these people is nothing other than that of the redeemer, who thinks of himself as part of θεός, of the μεγάλη δύναμις, or as τοῦ Χριστοῦ. For when we just noted that the false teachers *competed* as apostles with the apostle Paul, we were talking from the standpoint of Paul. From the standpoint of the Gnostics, Paul is no apostle at all, since he cannot (and will not) preach himself, but only out of mediated authority proclaims the crucified and accursed (I Cor. 12:3) Lord Jesus, while according to the opinion of the Gnostics the true apostle speaks in his own authority, which *as such* is the authority of Christ, because the Gnostic himself is τοῦ Χριστοῦ.

We reaffirm: The Gnostics in Corinth are not only τοῦ Χριστοῦ, not only πνεῦμα or πνευματικοί, but also ἀπόστολοι.

The same Gnostics appear also in others of Paul's congregations[355]; in our connection their agitation in Galatia is especially interesting. Down to our own days it has been, to be sure, scholarly dogma that in Galatia Paul had to struggle against the Judaizers, but I have tried to prove the untenability of this dogma in ZNW XLVII (1956), 25 ff. In Galatia also, Paul encounters Jewish Gnostics with the special self-understanding of the redeemer which we have been investigating.

What concerns us is the observation that the Galatian opponents charge against Paul that as an apostle he is dependent upon men and therefore his gospel is worth nothing; for the genuine apostle—so Paul understands his opponents—must be dependent upon Christ or upon God (Gal. 1:1, 11-12, 15 ff.). With this argument they pit their own authority against that of Paul. But this makes sense only if these new teachers themselves appear as apostles, and indeed not as ἀπόστολοι ἀπ' ἀνθρώπων, but as ἀπόστολοι Χριστοῦ in Galatia. If they themselves were apostles sent from men, they could not *accuse* Paul for his dependence upon men! [356]

In what sense these Gnostics were apostles of Christ we do not learn from the Galatian letter; we know it from the Corinthian epistles. But we do learn anew that they were apostles.[357]

[355] It is my conviction that the false teachers in Galatia, Philippi, Thessalonica, and Ephesus (Rom. 16:17-20) are also Jewish Gnostics.

[356] It is utterly inconceivable that these false teachers, allegedly as Judaists dependent upon the "apostolic" authorities of Judaism in Jerusalem, should accuse Paul of being dependent, like themselves, upon these "original apostles" and that therefore his gospel is of no value. Curiously, this is the prevailing view among the exegetes; cf. "Die Häretiker in Galatien," in *Paulus und die Gnostiker*, pp. 18-19.

[357] In connection with the Galatian epistle, I should like to refer also to the Ethiopic text of the Apocalypse of Peter (*ca.* 100-150), where it speaks of men "who circumcise themselves as apostles of a man" (Apoc. Pet. 10), but such a reference is forbidden by the well-grounded suspicion of serious textual corruption.

Gnostic apostles are further attacked in the letters of the Apocalypse.[358] In Rev. 2:2, the writer praises the congregation in Ephesus: ὅτι οὐ δύνῃ βαστάσαι κακούς, καὶ ἐπείρασας τοὺς λέγοντας ἑαυτοὺς ἀποστόλους καὶ οὐκ εἰσίν, καὶ εὗρες αὐτοὺς ψευδεῖς. These wicked people appear then, as in Corinth and Galatia, as apostles, and, as there, are called false apostles (II Cor. 11:13). That here we are dealing with representatives of essentially the same Jewish-Christian Gnosticism as that with which Paul struggled is shown by a look at the heresy which is attacked in the letters in general.[359] All that may with some probability be discerned from these letters points to that Gnosticism which already from general considerations must be the dangerous Christian heresy in Asia Minor in the time of the Apocalypse.[360]

Here it is apparently not a Gnosticism about which nothing can be more precisely determined, against which the letters are directed, but a Gnosticism of the type which concerns us here, not one in which the words of a redeemer are proclaimed, but one in which the redeemers themselves appear.

The Nicolaitans are a Gnostic sect (Rev. 2:6, 15).[361] Balaam (Rev. 2:14) is a title of disapprobation,[362] taken from the biblical history, for the Nicolaitans who in Rev. 2:15 are equated with the Balaamites.[363] The particular sin of Balaam is that he teaches the congregation φαγεῖν εἰδωλόθυτα καὶ πορνεῦσαι, the typical manner of conduct of Gnostic libertinism (Iren. I, 6. 3),[364] especially that of Simon and of Marcus (Iren. I, 13; 23. 3). Jezebel (Rev. 2:20 ff.) leads astray into the same sins. Her Gnostic position is also evident in the fact that she calls herself a prophetess, which reminds us of the prophets of Celsus and of the prophesying medium of Marcus, and that with those who belong to her she professes to know the "depths of Satan"—supposedly through their own ecstasy.[365] Gnostic also is the assertion growing out of pneumatic pride that one is "rich" and "has need of nothing," [366] which we have encountered in one form or another among

---

[358] Cf. E. Haenchen in RGG (3rd ed.), II, col. 1655.

[359] E. Lohmeyer in the *Handbuch, in loc.* calls these apostles "traveling missionaries." But the author of the letter of the Apocalypse does not understand ἀπόστολοι in such a general sense, but in the technical sense, for he continues: *that* they are not! Obviously these people are indeed wandering missionaries. The writer of the Book of Revelation only denies that they are *apostles*.

[360] See W. Bauer [1], p. 82.

[361] Cf. Iren. I, 26.3; III, 11.1; Th. Zahn, *Einleitung*, II, 623-24.

[362] Cf. the passage in Jude 11 which is also anti-Gnostic.

[363] See H. J. Holtzmann in the *Handkommentar, in loc.*

[364] Cf. *Die Gnosis in Korinth*, pp. 206 ff.

[365] See the article βάθος in TDNT, I, 517-18; U. Wilckens, *Weisheit und Torheit*, p. 82, n. 1.

[366] *Die Gnosis in Korinth*, pp. 168 ff.

all the redeemers of this type. These testimonies are supplemented by Rev. 2:9 and 3:9, according to which the Gnostics place value upon the fact that they are Jews. The author of the letters cannot or will not contest this, in spite of the accusation that they lie and that they belong to the synagogue of Satan. Instead, it becomes clear that the Gnostic false teachers count the apostles and prophets as their own, as in Galatia and Corinth representatives of the Jewish-"Christian" Gnosticism[367] do, and thus are native to that Near Eastern region in which also the Simonian apostles and the prophets of Celsus appeared.

Gnostic apostles are also testified to by Hegesippus, who according to Eusebius (CH IV, 22. 6) enumerated the older and the more recent Gnostic sects and then commented: ἀπὸ τούτων ψευδόχριστοι, ψευδοπροφῆται, ψευδαπόστολοι, οἵτινες ἐμέρισαν τὴν ἕνωσιν τῆς ἐκκλησίας φθοριμαίοις λόγοις κατὰ τοῦ θεοῦ καὶ κατὰ τοῦ Χριστοῦ αὐτοῦ. Hegesippus begins his enumeration of the sect leaders with Simon, Cleobius, and Dositheus. Naturally one cannot say that Hegesippus seeks the false apostles in them or among their disciples, but that does not alter the fact that Hegesippus is acquainted with Gnostic apostles. When these appear in connection with Gnostic prophets and Gnostic Χριστοί, we are dealing not only with the now familiar titles, but, certainly not accidentally, with that characteristic combining of such titles which testifies to the claim of the apostles and prophets to be themselves redeemers like Christ or as τοῦ Χριστοῦ.[368]

Hegesippus' contemporary, Dionysius of Corinth (in Eus., CH IV, 23. 12), calls the Gnostics who falsify his epistles οἱ τοῦ διαβόλου ἀπόστολοι. Therein also he may be repeating the Gnostic self-description, with a polemical turn added.

In any case Tertullian had become acquainted with such apostles also, and from him we learn something about their teaching: "Ceterum et Nigidius nescio qui et Hermogenes et *multi alii adhuc ambulant* pervertentes vias domini. Ostendant mihi ex qua auctoritate prodierint . . . probent se novos *apostolos* esse; dicant Christum iterum descendisse, iterum ipsum docuisse, iterum crucifixum, iterum mortuum, iterum resuscitatum" (de praescr. haer. 30. 13 ff.).

---

[367] The nearsighted doubling of the fronts (Gnosticism and Judaism) in the letters, still found in Lohmeyer (*op. cit.*, p. 41, n. 335) is just as outdated for this material as for the Ignatian epistles. For the first century after Christ, Jewish-Christian Gnosticism is the ordinary form of the Gnostic heresy in general.

[368] Hegesippus' formulation goes back to a widely known logion which also appears elsewhere: Just. Dial. 35; Ap. Const. VI, 13; Tert. de praescr. haer. 4; cf. Ps.-Cl. Hom XVI, 21, and doubtless is of anti-Gnostic origin. For the tradition of the early church, there are no false apostles other than those of Gnostic observance! Where the anti-Gnostic reference is not (any longer) understood or is of no interest, the concept of the apostle is also lacking: Mark 13:22 and parallels.

One should not suppose that these Gnostic apostles asserted that the entire Christ event of the ecclesiastical tradition has been repeated, as could be inferred from the formulation of Tertullian. What meaning could such an assertion have had? Undoubtedly what these apostles meant was that Christ had appeared again. Thus the assertion can only have had the meaning that "Christ has appeared in us, the apostles; we are τοῦ Χριστοῦ." This idea would then be the background of the following paragraph 16 if, as it appears, Tertullian here is still referring to the ideas of the Gnostics: "sic enim apostolos solet facere, dare illis praeterea virtutem eadem signa edendi, quae et ipse." It is further possible that these Gnostics connected the fate of their souls with the fate of the historical Christ in such a way that they (like Paul, who in conection with Gnostic terminology does it in a non-Gnostic way) spoke in the Gnostic sense of being crucified together, dying together, and rising together.

Perhaps Tertullian is thinking of these Gnostic apostles also where he (24. 5-6) turns against the Gnostics who reject the church's apostles in favor of—apparently their own—ecstatic heavenly journeys, as the Marcosians did according to Irenaeus (vide pp. 170-71). In that case we would find, still in this late time, the claim to be Χριστοῦ, the title of apostle, and the ecstatic technique combined, in other words, the characteristic marks of the plural apostolate.

The Didache, in the sections in which it alludes to "apostles," is to be understood only under the presupposition of a Gnostic apostolate which was current in Syria. The question as to place and time of the composition of the Didache can hardly ever be answered with finality, because the writing is a collection of pieces from various origins. The chapters which interest us, chaps. 11–16, may indeed be quite old and may belong to the Syrian region where the Christian apostolate was at home. Now Paul considered himself to be the last of the church's apostles (I Cor. 15:8).[369] In this he could have been mistaken. Yet we possess—apart from the Didache—no witness indicating that the ecclesiastical apostolate was continued after Paul.[370] Ignatius, the champion of the monarchical episcopate, rules out, as far as his time is concerned, the possibility that in Syria any ecclesiastical support could have been found for efforts toward the multiplying of office

[369] Cf. H. v. Campenhausen [2], p. 25; J. L. Leuba, op. cit., p. 59; E. Schweizer, op. cit., pp. 97-98, 195.

[370] "There is no apostle of the second generation" (W. Nagel, op. cit., p. 19). G. Klein, op. cit., n. 216, sees such testimonies also in Rev. 2:2 and in Eph. 4:11; 3:5; 2:20. I regard this as incorrect (see p. 238). Moreover, G. Klein does not establish how there is supposed to be found in Rev. 2:2 an orthodox apostolate, which of course in this passage is hardly possible at all.

holders in general and especially of apostles. For him the apostles are the holy figures of the past.

It is also noteworthy that already in Paul the church apostles and prophets appear as far less ecstatic-pneumatic than do the apostles and prophets of the Didache in a later time; instead, Paul is already consciously suppressing this ecstatic character (e.g., I Cor. 12–14). All this makes it likely that the apostles of the Didache belonged to circles at the outer fringes of the great church or of the heretics.

Now the Didache indicates in many features its nearness to Syrian Gnosticism. This is true for chaps. 9 and 10, whose eucharistic prayers stem from Gnostic tradition,[371] it is true for the triad of apostle-prophet-teacher (Did. 11–16),[372] it is true also in view of the fact that ecstasy in the worship service was still held possible (Did. 11. 9).

When one considers further that the apostles, who for Paul are the most prominent officeholders and according to Eph. 2:20 were the foundation of the church, are mentioned in the Didache only in 11.3-6 and even here are considered with very critical reservations, this arouses the suspicion that the writer of our lines here fears "that the false teaching of Gnosticism is being carried by wandering apostles into the congregations." [373]

Apostles in precisely the form in which they are portrayed to us by the Didache are, moreover, not known to us from the ecclesiastical context; for here we have to do not with apostles of the community, but with ἀπόστολοι Χριστοῦ, who speak with pneumatic authority.[374] But the ἀπόστολοι πάντες, whom Paul mentions in I Cor. 15:17,[375] form a limited and surveyable and even closed group, which according to the opinion of Paul has experienced no enlargement since his call, while the number of those called apostles in the Didache "must have been, even fundamentally and in their essence, unlimited and uncontrollable." [376]

The circumstances and relationships in Syria at the time of the turn of the century[377] are, to be sure, not very clear to us. However, W. Bauer[378]

---

[371] See *Die Gnosis in Korinth,* note on p. 234.

[372] See pp. 226 ff.

[373] According to R. Knopf in the *Ergänzungsband* to HNT, *in loc.*

[374] See G. Sass [2], p. 237. Cf. G. Widengren [3], p. 72: "The apostle—and that is really important—is to be received as the Lord Himself (Did. 11.4). This cannot make us astonished if we compare the conditions prevalent in Syrian Christianity, where the Apostle occupies a position much resembling that of Christ Himself."

[375] And who naturally are also ἀπόστολοι Χριστοῦ!

[376] G. Sass [2], p. 236.

[377] The traditions taken over by the Didache in 11.3-6 could of course have been still older and by the time of the final recension of the document could have been already without any basis in actuality.

[378] [1], pp. 70-71.

has correctly affirmed that the Gnostic movement appeared as overwhelming competitor of ecclesiastical Christianity, and with equal correctness H. Schlier[379] has judged the Syrian Christianity of Ignatius as "closely related in concepts and representations to the Gnosticism there."[380] Correspondingly, the mythological Gnosis can have been assimiliated to the Christianity of the church and in the course of this "syncretism" representatives of its free apostolate can have penetrated earlier or later to the very fringes of the church. Or—still more likely—the apostles of the Didache have been able to assert their suspected ecclesiastical position from that time when Gnostic and ecclesiastical Christianity were not generally sharply distinguished. In any case, it is certain that such a distinction in some places in Syria did not come about until very late; on the other side, the material which the Didache uses, in which the apostles are treated, may have already been fixed in the first century.[381]

More than this, of course, cannot be said, except that it is not possible to view the apostles of the Didache as successors of the church's apostolate, while they are easily understandable as offshoots of contemporary Gnosticism.[382] Therein also the Didache intimates the presence of an original plural apostolate of Gnosticism, and in spite of all the ecclesiasticizing, the apostles of the Didache still allow us to recognize the pneumatic-ecstatic character of these wandering preachers.

[379] H. Schlier, *Religionsgeschichtliche Untersuchungen zu den Ignatiusbriefen* (1929), p. 175.

[380] Still in the second century almost all the important heads of Gnostic schools came from the Syrian region.

[381] In his comprehensive work on *La Didachè, Instruction des Apôtres* (Paris, 1958), J. P. Audet places the composition of the Didache in the period between 50 and 70! This is certainly too early, though he has found agreement with this dating from J. Danielou, for example.

On the other side, E. Peterson, in his *Frühkirche, Judentum und Gnosis* (1959), p. 181, judges concerning the author of the Didache that he has "created a work which undoubtedly is less an expression of actuality than of a literarily mediated utopian portrayal of the early period of the church."

[382] G. Widengren ([3], pp. 65-79) rightly sees the apostolate of the Syrian Didache in close relation to the Gnostic concept of the apostle of the Syrian acts of the apostles, of which we shall speak shortly, and refers to the obviously " 'Gnostic' traits" of this conception of the apostle, which is explained by the gnosticizing character of Syrian Christianity.

G. Klein (*op. cit.*, p. 50, n. 209) objects: "It would be an absurd notion that since Paul there should have been within orthodoxy apostles only as half-heretical figures, without the congregations down to the time of the Didache having noted their doubtful character." This objection does not take into account the character of Syrian Christianity, which was still syncretistic in the later post-apostolic period. G. Klein diminishes its import still further when he admits (*op. cit.*, p. 52) that "more ancient material could have been simply compiled" in the Didache. This objection has no weight anyway in case of an early dating of the Didache itself (Audet: 70; Adam: 70–90/100).

Some passages in the Mandaean writings also are polemically directed against Gnostic redeemer-apostles, who are appearing in ever greater numbers:

Peoples and tongues stem from the nation of the Jews. My Lord called and commissioned me to instruct you about the peoples of the lie as well as about the prophets of the lie and the *emissaries* of falsehood; they develop in the wombs of the women, the women become pregnant with them and give birth to them. From the body of women they enter into bodies and take on bodily form. They distort the first teaching, and they bring lie, deception, and delusion into the world. They call themselves prophets and say, "We are *emissaries.* . . ." Now I say to you, my disciples: Do not listen to the lying words of the prophets, and do not waver from the way of your Lord. For the angels of error take on the form of ourselves, the three *emissaries,* we who have entered into Tibil. I told you: they too go about in the world, but they do not resemble us. . . . There is no one to whom the hidden things were revealed except the Great One, the Exalted, the Lord of Greatness, the Lord of all worlds.[383]

In the parallel passage it is said:

They call themselves God and set themselves up as *emissaries* (or: they call themselves "emissaries"). They take on a body and assume the form of men. They write a book of deception, set up warnings for them, and have a false prayer said. They cast lewdness, lust, and passion over the face of the earth and are called prophets.[384]

We remember that the Mandaeans at the outset were at home in the Palestinian setting and, in fact, in the primitive Christian time.[385] There and then they apparently encountered many redeemers, who at that time had the center of their activity there. Over against these they set the *one* emissary:

"I now, the first emissary, teach and say to all Nasoraeans who are now and who are yet to be born: Do not listen to their speech and do not wander from the way of life. My chosen ones! do not join with these who do not stand fast in *one* message." [386]

[383] Lidzbarski, *Ginza*, pp. 43.28–44.2, 21-25; 44.40–45.2.

[384] *Ibid.*, p. 25.26-30.

[385] The early dating of the beginnings of the Mandaean literature in the pre-Christian and early Christian period is less disputed today than ever. Cf., e.g., W. Baumgartner, "Der heutige Stand der Mandäerfrage," in ThZ, VI (1950), 401 ff.; R. Macuch, "Alter und Heimat des Mandäismus nach neuerschlossenen Quellen," in ThLZ (1957), cols. 401 ff.; O. Cullmann, *The Christology of the New Testament* (rev. ed.), p. 27; K. Rudolph, *Die Mandäer,* I (Diss., Leipzig); see the author's own note in ThLZ (1957), cols. 385-86, and *op. cit., passim;* ThLZ (1958), cols. 718-19; A. Adam, *Die Psalmen des Thomas* (1959), pp. 76 ff. It appears from the anti-Jewish polemic that our section comes from the early, Palestinian period of the Mandaeans (cf. Lidzbarski, *Ginza,* pp. VIII-IX).

[386] Lidzbarski, *Ginza,* p. 26.1-4.

Thus we learn that the apostles being opposed here are also called prophets and are represented as being God. Their commission competes with that of the *one* emissary[387]; thus they are themselves redeemers, who however appear in great numbers. They come from among the Jews and exhibit apparently libertine tendencies. They allege that the "hidden things were revealed" to them (Lidzbarski, *Ginza* 27. 1-2; 44. 40-41)! Consequently there can be no question that in these people we have to do, not with Gnostic apostles in general, but with apostles of that Gnosticism which has occupied us from the treatment of Simon onward.

Only briefly we refer once more to Mani, who was called "apostle" with a special emphasis. We have seen that as redeemer he laid claim to this title for himself and for some predecessors. According to his anthropogony, however, Mani can have made no special *anthropological* claim. He is part of the *one* light-substance which was left behind by the Primal Man in the power of darkness. With reference to being, he is thus identical with his predecessors in the apostolic office,[388] with the many apostles whom he again sends into the world [389] and who spread his teaching abroad, as well as with the genuine Gnostics in general. Now some of the Manichaean fragments discovered at the beginning of our century portray Mani as an ecstatic,[390] who is able also to transport others into ecstasy so that they behold the world of light.[391] However, if this ecstatic technique, to which Mani apparently owed the Gnosis which he proclaimed,[392] was widespread in the earliest Manichaeism, then the redeemer claim of Mani himself for the time of his appearing cannot have been exclusively intended, and his apostolate would deserve also to be mentioned at this point in our investigation.[393] This fact fits in with the observation of Kraeling (*op. cit.*, p. 34, n. 384), that "a broad gulf divides that which Mani said of himself and what his followers made of him." Unfortunately we know too little of the beginnings

---

[387] See pp. 190-91.

[388] Cf. C. H. Kraeling, *Anthropos and Son of Man* (New York, 1927), pp. 24 ff. The number of these apostles is not constant in the Mandaean writings, and their names vary. Cf. G. Widengren [3], pp. 58 ff.; E. Rose, *op. cit.*, pp. 30 ff.

[389] Cf. G. Widengren [1], p. 31: "The epithet of 'Apostle' has clearly a very wide meaning, because the successors of Mani, even in their ranks of 'teachers,' had inherited his designation of 'Apostle.' "

[390] Ed. Müller, AAB (1904), No. 47; No. 48 = pp. 83-84, 86-87.

[391] Cf. Al-Biruni, *Chronologie,* trans. by C. E. Sachau (London, 1879), p. 191.

[392] Al-Biruni reports concerning Mani that he frequently traveled to heaven in ecstasy, to spend some days there; cf. G. Widengren [3], p. 84.

[393] According to G. Widengren [2], p. 84, it is still true of Islam that "in Islam not only Muhammad but a great many sectarians within Shi'ak claimed to have ascended to heaven and to have been given a Heavenly Writing."

of Manichaeism to be able more surely to decide how far the Manichaean concept of the apostle goes back to the plural apostolate of Gnosticism.

Finally, the apocryphal acts of the apostles cannot here be passed over. With the help of the Acts of Thomas we can make clear the problem which interests us in our posing of the question. On this work, the splendid investigation of G. Bornkamm, *Mythos und Legende in den apokryphen Thomasakten*,[394] is available. The Acts of Thomas are witnesses to a Syrian *Gnosticism* of a Christian variety, even to the mythologizing of the narrative material. The church's influence is particularly inescapable in the fact that *Christ* takes the role of the redeemer. But he is not the only redeemer. The apostle Thomas can completely take his place.[395] In the Acts of Thomas there is a doubling of the representation of the redeemer,[396] and indeed the figure of Thomas, a representative of the Gnostic plural apostolate, is obscured by the superimposed figure of the church's Christ as the historical emissary. Basically the two figures are in competition with each other in the Acts of Thomas. This is, to be sure, obscured in various ways, but in a close examination one will see that either of these two figures is in a position by himself to achieve the work of redemption.

This combination of two typically utterly different redeemer-apostles finds its characteristic expression in the occasional designation of Thomas as the twin brother of Jesus.[397] Correspondingly, the fate also of Thomas is portrayed as quite parallel to that of Jesus: In the sale of Thomas as a slave the humiliation of Christ is repeated,[398] so that Thomas can be hailed in a hymn:

$$\text{ὃς ἐλεύθερος ὢν γέγονας δοῦλος}$$
$$\text{καὶ πραθεὶς πολλοὺς εἰς ἐλευθερίας εἰσήγαγες.}^{399}$$

In the final ascent of Thomas the heavenward journey of the redeemer is reenacted.[400] In the meantime there is the period in which the apostle has taken over the role of the redeemer and is leading men to the point where they can say: "You have led me to seek out and to know myself, who I

---

[394] FRLANT NF, XXXI.

[395] Cf. also Logion 13 in the newly discovered Coptic Gospel of Thomas (e.g. in Hennecke-Schneemelcher-Wilson, I, 287). There also on pp. 307-8 some important comments on the "Book of Thomas Athlete" from the Nag Hammadi find.

[396] G. Widengren ([1], pp. 27-28) speaks of "the repeated confusion in the Acts of Thomas between Christ and Thomas."

[397] Chaps. 31, 39; cf. chap. 11. Cf. G. Widengren [2], p. 174; Burkitt, *Early Eastern Christianity*, p. 198.

[398] G. Bornkamm, *op. cit.*, p. 19.

[399] Chap. 39 = Lipsius-Bonnet, 156.15 ff.

[400] G. Bornkamm, *op. cit.*, p. 15.

was and who and how I now am, so that I can again become what I was." [401]
We will pass over the particulars of the redeeming activity of the apostle
Thomas, in which numerous pagan, ecclesiastical, and Gnostic motifs are
mixed. We will indicate only two details: In chaps. 6–8, there is portrayed
a *rapture* of the apostle, out of which he sings the wedding song describing
the redeeming ἱερὸς γάμος. In chap. 11, Jesus appears in the form of his
twin brother Thomas in order to win, by means of a speech, the royal bridal
couple for the true heavenly marriage. G. Bornkamm[402] has rightly compared the already mentioned practice of the Marcosian apostles with this
redeeming activity.[403]

The redeemer-apostle Thomas is one of many apostles who are sent forth,
as he is, for the purpose of redemption and as redeemers. The fact that the
number of these apostles is limited to twelve belongs to the ecclesiasticizing
of the Gnostic traditions of the acts of the apostles during the second and
third centuries. The claim of Thomas is precisely that of all the representatives of the plural Gnostic apostolate, and his appearance corresponds to
that of these many redeemers, even to the occasional ecstasy. Naturally he
is no longer *called* God or anything similar, but he acts as such a one, and
the designation δίδυμος τοῦ Χριστοῦ is only a hardly veiled expression of
the view that in essence Thomas is equal to Christ.

The actual title of Thomas in the Acts of Thomas is "apostle." For
ecclesiastical circles this title is harmless. But Thomas is not an "apostle of
Jesus Christ," but a twin brother of Christ and an apostle of God [404] in
the sense in which the Gnostic redeemer in general and even Christ can be
called "apostle"; more precisely, in the sense in which Simon, as part of the
"great power," was called an apostle.[405] Not only in self-interpretation, but
also in the use of the title "apostle," the figure of the apostle Thomas in
the Acts of Thomas, a figure which in other particulars has been considerably ecclesiasticized, goes back to the Gnostic apostolate,[406] as it, in its

---

[401] Chap. 15 = Lipsius-Bonnet, 121.12-13.

[402] *Op. cit.*, pp. 75-76.

[403] See pp. 170-71.

[404] ὁ δίδυμος τοῦ Χριστοῦ, ὁ ἀπόστολος τοῦ ὑψίστου καὶ συμμύστης τοῦ
λόγου τοῦ Χριστοῦ τοῦ ἀποκρύφου (Act. Thom. 39 = 156.12-14).

[405] G. Widengren ([4], p. 174) judges: "The addresses to the Apostle Thomas in
these acts bearing his name constantly reveal the Apostle's being treated as the Saviour" and:
Thomas "is sent immediately from 'the true God' (chap. 39), or 'the new God' (chap.
42)." Widengren also rightly compares ([3], p. 68) Abgar's statement in his apocryphal
letter to Jesus, "Either you are God . . . or you are the Son of God," with the opinion
concerning Thomas in the Act. Thom.: "This man is either God or God's apostle."

[406] One may also observe that the vigorous production of acts of apostles and similar
literature precisely in the area of the influence of Gnosticism betrays the latter's original
interest in the apostolic office.

plural type, was current in precisely that Syrian region from which the Acts of Thomas come.[407]

Other "Acts" of apostles show similar relationships.

In the Acts of Andrew also, for example, the apostle himself is basically the redeemer. In the Acts of John, Christ himself would speak words of Andrew such as the following: "Help me, that I may become perfect. Come to my aid, so that you may recognize your own true nature. . . . Do I possess you because you have listened to me? Do I find myself in you?" (9-10.) Along with this, to be sure, Jesus also plays a traditional orthodox role, but for the act of redemption he is utterly superfluous. For his salvation the one to be redeemed requires no one but the apostle Andrew (12).

With reference to the Acts of Philip, it may be said in the words of E. Käsemann ([1], p. 92): "Thus the predicates . . . [of the redeemer] . . . are transferred to his envoy or the redeemer appears conversely in the form of his envoy—thus Christ in that of Philip (Act. Phil. 148 = Bonnet II, 89) or in the ἀπεικασία of Thomas (Act. Thom. 11 = Bonnet II, 116)."

On the Acts of Paul, see E. Peterson, *Frühkirche, Judentum und Gnosis* (1959), pp. 197-200; 23.

4. We summarize: Gnosticism knows two fundamentally different types of the redeemer figure. Either the redemption proceeds from a heavenly being who is sent into the world for the redemption of the fallen sparks of light, or these earthly sparks of light themselves appear as redeemers of the entire Pneuma. In the first case the redeemer is usually *one*, who once or repeatedly in the primeval time, or in the near or distant past, appeared. In the latter case the number of redeemers is in principle unlimited and their appearance is occasionally a present one. Both types of the redeemer present claims to the same significance and the same essential quality of being.[408]

---

[407] Cf. G. Widengren [3], pp. 65 ff.

[408] The basic identity and at the same time structural difference of these apostolic figures is also shown in much of the terminology which pertains to them. Thus, e.g., H. Schulte (*Der Begriff der Offenbarung im Neuen Testament* (1949), pp. 67 ff.) has proved that φανεροῦν or φανέρωσις are concepts of the special language of Gnosticism which denote the appearing of the redeemer or of his revelation. This is in keeping with the fact that the Corinthian Gnostics could use φανεροῦσθαι with reference to themselves in the same sense as ἐξιστάναι (cf. *Die Gnosis in Korinth*, p. 179; H. Schulte, pp. 20-21): for them in fact the ecstatic revelation of the Christ-Pneuma is the manifestation of the redeemer.

H. Windisch (*Paulus und Christus*, pp. 143-75) draws various parallels between the apostle Christ and the apostle Paul, but without even taking into account the actual backgrounds of his in part interesting observations and genuine parallels.

Led by an altogether different interest from that of our work, H. Becker (*op. cit.*, pp. 20 ff.) also comes to recognize the identity of "revelational address and missionary preaching," i.e., of the ministry of the *one* emissary and the ministry of the *many* apostles.

The two titles therefore coincide, and in both there appears under these titles also the concept of "apostle." [409]

The two types of the redeemer meet when a heavenly redeemer awakens one of the earthly sparks of light and sends it forth as a redeemer.[410] In this case the *one* function is allotted to two redeemers. This, too, makes it clear that in principle the two types are in competition with each other. They touch, to be sure, at the point of the communication of γνῶσις and ἐξουσία, but they cannot appear with each other as apostles-redeemers.

The often cited passage from Corp. Herm. X, 25 has already shown this. It is further shown, for example, in Od. Sol. 41. 15:

> The anointed one is in truth *one*,
> And he was known before the foundation of the world.

One may also compare John 10:7 ff. in the sense of the evangelist[411]:

Truly, truly I say to you, I am the door for the sheep; all those who have come before me are thieves and robbers.

Or John 5:43:

I have come in the name of my Father and you do not receive me; if another comes *in his own name*, him you will receive.

We recall the fact that it belongs to the characteristic marks of the plural apostolate that the apostles, as Paul formulates it, proclaim *themselves* (II Cor. 4:5).

Further, in John 3:31 [412] we read:

> Ὁ ἄνωθεν ἐρχόμενος ἐπάνω πάντων ἐστίν· ὁ ὢν ἐκ τῆς
> γῆς ἐκ τῆς γῆς ἐστιν καὶ ἐκ τῆς γῆς λαλεῖ.

On this passage we consider the fact that the many earthly redeemers appear in that region of the Near East in which also the Gospel of John may have arisen, and of this Gospel it is true that "in general we encounter ideas which can be understood only as current ones in their historical milieu." [413]

---

[409] G. Widengren ([4], p. 170) also has seen this, basically correctly: "There are above all two technical terms for the Saviour indicating his 'being sent,' *viz.* Apostle and Messenger. These names can, therefore, without any discrimination be given to the Divine Being sent down from on high, or to the earthly representative of this Saviour, and this both in Manichaeism and Mandaeism, on one side, and Christianity in its more Gnostic colouring, on the other."

[410] The examples of this, above, pp. 148 ff.

[411] R. Bultmann, *Das Evangelium des Johannes*, p. 287.

[412] Cf. John 3:13, and on this, S. Schulz, *op. cit.*, p. 106, n. 194.

[413] G. P. Wetter, *op. cit.*, p. 55.

Also behind Barnabas 3. 39, E. Peterson[414] suspects a polemic: τίς ἀνέβη εἰς τὸν οὐρανὸν καὶ ἔλαβεν αὐτὴν (sc., Wisdom) καὶ κατεβίβασεν αὐτὴν ἐκ τῶν νεφελῶν? Answer: No one; God sent Wisdom from above.

Therefore it may be said: *Where the apostle* is the authority, the apostolic authority of the Gnostic missionaries must disappear.[415] But *where the apostles* preach in nonmediated, demonstrable authority, the *one* emissary has no right to existence.

Thus it is only consistent that Paul, who employs the word group ἀποσ-τέλλειν, etc., for the plural apostolate, never uses it for Jesus Christ.[416] He manifestly stands in the same Gnostic tradition which, for example, is represented by the Corinthian apostles. Conversely, in the same way[417] is explained the noteworthy fact that in the Gospel of John the disciples are never called apostles. One can hardly imagine that the author of the Gospel of John would intentionally deny the title of apostle to the disciples, especially since he speaks (in 4:38; 17:18) quite casually of their being sent. Possibly John is still unacquainted with the later tradition which gives the title of apostle to the twelve. In any case, it was quite alien to *his* Gnostic tradition to give the earthly envoys this title[418]; for in the center of his Gospel stands the *one* emissary, Jesus Christ.

It is precisely the similarity of the task of the two different types of the apostolate that accounts for their actually, and sometimes explicitly, mutually exclusive appearance.

It is not surprising that the later the time, the less frequent is the occurrence of the *concept* of "apostle" for the many redeemers, while the title of "prophet" for these figures remains customary in Gnosticism (Valentinians, Marcosians, Celsus, *et al.*).[419] Very early the Gnostics

---

[414] *Frühkirche, Judentum und Gnosis* (1959), pp. 48-49.

[415] Hence the Mandaeans polemicize against the—equally Gnostic—"emissary of error" on behalf of the *one* heavenly emissary (see pp. 185 ff.).

[416] The sole exception, Gal. 4:4, is found in a pre-Pauline confessional formula.

[417] A different attempt at explanation in H. v. Campenhausen [2], p. 29.

[418] Only later are the distinctions between the two mentioned forms of the Gnostic apostolate effaced. This occurs most clearly in the Apocryphal acts of the Apostles which we have already considered (see pp. 187 ff.).
This mutual interpenetration in the relation of Jesus and the apostles also becomes clear in the *Pistis Sophia.* Cf., e.g., chap. 7 (Schmidt, pp. 6-7): "I brought with me from the beginning twelve powers . . . which I have taken from the twelve redeemers of the treasury of light according to the command of the First Mystery. These then I put into the womb of your mothers. . . . For these powers were given to you before the whole world, because you are they who will save the whole world . . ." (cf. chap. 8). Again: "Mary Magdalene and John . . . will be on my right and on my left, and I am they and they are I (chap. 96 = Schmidt, p. 148).

[419] Further, we cannot be surprised that a quite comprehensive body of literature has been preserved for us in which the *one* apostle is spoken of, delivers his addresses, proclaims

recognized the church's concept of apostle which restricted the apostolate to the first Christian generation. This they owed to the missionary interest of their "Christianity." [420] Conversely, at the same time the church eliminated the title of prophet for them in favor of Gnosticism. [421] But "apostle" and "prophet" are for early Gnosticism designations for the *same* "enthusiastic" (or fanatical) redeemer figure; the distinction concerns only the form of the ministry, [422] and hence the change from one to the other is easily possible. [423]

Still the title of apostle is understandably retained within Gnostic literature in the acts of the apostles, since these throughout concern themselves with figures from the circle of the twelve, although their concept of apostle, as we have seen, is the *Gnostic* one.

V

1. The question suggests itself as to whether the Gnostic concept of the apostle as we have just presented it had its own, still earlier, prototype. It is obvious that, with all the differentiation between types, yet a unitary

---

his message, while we seek in vain for the direct literary remains of the *plural* apostolate. In fact, it was noticeable that our account of the exclusive concept of the apostle rested essentially upon the "self-testimonies" and revelational speeches of these apostles, while the basis of the analysis of the plural concept of the apostles was almost exclusively a series of secondary reports of the *appearance* of these apostles. This difference is that of the apostolate itself. The *one* apostle is active by means of his *words handed down* from generation to generation. The activity of the *many* apostles consists in their *current appearance* at a given time. They do not write any books and in general will not even have given guidance to their communities, which were instructed by the Spirit, by means of letters, as Paul always did in exceptional situations.

[420] See p. 284. Thus with the Montanists only the title of prophet occurs, although the Montanist Maximilla can assert: "ἀπέστειλέ με κύριος . . ." (Epiph. Haer. 48.13). Nevertheless it is noteworthy that in spite of a certain ecclesiasticizing in their Christology, the Montanist prophets take up the claim of the plural Gnostic apostolate and set their revelations in opposition to the ecclesiastical tradition. Eusebius quotes as an expression of Maximilla: "ῥῆμά εἰμι καὶ πνεῦμα καὶ δύναμις" (CH V, 16.17). Cf. W. Bauer [1], pp. 180 ff.; G. P. Wetter, *op. cit.*, pp. 9-10.

[421] See pp. 226-27.

[422] See pp. 226-27.

[423] It is no accident that the two titles which earlier were common to the two tendencies were later divided precisely in such a way that the Catholic Church held to the apostolate and Gnosticism to prophetism, and not the reverse. The missionary office of the apostle, incomparably important at first, diminished in importance in comparison with the fixed officers of the community as time went on. It necessarily became an office with a great past; indeed it became a past office. As such, for enthusiastic Gnosticism it was without interest; yet for the tradition-bound church it was of ever-increasing importance. Conversely, the growing dependence of the church upon tradition rendered the office of the prophet suspect for it, while for pure Gnosticism this office continued to be indispensable.

concept lies at the basis of the representation of the "sent ones" in Gnosticism.

G. Widengren has concerned himself with this question in many of his splendid investigations[424] in which he has demonstrated that in Mesopotamia there have been "apostles of God" for a long time. He pursues these figures from the Sumerians through the Mandaeans and Manichaeans, Judaism, Samaritans and Christian Gnostics, down to Islam. Here we are interested only in the fact that in Mesopotamia, the home of Gnosticism and at the same time the second home of Judaism, already in pre-Gnostic times the heavenly emissary played a role, and technical expressions served to identify him.[425]

Above all else, the king served as emissary; yet he was not the only one.[426] Already *Lugalzaggisi* (about the middle of the third millennium B.C.) was called "king of Uruk, king of the country, the *Sent One* of Enlil, king of countries." [427] G. Widengren brings forward documentation for the royal "Sent Ones" from Lugalzaggisi down to the last Babylonian king, Nabonidus (556-39).[428] He characterizes these figures in summary: "The king is the possessor of divine knowledge imparted to him especially by the god of wisdom, but also of course as the possessor of the tablets of wisdom. He may also be called 'the sage scribe.' The king is the Sent One. He has ascended to heaven to receive, among other things, the tablets of destiny and to get his commission. Then he is sent out, i.e. he descends again. . . . As to the knowledge communicated to the king, it is of a mysterious character bearing upon the great mystery of heaven and earth, the hidden things, and it is a revelation of the hidden knowledge possessed by the gods (the god)" ([2], pp. 20-21).

It is clear that all the essential formal traits of the later Gnostic apostolate, and indeed particularly of the plural form, are here prefigured. The emissary is in possession of the divine mysteries, which are otherwise concealed. He is an earthly figure, who ascends to heaven in order thus to become an "emissary" of heaven; he in no way claims, however, to be the

[424] See the bibliography. Cf. also W. Staerk, *Soter*, II, 218 ff.

[425] K. Rudolph (*op. cit.*) has shown in several instances (e.g., pp. 200 ff.) that G. Widengren's studies on particular points may be used only with discrimination; still there can be no doubt about the correctness of the basic thesis (see *ibid.*, p. 128 *et passim*) which affirms a Mesopotamian apostolate which in essential features could become the formal prototype of the Gnostic apostolate.

[426] Already in the Gathas of the Avesta (32.1), but also in later Parsee literature (e.g., Dadistan-i Dinik 2.10; 48.30) Zarathustra and his friends and helpers also serve as *apostles* of Ahura Mazda.

[427] G. Widengren [2], p. 19. The expressions for "sent one" are in Sumerian "ki(n)-ki(n)-ma" and in Akkadian "nasparu," according to Widengren.

[428] Cf. also H. Gressmann, *Der Messias*, pp. 27, 41; E. Norden [2], p. 214.

only emissary. All this we meet again in the Gnostic apostolate, so that there can be no doubt of the fact that the Gnostic concept of the apostle already[429] had had its precursors.[430]

This knowledge is important for the understanding of the concepts ἀποστέλλειν–ἀπόστολος. According to what has been said above, an already given technical expression is translated with the word ἀποστέλλειν. In this case ἀποστέλλειν offered itself, because in secular Greek this stem already contained, in contrast with πέμπειν, the idea of the authority of the one sent.[431] It appears that not only in the case of the Gnostic apostle, but also in the case of his Mesopotamian prototype, an important stress was placed upon this element along with the idea of "being sent" itself. Since the Semitic equivalents of ἀποστέλλειν–ἀπόστολος were always formed from a single stem,[432] the now resulting adoption into use of the infrequent ἀπόστολος alongside the frequently used ἀποστέλλειν was a wholly natural development, which created a sharply delineated *terminus technicus*.

2. To be sure, still more important is the question whether the Gnostic concept of the apostle as sketched above continued in the post-Gnostic times. If this question is to be answered in the affirmative, then one could, in a given instance, draw conclusions from this later apostolate's characteristics concerning the Gnostic conception of the apostle. The connections between Gnostic and ecclesiastical apostolate which are most interesting to us will be treated shortly.

There is nevertheless in early Islam and among Iranian sects of the same time an expanded conception of the apostle to be demonstrated, a conception which contains all the essential characteristics of the plural apostolate of Gnosticism. Widengren ([3]) has explicitly dealt with this matter. On the basis of some of the examples offered by him, I shall set forth the structure, already well enough known to us, of the plural concept of the apostle. I shall reproduce the citations as given by Widengren; so far as it was possible, they have been checked with the sources.

The fact that in the Koran Mohammed is regularly called *rasul Allah* = "apostle of God" does not need especially to be documented (Widengren [3], pp. 7 ff.). To be sure, in the understanding of Islam he is not a representative of the plural apostolate, but rather the unique earthly apostle of

---

[429] On the existence of the emissary in Iranian religion, cf. A. v. Gall, *Basileia tou Theon* (Heidelberg, 1926), p. 126.

[430] Cf. further H. L. Jansen, *Die Henochgestalt,* Oslo, 1939.

[431] Cf. K. H. Rengstorf [1], pp. 398 ff.

[432] Cf., e.g., שלח—שליח in the Hebrew sources; and שאדאר—אישגאנדא in the Mandaean sources. Also in the later *Arabic* sources substantive and verb are formed from *one* stem; see G. Widengren [3], pp. 14 ff.

Allah. Mohammed's teaching rests upon "revelations," which were imparted to him in visions and auditions, and occasionally through the mediation of the archangel Gabriel. He himself recognized Moses, Jesus, and others (*ibid.*, pp. 23, 27-28, 35) as apostles *before* him. Soon after his death his self-interpretation, which ranged within the normal human sphere, was elevated into a superhuman one.

This development may have been strengthened in the defense against sectarian apostles. For alongside Mohammed there appeared others, for example *Musailimah* and *Tulayhah* (*ibid.*, pp. 16 ff.), as apostles; also before him, there are apostles attested in South Arabia, men whose names are mentioned in some instances in the Koran (*ibid.*, pp. 17 ff.). At about the same time such apostles appear also in Iran:

I am Bihafarid, the apostle of God to you.[433]

These apostles compete with one another:

I called him a liar and labeled his apostleship as false,[434]

says one apostle concerning the other. Particularly among the Shiites the apostolate was widespread. *Sahrastani* [435] reproduces the following as the opinion of a Shiite candidate for the office of Imam:

He believed further that he was the spark which fell from Heaven, and believed also that the apostles would never cease to be and that the apostolate never would be exhausted.

Many others similarly claim the apostolate (Widengren [3], pp. 29 ff.) which is passed on from the teacher to the pupils:

Bazig is a prophet and an apostle like *Abu-l-Khattab*,[436]

and

Al-Sari is an apostle like Abu-l-Khattab[437] (*ibid.*, pp. 31 ff., 42 ff., 88).

or passes on in a succession from the father to the sons:

[433] Houtsma in WZKM, III (1889), 33-34. See further [3], pp. 25 ff. G. Widengren correctly considers it difficult to determine whether here we encounter the last representatives of the Gnostic-Iranian apostle tradition or traces of Islamic influence.

[434] Al-Hamdani, Al-Iklil, ed. Nabih Amin Faris (Princeton Oriental Texts, Vol. VII, 1940), p. 142.7-8.

[435] Sahrastani, ed. Haarbrücker (Halle, 1850-51), I, 205.

[436] Al-Naubakhti, *Die Sekten der Schia,* ed. H. Ritter. Bibliotheca Islamica, IV (Istanbul, 1931), 38.15-16.

[437] *Ibid.,* p. 39.1 ff.

They hold that Ali was the apostle and that his children after him are apostles[438]

One Shiite sect believes that

all the apostles . . . are only *one* spirit and that revelation never ceases.[439]

The apostles assert that they are able to make their claim on the basis of a heavenly journey. *Sahrastani*[440] reports of *Abu Mansur al-Igli*:

He maintained . . . that he was lifted up to heaven and had seen the object of his worship, and he had patted him on the head with his hand and said to him: O my son, descend and convey a message from me; whereupon he had sent him down to the earth (*ibid.*, pp. 29-30, 85 ff.).

The one thus called in the course of a heavenly journey presents himself to men:

I am *Bihafarid*, the apostle of God to you.[441]

A heavenly journey of Mohammed himself is also reported (*ibid.*, pp. 96 ff.), and the later Islamic literature occasionally enlarges such reports considerably (*ibid.*, pp. 102 ff.):

Also *Bazig* claimed that he had ascended to heaven and that God had touched him and spat into his mouth, and that wisdom had grown in his breast like the truffle in earth, and that he had seen Ali sitting at the right hand of God.[442]

Thus the apostle has "knowledge" to proclaim, which for the most part is declared as "secrets":

Abu Muslim is a "sent prophet" who knows the hidden things, he whom *Abu Gafar al-Mansur* sent out [443] (cf. *ibid.*, pp. 43, 49, 83, 87).

In the Koran there are polemics against such a view:

I say not to you . . . : I know things secret.[444]

[438] Al-Bagdadi, *Moslem Schisms and Sects*, ed. A. S. Halkin (Tel Aviv, 1935), p. 67. (*ibid.*, p. 37).
[439] Mutahhar, *Le livre de la création*, ed. C. Huart (Paris, 1899-1919), IV, 28.
[440] Sahrastani, *op. cit.*, p. 205.
[441] WZKM, III (1889), 33-34.
[442] Mutahhar, *op. cit.*, V, 137.
[443] Al-Naubakhti, *op. cit.*, p. 46.15 ff.
[444] Sura 6.50.

Occasionally among the Shiites, Gabriel also appears as the mediator of such bits of heavenly wisdom (*ibid.*, p. 32).[445]

An example of the "I am" formula which was also common among these apostles has already been cited (cf. *ibid.*, pp. 48 ff.).

The lofty claim of these apostles also becomes clear in the following comment by *Al-Naubakhti* about a Shiite sect:

They said that the Imams are gods, and that they are prophets and that they are apostles and that they are angels.[446]

Of *Gafar al-Sadik* it is reported that with the following words he called a pupil to become an apostle:

O *Abu-l-Khattab*, I am God, and thou art my apostle unto my creation.[447]

Numbers of the passages adduced by Widengren ([3]) show that for the circles being described, prophet and apostle belong very close together and are often even interchangeable concepts (cf., e.g., pp. 30 ff.).

There is no question that the concept of apostle thus briefly described corresponds throughout to the plural apostolate of Gnosticism. To be sure, within Islam it is just as heretical as was Gnosticism within Christianity. However Mohammed himself may have understood his apostleship, for orthodox Islam Mohammed is simply *the*, even if earthly, apostle (cf. *ibid.*, pp. 47, 215-16).

Now one will hardly be able to prove definite connections between the here indicated Islamic concept of the apostle and the plural apostolate of Gnosticism. Naturally Mohammed himself and all the more his successors in the Shi'a were affected by strong influences of Christian and Jewish heresy. But even the concept of apostle in Gnosticism is only one special case of the conception, which was widespread in the Near East in numerous versions and at all times, of the heavenly or earthly emissary of God (*ibid.*, p. 216). The only thing we can say with *certainty* about it is that the plural apostolate of the Jewish and early Christian Gnosticism and the later concept of the apostle of Iranian and Islamic sectarians emerged in the same milieu; direct dependence cannot be *proven.*

[445] Al-Naubakhti, *op. cit.*, p. 55.1 ff.

[446] Al-Naubakhti, *op. cit.*, p. 32.6-7.

[447] Al-Dailami, *Die Geheimlehre der Batiniten*. Bibliotheca Islamica, II (Istanbul, 1939), 3.5 ff.

VI

Is there a connection between the plural apostolate of Gnosticism and the church's apostolate? [448] This is to be assumed as a matter of course when we reflect upon what has been said so far, and this assumption will be confirmed in the course of the comparison which now follows. At the same time, it will follow that the dependence lies on the side of the church's apostolate.[449] That Paul himself was not conscious of such a dependence should here be established once and for all.[450]

We employ, as a basis for the following section, the division presented in Part I of this work, and attempt to compare the individual characteristic traits of the church's apostolate there established with the Gnostic concept of the apostle. Not all points of correspondence between the two views of the apostolate are of equal significance, and not all are equally compelling and necessary. Still the comparison must be completely carried through; on the decisive characteristics it appears to me to be both convincing and inescapable.

1. We established first that the church's apostolate did not elevate its bearer out of the community and did not bestow upon him any special spiritual preference. The same is true for the Gnostic apostolate. There was at that time hardly any religious movement which in such radical fashion took away all distinctions between the members of their community as did Gnosticism. At first, to be sure, there was a fundamental distinction made between πνεῦμα and σάρξ, and thus between pneumatics and sar-

---

[448] Anyone who prefers to speak of a "gnosticizing" "charismatic itinerant apostolate" (thus J. Roloff, op. cit., pp. 80, 82) may do so; yet one may not, on the one hand, reckon firmly with the existence of such a charismatic itinerant apostolate (op. cit., p. 82) and, on the other hand, reject my attempt to derive the Pauline apostolate from it with the assertion that I have hardly succeeded in proving the existence of Gnostic apostles in the proper sense (op. cit., p. 20). For then one would, with E. Schweizer (TLZ [1962], col. 839), have to trace the apostle concept of Jewish and Jewish-Christian Gnosticism back to Paul, an undertaking which is for various reasons impossible; see the next note.

[449] G. Schille (op. cit., pp. 10-11) wishes conversely to trace the Gnostic concept of the apostle back to the early Christian one. But in view of the structural similarity of the heavenly and earthly emissaries in Gnosticism, this means also to derive the heavenly apostle from the early Christian apostolate—an unworkable undertaking!

[450] This is already shown from the fact that Paul only late, after his theology had long been formed, comes into direct contact with Gnosticism, namely in the mission fields of Asia Minor and Greece (see Die Gnosis in Korinth, first ed., pp. 124-25). Since Paul knew himself to be the last of the apostles, who moreover only received his call quite late, he in no case took part in the formation of the original ecclesiastical apostolate. In view of this state of things, to expect of Paul that he must have reflected upon the origin of his concept of the apostle and informed himself about it (thus E. Güttgemanns [2], p. 69) is an unreasonable demand.

kics,[451] the bearers of the spirit and the mere fleshly men. But the sarkics are in fact "nothing" (II Cor. 12:11); they are perishing substance which stems from the prince of this world, and are destined for extinction like all matter. Genuine existence belongs only to the pneumatics. Among these latter, however, every distinction has ceased to exist. All differentiations among men reside in their fleshliness; on the other hand, every true pneumatic being is a spark of the heavenly Anthropos, a member of the cosmic Christ, a fragment of the figure of the primal man which has been dismembered by the demons. "In Christ," i.e., in the eschatological existence of the pneuma which has been freed from the sarx, there is therefore neither Jew nor Greek, neither slave nor free man, neither male nor female; "in Christ" all genuine Being is the one pneuma.[452] Hence for the Gnostics it is sheer nonsense that the women should keep silence in the church[453]; their pneuma is not at all different from that which is found in men.

Therefore naturally there is also no "spiritual" distinction in the community, for—and here Paul's formulation is Gnostic through and through—"one and the same Spirit" (I Cor. 12:11) works all spiritual gifts. Thus God has set the apostolic calling as the most exalted service of the community, but one is an apostle only ἐκ μέρους (cf. I Cor. 12:27-28); the *whole,* to which the apostle belongs as *one* member alongside all the other pneumatics, is the σῶμα Χριστοῦ, as Paul puts it in still another bit of Gnostic terminology. We saw earlier how the representatives of the plural apostolate of Gnosticism are always concerned to assist their hearers in gaining that *same* self-understanding with which they themselves appear, so that the one thus redeemed can himself in turn become active as a redeemer. Simon, who is the "Great Power," gathers himself together by seeking the other parts of the "Great Power." The prophet Marcus awakens also in his "hearer" the prophetic gift, etc. The redeemer-apostle thus is no more than the ones who are to be redeemed. At this point, therefore, there appears a fully formal agreement between the Gnostic and the ecclesiastical apostolates. That Paul, however, achieves the identification of this side of his concept of apostle with the help of purely Gnostic categories is already an indication of his dependence.[454]

---

[451] The triad "pneumatics-psychics-hylics" stems from the later period of Gnosticism and is a sign of its internal softening.

[452] Cf. Gal. 3:28; Col. 3:11, and on the Gnostic origin of these ideas, *Die Gnosis in Korinth,* pp. 226-27. As clear evidence, I add to what is given there Pist. Soph. 143 (Schmidt, p. 245): ". . . to the place in which there is neither male nor female, nor are there forms in that place, but a perpetual, indescribable light."

[453] I Cor. 14:33*b*-36; cf. also E. Käsemann, *Der Dienst der Frau an der Workverkündigung nach dem Neuen Testament* (n. d.).

[454] I do not see that G. Klein (*op. cit.,* p. 277) has a conclusive argument against the derivation of the ecclesiastical concept of the apostle from the Gnostic one, in his objec-

2. The mission is entrusted to the primitive church's apostolate. For the Gnostic apostle the same holds true, of course. He too is called apostle for precisely this reason, because he is a "sent one," a missionary. The Gnostic apostles confront us not at all differently from the manner of Paul and his fellow apostles on missionary tours in the Gentile world. In Galatia, Philippi, and Corinth they do missionary work in the tracks of Paul and thus endanger the young congregations which he has founded. That they enter into the congregation from outside is shown by the fact that on their departure to travel further they apparently had letters of recommendation issued to them, with which they could introduce themselves into new situations (II Cor. 3:1). Simon travels in the West of the Empire, Mani in the East; he sends other apostles into all the world, so that in a short time Manichaeism is generally disseminated. Irenaeus meets the apostles of the Marcosians in Asia Minor as well as in the Rhone valley, and the prophets of Celsus are generally to be found in Phoenicia and Palestine. G. P. Wetter (op. cit., p. 70) correctly names as a distinguishing trait of these savior figures the fact "that they are always found on tours."

The Gnostics, for whom everything depends upon the free operation of the Spirit without hindrance, naturally do not think in terms of community organization.[455] The fact that the Christian apostle did not look upon the organizing and leading of a congregation as his task,[456] as Paul testifies,[457] is now easily explained.

At this point the question should be raised as to where the origin of the planned Christian mission is to be sought. It is well known that at the first the primitive community in Jerusalem gave as little thought to an organized mission as did Judaism of all periods. They waited in Jerusalem for the in-breaking of the kingdom of God, which they proclaimed as imminent. That the community was expanded during that eschatologically

---

tion that it makes the title of apostle in Paul a mere designation of function. For even if in Paul's thought the apostolate always appears at the head of the list of charismata bestowed by God (I Cor. 12:28 et passim), still Paul never ascribes to it more than a charismatic function. The specifics of this apostolic function, however, can be made understandable precisely from the perspective of the Gnostic origin, as will presently become evident.

[455] The absence of such community organization in the early period of Gnosticism and of all that pertains to such organization (e.g., a body of literature for use in worship, nonpneumatic offices, a fixed liturgy) must not lead us astray to the conclusion that there were no Gnostic communities. A glance at the similar character of the Pauline communities would have to rule out this conclusion.

[456] Although there naturally were functions of leadership in the Pauline communities, in contrast to the Gnostic conventicles (I Cor. 12:28).

[457] Of course the later period, Luke and the Pastoral Epistles, cannot conceive of it other than that even the community organization had been a special concern of Paul.

expectant time is no marvel, but in this time one could not arrive at the idea of a mission aimed at a goal. All the more puzzling is the beginning of the non-law-observing Gentile mission.

There can be no doubt that the beginnings of the Christian mission lie in the neighborhood of Antioch, in which also the apostolate is native. Could not only the apostolate but the organized mission in general be a gift from Gnostic circles? This is very probable. For Gnosticism there existed a necessary connection between the *eschaton* and the missionary work of the community. The Gnostics indeed no longer anticipated the eschatological intervention of God as did the primitive community in Jerusalem. God had already performed his final deed; the redeeming Gnosis has been sent. Now the responsibility lay with men themselves to bring about the culmination by gathering all the scattered sparks of light by means of Gnosis and by uniting them once again to the cosmic σῶμα Χριστοῦ, from which they had been kept at a distance by the malicious work of the demons. A comprehensive mission was thus the basic condition for the actualization of the redemption; for the individual Gnostic was only redeemed when, through the return home of all the scattered sparks of the spirit, the Christ-Primal Man had been restored, and the Pleroma had again become complete. Thus in Gnosticism there emerged necessarily a Gnostic mission and a Gnostic apostolate, and both were taken over by the ecclesiastical circles in the Syrian region.

This fact may be documented particularly with regard to the (non-law-observing) Gentile mission, on the basis of our sources. The discussions within the church about the non-law-observing mission among the Gentiles are well known; the "Judaizers" never took part in it. It is therefore inconceivable that the initiative for this Gentile mission is to be traced back to contemporary Judaism or indirectly by way of the primitive community in Jerusalem even to the intention of the historical Jesus.

Paul knew himself to have been set apart in his mother's womb by the exalted Christ to proclaim the gospel among the Gentiles (Gal. 1:15-16; 2:8; Rom. 1:5; 15:16).[458] But he was neither the first nor the only apostle to the Gentiles; he entered upon a work that had already been begun.[459]

---

[458] The emphasis with which Paul describes himself as apostle of the *Gentiles* naturally does not arise from a basic separation from the mission to the Jews (although this separation actually resulted from the arrangements of Gal. 2:9), but from the consciousness of the unprecedented newness of the fact that the Gentiles are fellow citizens of the kingdom of God.

[459] Cf. A. v. Harnack [1], I, 48. Therefore the question as to the origin of the Gentile mission free from the law cannot be answered with a reference to Paul's Damascus experience, whatever significance this experience had for Paul and his understanding of

Therefore the Gentile mission as such was apparently never a problem to him; it is foreseen in the Old Testament (Rom. 9:25 ff.) and has the visible blessing of God (Gal. 2:2). Only the question of the law in the Gentile mission becomes a problem for him, the former Pharisee, and the original contribution of Paul to the mission may lie in his answer to this question.[460] The fact that the Jews paid no attention to the mission also becomes a problem. But this problem evidently was solved by Paul in a Gnostic fashion.

Already in Jewish Christian Gnosticism, in fact, the question as to the justification of the Gentile mission had been posed. If one considers how heavily the Gnostic apostles with whom Paul had to battle in Galatia, Philippi, and Corinth stressed their Judaism (II Cor. 11:22; Phil. 3:4 ff.; Gal. 3:2), then the conclusion is unavoidable that they belonged to a circle of originally exclusively Jewish Gnostics, in which the possession of the Pneuma was regarded as reserved for the Jewish people.[461] The Gnostic material which is utilized in Eph. 2:11–3:21 [462] shows how people in the Gnostic circles then justified the change to the Gentile mission, which in view of the failure among their own people and of the widespread pneumatic-ecstatic manifestations in the Gentile world began almost under compulsion. Thereafter in the Gentile mission it had to do with a "mystery" which was "made known" through a "revelation." And in fact this "revelation" was issued "in the spirit" to the "holy apostles and prophets," from whom, through the "church" it even reached the "heavenly principalities and

---

the mission to the Gentiles; on the latter point, cf. Chr. Maurer, "Paulus als der Apostel der Völker," in *Ev. Theol.*, XIX (1959), 28 ff.

[460] Naturally Paul already found at hand the Christian mission to the Gentiles, free from the law—on account of it he persecuted the Christians; but the form in which Paul theologically solves the question of the law may be essentially his own theological achievement.

[461] Perhaps one may here recall the gnosticizing Wisdom literature of late Judaism, e.g.:
"Then the creator of all things gave me [*sc.*, Wisdom] a commandment,
And the one who created me gave to my dwelling place an abiding place
And said: Make your dwelling place in Jacob
And in Israel receive it as an inheritance" (Jes. Sir. 24.8).

[462] On the Gnostic background of this section, see H. Schlier, *Christus und die Kirche im Epheserbrief* (1930), esp. pp. 18 ff.; *ibid.*, *Die Kirche im Epheserbrief* (1949); *Die Gnosis in Korinth*, first ed., p. 108; G. Schille, *Liturgisches Gut im Epheserbrief*, Diss. (Göttingen, 1953). The kernel of the hymn in Eph. 2:14 ff. is apparently formed by the mythological idea of the bringing together of the sparks of the Pneuma imprisoned on earth with the substance of the Pneuma that remained in the Pleroma, into the one Primal Man. This material was reshaped into the clearly recognizable revelation hymn, the content of which is given above. I consider even this reshaping to have been done essentially within Gnosticism. The author of Ephesians then has finally built this hymn with an ecclesiastical commentary into his writing.

powers," while it was not "made known" to the other generations, and "in God" had been kept secret even from the "aeons." The content of this revelation is that the Gentiles are "fellow heirs, fellow members, and fellow participants" of the promises "in Christ." After this revelation takes place, the "dividing wall" between Jews and Gentiles is torn down, and both become, "in Christ" or "in one spirit," "one body," i.e., the "new Anthropos."

Here the Gnostic form of argument shows through with full clarity[463]: the Gentile mission is a mystery of God which was revealed to the apostles in the spirit. For the thoroughly antinomian and libertine early Gnosticism of a Jewish stamp, in contrast with Paul,[464] the question as to the validity of the law is not posed.[465]

But for this Gnosticism as well as for Paul, the fact of the blinding of Israel was a problem. Here now in Paul *himself* the Gnostic argumentation appears to have been preserved. In Rom. 11:25 ff. he is able to reveal to the community a "mystery" which stems from the "depth" of the "sophia" and "gnosis" of God and which was concealed from human cunning: Israel is in part hardened until the "Pleroma" [466] of the Gentiles has "entered in," and then all Israel will be saved.[467] "Language and thought forms of this prophetic speech are hebraicizing," as O. Michel (*op. cit.*, p. 249) correctly argues. But at the same time they are not genuinely Pauline. Not only does the statement that all Israel will be saved stand in tension with Rom. 9:6 ff., I Thess. 2:14 ff., and other passages. To say that the Parousia is to be dependent upon the success of the mission also contradicts the eschatological ideas of Paul when he says that the Parousia is to be expected at any moment. According to Rom. 11:25 ff., however, the Parousia must necessarily be delayed until first the Gentiles and then also the Jews have been converted. Both language and conception of this passage are, on the other hand, understandable in terms of Jewish-Christian Gnosticism[468]: The restoration of the Pleroma comes about according to the divine purpose in such a way that

---

[463] Cf. also Col. 1:26-27, and on this, *Die Gnosis in Korinth*, first ed. pp. 123-24.

[464] The theological problem of the law is easily solved for Gnosticism with the reference to the origin of the Old Testament from the hand of a lesser or even of the evil deity or of demonic angels. Even in Paul, who did not manage this problem so easily, there is found a remnant of this argument in Gal. 3:19; cf. H. Schlier, *op. cit.*, pp. 111-12.

[465] The fact that the libertine Gnostics in Galatia practiced circumcision has nothing to do with nomism, as I have tried to show in ZNW, XLVII (1958), 46 ff. (*Paulus und die Gnostiker* [1965], pp. 27 ff.).

[466] On πλήρωμα, cf. H. Schlier, *Der Brief an die Epheser* (1958), pp. 96 ff.; H. Jervell, *Imago Dei*, pp. 221-22.

[467] On this passage, cf. O. Michel (in Meyer's *Kommentar, in loc.*) who considers it likely "that an earlier divine utterance was re-formed by Paul" (p. 250, n. 2).

[468] On this, cf. E. Norden [2], pp. 295 ff.

first the *Gentiles* and thereafter the Jews enter into the Pleroma through reception of Gnosis.

If one accepts what has been said, then it not only becomes clear that the church's apostolate has a Gnostic prototype; it also shows that the apostolate only as the integrating part of the *entire*[469] missionary concern of the earliest church of Syria was taken over[470] from circles of still Jewish or of already Christian Gnosticism.[471]

This begins to answer the question why only a part of the Christian missionaries bore the name of "apostles." In Gnostic circles, as the Didache shows, actually every missionary might also have been an "apostle." In contrast, not every Christian missionary fulfilled the prerequisites of the apostolate. The reason will be discussed in the following.

3. The apostle is "called" by the exalted Christ *himself*. The Gnostic background of this conception is evident. The relationship of the genuine Gnostic to Christ is one of identity of being. He is Χριστοῦ, i.e., a part of

---

[469] Syria is also explicitly presupposed as the place of origin of the mission to the Gentiles in Ep. Ap. 33. It is incomprehensible to me how J. Roloff (*op. cit.*, p. 20; cf. also E. Schweizer, TLZ (1962), col. 839), in spite of these statements, which he apparently has not even read, can write that the "most serious objection" to my derivation of the apostolate from Gnosticism is "that from it precisely the *proprium* of the Pauline concept of the apostle, his being sent on the mission to the Gentiles, remains unexplainable; for Gnosticism provides no point of contact for this." It is, rather, true that *no* point of contact for the Pauline mission to the Gentiles is provided in the derivation, also preferred by Roloff, of the Pauline apostolate from the Jewish *Schaliach* institution or from other phenomena of official Judaism. In the fact that the apostolate to the Gentiles necessarily appears early in Jewish Gnosticism—the pneumatic-ecstatic phenomena which are fundamental to Gnosticism do not allow a national limitation—there is, in view of the coupling of Gentile mission and apostolate, a strong point for the derivation which I have undertaken.

[470] Already Jewish Gnosticism, following the principle of τὰ ἔσχατα ὡς τὰ πρῶτα (Barn. 6.13), had identified the Primal Man and Christ and was thus a *Christ* Gnosticism. One cannot speak of *Christian* Gnosticism in our sense of the term until the figure of Jesus of Nazareth or the Pneuma dwelling in him explicitly acquired a *special* significance.

[471] The ecclesiastical mission naturally was not limited to the Gentiles, but with its freedom with respect to the law was also directed to the Jews of the Diaspora. This called forth the primitive community in Jerusalem, whose existence in the holy city was assured only if it held fast to the law and did not fall under the suspicion that it was conspiring with the non-law-observing Jewish missionaries. It was thus compelled to draw up plans for a mission to the Jews which would be faithful to the law, in order to prove the seriousness of its adherence to the law. In the Diaspora, this new work was borne chiefly by Peter, while James took over the leadership of the community in Jerusalem. At the so-called apostolic council, of which Paul tells in Gal. 2, it was agreed that the Antiochians should turn εἰς τὰ ἔθνη, but the Jerusalem missionaries εἰς τὴν περιτομήν. Thus there is found in Corinth, e.g., a Jewish-Christian Petrine community alongside the Gentile-Christian community of Paul or of Apollos, which are joined in a common defense against the Gnostic Christ party (I Cor. 1:12). Cf. on this my book *Paul and James*, StBTh, XLVI (1965), 1 ff.

Christ [472]; as a redeemed one he is ἐν Χριστῷ, and Christ is redeemed only when he has united with himself all the members that are scattered abroad in the world. The sending forth of many ἀπόστολοι into the world is therefore not to be regarded differently from the sending forth of the ἀπόσ-τολος κατ᾽ ἐξοχήν (*vide* pp. 189 ff.). For the Gnostic, no special call is required for such apostolic service. His right to the apostolate is given in principle when he can show that he is Χριστοῦ, that is, that he bears Christ himself within himself or is himself "Christ." He has, indeed, nothing other than this "inner Christ" (Col. 1:27), and thus just "himself" (II Cor. 4:5), to proclaim. If he does this, he is automatically "Christ's apostle." [473] Whoever, on the other hand, cannot show that Christ actually is "in him" is at best ἀπόστολος ἀπ᾽ ἀνθρώπων. [474]

With the taking over of the apostolate by the church, naturally the intolerable anthropological or christological [475] ideas of Gnosticism had to be dropped. The pneumatic is no longer identical with Christ. But the empty formulas of these ideas were preserved and were in part filled with new contents. Thus for Paul, somewhat in conflict with the later Lucan tradition, only the *exalted* Christ comes into consideration as the one who calls. [476]

[472] Or of the "Great Power," the "Pneuma," the "Primal Man," or however people named this heavenly Being who had fallen into matter. Here and in the following we prefer the title "Christ" because it was the designation of the Primal Man in that branch of Gnosticism from which Paul's conception of the apostle was derived, and also because the Gnostics in Corinth, among whom esp. we demonstrate the Gnostic apostolate, use this title. It no longer needs esp. to be stressed that any sort of conception of ecclesiastical Christology may not be applied to this Gnostic title. Cf. *Die Gnosis in Korinth*, pp. 32 ff.

[473] Perhaps the conception of the original identity of Christ and apostle in the Gnostic apostolate has been unconsciously retained in many of the ecclesiastical passages in which later Christ and the apostles are seen as closely bound together; e.g., in the passages cited by A. v. Harnack [1], I, 320; John 20:21 *et passim*.

[474] R. Reitzenstein (Reitzenstein-Schaeder, *Studien zum Antiken Synkretismus* [1926], p. 141) had already recognized these connections: "The Oriental believes that he comes to know the world when he gains a vision of God in his true form. But God is also the Self within him, in himself one sees the world, and only through God himself can one get a vision of him; indeed, through this vision he enters wholly into us. This is the basic idea of all Gnosticism . . . , the experience from which Paul . . . derives his apostolate. Of course speculation is also developed here . . . ; but its foundation and its aim are always ecstasy, revelation."

[475] For original Gnosticism these two concepts are interchangeable; Christ is not only the Primal Man, but as such also the individual man.

[476] The reshaping which we have here of the Gnostic apostolate, which spoke of the identity of being with the Spirit-Christ, into the ecclesiastical apostolate, which speaks of the calling and commissioning by the Spirit-Christ, is naturally significant. Anyone who wishes to assume that this reshaping was influenced by the legal institution of the *Schaliach* may do so. But such an assumption is unnecessary and improbable; for then it would be expected that the authority of the apostle is the Christ who does the calling, while in fact the apostolic authority, in good Gnostic fashion, resides within the message itself.

Any connection of the historical Jesus with the apostolate lies completely outside his range of vision. This corresponds to the Gnostic conception,[477] which recognized only the spiritual Christ and abused the historical Jesus with anathemas.[478]

All the more for Paul, in agreement with Gnosticism, a call for the apostle that comes through *men* (in contrast with the *Schaliach*) is not conceivable (Gal. 1–2; *vide infra*).

To the Gnostic forms of the "call" belongs also the fact that Paul, in contrast with the Old Testament prophets, tells nothing at all about an actual experience of a call, and apparently cannot do so. He hands on no vocational message of any kind. Instead, he constantly refers to the ὅρασις or ἀποκάλυψις κυρίου, which to be sure does not *necessarily* make one an apostle, as I Cor. 15:5 ff. shows, but which *can* make one an apostle.

Now, however, the chief demand of the Gnostic apostles, who require of Paul a proof of his apostolic rights, apparently is to hear of ὁράσεις or ἀποκαλύψεις Χριστοῦ in Paul's experience. In his apology, Paul always goes into this requirement first; in II Cor. 12:1-10 he complies with this demand with the greatest explicitness. It is interesting to note that apparently for Paul there are two different things to be distinguished here: One of them is to be "called" through an ἀποκάλυψις Ἰησοῦ Χριστοῦ (Gal. 1:12); the other is to experience an ἀποκάλυψις κυρίου as he describes it in II Cor. 12:1 ff.; for on this point the exegetes rightly agree, that in II Cor. 12:1 ff. Paul does not at all have in view his experience of being called, and therefore certainly would not have been able to describe it in the terms in which he describes his journey to heaven in II Cor. 12:1 ff.

There can be no serious doubt, however, that the expression ἀποκάλυψις Ἰησοῦ Χριστοῦ in Gal. 1:12 *originally* was intended to designate nothing other than does the expression ἀποκάλυψις κυρίου in II Cor. 12:1. In its origin, namely in Gnosticism, the ecstatic "heavenly journey of the soul" which Paul appears to describe in II Cor. 12:1 ff., is precisely that ἀποκά-λυψις[479] which every person who claims to be an apostle must be able to

---

[477] The Gnostic structure of this motif of the Pauline concept of the apostle was very probably clear to later times. Thus there is found in Ps. Clem. Hom. 17.14-19 a detailed polemic of Peter against Simon-Paul, in which Peter maintains the view that only the encounter with the historical Jesus and not a "revelation" makes one an apostle. H. J. Schoeps, who more than once has referred to this text (*op. cit.*, pp. 14 ff.; *Paulus* [1959], pp. 78 ff.), could be correct in his surmise that this polemic is directed against Gnostics. But that therein the arguments of the Jerusalem Judaists against Paul again emerge is, of course, an assumption by Schoeps which is impossible.

[478] I Cor. 12:3.

[479] The concept ἀποκαλύπτειν or ἀποκάλυψις is *in this usage* genuinely Gnostic, but neither Old Testament nor common Greek usage. To be sure it had already found its

produce.[480] To the Gnostic, therefore, Paul's portrayal in II Cor. 12:1 ff. must have seemed to be a fuller exposition of the assertion which he had made, e.g., in I Cor. 9:1, that he had "seen Jesus the Lord"—which Paul was not even remotely considering.

Paul may have transmitted faithfully the form of the Gnostic concept of the apostle in the idea that the capacity to receive ἀποκαλύψεις does not necessarily and unconditionally make one an apostle (I Cor. 15:5 ff.), but that every apostle has to demonstrate this ability. We probably may assume that even early Gnosticism did not expect *every* pneumatic to be able to report or produce his own "revelations." Still ὀπτασίαι and ἀποκαλύψεις were the major part of the σημεῖα τοῦ ἀποστόλου (on this, *vide* pp. 213-14).

The Gnostic apostolate certainly never knew an actual "call" in addition to these. Perhaps the sending forth of the apostles by the Gnostic communities was regulated in some fashion; but every one who was equipped with the σημεῖα τοῦ ἀποστόλου could perform the ministry of the apostle at any time.[481] There is no place in the Gnostic world of thought for an act of calling which goes beyond these signs. The person is himself Christ; how then could Christ also call him?

Now Paul's inability to picture an experience of a call becomes understandable. When it is demanded of him, he employs the terminology given to him by the tradition, and he is probably able to do this only because he no longer knows about its original meaning—as II Cor. 12:1 ff. shows. In view of such a connection with the pre-given formulas, one will have to take care not to ask how Paul's experience of the call looked in its particulars. Like his Gnostic colleague, the apostle of the church knows himself (without taking over the ecstatic Gnostic principle) to be called through an encounter with Christ of the closest possible kind. The Gnostic, to whom this encounter, repeated constantly in his ecstasies of all kinds,

---

way into late Judaism from Gnosticism. In the Pauline corpus it is frequently found in this originally Gnostic sense; in addition to Gal. 1:12, 16, it is also in Gal. 2:2; I Cor. 14:6, 26, 30; 2:10; Eph. 1:17; 3:3, 5. A more exhaustive investigation of the concept would go beyond the limits of the present work. Cf. further E. Pax, *op. cit.*, p. 217.

[480] This ecstatic process is described in detail by Paul in I Cor. 14:26, 30: ἕκαστος ψαλμὸν ἔχει, διδαχὴν ἔχει, ἀποκάλυψιν ἔχει, γλῶσσαν ἔχει, ἑρμηνείαν ἔχει . . . ἐὰν δὲ ἄλλῳ ἀποκαλυφθῇ καθημένῳ, ὁ πρῶτος σιγάτω. It is of course characteristic for Paul that he names ψαλμός and διδαχή *before* the ecstatic charismata. But then follows at once the ecstatic "vision" with the "speaking in tongues" in which the ecstatic person describes the celestial world and which requires an interpreter, so that the content of the "revelation" can be determined. I should not assume that Paul introduced this kind of worship service into his congregations. But he is familiar with it and therefore, in his writing to the Corinthians, who had inquired about this form of worship because the Gnostics practiced it (I Cor. 12:1), he can go into the matter.

[481] There was no apostolic *office*, but only an apostolate.

mediates the consciousness of his identity with Christ, is operating here in a sphere which is most fundamentally and originally his own. Yet the Christian of the church is so little at home here that Paul only under compulsion and even then in a surprisingly formal way defends a right which for him rests much more upon an inner justification than upon external legitimation. The fact that Paul can portray the experience of II Cor. 12:1 ff. in the same concepts with which he speaks of the experience of his call, without seeing anything in common between the two events,[482] shows in any case how little his call, for him, has to do with an event such as the one described in II Cor. 12:1 ff.

Now it no longer appears surprising that in Paul no fixed terms and set formulations other than the *termini* ἀποκάλυψις and ὀπτασία are used to describe the "call." Still there was for the Gnostic prototype of the church's apostolate no other origin and no other assurance of the apostolic right than the ecstatic experience of the "Christ in us" and the knowledge, gained through heavenly revelations, of the way to life. With the concept, taken over by Paul, of the ἀποκάλυψις Χριστοῦ the entire "call event" of the Gnostic apostolate is described.[483]

On the basis of the Gnostic apostolate it also becomes understandable that indeed the resurrected One, i.e., the Spirit-Christ, testifies for the apostle, but not that the apostle becomes the resurrection witness κατ' ἐξοχήν. For the resurrection of Christ in the sense of the church, namely as historical fact as also Paul has to proclaim it (I Cor. 15), is for pure Gnosticism no more a relevant or even possible idea than the cross is for it an eschatological event.

When Paul customarily attributes to the apostle an authority that is indeed absolute but by no means exclusive, this corresponds to the historically given state of things that not all authoritative preachers were also apostles and the material of faith that was handed down was not of apostolic

---

[482] Cf. U. Wilckens, "Die Bekehrung des Paulus als religionsgeschichtliches Problem," in ZThK, LVI (1959), 274.

[483] This Gnostic conception has been preserved in the Ephesian epistle even more clearly than in the writings of Paul himself. In Eph. 3:1-5 it is presupposed that the *apostles* and prophets learn through ἀποκαλύψεις the μυστήρια of the divine plans which had previously been hidden from all creatures. The charisma of receiving such "revelations" makes one an apostle. Here the generally apostolic charisma still has not been reduced to the once-for-all experience of the call: κατὰ ἀποκάλυψιν ἐγνωρίσθη μοι τὸ μυστήριον, καθὼς προέγραψα ἐν ὀλίγῳ, πρὸς ὃ δύνασθε ἀναγινώσκοντες νοῆσαι τὴν σύνεσίν μου ἐν τῷ μυστηρίῳ τοῦ Χριστοῦ, ὃ ἑτέραις γενεαῖς οὐκ ἐγνωρίσθη τοῖς υἱοῖς τῶν ἀνθρώπων ὡς νῦν ἀπεκαλύφθη τοῖς ἁγίοις ἀποστόλοις αὐτοῦ καὶ προφήταις ἐν πνεύματι (Eph. 3:3-5). We also recall that in the consideration of the plural apostolate of Gnosticism we repeatedly encountered the "revelations" which established the apostolate; cf. pp. 159 ff.

origin; naturally Paul understood clearly that the concept of the apostle was native to Hellenistic Christianity. However, in Gal. 1:17 ff., for the apologetic reasons mentioned earlier, Paul apparently avails himself of a feature of the original Gnostic concept of the apostle when he views the fundamental Christian authority as exclusively apostolic; for to Gnosticism indeed every missionary who imparted the redeeming knowledge was an apostle in the technical sense.

4. This easily explains the remarkable fact that not only are the manifestation of Christ and the beginning of the apostolate a *single* act, but Paul is furthermore of the conviction that in the same moment he also received the gospel. For the Gnostic the gospel is indeed nothing other than the Christ who is in him. In the very moment in which this Christ is revealed in ecstasy, the Gnostic knows that he has life, that he, to put it in the church's language, is converted, and that he now can go forth in order to repeat just this gospel, or to repeat it in ecstasy[484]: Christ is in you! Because the ecstatic revelation of the Pneuma-Christ as the human "I" is the gospel itself, the Gnostic cannot separate the two. The thought of Paul that he has received his entire gospel at the very moment of the call or of the manifestation of Christ, which has rightly puzzled the exegetes, is thus so much a matter of tradition that one will properly refrain from burdening this statement of Paul with too many implications.[485]

5. Now we can also comprehend Paul's claim to have received his gospel at the moment of the "call" directly from Christ and without human mediation. For the Gnostic apostle, Christ himself is the gospel. The joyous message consists in the fact that it can be said and shown to men that Christ is man's own self, that man is a piece of the Christ-Primal Man. We saw earlier how Paul also could freely set up the equation of Christ = gospel (see above, p. 31), even though he fills it with an entirely different content from that which Gnosticism used. In general, to be sure, Christ serves for him as the *mediator* of the gospel, and Paul places value upon the argument that he has received his message without any *human* mediation. This is only another expression of the selfsame original state of affairs. Because the Christ who dwells within men is himself the gospel, the pneumatic is always in a position to repeat and hand on the gospel on his own authority. Men can

---

[484] Cf., e.g., the characteristic portrayal of such an ecstatic demonstration, as not only the Gnostics produced them, in Apuleius, Metam. VIII, 27.

[485] There can indeed be no doubt at all that Paul the persecutor of the Christians was already acquainted with the basic features of the church's gospel during the time of his persecuting activity. Otherwise why would he have become a persecutor? See below and cf. R. Bultmann [1], I, 187-88.

indeed awaken the "inner Christ" from sleep, can thus call forth the gospel in others, but their effort is successful only when the "message," i.e., the Christ, already slumbers within men. Thus it is not even conceivable that the Gnostic apostle speaks in an alien authority, that he is an "apostle from men." When he goes into ecstasy and speaks with tongues, Christ indeed speaks from him (II Cor. 13:3). But further, the ὀπτασίαι καὶ ἀποκαλύψεις κυρίου which are to be achieved in one's own power open to the Gnostic directly and immediately the knowledge of the heavenly world and of the ways to that world. Through his heavenly journeys he possesses *all* Gnosis, and he possesses it from his own vision, without alien mediation of any kind.

It is hardly necessary to point out that here again Paul takes over only an external form when he, like the Gnostics, asserts the immediacy of his apostolic gospel, regardless of whether he equates Christ and the gospel or introduces Christ as the mediator of the gospel. Unfortunately, he does not tell us with what content he fills this form; indeed it is only against his will that he is compelled to the exposition, for him basically quite uninteresting, of his concept of the apostle at all. His own content in this alien form may have been quite scanty.

In any case, Paul can hardly have believed that he had received the "historical facts of salvation" as such immediately from Christ; for these facts Paul must already have known as persecutor of the community. Even the wording of the primitive Christian confessions of faith, such as, e.g., the formula handed on by Paul himself in I Cor. 15:3 ff., or the wording of other bits of tradition such as, e.g., the account of the last supper, may have been known to him for a long time; at any rate, they were not later communicated to him without human mediation. Thus his revelation can have been only *that* these lifeless words are gospel for him, and *why* they are gospel. The kerygmatic truth of the tradition was the inner substance of the "revelation of Jesus Christ." [486] By receiving, in the encounter with the

---

[486] It may be that the ἀπὸ τοῦ κυρίου (I Cor. 11:23; cf. I Thess. 4:2) is also to be understood in this sense. Paul naturally is not of the opinion that he has received the words of the Supper directly from Christ, but he also hardly intends to say that the tradition which has come down to him from men in an unbroken line goes "in the final analysis back to the Lord" (W. G. Kümmel in HNT, IX [4th ed.], 57, l. 32; cf. J. Jeremias, *The Eucharistic Words of Jesus*, p. 202). H. Lietzmann is correct when he writes on this passage: "The Lord has revealed to him the essential meaning of this history." Cf. H. Lietzmann in *Kleine Schriften* II, TU, LXVIII (1958), 21 ff.; G. Sass [1], p. 115 and the references to literature there; H. v. Campenhausen [4], p. 26; W. Bauer [2], p. 99. G. Bornkamm (ZThK [1956], pp. 320 ff.) again correctly points out that the pair of concepts παραλαμβάνειν—παραδιδόναι (I Cor. 11:23) corresponds to the language of the rabbinical schools. Paul thus places himself as a link in a chain of tradition. Nevertheless it is not correct when G. Bornkamm concludes from this that con-

resurrected One himself, the gift of πίστις, he received the gospel directly from the hand of the Lord. In the conversion of Paul lies the revelation of the gospel complete.

In particular, this will have convinced Paul of the truth of the specific message on account of which he had persecuted the Christians: Christ is the end of the law. Yet it is clear that Paul has hardly reflected upon these questions. He employs without prejudice alien, and for his purpose often inadequate, representations and concepts, and he is able to do this because his own theology would never compel him, as it would the Gnostics, to fill these ideas and concepts with life[487] appropriate to them.

6. We established earlier that Paul intends to secure his apostolic rights which are under attack by alluding to his "call" by Christ, but that with this apparently traditional argument he is not at all successful. No wonder! The Gnostic apostle was always in a position objectively to produce the proof that Christ himself was speaking in him; through his ecstasies and trances he was able convincingly to present the legitimacy of his message and thus of his office at any time. He had no notion of reporting on a past ἀποκάλυψις; he produced his trances in the present.[488] Therefore the people in Corinth expected also from Paul a sign of the Christ who spoke in him,[489] they expected a "revelation of Christ."[490] But the assertion with

---

sequently Paul must also have received the tradition which is to be handed on *from the community.* Paul himself explicitly says in Gal. 1:12-13 that this view in any case for him is *not* implied in the παρέλαβον (contra I Cor. 15:1 ff.). Thus he stands at least *also* in the Gnostic tradition which G. Bornkamm has overlooked, which already occurs in the mystery cults with the technical expressions παραλαμβάνειν—παραδιδόναι and on which one should consult E. Norden [2], pp. 288 ff. See also W. Bauer, *Der Wortgottesdienst der ältesten Christen* (1930), pp. 40-41.

[487] Like the revelation of the gospel, conversion is not a result of human effort and achievement, but God's gift; this is perhaps the "existential" content of the tradition-bound Pauline statement that he had received his gospel directly from Christ.

[488] With this, the Gnostic apostle, altogether in contrast with Paul, is classified in the circle of the θεῖοι ἄνδρες of Hellenism and of Oriental syncretism, among whose distinguishing marks was the fact that they were authenticated as divine beings by means of their miraculous *activity.* The finest example of such a θεῖος ἀνήρ is probably offered by Empedocles in Diels, XXI B, 112-14.

[489] II Cor. 13:3.

[490] In this connection I refer once again to Ps. Cl. Hom. XVII, 13-19, where Peter argues against Simon's position that one can be an apostle on the basis of ὁράματα, ὀπτασίαι, ἀποκαλύψεις, and ἐνύπνια. One must, rather, be called by the historical Jesus. Ecstatic experiences are not subject to testing and may even be prompted by evil spirits. Against this argument, Simon defends his "revelations." Behind the Simon of this discussion, doubtless Paul is hidden (G. Strecker, *Das Judenchristentum in den Pseudoklementinen*, TU, LXX, 194-95). But this Paul is portrayed on the basis of his own terminology as a Gnostic apostle, so that the identification with Simon is not without a certain justification, and H. J. Schoeps (see n. 477) may be correct in his surmise that the speech of Peter against Simon-Paul *actually* is directed against Gnostics. Tert. de

which Paul thought to comply with this expectation, i.e., that he is an apostle on the basis of an ἀποκάλυψις Χριστοῦ, indeed no longer has for Paul the Gnostic meaning. He cannot, and he does not intend to, "reveal" the "Christ in him" in ecstasy. He is able only to refer to a quite unprovable and, for the Gnostics, uninteresting "call," and his description of it in Gnostic concepts[491] cannot have made it more powerfully convincing for his opponents.

Since at this decisive point of the discussion he himself becomes aware that the traditional proof, when he must use it, does not achieve its function, Paul tries for a more effective proof of the legitimacy of his apostolic office, one which contains the demanded and requisite immediacy: The success of his preaching identifies him as an apostle.

It is clear that here a genuinely Pauline motif enters alongside that of the Gnostic tradition which is alien to his own concept of the apostle, and that this motif could wholly convince his congregation but not at all the Gnostics.[492] Now we established earlier that this "dialectical" argument is indeed successful, because it is just as immune to testing as are the Gnostic ecstasies, but it yields nothing of particular value for the apostolate. This argument places the apostle in line with *all* primitive Christian missionaries; "apostles from men" can also appeal to this argument, and Paul certainly would have had nothing to object against that. But this means: The actual intention of the *church's* apostolate, as Paul represents it, is uninterested in a special *apostolic office* with everything that pertains to it. The only important thing is that there are missionaries and that they preach with success, regardless of how they have come to their divine mission.

This shows again that the apostolic office which was quite exclusive also in Hellenistic Christianity cannot have had its origin in ecclesiastical Christianity. It is native to Gnosticism, where it is simply the missionary

---

praescr. haer. 24.5-6 also is apparently directed against such Gnostics, who appeal to their own "revelations" instead of to the ecclesiastical tradition.

[491] The ἀποκαλύψαι τὸν υἱὸν αὐτοῦ ἐν ἐμοί may also belong to this Gnostic conceptualization. In its original sense, indeed, this formula means that the Pneuma-Christ living *in him* is revealed to a man, that he comes to know himself as a pneumatic, and the outward process of this "revelation" is the ecstasy. If one recognizes this, one will be careful about inserting too much into the Pauline understanding of the ἐν ἐμοί. In non-traditional language Paul would certainly have used the simple dative: God has revealed his Son to me. This is all he intended to say.

On the ἐν ἐμοί, cf. H. Schlier, *op. cit.*, pp. 26-27; W. Prentice in ZNW (1955), pp. 250-51; A. Fridrichsen, *op. cit.*, n. 23.

[492] In Ps. Cl. Hom. XVII, 13, Simon says to Peter: ὁ ἐναργῶς ἀκούων τινὸς οὐ πάνυ πληροφορεῖται ἐπὶ τοῖς λεγομένοις· ἔχει γὰρ ὁ νοῦς αὐτοῦ λογίσασθαι μὴ ἄρα ψεύδεται ἄνθρωπος ὢν τὸ φαινόμενον. ἡ δὲ ὀπτασία ἅμα τῷ ὀφθῆναι πίστιν παρέχει τῷ ὁρῶντι ὅτι θειότης ἐστίν.

office. Taken over by the church at the beginning of her mission, it very soon disappeared as a missionary office, because its peculiarities must have appeared unexplainable and superfluous for ecclesiastical Christianity, especially outside Syria. The church needs no missionary office raised to a higher power, and indeed especially not the Pauline church. Paul knows himself to be the last of the apostles but by no means the last of the missionaries (I Cor. 15:8 ff.). The example of Paul in II Cor. 10–13 shows into what perplexities the church's apostle enters in view of this state of things when he discusses his office with the Gnostics. The Gnostics are able so to drive Paul into a corner that, under compulsion and under constant protest, he attempts to show that he, too, fulfills the Gnostic conditions for the office of apostle. Thus on one side he is conscious that it is not unjustified to set up these conditions, apparently because they stand in a traditional connection with the apostolic office. But on the other side he rightly senses that these conditions have no longer anything to do with *his* concept of the apostle.

Therefore he only quite formally mentions (II Cor. 12:12) that the σημεῖα τοῦ ἀποστόλου in Corinth have happened with σημείοις τε καὶ τέρασιν καὶ δυνάμεσιν. We have already noted that it is quite difficult to recognize with what content Paul filled this formula. Its original meaning was, as the parallel passages Rom. 15:19 and Heb. 2:4 let us see more clearly, that the apostle must be in a position to exhibit before the community in a marvellous fashion the power of his Pneuma, that is, through ecstasies, speaking in tongues, trances, etc., both to deliver his message and to prove his authority.[493] One could hardly place these high demands in their totality upon every Gnostic; for the apostle they were indispensable if his mission was to have success. He had to be able to demonstrate *ad oculos* that he was not delivering his own words, but that Christ *himself* spoke in him (II Cor. 13:2).[494]

To these special signs of the apostle belong, above all, those manifestations which Paul in II Cor. 12:1 ff. calls ὀπτασίαι and ἀποκαλύψεις κυρίου. We have already attempted (*vide* pp. 206 ff.) to make clear the significance

[493] Cf. Exc. ex Theod. 24; here it must suffice to refer to our examination of the plural apostolate, where we repeatedly encountered the ecstatic phenomena of the Gnostic apostles which were scornfully called "magic" by the church fathers.

[494] The demand for "signs of an apostle" is for the Gnostics identical with the demand made upon Paul that he should prove that he is not a σαρκικός (II Cor. 10:2) but a πνευματικός (II Cor. 10:7). Paul is not aware of this identity. Since he has made full use for his theological thought of the general conceptual framework in which these latter demands are enclosed, he can affirm these demands. For him also the apostle naturally must be a pneumatic. On the other hand, he maintains a critical stance with respect to the special demands for the various ecstatic signs of the apostle; he is aware of their alien character for his conception of the apostolic office.

of these and their connection with the Pauline "call narratives." To be sure Paul must go back fourteen years when he, in traditional terms of Hellenistic mysticism,[495] wishes to portray how he once had been caught up into the third heaven.[496] In the Gnostic circles indeed people had expected that the apostle could, at any time in the meetings of the community, demonstrate how his Pneuma left his body, which remained behind, lifeless, and after a certain time returned to it, in order to report concerning the ἄρρητα ῥήματα.[497] But even though Paul cannot comply with this expectation, yet nowhere does he so fully comply with the Gnostic demands as in II Cor. 12:1 ff.,[498] where he, without knowing it, describes just that event which according to the opinion of his opponents is connected with the assertion that he had "seen Jesus the Lord."

In *Die Gnosis in Korinth,* I have shown how little Paul wishes to describe a heavenly journey of the *soul* (pp. 197 ff.). Nevertheless, one can hardly wish for a better description of that event which the Gnostic experienced as a "heavenly journey of the soul" than what Paul offers us in II Cor. 12:1 ff.

Now there are, to be sure, many parallel portrayals which point to the necessary connection between apostolate and ἀποκάλυψις. We have already met an abundance of examples of this ecstatic "magic" where we examined the plural apostolate. Here I shall refer merely[499] to the following fragment, first published by A. Jakoby, from a Coptic-Gnostic Gospel, in which Jesus says:

> (that I) may reveal to you my entire splendor
> and show to you
> your whole power and the secret
> of your apostleship. . . .

On the back of this fragment it goes on to say:

> Our eyes penetrated all places,
> we viewed the splendor of his
> Deity and the entire splendor
> ((of his)) lordship. He clothed ((us))

[495] Of course these terms had already gained entry into certain circles of late Judaism.
[496] Cf. R. Reitzenstein, *op. cit.,* pp. 369-70.
[497] Cf. n. 480.
[498] So also the Gnostics later like to appeal to the passage, when they claim Paul for themselves (cf. Hipp. 5.8 = Wendland, pp. 93-94).
[499] Characteristic of this also is the beginning of Saying 65 of the Gnostic Gospel of Philip: "An ἀποστολικός saw in a vision (ὀπτασία) . . ." (following the trans. of H.-M. Schenke in TLZ, XC [1965], col. 329).

((with)) the power ((of our)) apostle-
((ship)). . . .[500]

Here the conception is clearly "ecclesiasticized." The apostles are the twelve, and the ἀποκάλυψις appears to be a *unique* occurrence, yet the Gnostic basic conception remains undisturbed, in that the apostolate is based upon the ecstatic experience of the heavenly world.[501]

7. We have already learned that Paul refused to emphasize his message by validating his claim as an apostle, even though he must have been in a position to do so, from the structure of his concept of the apostle. This refusal is now explained by the fact that the Pauline apostolate has its source in the Gnostic apostolate, even though the Christian and "dialectical" theologian Paul would not have been able to take over the identity and the objective demonstrability of office and message.

8. Now, with the help of the Gnostic concept of the apostle, we find the explanation of the radicality with which Paul speaks of his authority and of the fact that this authority does not lie in the office as such but rather in the message itself. In the Gnostic apostle, indeed, Christ himself speaks.[502] There is, therefore, no higher authority than the apostle, and no other apostolic authority than that of Christ himself. From this, one understands that Paul also, who claims to speak ὑπὲρ Χριστοῦ (II Cor. 5:20),[503] can pronounce a curse upon the angels from heaven if they preach anything other than what he preaches; for Christ stands above all the angels. There is no question that such a radical claim had more convincing power for the Gnostics, who bring Christ himself to expression, than for Paul, who can only assert that his message comes from Christ. The Gnostic is not an envoy of Christ, but Christ himself is in him; therefore he can demonstrate his authority at any time. Paul, as an envoy of Christ, can only assert his. The grounding of his authority, Gnostic in structure, thus appears in his case

[500] See in Hennecke-Schneemelcher-Wilson, I, 230; cf. Pist. Soph. 46 = Schmidt-Till, p. 53.

[501] Cf. further the following quotation from an apocryphal writing of Moses: "God said to Moses: Moses, my servant! Thou camest up here and hast been worthy of the privilege of seeing all with thy power; and I have made thee ascend seven heavens, and have shown thee my royal treasures and I have given thee my law" (Gaster, *Journal of the Royal Asiatic Society* [1893], p. 550; cf. G. Widengren [2], p. 40).

[502] "You are he who will preach through us" (Ep. Ap. 41); cf. II Cor. 13:3. This Gnostic tradition also stands behind the formulation of Paul in Gal. 4:14, according to which people have received him, the apostle, ὡς Χριστὸν Ἰησοῦν.

[503] H. Becker (*op. cit.*, p. 21, esp. n. 3) has already recognized the connection of this Pauline claim with the Gnostic apostolate.

quite sharply disjointed; it becomes "dialectic" when he like the Gnostics appeals to Christ.[504]

This grounding appears less disjointed when he refers to his ἐξουσία, in other words, to his *unmediated* authority as a pneumatic. But this is a sideline of his argumentation, one which does not lead anywhere. He speaks in the traditional Gnostic conceptualization, and if *we* can hardly recognize how he conceived of the practical application of his ἐξουσία, Paul himself may already have had the same difficulty. In this sideline we are faced with something other than an assimilation of the *apostolic* tradition of Gnosticism. This ἐξουσία is not the special authority of the apostle, but the general authority of the pneumatic.

9. Perhaps now the somewhat puzzling idea of μίμησις in Paul also becomes understandable. Unfortunately we still do not have the frequently demanded monograph on the concept of μίμησις.[505] But for our purposes it will suffice to refer to a small segment of this problem. Since Plato the idea had been current that men should be imitators of Deity, and this idea is found in the general Hellenistic-Oriental syncretism.[506] In the cultus of the mysteries, especially in Syria, it had gained considerable significance, and had found acceptance also in Gnosticism.[507] The emergence of the concept of μίμησις in the apostolic fathers, especially Ignatius and Polycarp,[508] is explained in terms of its use in the mystery religions and in Gnosticism.

The imitation motif in Gnosticism is most frequently found in the form that the pneumatic is to follow after the *one* redeemer who has preceded him on the way into the Pleroma and thus has opened up the salvation-bringing possibility of the μιμεῖσθαι. That the imitation motif which permeates the book of Hebrews is also to be explained on this basis has been correctly asserted by E. Käsemann ([1], pp. 114 ff.). Yet there is no fundamental distinction between the imitation of the *many* apostles and the imitation of the *one* emissary (*vide* pp. 189 ff.).

---

[504] Paul speaks with the authority of the *proclaimed* Christ; the Gnostics are themselves this authority of Christ without any mediation.

[505] In the meantime the following have appeared: W. P. de Boer, *The Imitation of Paul, an Exegetical Study*, 1962; E. Larsson, *Christus als Vorbild*, 1962; A. Schulz, *Nachfolgen und Nachahmen*, 1963. The religious-historical problems which are of chief interest to us are only inadequately considered in these studies. On the other hand, the book by H. D. Betz, *Nachfolge und Nachahmung Jesu Christi im Neuen Testament*, 1967, displays a strong religious-historical interest.

[506] See TDNT, IV, 659 ff. and the references to the literature given there.

[507] See G. P. Wetter, *Altchristlichen Liturgien*, I, *Das christliche Mysterium* (1921), pp. 67-68; H. Schlier, *op. cit.*, pp. 164 ff., n. 497; TDNT, IV, 662, n. 4; *Der Brief an die Epheser* (1958), pp. 230 ff.

[508] Cf. H. Schlier, *Religionsgeschichtliche Untersuchungen zu den Ignatiusbriefen*, BZNW, VIII (1929), 158 ff.

The significance of μιμεῖσθαι for the Gnostic apostle lies in the fact that he demands of his "hearers" the imitation of his ecstasy, his speaking in tongues, and his trances,[509] so that he may give to them the certainty that they too are Χριστοῦ, or τῆς δυνάμεως, or similarly, i.e., a part of the cosmic Primal Man-Christ.

Hippolytus describes precisely this procedure when he (6. 42 = Duncker-Schneidewin, 302. 11 ff.) presents the relationship of the Gnostic Marcus to his teacher Valentinus, two representatives of decisively apostolic self-interpretation: ὁ δὲ Μάρκος μιμούμενος τὸν διδάσκαλον καὶ αὐτὸς ἀναπλάσσει ὅραμα . . . καὶ γὰρ Οὐαλεντῖνος φάσκει ἑαυτὸν ἑωρακέναι. And in what way Marcus himself in turn demanded ecstatic imitation of himself, Irenaeus tells us in a polemical distortion (I, 13. 3); cf. pp. 170 ff.

A similar report is found in Hippolytus' account of Simon. Simon has come in order to redeem Helena, the "lost sheep," from her bonds. To such "redemption" belongs the scorning of corporeality through sexual libertinism: οἱ δὲ αὖθις μιμηταὶ τοῦ πλάνου καὶ Σίμονος μάγου γινόμενοι τὰ ὅμοια δρῶσιν, ἀλογίστως φάσκοντες δεῖν μίγνυσθαι . . . (Hipp. 6. 19 = Duncker-Schneidewin, 254. 79 ff.). The concept of μιμεῖσθαι here does not need to be a necessarily technical usage; still the examples make clear the nature of Gnostic existence as existence in the following or imitating of the apostle as the ἀρχηγός or πρόδρομος.[510]

To imitate the apostle means to awaken the sleeping Pneuma, to leave the body, and to find one's way back into the Pleroma, just as he does. Such imitation of the apostle is at the same time *imitatio Christi*, who indeed in every pneumatic once again finds the way upward: μιμηταί μου γίνεσθε, καθὼς κἀγὼ Χριστοῦ (I Cor. 11:1).[511] The μίμησις concept thus stands in an organic connection with the Gnostic apostolate.[512]

---

[509] Naturally also of his asceticism (see pp. 222 ff.), his libertinism (see below), his suffering (see pp. 222 ff.), and so on.

[510] Cf. Heb. 2:10; 6:20; 12:2; Col. 1:18, and the Gnostic parallels to these in E. Käsemann [1], pp. 80 ff.

[511] The Gnostic background of this imitation of Christ very clearly comes to light in Origen's Comm. in Joh., VI, 42: οἱονεὶ γὰρ καθ' ἕκαστον ἅγιον Χριστὸς εὑρίσκεται καὶ γίνονται διὰ τὸν ἕνα Χριστὸν πολλοὶ Χριστοὶ οἱ ἐκείνου μιμηταί.

[512] H. D. Betz (*op. cit.*, p. 159, n. 2) calls the above described mimesis conception "utterly fantastic"—rightly so, insofar as he obviously understands it as an exposition of the *Pauline* conception of the *imitatio*. But it is incomprehensible to me how he can *misunderstand* it in this way. I am talking about the *religious-historical background*, which I suspect in Gnosticism, of the Pauline concept of an *imitatio* of the apostle or of Christ. Naturally it is beyond question that Paul himself does not understand this *imitatio* in a Gnostic sense. (H. Güttgemanns, by the way, has rightly considered [[1], p. 192, n. 134] this difference between the religious-historical background and the Pauline understanding of the Pauline mimesis conception.)

The proper reflections which H. D. Betz undertakes on the religious-historical origin

Knowledge of this allows the supposition, to be formed in connection with our investigation with some certainty, that the μίμησις idea of Paul together with the fundamental characteristics of his concept of the apostle has been taken over from the Gnostic apostolate. For this reason one need not be surprised that it does not function in a highly organic fashion when Paul employs this concept, to be sure only occasionally and quite formally, in connection with his apostolic activity.

10. We do not need to prove in particular that in its essence the Pauline no less than the Gnostic apostolate is eschatological. This is self-evident as a result of all that has been said.

It is now also easy to see that the special eschatological presentation mentioned earlier, which is connected with the apostolate,[513] operates in purely spatial categories, free from all temporal ideas, because it is the essence of Gnostic eschatology, in contrast with the church's future expectation, not to be interested in time, but only in the penetration of the Gnosis into all areas of the world.[514] When the call to the slumbering ones has been voiced generally, the restitution of the Pleroma by itself proceeds.[515] It is important not to omit any areas, since otherwise the "complete Anthropos" cannot be restored. The call once sounded forth reproduces itself. Urgency in view of the threatening end of the world is unknown to the Gnostic. It is indeed his own task to bring about the end.[516]

It is interesting to observe how much Paul, in connection with his apostleship, takes over this Gnostic thought, although the tension which thereby enters into his eschatological conceptions is evident.

---

of the Pauline mimesis concept unfortunately remain wholly inadequate. The reference to the Hellenistic-mystery mimesis conception (*op. cit.*, pp. 137 ff., 186) not only is much too general, but also leads astray with the mention of the mystery cults. For evidence that the mystagogue requires the initiate to imitate *him* does not occur, and with good reason, in the orbit of mystery piety in which it is always a matter of the deifying imitation of the *cult god*. Since Paul on the contrary presents *himself* as a model, one cannot find the origin of his concept of imitation in the mysteries, but indeed in Gnosticism, in which the apostle functions *as God*.

[513] No evidence is to be found to support the assertion of H. v. Campenhausen ([1], p. 110, n. 4), that it does not belong "to the essence of the apostolate but is only a special principle of Paul, to begin work merely in those places where he has had no predecessor."

[514] Therefore we constantly find in Gnosticism such remarks as "I have gathered myself together from all *places* (Epiph. Haer. 26.13) or "ut omnium *locorum* gentes illius passione salventur" (Orig. de princ. IV, 3.13 = Koetschau 344.8 ff.).

[515] "Smaller and smaller from day to day grows the number of souls [on earth] while they rise upward, purified" (Ephraem, quoted in Hans Jonas, *The Gnostic Religion* [1958], p. 234).

[516] "The end will come when the entire sprinkling of the light-pneuma is gathered together and is carried away into the incorruptible aeon" (Iren. I, 30.14).

11. The fact that the ecclesiastical apostle is called for a lifetime is in agreement with the obligation of the Gnostic apostolate. Here also no break within the church's concept of the apostle is discernible. The eschatological orientations of Gnosticism *and* church would make an apostolate that disappears before the "end" meaningless.

Similarly, the Gnostic and the ecclesiastical apostolates agree in the fact that there can be no "apostle in retirement." The title "apostle" in Gnosticism designates not an office but a *charisma,* and the situation is no different in the case of Paul (I Cor. 12:28 ff.), to whom as a Jew a static concept of office could have been conceivable.

12. It is interesting to ask whether Paul stood, perhaps even unconsciously, in the Gnostic tradition when he refused support from the congregations. To be sure, the exegetes with great unanimity suppose that the Gnostic apostles in Corinth stand on their rights to be supported by the congregation, and that they contest Paul's apostolic rights for this very reason, because he himself earns his own living. What is there to support this supposition?

First of all, II Cor. 11:20. Κατεσθίειν is supposed to mean, he lives "as 'apostle' at the expense of the congregation," and λαμβάνει is supposed to have the obvious secondary meaning of "exploit" (Lietzmann, HNT, *ad loc.*). But it would be natural to give these two words this concrete connection only if it were established that the Gnostic apostles were exploiting the congregations. But apart from this passage, that is by no means established. Thus it is first of all more natural to understand κατεσθίειν quite generally, as in the other places where Paul uses the word, such as Gal. 5:15: one "consumes you, intends to cause you harm." This concept, then, is easily fitted into the other equally general expressions of II Cor. 11:20, the object of which is always ὑμᾶς, not τὰ ὑμῶν. Then λαμβάνειν also naturally means simply "to capture," "to win," as in II Cor. 12:16, or still better, "to seize," "to lay hands upon," as C. Lattey[517] translates the expression, referring to parallels in the LXX.

There remains then only I Cor. 9:12: εἰ ἄλλοι τῆς ὑμῶν ἐξουσίας μετέχουσιν, οὐ μᾶλλον ἡμεῖς. Thus other teachers in Corinth have actually accepted support from the congregation. But rather than to think here of the Gnostic apostles, it is more natural to refer with Lietzmann (*loc. cit.*) to Apollos and Peter.

Thus on the basis of these passages there exists a real possibility that the Gnostics did *not* have themselves supported by the congregation. Now it must be added that their charge against Paul was not that he refrained from his apostolic right of support. Indeed it does not even make sense that one could have made such a charge against him. At the most one could have said: Paul does not allow himself to be supported by the congregation, thus he does not intend to be taken as an apostle.[518] But the charge cannot have been like this, because with all the other arguments which the Corinthian letters disclose, the opponents are contesting precisely the apostolic *claim* of Paul. In addition, it would have been absurd against such a charge first explicitly to establish the apostolic rights, as Paul did in I Cor. 9:4 ff.; for this charge in fact proceeds from the idea that the apostle *has* this right. The charge which people were directing against Paul in financial matters is rather that in II Cor. 12:16: Like a base sorcerer, Paul is exploiting the congregation with cunning, by means of the collection.[519] He is only acting *as if* he would accept no money; in truth he is zealously collecting it for himself.

But *this* charge also stands back of I Cor. 9:4-23. In this section Paul offers himself as an example of the proper preservation of Christian freedom, of which he had spoken in chap. 8: He may live of the gospel, but refrains from doing so, in order to become an offense to no man. His declarations are indeed quite appropriate to chap. 8; but the form and the extent in which Paul speaks of his refusal to exercise his apostolic rights show that he did not choose this example by chance in order to explain his fundamental declarations of chap. 8. Precisely as in 9:1-3, only in a much more restrained manner, he arms himself against charges[520] which people were making against him with respect to his right to support; charges however which he probably heard only as rumors and himself hardly connected with the matter of the collection.

The decision about the conduct of the Gnostic apostles rests on the exegesis of II Cor. 11:12. In the preceding verses Paul arms himself, it appears, against the assertion that he has exploited the congregation, and yet still without having conceived that this charge is related to the collection. He solemnly affirms that he has not burdened the congregation, and that for the future he does not intend to allow the reputation of accepting no support from the Corinthians to be destroyed. In the future he will still act in such a way ἵνα ἐκκόψω τὴν ἀφορμὴν τῶν θελόντων ἀφορμήν, ἵνα ἐν ᾧ καυχῶνται εὑρεθῶσιν καθὼς καὶ ἡμεῖς; in other words, analogously: "In

---

[518] Thus H. Lietzmann in HNT, IX (4th ed.), on I Cor. 9:4.

[519] Thus correctly H. Lietzmann, *in loc.* Paul also very explicitly refutes the same accusation in I Thess. 2:3-12 (cf. II Cor. 6:8), where in my opinion he is defending himself against the same opponents.

[520] Anyone who connects vs. 3 to the following for this reason can have no doubt about it. But in my judgment, vs. 3 is the close of the preceding polemic.

the future also I will accept no money, so that I will give no occasion to those who seek an occasion to disparage me; in that in which they glory they are to be found just as are we also." The two ἵνα sentences are parallel.[521] The boast of the Gnostics is the same as that which Paul claims in vs. 10: not to live at the expense of the congregation. Paul does not intend to give his opponents the satisfaction of seeing him accept money from the Corinthians so that they could elevate themselves above him. If they boast, they are to have no other boast than he himself possesses.[522] This means, then, that the Gnostic apostles, like Paul, boast of their unselfishness. Even Windisch in the Meyer Commentary on this passage concedes that this explanation,[523] which the earlier exegetes from the time of Chrysostom onward have held to be correct, is the only one that makes sense. But since he is bound like all modern exegetes through a false interpretation of vs. 20 to put the blame on the superapostles for accepting support, he decides rather that the text of vs. 12 has been corrupted!

It is certainly no accident that in the consideration of the plural apostolate we nowhere encountered the assertion that the Gnostic apostles were preaching for the sake of money, even though the church fathers otherwise were not reluctant to ascribe to these people all sorts of evil. Apparently their conduct must have been such as to rule out this charge as malicious.

Further, if our supposition was correct in seeing a Gnostic origin for the apostles of the Didache, it is noteworthy that the authenticity of the wondering apostles and prophets may be recognized by the fact that they do not covet money (11:6, 12), and do not even demand food (11:9), but rather labor (12:3 ff.). For the noncharismatic local officeholder, on the other hand, there is characteristically the sharpening of the primitive Christian rule that every laborer is worthy of his hire (13:1 ff.).

But if it is the practice among the Gnostic apostles not to allow themselves to be supported by the congregation, then we may suspect that Paul and the ecclesiastical apostolate of his time are dependent upon the original Gnostic concept of the apostle in this point as well. I Cor. 9:5 appears to speak against this suspicion. The λοιποὶ ἀπόστολοι are indeed mentioned, probably because they, like all other servants of the congregation, are accustomed to accept support. But to be exact, Paul says of them only that they travel in company with their wives. For this reason they will naturally

---

[521] Cf. II Cor. 9:3; Eph. 5:26-27.

[522] Paul deliberately does not say "that I may be found as they"; he makes *himself* the measure for comparison, not his opponents.

[523] It is already rendered probable by the fact that II Cor. 11:7 ff. stands within the section in which Paul sets his own κἀγώ alongside the ἐγώ of his opponents, but does not dwell upon his incomparable advantages over against them.

have been more likely to be dependent upon the help of the congregations, which Paul indeed had not always scorned (II Cor. 11:8-9), than were single persons. But that it is basically the practice of the apostle to earn his own livelihood is seen also in I Cor. 4:9 ff., where Paul says of the apostles in general: καὶ κοπιῶμεν ἐργαζόμενοι ταῖς ἰδίαις χερσίν (I Cor. 4:12).

Thus it may have been a general principle in primitive Christianity, taken over probably from Judaism, that the servants of the gospel are also to live of the gospel (I Cor. 9:4 ff.), a principle which the brothers of the Lord, like Peter, along with their wives would also have followed (I Cor. 9:5). On the other hand, it appears to have been the special duty of the church's apostle, after the pattern of the Gnostic apostolate, to refrain from exercising this right, in order not to appear as a charlatan, a danger which naturally was much more acute in the case of the missionaries than in that of the preachers who worked in existing congregations to whom their sincerity was known. That Paul (II Cor. 11:8) as well as the "other apostles" (I Cor. 9:5) allowed exceptions to this rule and, probably only from old and trusted congregations, accepted gifts does not nullify the rule.

The knowledge that Paul's refusal of support apparently is the apostolic refusal of support generally still does not bring into question the fact that Paul views his refusal of support as a noncompulsory personal decision (I Cor. 9:15 ff.). But he says nothing to indicate that there were not others before, beside, and after him *also* who took this same position. The fact is, rather, that he did *not* hold this decision to be a unique one (I Cor. 4:12; II Cor. 11:12; 12:18; cf. Matt. 10:8); and he never viewed himself as the first of the apostles (I Cor. 9:6)—surely Barnabas did not feel himself to be prompted by Paul to renounce his right to support! Rather the opposite is to be assumed and shows the renunciation of support to be a piece of "apostolic tradition" which Paul determined to take over in the service of the proclamation.

13. May the apostolic sufferings, also, be understood in the context of the Gnostic apostolate? We have already called attention to the unique basis which Paul gives in II Cor. 4:7 ff. for the apostolic suffering: The more the body of the apostle is given over to death, the more clearly evident does the life of Jesus ἐν τῇ θνητῇ σαρκί of the apostle become for the community. We have mentioned that the other basis which Paul offers in II Cor. 1:3 ff. is much more probable: In all our sufferings we are comforted, so that we may pass on to others the comfort which we have received.

In fact the former motivation becomes understandable only when we again trace it back to the Gnostic self-understanding in general, and in particular to the actualization of that self-understanding in the Gnostic apostolate. Hand in hand with the proclamation of the Pneuma-Christ which is imprisoned in the human σάρξ goes the radical derogation of the flesh by the Gnostic charismatics. The Gnostic stakes his honor on demonstrating the nothingness of the flesh, through asceticism and self-castigation, through libertinism and dissipation, through denial of the resurrection, and so on.[524] The more he scorns and disparages his body and becomes indifferent to all the sufferings of the body, and the more the body is daily given over to death, all the more radiantly does the life become recognizable which lies concealed within the mortal body as within a prison: the inner "Christ," the Pneuma itself. Thus not only is the Gnostic elevated above all suffering; he could even welcome the daily suffering of the body which led him to a disdainful endurance,[525] as a welcome undergirding of his missionary activity.[526] In this sense, then, even the suffering of Jesus could acquire a significance in certain Gnostic circles, and the apostle could identify his suffering with that of Jesus, as has occurred in the tradition which stands behind II Cor. 1:5 and Col. 1:24.

Here I can leave aside the task of explicitly setting forth and documenting the meaning of suffering for the Gnostic and in particular for the Gnostic apostle, since H. Schlier[527] has already performed these tasks in splendid fashion. I repeat here only one of Schlier's numerous examples. In the Act. Andr. it is reported that Andrew has moved Maximilla, the wife of the proconsul Ageates, to refrain from marital intercourse. Because of this he is threatened with death, if Maximilla holds to her intention. But just for this reason Andrew urges Maximilla to do so, for: συμπάθησόν μου τῷ πάθει, ἵνα γνωρίσῃς ὃ πάσχω καὶ τοῦ παθεῖν φεύξῃ (Act. Andr. 9). To paraphrase, it means: Transfer yourself into my suffering of death, so that you may grasp what this suffering signifies, namely the freeing from the fetters of the body (cf. chap. 6), and that you, too, in following me, may escape that suffering which is the state of being enslaved in the body. The suffering of the apostle thus leads his hearer to salvation: "So death is at work in us, but life in you" (II Cor. 4:12).

[524] I refrain from listing documentation for this basic Gnostic outlook.

[525] Cf. in the Gnostic Act. Joh. 96: εἰ τὸ πάσχειν ᾔδεις, τὸ μὴ παθεῖν ἂν εἶχες, τὸ παθεῖν σύγγνωθι καὶ τὸ μὴ παθεῖν ἕξεις.

[526] The self-mutilation of many ecstatics (cf. e. g. in Apul. Metam. VIII, 27) finds its explanation here.

[527] In n. 497, op. cit., pp. 102 ff.; 158 ff. H. Schlier was not yet acquainted with the Coptic Gospel of Thomas; there, Saying 58 reads: "Blessed is the man who has suffered. He has found life." On this, E. Haenchen (Die Botschaft des Thomas-Evangeliums [1961], p. 42) rightly comments: "The Gnostic suffers under the world. But that which thus suffers cannot itself be a piece of the world, but is extra-terrestrial and supra-terrestrial." Thus suffering leads to the knowledge of salvation.

It is understandable that the church fathers do not publicize the fact that the Gnostic apostles also knew how to suffer as persecuted ones and martyrs, even though among them were found proportionately no fewer martyrs than among the Christians; and the Gnostic apostles against whom Paul contended were persecuted by Jews and Gentiles no less than he was, and, also no less than he, they knew how to suffer and to die, especially because ἅμα τῷ ἀποθνήσκειν τὰς ψυχὰς αὐτῶν ἀναλαμβάνεσθαι εἰς τὸν οὐρανόν (Justin, Dial. 80). Instead, the church fathers preferred to picture the *active* disparagement of the body by the Gnostics, which however, including libertinism, grew out of the same motives as did the passive readiness to suffer.

If Paul explained his apostolic suffering only as he does in II Cor. 1:3 ff., then one could conclude that he is moving altogether along a way of his own when he speaks of the suffering of the apostle. Yet the explanation of II Cor. 4:7 ff. shows that even the suffering was an integrating component part of the Gnostic concept of the apostle which was taken over, only that Paul himself senses that *his gospel* does not gain in convincing power even through the supposedly unmistakable meaning of his suffering, as was the case with his Gnostic colleagues whose gospel was the Christ imprisoned within the body and whose judgment concerning the body as such was wholly different from that of Paul. For this reason Paul forms his own thoughts about the meaning of the sufferings of the apostle. It is only consistent when these sufferings in II Cor. 1:3 ff. apparently can also be of an inner sort, while in II Cor. 4:7 ff. in agreement with the Gnostic tradition Paul is thinking only of the bodily suffering. But in any case it is established also for Paul, out of the Gnostic background, that there is a special, theologically relevant apostolic suffering.[528]

---

[528] E. Güttgemanns ([1], pp. 124 ff.) critically discusses my attempt to understand the "apostolic suffering" in Paul in terms of the Gnostic apostolate. First he objects that the Gnostics could not have had a positive estimate of the apostle's sufferings, since for example the Gnostics in Corinth had taken offense at the sufferings of the apostle, as I myself also assume. But this offense is aroused by the fact that Paul is not willing to regard the body as the anti-godly prison of the Pneuma! The *positive reference* to the body is rooted for the Gnostic precisely in the *negative evaluation* of the body! Hence the rejection of the cross of Jesus and the identification of the sufferings of the Gnostic with Jesus' sufferings on the cross belong *together* for the Gnostic (*op. cit.*, p. 126). Further, Güttgemanns thinks that in the New Testament there is no apostle other than Paul who has made his sufferings a theological theme (p. 125). Correct! But why does Güttgemanns here suddenly forget that we encounter in the New Testament no literary remains at all of any other apostle? Elsewhere he himself does remark "that we know simply nothing at all about the self-understanding of any apostle other than Paul, since the Pauline letters are the only authentic documents of an apostle in the entire New Testament" ([2], p. 66). The correct acknowledgment on Güttgemanns' part that the theological intention of Paul and the religious-historical origin of his motifs are to be

14. If the primitive Christian concept of the apostle is of Gnostic origin, then one no longer marvels over the fact that the apostle is concerned with μυστήρια which he receives through ἀποκαλύψεις. Whoever in his trances by way of anticipation can view the heavenly splendor—and this is achieved by the Gnostic apostle—knows also the divine secrets which remain concealed from one who is not able to escape from the body.[529] μυστήριον is therefore one of the most frequent[530] and most characteristic technical expressions of Gnosticism.[531]

Naturally not only the *apostle* receives such μυστήρια, which are accessible to the Gnostic in general insofar as he is an ecstatic.[532] But in view of the connection between the apostolate and μυστήριον in Paul, his understanding of such μυστήρια may have come to him along with the concept of apostle. We have seen above that the ecstatic praxis which leads to the ὀπτασία and to the reception of the μυστήρια was an indispensable presupposition for the function of the Gnostic apostle.

distinguished leads further to the conclusion: "Therewith, however, the methodological possibility of inquiring at all about a religious-historical 'derivability' of the motif is blocked." I can only regard this conclusion as absurd, esp. since without the religious-historical motif research even the difference in intentions could hardly be discovered. Naturally I cannot contest Güttgemanns' reference to the generally post-Pauline origin of the Gnostic evidence that is cited for the "suffering." But this would be significant only if the conception of suffering that occurs in this documentation were the genuinely Pauline conception; but Güttgemanns himself rightly holds precisely that to be "completely ruled out" (p. 125).

[529] Cf. e.g., the beginning of the so-called Mithras Liturgy (following A. Dieterich, *Eine Mithrasliturgie* [3rd ed., 1923], p. 2): Τὰ πρῶτα παράδοτα μυστήρια . . . ἦν ὁ μέγας θεὸς ῞Ηλιος Μίθρας ἐκέλευσέν μοι μεταδοθῆναι ὑπο τοῦ ἀρχαγγέλου αὐτοῦ ὅπως ἐγὼ μόνος αἰητὸς οὐρανὸν βαίνω καὶ κατοπτεύω πάντα. The section Rom. 11:25 ff. (see pp. 203-4) still preserves throughout in Paul the traditional form of the Gnostic revelational discourse, as E. Norden ([2], pp. 295 ff.) has shown. Norden offers (*op. cit.*, pp. 290 ff.) numerous other examples of this form of the proclamation of mysteries in the "earliest Jewish-Christian Gnosticism." For our purposes, it is noteworthy that throughout it is not *the* emissary, but *an* apostle who speaks of many of these mysteries. I refrain here from giving again the frequently collected evidence.

[530] This frequency of occurrences prohibits our giving even a selection of passages. It may be that the concept μυστήριον passed from the older mystery cults into Gnosticism during the early period of the latter; still, in view of the close connection already present between Gnosticism and the mystery cults at the time around the birth of Christ, this is unimportant for our purposes.

[531] Cf. G. Bornkamm, article on μυστήριον in TDNT, IV, 802-28; H. Schlier, *Der Brief an die Epheser* (1958), pp. 59 ff.; esp. p. 60, n. 3.

[532] This means that in addition to the apostle, at least the Gnostic prophet also was the recipient of the "mysteries." Eph. 3:2-6 has preserved the Gnostic tradition well: "Apostles and prophets possess a spiritual insight into the mystery of Christ which distinguishes them from the rest of the community" (G. Bornkamm in TDNT, IV, 821). Naturally this does not mean a special spiritual quality, but a functional "something more."

15. We observed earlier that the answer to the question about the origin of the apostolic office must at the same time clarify the origin of the office of the New Testament prophet. Now there can in fact be no doubt that the New Testament prophetic office also was an originally Gnostic community office[533] and that the connection of apostle and prophet stems from Gnosticism.

If we keep in mind that from the beginning there existed, alongside the Jewish-Christian primitive community, Hellenistic and Gnostic communities of a Christian observance which occasionally had their own development, then we will have to divide the officeholders who were present in the primitive Christian time as follows: The πρεσβύτεροι belong originally in the Jewish-Christian communities; the Jewish origin of their office may be regarded as established.[534] Jewish Christianity at the beginning knew nothing of missionaries. To the Hellenistic community belong the ἐπίσκοποι,[535] the διάκονοι,[536] and, apparently especially for missionary service, the εὐαγγελισταί.[537] In the Gnostic communities, on the other hand, the προφῆται[538] (and διδάσκαλοι[539]) are at home as locally fixed [540] "office-bearers," while

[533] See *Die Gnosis in Korinth* (first ed.), p. 129.

[534] See H. v. Campenhausen [2], pp. 82 ff.; TDNT, II, 91 (Beyer); TDNT, VI, 662 ff. (Bornkamm).

[535] Their origin is still as much as ever disputed; see H. v. Campenhausen [2] p. 84, and more recently W. Nauck, "Problem des frühchristlichen Amtsverständnisses," ZNW (1957), pp. 203 ff.; A. Adam, "Die Entstehung des Bischofsamtes," (Bethel-Jahrbuch, 957).

[536] See H. v. Campenhausen [2], p. 84; TDNT, II, 91.

[537] See TDNT, II, 736-37 (Friedrich); W. Grundmann, *op. cit.*, p. 122; *ibid.*, *Die Geschichte Jesu Christi* (1956), p. 22.

[538] One should note that the Christian prophet emerges in the "gnosticizing" writings of the New Testament, and indeed always in the passages that have a strongly Gnostic flavor (Eph. 2:20; 3:5; 4:11) or in the dispute with Gnosticism (I Cor. 12–14). In the book of Acts we encounter the prophets in the Syrian-Antiochian region (13:1; 15:32). Gnostic prophets are known to us from all periods: Rev. 2:20; Did. 11 ff.; Herm. Mand. XI, 12 ff.; Eus., CH IV, 7.7; 22.6; V, 13.2; Clem. Alex. Strom. VI, 6.53²; Epiph. Haer. 40.7; the Montanist prophets and prophetesses; Tert. carn. 6. Cf. W. Bauer [1], pp. 182 ff.; E. Hennecke (2nd ed.), pp. 290 ff.; H. v. Campenhausen [2], pp. 198 ff. The pairing of apostles and prophets in Gnosticism is found, in addition to the New Testament passages cited, e.g. in Rev. 2:2, 20 (Did. 11.3 ff.; see pp. 182-83); the passages from Mandaean writings cited on pp. 185-86 above; Eus., CH IV, 22.6. This last-named passage is interesting because of the ancient addition of "pseudo-Christs" to the "pseudo-apostles" and "pseudo-prophets" (cf. Justin Dial. 82.2). "Christ" is the authorized self-designation of the Gnostic of the early period. Cf. further Ps. Cl. Hom. XI, 35. It may be of interest in this connection that Josephus (*Wars* II, 159) tells of prophetic discourses which played a role among the Essenes and which quite certainly were not speeches of Old Testament prophets.

[539] The fact that the teacher is added to the pair "apostles—prophets" only with some interval separating them is due to the fact that he did not have, as they did, a pneumatic office in the narrower sense. His commission apparently was to speak and to teach, not ἐν ἐκστάσει but ἐν νοΐ.

the ἀπόστολοι attend to the ministry of the mission. The coordination of apostles and prophets is thus originally Gnostic.[541]

Paul has taken over in essence the Gnostic "offices," though with the sharpest suppression of their predominantly pneumatic-ecstatic character[542] (I Cor. 14!).[543] While the early Catholic Church was able completely to usurp the apostolic office for itself, though with an essential reshaping of the original concept of the apostle, the prophetic office had to be eliminated later, because it could not be clearly separated from the earlier activities of the Gnostic "pseudo-prophets" and from the later ones of the Montanists.[544]

16. It is uncertain whether the fact that the primitive Christian apostles usually were sent out by two's goes back to a corresponding practice of the Gnostic apostolate. The sending out δύο = δύο is in primitive Christianity in general very widespread, as the selected passages presented earlier (pp. 53-54) show.[545] It is found occasionally also in late Judaism[546]—not in the

---

Even Gnosticism could not dispense with such teaching. One may compare, e.g., from Hippolytus' discussion of the "Great Proclamation" the remark that the Dynamis τοῦ λόγου τοῦ προσήκοντος καὶ διδασκαλίας which resides in man is destined for perfection.

[540] H. Greeven, op. cit., p. 9; we do not have documentation of itinerant prophets for the time of the ecclesiastical apostles.

[541] For Mani the two designations are equally appropriate: cf. G. P. Wetter, op. cit., p. 15; H. Jonas, Gnosis, I, 312. With the decline in the use of the title of apostle in Gnosticism (see pp. 191-92), "prophet" also becomes the designation for the itinerant pneumatic. However, in the Didache the functional distinction between apostles and prophets still may be clearly observed, as H. Lietzmann has correctly seen: "It portrays the 'apostles' as without possessions and restless, missionaries who wander from place to place, and the 'prophets' as the bearers of revelation who have been inspired by the divine spirit and high priests (ἀρχιερεῖς, 13.3) of the individual congregation" (Kleine Schriften I, TU, LXVII [1958], 142).

[542] This character however still comes out so clearly that down to the present time one speaks generally, and rightly, of the "apostles, prophets, and teachers" as the charismatic officeholders in the actual sense, even though Paul himself had already said that one and the same Spirit works in all the "offices" (I Cor. 12:11). On this, cf. Bultmann [1], II, 103-4, who fittingly observes that "by the person and work of the apostles, prophets, and teachers the Ecclesia is represented as the one Church." This also shows the Gnostic origin of this triad: As the one body of Christ, the church is the one church.

[543] Paul already separates the ecstatic speaking in tongues from the loftier prophetic discourse, while originally the speaking in tongues was precisely a significant activity of the prophets (Iren. I, 13.3; Orig. Cels. VII, 8-9; Eus., CH V, 16.7-9; R. Reitzenstein, op. cit., pp. 323 ff.).

[544] Rev. 2:20; Did. 11 ff.; Herm. Mand. XI, 12 ff.; Eus., CH IV, 22; V, 17; A. Ehrhardt, op. cit., p. 83; H. v. Campenhausen [2], pp. 195 ff.; H. Kraft in ThZ (1955), pp. 264 ff.; A. v. Harnack [2], pp. 59 ff. The book of Revelation was accepted in spite of its prophetic character, because it qualified as apostolic.

[545] Cf. the more complete compilation of New Testament references in J. Jeremias, "Paarweise Sendung im Neuen Testament," Manson Festschrift (1959), pp. 138 ff. (Cf. also Act. Petr. 3 near the end.)

[546] Cf. ibid., pp. 136 ff.

Old Testament—yet, in spite of contrary assertions, it is not characteristic for the legal institution of the *Schaliach* (*vide* p. 108). J. Jeremias (*op. cit.*, p. 139, n. 532) conjectures that the heretical apostles in Corinth also appeared in pairs; this is, however, completely uncertain. In the passages mentioned above (pp. 159 ff.), the Gnostic apostles appear throughout in undetermined numbers; it could have been two, it could occasionally, however, also have been more. Nevertheless it is interesting that the Corinthians, in their apocryphal letter to Paul (1. 2; *vide* Hennecke-Schnee-melcher-Wilson II, 374), introduce their complaints about the Gnostics who have come to them with these words: "There are *two* men, named Simon and Cleobius, who have come (here) to Corinth, who are perverting the faith of some through corrupt words." In Ep. Ap. 1, Simon and Cerinthus appear as a pair of Gnostic apostles; and certainly I Tim. 1:20 should be remembered, where Hymenaeus and Alexander are represented as false teachers, just as in II Tim. 2:17 Hymenaeus and Philetus are named as Gnostic heretics. The more widespread a sending forth δύο = δύο in the context of late Judaism and of Hellenism was, the more probable it is that it was mediated to the primitive Christian apostolate through its Jewish-Gnostic prototype.

17. Finally, the genuine apostolic καύχημα which we have noted with Paul does not seem to have a direct Gnostic prototype. The constant connection of this καύχημα with the "day of the Lord" alone suggests that in this passage we have hit upon a thought that is Pauline in its essence. To be sure, we may ask whether in this apostolic καύχημα of Paul there is not reflected in a completely altered form the clearly accented boasting of the Gnostic apostles which Paul contests (e.g., I Cor. 4:7 ff.; 5:2; II Cor. 10:12-13; 5:11-15; Gal. 5:26; 6:3) and for which Gnostic parallels may be cited in abundance (e.g., Iren. I, 13. 6; III, 15. 2; Rev. 3:17; Herm. Sim. IX, 22; Clem. Al. Strom. IV, 23. 149). In any characterization of the apostolic boasting of Paul in his Christian understanding of existence one does not escape the impression that the brave battler against all human glory cannot deny a remnant of foreign influence when he boasts of his apostolic ministry. But more than an open consideration of this question is hardly permissible.

18. It seems certain to me, though, that the remark of Paul in I Cor. 1:17 to the effect that Christ has *sent* him not to baptize but to preach is based upon a characteristic trait of the Gnostic apostolate. The attitude of the Gnostics to baptism is varied; occasionally it is quite positive,[547] but

---

[547] Namely where Gnosticism and the baptist movement meet. And this apparently happened in significant measure in the Palestinian as well as in the Mesopotamian region.

frequently negative or critical. The more nearly original the gnosis is, and the more it is pure "knowledge" which brings redemption, the more meaningless do sacramental actions become (cf. Iren. I, 21. 4). I have earlier (*Die Gnosis in Korinth*, pp. 233 ff.) demonstrated that precisely that branch of the Gnostic movement to which Paul was indebted for the greater part of his Gnostic terminology and for his representation of the apostle, and to which the Gnostic apostles in Corinth belonged, placed no value upon baptism; and our present investigation of the plural apostolate has not produced any evidence to the contrary. Accordingly the Gnostic apostles appear not to have baptized; they did not concern themselves with such unspiritual activities.

From this it becomes comprehensible that even Paul still did not hold it to be the task of the *apostle* to baptize. That he nevertheless did not disparage baptism is beyond question. With his positive evaluation of baptism in general he stands in the Hellenistic tradition of primitive Christianity which also in other respects is dominant in his thought, a tradition which however in this problem could not prevail against the concept of apostle determined by Gnosticism. Thus is explained the noteworthy inconsistency, that Paul indeed highly values baptism but does not consider it to be a task of the apostle.

Conclusion

In my opinion, after what has been said, there can be no doubt that the primitive Christian apostolate was an appropriation of the missionary office of Jewish or Jewish-Christian Gnosticism native to the same Syrian region in which the church's apostolate is at home. The original relationship of the two "offices" is evident, and the comparison which was carried through above shows with utter clarity that the dependence lies on the side of the church's apostles. The original conception of the apostle is Gnostic. The various gaps and discontinuities of the ecclesiastical concept of the apostle, which become apparent especially in the dispute of Paul with the Gnostic apostles, are explained as a necessary consequence of the transplanting of the office, which was first conceived for the essential mythological thought of Gnosticism, into the world, conditioned by historical thought, of Jewish-Hellenistic, characteristically Pauline, Christianity.

In addition to the actual dependence there is the dependence in terminology. In Gnosticism as in the church, for the related office-bearers we find the technical designation ἀπόστολος, and as a verb, correspondingly,

---

But it clearly shows that the high estimation placed upon baptism in such syncretistic circles is not of Gnostic *origin*.

ἀποστέλλειν (Rom. 10:15; I Cor. 1:17). A glance at this terminology should destroy even the last vestige of doubt whether the apostolate is of Gnostic origin; for ἀπόστολος and ἀποστέλλειν belong to the most characteristic and most original technical expressions of Gnosticism in general, and can only have been given by Gnosticism to Christianity, but never by Christianity to Gnosticism.

Thus actually as well as linguistically, quite a clear line seems to lead from the emissaries of Mesopotamia, by way of the Gnostic concept of the apostle which emerged there, to the primitive Christian apostolate, which developed first in its Gnostic form in the Syrian region closely connected with Mesopotamia, and then was taken over by ecclesiastical Christianity.[548]

---

[548] For a long time, however, Syrian-Mesopotamian Christianity continued to be gnostically oriented; cf. K. Rudolph, *op. cit.*, p. 49, and the references to the literature given there.

PART FOUR

The Transference of the Apostolate to the Twelve and Its Restriction to the Twelve and Paul

Jerusalem remained essentially untouched by the development which has been presented up to this point. Nevertheless, later on the twelve not only qualify in general as apostles, but indeed the ecclesiastical apostolate is limited to them! Only Paul retains, beside them or even among them, a not always unassailed right to claim the title of apostle. The development of the primitive Christian concept of the apostle reaches its conclusion only when it comes to the point where the twelve and Paul serve as apostles. What motives led to this shifting and narrowing of the title of apostle?

I

This question has often been propounded, even though most of the investigators have been of the opinion that it suffices to explain the *limitation*[1] of the title of apostle to the twelve,[2] while in truth the problem lies above all in the *transferral* of the apostolate to the circle of disciples.

The answers are varied. W. Seufert, who with his otherwise splendid investigation stands wholly under the influence of the Tübingen school, rightly recognizes the late origin of the apostolate of the twelve. In his opinion the conception of the apostolate of the twelve as an external institution is formed by a reaction, resulting after the apostolic council, of the Jerusalem

---

[1] For P. Wernle ([1], pp. 112 ff.), and not for him alone, the real problem is in fact Paul's taking over of the title of apostle in association with the twelve "apostles."

[2] A. v. Harnack (*Die Lehre der zwölf Apostel* [1884], p. 116) then gives the following explanation: "In the concern for his own recognition he increased the recognition of the twelve apostles, with whom he put himself on a level, and, at least so far as our knowledge of the matter goes, he is quite actually the founder of the view of the extraordinary position of the twelve apostles as apostles." J. Wagenmann, *op. cit.*, pp. 39-40, 49-50, agrees.

congregation to the Pauline "subjectivism" and missionary success (*op. cit.,* p. 44), and "the increasingly strong reaction against the successful Gentile mission of Paul appears to have pulled back to the recognition of the twelve as apostles, as one pulls back to a base of operations, from which the apostolic rights could be denied Paul" (*op. cit.,* pp. 47-48). Thus the struggle between Paul and the Judaists is a struggle over the apostolate. This way of construing the matter stands or falls with Baur's interpretation of primitive Christian history; it collapses when one recognizes that the discussions about the apostolate in Galatia and Corinth were occasioned by Gnostics. W. Seufert himself senses some of the difficulties which follow the presupposition of Baur's picture of the history: "This catchword (*sc.* apostle), about which the struggle at one time revolved (I Cor. 9:1), is avoided by Matthew and Mark wherever possible,[3] . . . while in Luke the kinship with Pauline thought . . . is betrayed by a greater preference for this word" (*op. cit.,* p. 65). W. Seufert apparently has completely overlooked the fact that Luke, the "friend of Paul," deliberately gives the name of the apostle only to the twelve and never to Paul [4]; and the silence of Matthew and Mark naturally testifies to the fact that at their time the twelve still were not apostles.

Still more recently H. v. Campenhausen ([1], pp. 117-18) offers a solution to the problem based upon presuppositions like those of W. Seufert.[5]

W. Seufert's thesis has found considerable agreement, as for example in A. v. Harnack (*vide* n. 2), M. Goguel ([2]) and many others, so that with respect to this thesis one can speak of a "critical consensus" (cf. G. Klein, *op. cit.,* pp. 52 ff.). In fact none of the critical investigators after Seufert can deny the impression which his work has made.

Further, H. Mosbech ([1], p. 191), in a quite adventuresome fashion and with "the help of imagination" (p. 200), sees the title of apostle as developed first by Paul as a *terminus technicus* during his discussions with those of Jerusalem and then as being taken over by the twelve. A reading of his argument—the weakest passage in his fine essay—makes any refutation unnecessary. Much the same holds true in the case of E. Meyer (*op. cit.,*

---

[3] On account of their "synthetic" interest?

[4] On Acts 14:4, 14, see pp. 248-49.

[5] It is true that his explanation signifies a noticeable advance beyond the earlier study of the problem, in that H. v. Campenhausen places the emergence of the exclusive apostolate of the twelve at the *end* of the apostolic age (on this, cf. G. Klein, *op. cit.,* pp. 60 ff.); but at the same time he remains behind many of the more recent efforts at solving the problem when he expresses the opinion that it is sufficient to account for the *limitation* of the title of apostle to the twelve, while he apparently considers that the *transfer* of the title to them had already taken place in the pre-Pauline era ([1] pp. 105 ff. Cf. further pp. 265-66 below).

II, 255 ff.).[6] Without any more precise proof, E. Bammel (*op. cit.*, p. 417) presents his assumptions that James (!) was the driving force behind the introduction of the title of apostle in Jerusalem.

Quite different is the fanciful construction of H. Vogelstein ([1], pp. 447 ff.). According to him the twelve disciples were apostles in the sense of the Jewish שלוחים, even before Paul, and thus were men set apart for their ministry by the laying on of hands. Paul, on the other hand, was originally a Christian prophet, and as such he possessed in Jerusalem a higher authority than that of an apostle.[7] But after the death of Jesus the apostles are advanced in rank to a position ahead of the prophets: apostles, prophets, teachers. Therefore the "prophet" Paul, in order not to stand below the apostles in Jerusalem, had to make good his claim that he also was an apostle. Thus there came about with him and in his circle of missionaries a complete alteration in the concept of the apostle. The Christian apostle, resembling the Old Testament prophet, called of God and possessing authority, developed out of the *Schaliach*.

The view of E. Lohse ([1], pp. 269 ff.) remains quite unclear. In his essay, rich in fitting observations, he quite rightly sees that Paul formed the primitive Christian concept of the apostle. Then, however, Paul is supposed to have understood the office of the twelve in terms of his own office and to have given to them the title of apostle. That is indeed correct for Peter, the only provable "apostle" among the twelve.[8] But how could Paul have given the title of apostle to the δώδεκα in general, who even in Lohse's opinion were not missionaries ([1], pp. 263 ff.), and who at the time of the conversion of Paul had already ceased to exist as a closed group ([1], p. 265)? And actually he never did so. Lohse also neglects to explain the *limitation* of this title to the twelve.

The construction offered by G. Sass ([1], pp. 132 ff.) is likewise without any connection with the tradition. He says that the circle of the twelve belonged originally to Galilee—which is quite possible—and knew nothing

---

[6] "Thus the inference will not be too daring that it (*sc.,* the designation of the twelve as apostles) first came into use by Paul in his conflict with the church of Jerusalem. Paul claims, as an apostle and an independent missionary for the Gentile world, to have been called immediately by the Lord, without human intervention and without any support or commissioning on the part of the mother church, and therefore claims also to stand completely independent and with equally valid authority alongside this church and its leaders; he recognizes the latter only as persons of equal authority and not as superiors. This leads to the fact that now the title of apostle is transferred to these also, and indeed, in opposition to Paul's claim from the other side, is restricted to the twelve alone" (*op. cit.,* pp. 256-57). Meyer does not give a reason for this construction.

[7] H. Vogelstein thus erroneously sees the Christian prophets in a line with those of the Old Testament.

[8] See pp. 62-63, 94-95; E. Lohse [1], p. 265.

of the concept of the apostle; the twelve served as witnesses of Christ. The circle around James belongs in Jerusalem; James sends forth ἀπόστολοι (= שלוחים). Then come members of the circle of the twelve to Jerusalem, of whom also some are sent out by James. Thus the concept "apostle" is connected with the twelve, nevertheless in such a way that these "witnesses of Christ" now become apostles of Christ and claim a lifelong commission. Paul did not call himself an "apostle of Christ" immediately after his conversion. It was only in the discussions with the "original apostles" and those whom they had sent out that Paul also was compelled to call himself an apostle and ultimately to think of himself in a unique sense as an apostle. This construction also needs no refutation.[9]

All these explanations—the number could be enlarged considerably—do not advance our investigation.[10] They misplace the transference of the concept of apostle to the twelve as a group by placing it in a much too early time.[11] We must proceed from the knowledge that neither Paul nor Mark and Matthew have any knowledge of twelve apostles, and therefore we must seek in the so-called *postapostolic* age the motives which made the δώδεκα into apostles,[12] and stirred the stream of tradition.[13]

[9] G. Sass [2], pp. 237 ff., pictures an essentially different development.

[10] Cf. also H. Mosbech [1], pp. 178 ff.; G. Klein, *op. cit.*, pp. 52 ff. With great reticence A. Fridrichsen (*op. cit.*, n. 12) asserts only "that Paul has laid the foundation of this view." That is to say, he gave to Peter as the first of the twelve the title of apostle. This is correct, but it still does not explain the emergence of the apostolate of the twelve.

[11] G. Sass ([2], p. 236) suggests very cautiously the possibility of a post-Pauline origin of the apostolate of the twelve. J. Munck programmatically defends this thesis. Cf. the discussion by G. Lindeskog in ThR (1950), p. 234: "Paul is the decisive factor in the development of the concept of the apostle. He employed it to designate the person called and chosen by God in a preeminent sense. As a result, in the post-apostolic age people transferred the concept of apostle to the twelve." Cf. further J. Munck ([1], pp. 101 ff.: "The twelve disciples are not called apostles until the post-Pauline period" (p. 104). His explanation for the transfer of the concept of apostle to the twelve out of the battle over the apostleship of Paul is of course unacceptable ([1], p. 109). Already in 1957, G. Klein cited Munck's work in agreement (ZKG, LXVIII [1957], p. 369). Similarly also A. Fridrichsen, who correctly affirms: "Paul never calls the Twelve 'Apostles' " (*op. cit.*, n. 12). For H. v. Campenhausen's view, see n. 5. As much as the advance in the investigation of the apostolate of the twelve which is characterized by the references given here is to be welcomed, it does not suffice to seek the origin of the new concept of the apostle in the (early) post-Pauline era, but for the rest, as previously, to take into account the rivalries between Paul and Jerusalem on this matter. Further investigation will demonstrate this.

[12] G. Klein, *op. cit.*, who divides the preceding research into the "conservative consensus" which affirms an original apostolate of the twelve, and the "critical consensus" which traces the apostolate of the twelve to Paul, also comes to this understanding of the matter. This division of his is indeed somewhat schematic and is not capable of being completely fair to all the variations of the study of the apostle; nevertheless the refutation of both consensuses is thorough and convincing.

[13] G. Klein also devotes himself to this task. Even if his answer is essentially different from the one given below, which he had before him, still the two investigations run

Are these motives native to the Pauline tradition? If not, where else?

II

1. Paul and the Gnostics are agreed that "Christ" is the only authority of the community. Agreement also governs the affirmation that Christ comes to the communities through the apostle. Thus the Gnostic apostles in Corinth appeal to their current apostolic authority: Christ speaks here and now, in us; we are Christ's. [14] When the congregation in response to these "Christ people" appeals to its apostolic teachers,[15] Paul, who does not yet have a clear picture of the situation in Corinth, rebukes them: One cannot appeal to men[16]; the only proper motto is: ἐγώ εἰμι Χριστοῦ (I Cor. 3:23)! But what else was there for the congregation to do, in response to the "apostles of Christ," but to appeal to Paul? Paul indeed has received his gospel directly from Christ; to appeal to Paul means to recognize the *gospel* of Paul and with it the authority of Christ himself. In his later correspondence Paul does not repeat his rebuke.

This discussion in Corinth makes it clear that in the Gnostic congregations, even after the departure of the apostle, Christ *himself* remains present, namely in the pneumatics, who give utterance to him in προφητεύειν and in all other forms of ecstasy. The person of the apostle, who has awakened the Christ-Pneuma, is for the community uninteresting. In him indeed the same Christ spoke who, once awakened, now can speak further in all the pneumatics.

The same does not hold for the Pauline congregations. When Paul leaves the congregation, the *Word* of Christ remains behind, which the congregation however could receive and still can receive only through him. Even after his departure the apostle remains necessarily the person to whom one must appeal about the true gospel of Christ as proclaimed in the congregation.[17]

Thus the Gnostic apostolate has significance only *in actu*. The abiding thing is the authority of the Christ-Pneuma. The Christian congregation on the contrary always holds in memory its apostle as the guarantee of its "Christian-ness." It is compelled always to appeal to the message of the historical apostle.[18] If for the genuine Gnostic the Χριστοῦ εἶναι is im-

---

[14] I Cor. 1:12; II Cor. 10:7.

[15] That is to say, to Paul, Peter, and Apollos: I Cor. 1:12.

[16] I Cor. 1:13 ff.; 3:1 ff.

[17] In order not to be misunderstood, this sentence requires the supplementary reference to I Cor. 1:12 ff.; 3:5 ff.; 21 ff.

[18] There is in Paul himself no unequivocal indication of what significance such an appeal has. On the one hand, he forbids the appeal to his name (I Cor. 1:12) and wishes

parallel for a good distance, so that I can refer to Klein's work as a solid, detailed, and thoroughly independent enlargement of many passages in the following statements.

mediately valid, still the Pauline Christian must necessarily say first: ἐγώ εἰμι Παύλου, and therefore: ἐγώ εἰμι Χριστοῦ.

For this reason, in ecclesiastical circles already long before the turn of the century people had collected the letters of Paul [19] and had circulated them among the congregations; naturally not as "canonical" scriptures, but still as the standard tradition of the true Christian doctrine. The Christian congregations, in contrast with Gnosticism, also handed on the names of their actual or alleged founders.

For this reason we cannot see what necessities could have compelled the congregations of the Pauline tradition to appeal to the twelve disciples instead of to Paul. Certainly these congregations, in confronting Gnosticism, whose nonmediated apostolic authority must have been much more powerfully convincing than the Pauline variant of the original Gnostic office, had a difficult position. One could thus imagine that the church communities were looking around for still higher authorities and that they found these in the twelve disciples and their connection with the *historical* Jesus. But this did not happen, for precisely the reason that the circle of the twelve together with the historical Jesus never entered into the immediate horizon of the Pauline tradition.

But in addition, the deficiency in the Pauline congregations was not a lasting one. The pneumatic high pitch could not be maintained for long in most of the Gnostic communities, and Gnostics soon began to appeal to Paul [20] and to make use of his epistles. In view of the considerable Gnostic contribution to the theological terminology of Paul, this was not difficult,[21] and writings of their own apostolic authorities from the earliest times, to which they might have gone back and appealed, naturally were not available.

This phenomenon shows, however, that the turning away of the Pauline

---

to be judged only in terms of the success of his preaching. On the other hand, however, in the anti-Gnostic struggle over the apostolate, in taking up Gnostic traditions he asserts the demonstrable immediacy of his message and for this reason pronounces a curse upon all those who preach something else (Gal. 1). Since the battle against Gnosticism for a long time helped to determine the internal development of the church, the anti-Gnostic gnosticizing construction of Paul's concept of the apostle, which was alien to his actual intention, became the dominant one.

On the de-eschatologizing of the concept of the apostle, cf. C. K. Barrett, "The Apostles in and After the New Testament," *Svensk Exegetisk Årsbok*, XXI (1956), pp. 30-49.

[19] Cf. P. Feine, *Einleitung in das Neue Testament* (5th ed., 1930), pp. 243-44 (Feine-Behm-Kümmel, *Introduction to the New Testament* [1966], p. 339); W. Schmithals, "Zur Abfassung und ältesten Sammlung der paulinischen Hauptbriefe," ZNW, LI (1960), 225-45; *Paulus und die Gnostiker* (1965), pp. 175-200.

[20] Epiph. Haer. 38.2; Iren. I, 21.2; III, 1-2; 8.2 ff.; 13.1; V, 35.2; II Peter 3:15 ff.; Clem. Alex. Strom. VII, 17.106; Exc. ex Theod. 23.2-3; 35; Muratorian Canon, ll. 63-68; Marcion; cf. W. Bauer [1], pp. 184-85; 227.

[21] Cf. J. Wagenmann, *op. cit.*, p. 121.

congregations to Gnosticism in some places was considerable.[22] For the acceptance of Pauline authority by the Gnostics can be understood only if apostatizing Christians took with them the Pauline tradition.

2. The orthodox community now faced the task of assuring its own interpretation of the Pauline tradition in opposition to the understanding of that tradition among the Gnostics. The Pastoral Epistles show how this occurred in the church's congregations. The historical significance of these epistles does not lie in those passages in which they transmit Pauline ideas with passable correctness, but in general in those places where they mark out new lines, partly in connection with Paul.

The actual concern of these post-Pauline writings is the preservation of the correct *doctrine* in opposition to the false teaching of Gnosticism.[23] H. Schlier[24] has collected thirteen different concepts representing the idea of "teaching" which are repeatedly encountered in the Pastoral Epistles! The "wholesome doctrine" (Titus 2:1; I Tim. 1:10) comes from Paul himself. He has the "office" (I Tim. 1:12); he is κῆρυξ καὶ ἀπόστολος, as he solemnly affirms (I Tim. 2:7; II Tim. 1:11); he is an apostle according to the ἐπίγνωσις ἀληθείας (Titus. 1:1); the "sound words" of Christ are entrusted to him (I Tim. 1:11). Paul has handed over the correct doctrine to his pupils Timothy and Titus, part of it orally (I Tim. 1:3, 18), but part of it also in writing (I Tim. 1:18; 3:14). They are to preserve it (I Tim. 4:16; 6:20) and to hold fast to the pattern of the "sound words" they have heard from Paul (II Tim. 1:13-14), which they have already been doing, as Paul explicitly testifies (I Tim. 4:6; II Tim. 3:10). They have all the more reason for doing so since they know that this doctrine comes from the apostle Paul (II Tim. 3:14). But they are also to hand on to others this doctrine (I Tim. 4:6, 11; 5:7; Titus 2:1), as if Paul himself were doing it (I Tim. 4:13). They must keep themselves aloof from all other teachings (I Tim. 4:7; Titus 3:9) and must faithfully administer their teaching office. It is especially important that still other new preachers who stand in this apostolic tradition be trained (II Tim. 2:2), and that elders and bishops be installed who are able to preserve the apostolic ordinance, to proclaim the sound doctrine, and to confute the Gnostic false teachers (Titus 1:5 ff.). In view of the importance of correct tradition, caution in the calling of new officeholders is quite appropriate (I Tim. 5:22). Thus,

---

[22] Cf. I Tim. 5:15; 6:20-21; II Tim. 1:15; 2:16 ff.; 4:3-4, 10, 15; Titus 1:10 ff.; 3:9 ff. Even the controversies in Corinth attested by I Clement certainly go back to the efforts of the gnosticizing circles to gain power (cf. W. Bauer [1], pp. 99 ff.). Cf. Acts 20:29-30.

[23] On the following, cf. Dibelius-Conzelmann, *Die Pastoralbriefe* (3rd ed., 1955), pp. 1-2; article, "Pastoralbriefe" in RGG, IV, 3rd ed.

[24] Gogarten *Festschrift* (1948), p. 47; cf. H. v. Campenhausen [2], pp. 118-19.

as Timothy received his office solemnly through the laying on of hands (I Tim. 4:14; II Tim. 1:6),[25] so is he to hand it on through the laying on of hands (II Tim. 5:22). Thereby, following the Jewish example,[26] the taking over of the correct tradition is legally symbolized and the charisma of the office is transmitted.

The Pastoral Epistles thus are familiar with the fully developed schema of the apostolic tradition.[27] To be sure, one can hardly speak here of a monarchical episcopate in the strict sense. There are ἐπίσκοποι and πρεσβύτεροι, although their relationship one to another is not completely clear[28]; if the bishop has a special position among the elders, it still is nothing more than that of *primus inter pares*. But in any case, in the chain of tradition exhibited by the Pastoral Epistles the inviolability of the Pauline tradition is assured. In it one possessed a strong weapon against Gnosticism; for wherever Gnosticism had insinuated itself into the historic tradition and appealed to the Christ of Paul instead of the "inner Christ," it was always subordinated to the ecclesiastical line of argument, which with greater justification claimed for itself the genuine tradition.

It is clear that all these inner developments as to the relationships of tradition within the Pauline congregations are wholly attuned to Paul and leave no room for an apostolate of the twelve.[29] With the Pastoral Epistles we are already at the end of the first century,[30] and it is unlikely that in the second century people would have undertaken to reforge the weapons against the heretics which, according to the evidence of the Pastoral Epistles, were already well forged. For this reason the possibility that the transferral of the apostolate to the twelve took place within the realm of influence of the Pauline congregations is ruled out.[31]

[25] I regard as ruled out the possibility that the ordination of Timothy by Paul is historical, as E. Lohse ([2], p. 81) asserts.

[26] Cf. E. Lohse [2], pp. 80 ff.

[27] On pagan and Jewish prototypes of the idea of tradition, cf. H. v. Campenhausen [3], pp. 240-44, and the literature given there.

[28] On the discussion of this question, see H. v. Campenhausen [2], p. 117; H. Schlier, *op. cit.*, p. 53, n. 24, esp. n. 31, and the literature indicated there.

[29] For this reason alone, even the Pastorals cannot be an attempt "to enrol Paul unmistakably in the antiheretical front and to remove the lack of confidence toward him in ecclesiastical circles" (W. Bauer [1], p. 228). The epistles contain no sort of concession to ecclesiastical circles outside the Pauline communities.

[30] I should not place them any later. The Gnostics who are being opposed in them belong to a quite early period; Polycarp is already acquainted with I Tim. (cf. I Tim. 6:7, 10 with Polyc. 4.1). I regard as improbable the theory that he himself is the author of the Pastorals, as H. v. Campenhausen has attempted to make plausible in a splendid study (*Polycarp von Smyrna und die Pastoralbriefe* [Heidelberg, 1951]).

[31] That in Eph. 2:20, 3:5, and 4:11 such a transfer is not yet intended should be self-evident, in spite of the frequently encountered opposite view.

3. We must, therefore, look elsewhere. Among the other streams of tradition in early Christianity which we have come to know, the Johannine is eliminated at the outset. We have already established that the Gospel and the Epistles of John do not know the disciples as apostles. The probable reasons for this have been shown. The Johannine position cannot have changed so soon, for according to its very essence the Johannine Christianity does not tolerate any historical guarantees such as are given by the tradition which is bound up with the apostolate of the twelve. John knows no "doctrine" which must be correctly transmitted. He knows only the Word given in the person of the revealer. Its verification is impossible, but for precisely that reason it demands *decision*.

Further, the consideration of *time* factors precludes that the title of apostle could have been first transferred to the twelve in a later development of the Johannine tradition. Even if one places John before Luke, who already knows the δώδεκα as uncontested apostles, there still is lacking the necessary period of time in which one could place the emergence of the new idea and its transferral into the Lucan tradition, quite apart from the fact that any contacts between the thought world of John and that of Luke are ruled out.

4. Between Paul and John stands Ignatius of Antioch, who represents the ecclesiastical tradition of Syria at the beginning of the second century. Naturally he knows the apostles. For him also they are the guarantors of the true gospel, with whom one must be in agreement (Eph. 11:2); for from them come the δόγματα (Magn. 13:1-2) and διατάγματα (Trall. 7:1), which are in conformity with the will of God (Magn. 7:1). But an actual theory of succession like that in the Pastoral Epistles is lacking.[32] For Ignatius the assurance of pure teaching is not the central concern. This is bound up with the fact that in Syria Gnosticism was strong enough not to allow itself to be drawn onto the platform, alien to its nature, of a doctrinal struggle. In Antioch people were not battling over the genuineness of the tradition; it was rather a matter of tradition versus spirit,[33] of the "Christ outside us" against the "Christ within us." Thus in the Syrian

---

The interpretation of the passages to refer to apostles (and prophets) who are living in the time of the author of the Ephesian epistle seems to me to be just as impossible as the connection of them with the apostolate of the twelve. G. Klein (*op. cit.*, pp. 66-75) proposes this interpretation, with arguments which in my judgment are not supportable. Even this explanation rules out for the Ephesian epistle any knowledge of the apostolate of the twelve.

In the Ephesian epistle, in fact, the Pauline concept of the apostle is simply reproduced, the concept which for the author of the epistle correctly appears to be restricted to the first generation.

[32] H. v. Campenhausen [2], p. 106.

[33] Cf. W. Lütgert, *Amt und Geist im Kampf*, 1911.

context the dispute between church and Gnosticism has continued to preserve the original character which, for example, the Corinthian correspondence exhibits. The Christians of the church in Corinth appealed, against
the Gnostics, to Paul, Peter, and Apollos; similarly, at the time of Ignatius,
the current bishops, presbyters, and deacons were the guarantors of the
true gospel. Whoever associated himself with them and recognized them
as teachers had thereby denied the unstructured authority of the Gnostic
pneumatics. The subjection to the monarchical episcopate, which Ignatius
furnishes with every conceivable authority,[34] is also doctrinally the sharpest
rebuff to Gnosticism, which could never limit the spirit to the leaders of
the congregation.

For this reason the significance of the apostles is not nearly so great for
Ignatius as it is for the Pastoral Epistles. For him they are holy figures of
the past whom one must honor (Trall. 12:2; Philad. 9:1). He cannot place
himself on a par with them (Trall. 3:3).[35] But he often compares them
with the presbytery: Subject yourselves to the presbyters, as to the apostles
of Christ, for the presbyters act in the place of the συνέδριον of the apostles
(Trall. 2:2; 3:1; Philad. 5:1; Magn. 6:1; Smyrn. 8:1). Thus Ignatius knows
the apostles primarily as a group of several persons. From among their company only Paul and Peter are mentioned in particular and by name, and in
fact jointly in the epistle to the Romans (Rom. 4:3). Apparently Ignatius
is familiar with the old Roman tradition which places these two apostles in
close connection with the capital of the Empire. Paul, the chief apostle, is
also mentioned explicitly in Eph. 12:2 and is adorned with extravagant
adjectives.

But who are the apostles in general whom Ignatius has in mind? "The
apostles are for Ignatius the intimate personal companions of Jesus and, in
addition, Paul," says W. Bauer (HNT, *Ergänzungsband*, on Eph. 11:2),
and I have found no one who is of a different opinion.[36] But I have also
failed to find anyone who offers reasons for this assertion. Most likely still
is the assumption that Ignatius means the *actual* apostles when he speaks of
the ἀπόστολοι, i.e., that host of missionaries who were native to the Syrian
region, to whom Paul belonged as prominent representative, and among
whom also Peter was very early counted. It would indeed be remarkable if
Ignatius himself were to speak of the twelve as *the* apostles, as an obvious
designation, and were to treat the host of apostles in his home country,
who still were active in his youth, as nonexistent. That is all the less con-

---

[34] See H. v. Campenhausen [2], pp. 109 ff.; W. Bauer [1], pp. 65 ff.
[35] This does not happen even in the Inscription to Ign. Trall.
[36] Cf. J. Wagenmann, *op. cit.*, p. 89; A. v. Harnack, *op. cit.*, I, 326.

ceivable since Ignatius generally stands quite aloof from the Jerusalem tradition, including that concerning the historical Jesus.

When one has once freed himself from the erroneous idea that the twelve had been considered apostles already in the first period of primitive Christianity, then every motive disappears for presupposing the apostolate of the twelve in Ignatius. He does not yet know the twelve as apostles.[37] Possibly they are rather designated by the expression οἱ περὶ Πέτρον (Smyrn. 3:2).

5. Now if we turn to Jerusalem and to the strict Jewish Christianity there, in the land east of the Jordan and in the Dispersion, it is understandable that the authority of the apostle Paul was not recognized in these circles.[38] But *the* authority of Jewish Christianity was not the twelve disciples, however much they were honored, and, naturally, especially not the twelve "apostles," but James,[39] who had not belonged to the circle of the twelve. In the Κηρύγματα Πέτρου, the Jewish Christian literary source of the Pseudo-Clementines,[40] he is regarded as ἀρχιεπίσκοπος, to whom even Peter, who has only the status of the teacher of the law, must be subordinated.[41] His authority is uncontested.

This appeal of the Jewish Christians to James is historically justified and goes back to the time in which Peter surrendered the leadership of the community in Jerusalem to James. There is no possibility that the apostolate of the twelve could have developed in this unbroken tradition of James.

6. Again, we must turn our gaze more to the West. There we meet Polycarp, Bishop of Smyrna (Ign. Magn. 15), whose congregation is situated in the former missionary territory of Paul. Polycarp is, quite naturally, strongly influenced by Paul, as his epistle to the Philippians demonstrates. Possibly he already knows the Pastoral Epistles; at any rate, he is acquainted with their theological tradition.[42] The relationships of the various offices in his congregations may correspond more to those of the Pastoral Epistles than to the ideas of Ignatius. Polycarp has no interest in the success of the monarchical episcopate. He is indeed a bishop, as Ign. Magn. 15 and Ign. Pol. inscr. show, but he never calls himself one. Instead, he rather places himself

---

[37] G. Klein (*op. cit.*, pp. 90 ff.) agrees with this judgment and gives detailed reasons for it.

[38] Iren. I, 26.2; III, 15.1; Orig. Cels. V, 65; Epiph. Haer. 30.16, 25.

[39] H. v. Campenhausen [2], pp. 197-98.

[40] See H. J. Schoeps, *Theologie und Geschichte des Judenchristentums* (1949), pp. 37 ff.

[41] H. J. Schoeps, *ibid.*, p. 292.

[42] See W. Michaelis, *Einleitung in das Neue Testament* (2nd ed., 1954), p. 238.

with the presbytery (Pol. inscr.).[43] For him as for the Philippians, Paul is the authority only for the reason that both orally and in writing he has perfectly taught the Word of truth (Pol. 3:2; 11:3). Polycarp repeatedly refers to Paul's letters, with which he is thoroughly conversant, while he stands quite remote from the Synoptic tradition.

But who are οἱ εὐαγγελισάμενοι ἡμᾶς ἀπόστολοι (Pol. 6:3), to whom the community is indebted for the joyous message? Who are the λοιποὶ ἀπόστολοι who appear alongside Paul (Pol. 9:1)? Once again there is no occasion for taking this to mean the twelve.[44] Anyone who stands in the Pauline tradition as does Polycarp knows as little of the twelve apostles as does the author of the Pastoral Epistles. Paul, probably Peter, and then the λοιποὶ ἀπόστολοι of I Cor. 9:5 most likely are the apostles whom Polycarp knows.[45]

I Peter also belongs to Asia Minor. It purports to have been written by Peter, the *apostle* of Jesus Christ. But it is generally acknowledged that the author lived to a large extent in the Pauline thought world.[46] It is surprising that in the circle of Pauline congregations Peter could be called up as an apostolic crown witness. A. Jülicher[47] thinks that the author sought "naturally one of the pillar apostles, who at the same time enjoyed the glory of martyrdom." Since the book of Acts offered only Peter and Paul as possible choices, he attempted to make use of Peter rather than Paul, "because he feared too strong a contrast with the great letter writer Paul." Perhaps this was the actual state of things, although it is quite certain that the book of Acts was still unknown to the author of I Peter. But the simplest assumption is that the author, who stands close to Paul, knew about the Petrine tradition which was actually present in the Pauline missionary territory. I have earlier sought to show[48] that already in the time of

---

[43] Polycarp apparently still knows of no bishop in Philippi, for he does not mention him in his writing (see W. Bauer in HNT, *Ergänzungsband*, p. 284). This corresponds to the situation in the Pastoral Epistles, which likewise provide no clear decision as to the relation of elders and bishops (see p. 238).

[44] This assumption of course is repeatedly made as though it were self-evident, without any supporting argument (cf. W. Bauer, *op. cit.*, p. 293, n. 43; J. Wagenmann, *op. cit.*, p. 91). Now *contra*, and properly, G. Klein, *op. cit.*, pp. 105 ff.

[45] In Mart. Polyc., it is said of Polycarp that he σὺν τοῖς ἀποστόλοις καὶ πᾶσιν δικαίοις ἀγαλλιώμενος δοξάζει τὸν θεόν (Mart. Polyc. 19). Even in this passage there is no necessity for including the twelve among the apostles, all the less since Polycarp himself can be described as διδάσκαλος ἀποστολικός (Mart. Polyc. 16; cf. Eus., CH V, 20.7).

[46] One may also observe the wholly "Pauline" context of I Peter. I Peter 1:1: the Pauline missionary territory; 5:12: Silvanus; 5:13: Mark; cf. Acts 12:12, 25; I Tim. 4:11.

[47] *Einleitung in das Neue Testament* (6th ed., 1906), p. 185.

[48] *Die Gnosis in Korinth*, pp. 191 ff. "His labours in the mission-field must have brought him [Peter] to the side of Paul," writes A. v. Harnack ([1], I, 62, n. 2), who

the conflicts testified to in the Corinthian correspondence, "Paul's people" and "Peter's people" formed a united front in Corinth against the invading Gnostics. Even if the Jewish Christians were quickly absorbed into the sphere of influence of the strongly Pauline congregations, still the consciousness would have been preserved that the apostle Peter was also co-founder of the congregations.[49] The Pauline I Peter then is no longer surprising to us,[50] and at the same time we shall not fall into the error of having the apostle Peter in I Peter 1:1 introduced as one of the twelve apostles.[51] He is indeed represented as one of the apostles, as already done by Paul (Gal. 1:18-19), but, precisely as in Paul, as one of the *actual* apostles.

Irenaeus transmits to us in IV, 27.1–32.1 a complete anti-Marcionite excerpt which he ascribes to a "presbyter." According to general opinion this "presbyter's sermon" as a whole is pre-Irenaean (*vide* M. Widmann in ZThK [1957], p. 160, and the literature mentioned there); whether it is Roman or from Asia Minor is uncertain. In this excerpt Paul serves as "the apostle" (27. 3,4; 28.3; 32.1). In one instance the twelve appear beside him as the "disciples" (29.1), and likewise John as "discipulus" (30.4). That "the apostles" in 28.3 are also the twelve is not so certain that one could not reckon with an ignorance of the *apostolate* of the twelve on the part of the presbyter. Further, the citation of the presbyter in Iren. V, 5.1 shows acquaintance only with the "apostle Paul."

The Epistle to Diognetus, which is difficult to ascribe to a particular place and time, also belongs to the circle of this literature. The *Autor ad Diognetum,* like any other author of the second century, is both internally and externally indebted to Paul, while no knowledge of the Synoptic tradition is to be traced to him. The concept of apostle occurs in the last two chapters[52] of this missionary-apologetic writing. The author is represented as ἀποστόλων γενόμενος μαθητής (11.1). The Logos, which was rejected by the people of the Jews, has been preached διὰ ἀποστόλων and believed by the Gentiles (11.3). For these believers it now may be said: ἀποστόλων παράδοσις φυλάσσεται (11.6), as it then generally is a sign of the time of salvation that ἀπόστολοι συνετίζονται = apostles receive knowledge

---

on the basis of this understanding can even decide for the genuineness of I Peter ([1], 62, n. 2).

[49] Bishop Dionysius of Corinth (*ca.* 170) names Peter and Paul as founders of the Corinthian congregation (Eus., CH II, 25.8); one may also recall the Roman tradition about Peter and Paul.

[50] The question should be posed whether the composition of I Peter was not decisively conditioned by the motivation of drawing the Petrine congregations to the Pauline congregations in the critical times of persecution and the Gnostic peril, by exhibiting the theological affinity of Peter and Paul.

[51] Thus now also G. Klein, *op. cit.,* pp. 83-84.

[52] By many students, these chaps. are not ascribed to the author of chaps. 1–10.

(12.9). There is nothing to suggest that these apostles in particular or in general are the twelve; on the other hand, only Paul qualifies as ὁ ἀπόστολος (12.5). The fact that ἀπόστολοι always appears without the article points to an open concept of the apostle which indeed belongs to the past, but in this past does not designate a closed circle.[53]

7. What is the situation in Rome? That even Hermas[54] betrays no knowledge of the twelve apostles is indeed little contested,[55] even though J. Wagenmann (*op. cit.*, p. 88) assumes that the twelve obviously have been drawn by Hermas into the (larger) apostolic circle. But there is nothing to require this assumption. The apostles are consistently placed together with the teachers in a quite formal fashion, a sign of that old and original tradition which does not yet know the apostolate of the twelve[56] (Vis. III, 5.1; Sim. IX, 15.4; 16.5; 25.2). Only in Sim. IX, 17.1 do the apostles appear without an explicit mention of the teachers. The number of the apostles and teachers is given as forty (Sim. IX, 15.4; 16.5), and one does not gain the impression that Hermas could precisely distinguish between the two groups of officeholders. Basically the question of the office does not interest Hermas at all. He operates only with some already present traditions.[57]

First Clement is more important. Also for him it may be said that the office in Rome itself has not yet become a problem—different from Corinth, where the approved bishops were deposed by the majority of the congregation, probably in connection with disputes between ecclesiastical and Gnostic Christianity.[58] In view of this state of things, Clement takes up approximately the position which the Pastoral Epistles represent with great emphasis: God has sent Christ; Christ has entrusted the gospel to the apostles; the apostles installed bishops or presbyters[59] and deacons, and at

---

[53] The concept of the apostle in the Epistle to Diognetus speaks in favor of a relatively early time for the composition of the document.

[54] That Hermas belongs to *Rome* has of course recently been sharply contested by E. Peterson, who, not without reason, sees rather an Eastern, Palestinian "local color" in the "Shepherd"; cf. E. Peterson, *Frühkirche, Judentum und Gnosis*, pp. 254-309, esp., e.g., p. 283.

[55] To be sure, E. Meyer (*op. cit.*, I, 270) is of the opinion that the "Shepherd" knows only the twelve as apostles.

[56] See pp. 51 ff.

[57] The tradition utilized in Sim. IX, 17.1 *could* presuppose that there were *twelve* apostles: "The twelve mountains are the twelve tribes which dwell in the whole world. The Son of God was preached to them by the apostles." But such a presupposition is improbable; the number twelve is connected only with the twelve tribes. Cf. A. v. Harnack [1], I, 320; G. Klein, *op. cit.*, pp. 97 ff.

[58] W. Bauer [1], pp. 99 ff.; *Die Gnosis in Korinth* (first ed.), p. 254, n. 2.

[59] The two titles are interchangeable—as they are in the Pastoral Epistles—as I Clem. 44:4-5 shows; cf. also I Clem. 44:1 with 47:6.

the same time gave command to them that after their death other approved men should be entrusted with these offices by the whole community (I Clem. 42-43). In Clement as in the Pastorals, with whose understanding of office he is in closest contact, we find a complete order of the apostolic tradition.[60] It is, to be sure, still less legally structured than in the Pastorals; nothing is said about the laying on of hands. But the line of succession in office drawn by I Clem. still can only have the meaning of identifying the men who stand in this tradition as apostolic. H. v. Campenhausen ([2], p. 172) to be sure correctly thinks: "With respect to the apostles the concept of tradition plays no role." The question of doctrine thus—similar to the case of Ignatius and different from that of the Pastorals—is not yet broached. In a representative of the Roman community which at the end of the first century is still untouched or only lightly touched by Gnosticism, this should not be surprising. In I Clem., likewise, one cannot yet speak of an apostolic succession in the sense of the later monarchical episcopate.

But who are the apostles who have received the divine gospel from Christ and have handed it on to the community through approved men? Two of the "good apostles" are named by name: Peter and Paul (I Clem. 5:3). Both qualify also in I Clem. 47:4, in distinction from Apollos, as apostles. In I Clem. 47:1 Paul by himself is called "blessed apostle." Thus in no case does Clement know the idea of the twelve simply as the apostles. In I Clem. 5:2 ff., moreover, the apostles are distinguished from the "pillars" (following Gal. 2).[61] This also makes it quite improbable that by the term ἀπόστολοι I Clem. means the twelve and Paul. On the contrary, these passages fit quite well into the original picture of the apostle which was well known to Clement from the letters of Paul and which lay close at hand, a picture which did not include the twelve.

Now to be sure there is still another tradition which permits it to appear, e.g. to R. Knopf[62] and J. Wagenmann,[63] as a settled fact that by the term "apostles" I Clem. means the twelve and Paul. I Clem. 42:1 ff. reads thus:

οἱ ἀπόστολοι ἡμῖν εὐηγγελίσθησαν ἀπὸ τοῦ κυρίου Ἰησοῦ Χριστοῦ, Ἰησοῦς ὁ Χριστὸς ἀπὸ τοῦ θεοῦ ἐξεπέμφθη. Ὁ Χριστὸς οὖν ἀπὸ τοῦ θεοῦ καὶ οἱ ἀπόστολοι ἀπὸ τοῦ Χριστοῦ. ἐγένοντο οὖν ἀμφότερα εὐτάκτως ἐκ θελήματος θεοῦ. παραγγελίας οὖν λαβόντες καὶ πληροφορηθέντες διὰ τῆς ἀναστάσεως τοῦ κυρίου Ἰησοῦ Χριστοῦ καὶ πιστωθέντες ἐν τῷ λόγῳ τοῦ

---

[60] "I Clement not only hints at the doctrine, in an imperfect and tentative way, but uses it clearly and competently, as a well-established tenet of the Christian faith" (A. Ehrhardt, op. cit., p. 77).

[61] R. Knopf in HNT on I Clem. 5:2.

[62] Ibid. on I Clem. 5:3 ff.

[63] Op. cit., p. 87; further, E. Lohse [1], p. 259; A. v. Harnack [1], I, 325.

θεοῦ, μετὰ πληροφορίας πνεύματος ἁγίου ἐξῆλθον εὐαγγελιζόμενοι τὴν βασιλείαν τοῦ θεοῦ μέλλειν ἔρχεσθαι. κατὰ χώρας οὖν καὶ πόλεις κηρύσσοντες καθίστανον τὰς ἀπαρχὰς αὐτῶν. . . .

This passage may most simply be understood in terms of the Synoptic-Lucan tradition, which excludes Paul: The twelve apostles were entrusted by the historical Jesus with the gospel, received from him the missionary commission (Matt. 10:1 ff.), were fully convinced by the resurrected One (Matt. 28:19) and confirmed in the Word of God, and then set about preaching everywhere that the kingdom of God was dawning (cf. Matt. 10:7).

It is certainly possible also to explain the passage cited above wholly in the sense of the original view of the apostolate as presented in Gal. 1–2.[64] In this the διὰ τῆς ἀναστάσεως in vs. 3 is also to be connected with the παραγγελίας οὖν λαβόντες: The entire apostolate is the work of the *exalted* Lord. In this connection one may appeal to the fact that otherwise I Clem. betrays hardly any acquaintance with the Synoptic tradition.[65] Further, the reference to the ἀπαρχαί installed by the apostles (I Clem. 42:4) is certainly dependent upon Rom. 16:5 and I Cor. 16:15, so that in chap. 42 of his epistle Clement has Paul in mind, who in no way fits into the Synoptic scheme. The vs. I Clem. 42:1, which contains the term ἀπόστολος, is so strongly reminiscent of Gal. 1:11-12, that one can hardly avoid assuming that Clement has in view the Pauline concept of the apostle. And the line "God-Christ-apostles" (I Clem. 42:1-2) is good Pauline thought (II Cor. 5:20).

If we used the "synoptic" meaning in I Clem. 42, we would be dealing with the earliest witness to that interpretation which sees in the twelve disciples the true apostles, and would at the same time acknowledge that Clement had taken over this view, which would not fit in with his familiarity with the *apostle* Paul, from the stream of tradition which had come to him. On this question, cf. *infra* p. 265, n. 152.

III

1. The Apocalypse of John offers a testimony[66] which is possibly *much* later. Rev. 21:14 speaks of the δώδεκα ὀνόματα τῶν δώδεκα ἀποστόλων τοῦ ἀρνίου which are written upon the twelve foundation stones of the

---

[64] Even Matthew (28:19-20) and Luke (Acts 1:8) put the missionary commandment in the mouth of the *resurrected One!*

[65] He quotes words of the Lord only twice (I Clem. 13:2; 46:7-8), and indeed in both instances from apocryphal or oral tradition; see R. Knopf in HNT, *in loc.*—G. Klein, *op. cit.,* pp. 84 ff. follows *this* interpretation of the passage I Clem. 42:1 ff.

[66] The Apocalypse is not certainly attested before Justin (Dial. 81; Eus., CH IV, 18.8).

wall of the heavenly city. For the author of this sentence, only the twelve are the apostles[67]; there is no place for Paul alongside them. If one places next to this passage Rev. 18:20[68] (and 2:2), where the original concept of the apostle is still found, then the use of different and distinct ancient materials in the Apocalypse becomes clear.

2. Very soon, alongside these isolated traces,[69] Luke appears with his writings. In his Gospel the disciples are five times identified as apostles (6:13; 9:10; 17:5; 22:14; 24:10; on 11:49, see p. 97), and in the Acts about twenty-six times, last of all Acts 16:4; in addition, there is found one time the word ἀποστολή (Acts 1:25). The relatively infrequent occurrence of ἀπόστολος in the Gospel is explained by the fact that the Synoptic sources of Luke did not yet have the word.[70]

The picture which Luke has of the apostles is clearly recognizable.[71] Their special task is the mission, indeed the world mission (Acts 1:8). The call to their ministry had already come during the lifetime of Jesus[72]; even Judas had in fact been a called apostle (Acts 1:16 ff.).[73] A precondition for their ministry was that they had been together with Jesus during the whole time in which Jesus was at work, thus from the baptism of John

[67] G. Klein disputes this (op. cit., pp. 76 ff.). He thinks that the number twelve is determined by the context and has nothing to do with the twelve disciples, and all the more has nothing to do with twelve apostles. This is more than improbable. How does "John" come to introduce the apostles at all unless the number twelve were already connected with the apostles for him? There is no occasion for introducing them in the context. G. Klein also rightly sees the special parallelism which exists between the twelve tribes of Israel (vss. 12-13) and the twelve apostles. But then for the latter as for the former it must hold true that the number twelve is already given. Finally, the author of the Apocalypse would have had to use a different formulation if the number of the apostles was basically unlimited and would have had to write somewhat as in the case of the angels: καὶ ἐπ' αὐτῶν τὰ ὀνόματα δώδεκα ἀποστόλων. The actual formulation, ὀνόματα τῶν δώδεκα ἀποστόλων, unequivocally limits the number of the apostles to twelve. This limitation is either tradition or—hardly—the author's own doing.

[68] See p. 52.

[69] Asc. Jes. 3.13 ff., where twelve apostles are mentioned, could also come from a relatively early period. The placing of this passage around the turn of the first to the second century, to be sure, appears to me to be too early by far (thus H. Duensing in Hennecke) and is unfounded. On the question of date, see G. Klein, op. cit., pp. 107-8, who rightly rejects too early a dating of the entire document.

Cf. also E. Stauffer, Jesus (1957), p. 138, who dates it even in the early part of the year 68!

[70] The same observation may be made with reference to the early source fragments of the book of Acts; they are not acquainted with the concept ἀπόστολοι for the twelve; see E. Lohse [1], p. 264.

[71] On the following cf. W. Mundle, op. cit., pp. 38 ff.; H. v. Campenhausen [1], pp. 115 ff.; J. Wagenmann, op. cit., pp. 65 ff.; G. Klein, op. cit., pp. 114 ff.

[72] Cf. J. Wagenmann, op. cit., p. 67. On the fact that according to Luke, then, the twelve were hardly active as missionaries, cf. n. 144.

[73] E. Haenchen, op. cit., in loc.

onward; and further, that they were witnesses of his resurrection (Luke 24:48; Acts 1:21-22).[74] Therefore they know everything which the Lord has proclaimed during his earthly activity, and are likewise acquainted with the words of the resurrected One which he spoke to them about the kingdom of God during the forty days between the resurrection and the ascension (Luke 24:45 ff.; Acts 1:3). No one equals them in knowledge of these things.

But they are also the actual bearers of the Pneuma. The possession of the spirit is a precondition for the exercise of the apostolic ministry (Acts 1:8). Thus the twelve awaited in Jerusalem the reception of the Pneuma, as they had been commanded to do (Luke 24:49; Acts 1:4-5). On Pentecost the promise is fulfilled. The Spirit sat upon the twelve and they began to preach[75] (Acts 2), "full of the Holy Spirit" (Acts 4:8).

In view of such significance of the apostles every Christian must be dependent upon the twelve. We know how unhistorical this presentation is.[76] But Luke takes it so much for granted that he makes even Paul always act in the sense of the Jerusalemites; for however little Luke is concerned artificially to *subordinate* him to the twelve, and however little, on the other hand, he ascribes to Paul less authority than to the twelve, still for him it remains unshakably true that besides the "apostles" there can be no *independent* authority. We find Paul repeatedly in Jerusalem, where his mission is confirmed by the "apostles" (Acts 9:26; 11:30; 12:25; 15:2, 6, 25; 18:22; 21:15 ff.). Paul does not constantly qualify as an apostle, which is self-evident in view of the fact that he does not meet the Lucan conditions for the apostolate[77]; to be sure, it does not disturb Luke so to call him and Barnabas in Acts 14:4, 14, supposedly following a source,[78] but in this case

[74] Cf. E. Haenchen in ZThK (1955), p. 208.

[75] The Spirit will hardly have been poured out upon the community, which indeed did not yet even exist, but upon the apostles. Only thus does it become understandable that later the further bestowal of the Spirit can be bound up with them. *Contra* E. Haenchen, *op. cit.* on Acts 2:1, because the οὖτοι of vs. 15 must be other Christians. But Peter refers in vs. 15 to his eleven fellow apostles.

[76] H. J. Schoeps of course intends "to represent the original Jerusalem concept of the apostle, as the Lucan portrayal exhibits it"! (*Urgemeinde—Judenchristentum—Gnosis* [Tübingen, 1956], p. 14).

Such a judgment today, of course, forms a rare exception. On the whole the view has prevailed that "the Lucan concept of the apostle . . . corresponded neither to the original usage nor to the state of things as they were after Jesus' death" (P. Winter in ThLZ [1957], col. 835).

[77] The story of Paul's call, told three times by Luke, is not supposed to, and cannot, take the place in any wise of the special advantages of the twelve as witnesses of the life of Jesus and of his resurrection; cf. J. Wagenmann, *op. cit.*, pp. 76-77.

[78] Thus the majority of scholars; cf. K. Lake, *op. cit.*, p. 51; G. Sass [2], p. 234; A. Hilgenfeld, *Einleitung*, p. 585. Even Haenchen, who is very critical with respect to sugges-

he thinks of them obviously as "emissaries" in the nontechnical sense.[79] But Luke shows himself to be completely uninterested in an ordered apostolic succession.[80] The laying on of hands in the commissioning of the seven protectors of the poor is not to be taken as a bestowal of authorization to teach, especially since for Luke the seven are not teachers. It has to do simply with an ordination[81] which underscores the self-evident fact that all power lies in the hands of the twelve. Only the speech of Paul in Acts 20:18 ff. clearly shows connections with an anti-Gnostic doctrinal tradition (Acts 20:20, 27 ff.). But this speech, in my opinion, is not a Lucan construction, as E. Haenchen[82] has again recently emphatically asserted. Its kinship with the wholly non-Lucan Pastorals has impressed the exegetes in general. I consider the speech to be a piece, reworked by Luke, of the so-called "itinerary," [83] the author of which stood close to the author of the Pastorals or was even identical with him, though I cannot at this time more fully establish this assumption. At any rate, even Acts 20:18 ff. cannot serve as proof that Luke let the correct tradition of the apostolic doctrine worry him in any way.[84]

All this is not to dispute that Luke *consciously* presented the twelve in Jerusalem as the authorities upon whom all Christians, even Paul, depend.[85] Luke writes the Acts of the Apostles essentially out of the tendency to present Christianity as the true Judaism.[86] This tendency includes the em-

---

tions about sources of the book of Acts, assumes for the scene in Lystra (Acts 14:8-20) an earlier individual tradition (*op. cit.*, p. 381). Paul and Barnabas must have been named in this early tradition.

[79] Cf. E. Lohse [1], p. 273, n. 46; H. v. Campenhausen [1], p. 115.

[80] H. v. Campenhausen [2], p. 169.

[81] Cf. E. Lohse [2], pp. 77-78.

[82] *Op. cit.*, pp. 533 ff.

[83] The misleading designation "itinerary" should be abandoned. More appropriate, certainly, would be the characterization as "mission aretalogy."

[84] Even Acts 14:23 does not have the tendency to assure the apostolic doctrinal tradition.

[85] G. Klein has shown this (*op. cit.*, pp. 114-85) in a completely convincing way.

[86] E. Haenchen (*op. cit.*, p. 565 *et passim*) thinks that this presentation has the aim of maintaining protection for Christianity as *religio licita*. According to H. Conzelmann (ThLZ, LXXXV [1960], cols. 244-45), the texts mean "rather that Luke is offering a dual line of argument: one, basically in terms of salvation history, for *use within the church;* here he shows the salvation-history *continuity* of Israel and the church; and the other, topical-apologetic; here, in the address to the *imperium,* he sets the church *at a distance* from the 'Jews.' " Over against this, Haenchen, in the new edition of his commentary, holds to his thesis.

That the apologetic interpretation of the continuity Israel-church does not exclude the salvation-history interpretation is clear. This was a time when persecutions by the state— not in the last analysis prompted by the Jews—were already underway, while even after this, Judaism could practice its cult freely and without making sacrifices to the emperor in the Roman Empire. H. Conzelmann should be asked what interest the church

phasis that Jerusalem is the center and the departure point of Christianity and that all manifestations of Christianity, even Paul and his work, are rooted in the Jerusalem tradition of the twelve apostles, which in turn is the tradition of the historical Jesus.[87]

3. Justin has the same concept of the apostle as has Luke. For him Paul apparently did not exist. He is never mentioned. Whether Justin knew of any letters of Paul is very doubtful to me. To be sure Goodspeed[88] has sought to show in the *Dialogue* no less than sixty-two allusions to the letters of Paul,[89] but a close examination shows that in none of these passages is it necessary to presuppose a knowledge of Paul.[90] However that may be, for Justin only the twelve qualify as apostles.[91] Their authority is demonstrable, since already the Old Testament, for example, established the number of twelve for the apostles, and since it had frequently been foretold that the twelve disciples would proclaim the gospel to all the world from Jerusalem (Apol. I, 31; 39; 40; 42; 45.5; 49.5; 50; 53).[92] In particular, Peter (Dial. 106.3), John (Dial. 81) and the Sons of Thunder (Dial. 106.3) are men-

---

could have had in such a time in keeping its distance from the Jewish religion, something that indeed does not occur either in Acts or in the comparable apologies. But Haenchen's interpretation of the Lucan tendency likewise is hardly adequate. G. Klein (*op. cit.*) goes further; see pp. 270-71.

[87] One should not, however, speak of "apostolic tradition" or "succession," since these concepts, because of their unmistakable origin in church history, describe an equally definite situation in the realm of church order. But the Lucan concept of tradition does not refer to the legal ordering of matters within the church. The speech in Acts 20:18 ff., which is intended essentially in the sense of the apostolic tradition, has for Luke only the significance of undergirding *his* concept of tradition. Cf. also H. Conzelmann, *The Theology of St. Luke*, pp. 217-18.

[88] *Die ältesten Apologeten,* Index.

[89] In the Apologies, on the other hand, only five.

[90] I owe this proof in particular to G. Klein, *op. cit.*, pp. 192-201; cf. also W. Bauer [1], p. 218.

[91] This does not mean that Justin was opposed to Paul. His attitude toward Paul may have been no different from that of Luke, who indeed also has nothing against Paul but nevertheless neither reads his letters nor recognizes him as an apostle. But naturally it is all the more wrong to conclude that, in spite of his utter silence on the matter, Justin, because he did not fight him, recognized Paul as an apostle (thus J. Wagenmann, *op. cit.*, p. 169).

G. Klein (*op. cit.*, p. 200) considers it impossible that Justin was not acquainted with any writings of Paul. "At this time and in this place that would be impossible." This is not at all certain. On the assertion that *around 150* every Christian theologian must have been acquainted with Paul, see p. 261, n. 138. That in *Rome* they were acquainted with Paul is naturally certain. But Roman Christianity around 150 consisted of a multiplicity of different communities with differing traditions. That the Oriental Justin must have devoted himself in Rome to the Pauline tradition is an unreasonable demand. Did Rudolf Bultmann in Marburg devote himself to the literature of Hans Bruns, or Billy Graham in Berlin to the writings of Ernst Fuchs? Hardly!

[92] Cf. J. Wagenmann, *op. cit.*, p. 165.

tioned. The twelve apostles are the missionaries to all the world, εἰς πᾶν γένος ἀνθρώπων ἐλθόντες (Apol. I, 39; 50; 53.3), thus particularly to the Gentiles (Apol. I, 42.4; Dial. 53.1; 109). As apostles of Christ they begin their world mission in Jerusalem (Dial. 114.4; 119.6—Dial. 110.2; Apol. I, 45.5; 49.5). They are the first ones to have been convinced of the necessity of Christ's suffering (Dial. 76; 106), and this was done by the resurrected One, to whose resurrection they can bear witness (Apol. I, 50.12). Through the Gospels (Apol. I, 66.3; Dial. 88.3), the ἀπομνημονεύματα τῶν ἀποστόλων (Dial. 100.4; 101.3; 102.5; 103.6, 8; 104; 106.1, 4; Apol. I, 67.3), they disseminate the knowledge of the prophecies of the Old Testament which are fulfilled in Christ, and of the proper use of the sacraments (Apol. I, 61.9; 66.3). The Gentiles never would have heard anything of Christ if it had not been for the apostles' proclamation to them (Apol. I, 49). What the apostles already have taught in the name of Christ is still transmitted today by the church, thus also by Justin (Apol. I, 45.5; 50; 61; 66; 67.8).

As in Luke, so also in Justin any reference to an apostolic succession is lacking. The teachers of the church teach nothing other than what the apostles taught; but the unity of teaching is not guaranteed by the ecclesiastical office which for Justin has no weight, and even less by an "official" tradition, but rather by what is accessible to everyone, the ἀπομνημονεύματα τῶν ἀποστόλων· οἱ γὰρ ἀπόστολοι ἐν τοῖς γενομένοις ὑπ' αὐτῶν ἀπομνημονεύμασιν, ἃ καλεῖται εὐαγγέλια, οὕτως παρέδωκαν (Apol. I, 66.3).

4. The Epistle of Barnabas belongs to this circle as still another writing. The connections between Barnabas and Justin are uncommonly numerous, as a look at Windisch's commentary on the Epistle of Barnabas in HNT will show. That Justin made use of Barnabas, as Windisch presupposes,[93] appears to me unlikely. It is more probable to assume common traditions, particularly in view of the complicated literary character of the Epistle of Barnabas, which certainly is not a writing from a single mold.[94] But for us this question is of no importance. Barnabas also never mentions and cites Paul, but neither does he do battle with him. No passage in his work shows with certainty that he was acquainted with the Pauline letters. It is altogether obvious that for him only the twelve qualify as apostles. The fact that he alludes to them only twice shows how little he thought it necessary to be concerned about the recognition of the apostolate of the twelve.

As for Justin, so also for Barnabas the apostolate in general as well as the number of twelve for its bearers is predetermined in the Old Testament

---

[93] In HNT, *Ergänzungsband*, p. 301.
[94] *Ibid.*, pp. 411-12.

(Barn. 8.3), even though the scriptural proof is different from that of Justin (Dial. 42). Barnabas declared even more strongly than had Justin (Apol. I, 50; Dial. 53; 106) that before their call the twelve had been extraordinarily great sinners, because Jesus wished to show that he had come not to call the righteous but sinners (Barn. 5.9).[95] Obviously, the authority of the twelve was utterly unassailed.[96] It is they who have proclaimed the gospel upon the commission of Jesus Christ; they have τὴν ἐξουσίαν τοῦ εὐαγγελίου (Barn. 8.3; 5.9).[97] But Barnabas had no kind of interest in apostolic succession. In general the whole question of the ecclesiastical office played for him, as for Justin (and Luke), so small a role that one is not able to tell just how his congregations may have been organized.

II Peter and Jude also belong to the circle of this literary tradition. The relationship between these two pseudepigraphical writings need not detain us; their internal and external kinship is plain enough.[98] The existence of Paul's letters is known to II Peter. He knows that the Gnostics improperly use these letters in support of their own doctrine (II Pet. 3:15-16). Whether the author of II Peter, for his part, knows the content of the letters of his "dear brother Paul" is uncertain. Clear reminiscences of Paul's letters are not found here. The same is true of Jude. In II Pet. 1:1, ἀπόστολος appears in the singular; Peter introduces himself as servant and apostle of Jesus Christ. In II Pet. 3:2 and Jude 17 there is an occasional recollection of the words of the ἀπόστολοι τοῦ κυρίου ἡμῶν 'Ιησοῦ Χριστοῦ. One will be able to assume with certainty that by these apostles the author means the twelve, when one notes the late date of writing and the theological orientation of these letters within the circle of the writings already mentioned, writings which know only the apostolate of the twelve.[99]

Above all, a comparison of II Pet. 1:1 with 1:16 ff. shows that the decisive characteristic mark of the apostle here, as in Luke's writings, consists in his being a witness of the *historia* of Jesus.[100] In view of the late date of

[95] Cf. also H. Köster, Synoptische Überlieferung bei den apostolischen Vätern, TU, LXV (1957), 141 ff.

[96] G. Klein (op. cit., pp. 96-97) excises Barn. 8.3 as a gloss, and on the basis of Barn. 5.9 admits only that in Barnabas the apostles are rooted in the *historia* of Jesus, but denies that in them we have to do with the twelve. But at the time of Barnabas an apostolate other than that of the twelve in the vicinity of Jesus is hardly conceivable and furthermore is never proven anywhere.

[97] There is no occasion for the assumption that in these passages Barnabas is conducting a polemic against the apostolic claims of others (than the twelve; see M. Barth, Der Augenzeuge, p. 337).

[98] The generally assumed position of Jude as earlier than II Peter appears to me not *absolutely* necessary. Composition by the same hand is not *completely* to be ruled out.

[99] See below, p. 261.

[100] Thus for the author of II Peter, Paul apparently is not an apostle. Cf. G. Klein, op. cit., p. 105.

II Peter, his acquaintance with the Synoptic tradition, and the fact that the matter of being an apostolic eyewitness appears only in connection with the apostolate of the twelve, we must conclude that the apostles of II Peter are the twelve disciples of the historical Jesus.[101]

The teaching is apostolic, but it does not need especially to be guaranteed as such. In any case, the office in general and the apostolic succession in particular do not play any role either for II Peter or for Jude.

Other personages of this relatively early time, who probably must be counted among the above-mentioned authors, have not left us adequate evidence to form final judgments.[102] Among them is counted Papias of Hierapolis, who wrote as his single work five books λογίων κυριακῶν ἐξηγήσεις, which probably means rather an exposition of the words and deeds of Jesus known to him from Matthew and Mark than a new collection of such words and deeds (Eus. CH III, 39). He attempts to inquire back into the opinion of the disciples, and he enumerates seven "disciples of the Lord," though in the fragment preserved by Eusebius the title ἀπόστολος does not appear. Neither does it appear in any of the other extant fragments from his writing, "although in them there are fairly frequent references to men of whose position as apostles he can have had no doubt." [103] It seems, then, that to Papias, who wrote before the middle of the second century, the title ἀπόστολος for the twelve was still unknown. This corresponds to the fact that the Gospel of Luke was still unknown to Papias (*vide* p. 255).[104] Eusebius reports nothing about any acquaintance of Papias with Paul.[105]

One must also count Tatian, the pupil of Justin and later a Gnostic, in this group, at least for the period when he was within the church. The positive attitude of Tatian toward the alleged tradition from the circle of the twelve is beyond question, since he composed the Diatessaron. His attitude toward Paul is unclear. He is said (Eus. CH IV, 29) to have altered passages of the "apostle"; but at the same time, in his school Paul, together with the book of Acts, is said to have been rejected (*vide ibid.*).[106]

The Athenian Aristides, who does not mention Paul,[107] speaks in conclu-

---

[101] Thus also G. Klein (*op. cit.*, pp. 100 ff.), who, following the example of others (cf. esp. E. Käsemann, "Eine Apologie der urchristlichen Eschatologie," ZThK, XLIX (1952), p. 279) gives detailed proof for this opinion.

[102] The loss of the epistles of Dionysius of Corinth is esp. grievous for us. The concept of the apostle is lacking in the fragments which are preserved in Eusebius.

[103] Th. Zahn, *Apostel und Apostelschüler in der Provinz Asien* (1900), p. 135.

[104] Papias perhaps never left his Phrygian homeland; cf. W. Bauer [1], p. 110.

[105] W. Bauer ([1], p. 217) has attempted to show it unlikely that we can assume any acquaintance with Paul's letters on the part of Papias.

[106] On Tatian, cf. M. Elze, *Tatian und seine Theologie*, Forschungen zur Kirchen- und Dogmengeschichte, IX, 1960.

[107] Cf. J. Wagenmann, *op. cit.*, pp. 158-59.

sion of the fact that Jesus "had twelve disciples who, after his ascension, traveled into the various kingdoms of the earth in order to proclaim his greatness." [108] He also must have belonged to the circle bound to the twelve apostles,[109] and one may assume the same of Quadratus.[110]

In this connection we must also mention the Didache, which as διδαχὴ κυρίου διὰ τῶν δώδεκα ἀποστόλων τοῖς ἔθνεσιν was certainly put into circulation in the twelve-apostle tradition; just as certain, however, is the fact that individual parts of its appendix (chaps. 7–16) stem from an entirely different tradition.[111]

The fragment of the "Gospel of the Hebrews" cited by Epiphanius (Haer. 30.13.2-3) also is acquainted with *twelve apostles*. On the other hand, in the extant parts of the Gospel of Peter (and in the Apocalypse of Peter) only the *twelve disciples* are spoken of (Hennecke-Schneemelcher-Wilson, I, 187). Both writings may stem from the time before *ca.* 150. Equally ancient is the fragment of the "Preaching of Peter" preserved by Clement of Alexandria (Strom. VI, 6.48), which names *twelve apostles;* still, it is possible that the allusion to them was first inserted by Clement himself.

5. Thus we find a rather large circle of writings and writers to whom it is just as obvious that the twelve are apostles as it is that Paul does not qualify as an apostle.[112] If we ask in what time these writings with their new (in contrast with the original concept of the apostle) understanding of the apostolate belong, the answer is unequivocal: in the first half of the second century, and rather in the second quarter than in the first quarter. Quadratus presented his Apology to the Emperor Hadrian (who died in 138), and Aristides probably presented his to Antoninus Pius (who died in 161). About 165 Justin suffered martyrdom; Tatian had been his pupil.

---

[108] The text is preserved in the legend of Barlaam and Josaphat. I quote following the translation of Ludwig Burchard which appeared in the Theatiner-Verlag, München. The passage quoted above is found in R. Raabe, *Die Apologie des Aristides*, TU, IX.1 (1892), p. 3.

[109] Of course it remains uncertain whether he gave the title of apostle to the twelve.

[110] Cf. also the apologist Apollonius (*ca.* 197) in Eus., CH V, 18.14.

[111] Cf. G. Klein, *op. cit.*, pp. 80 ff. Following the example of others, Klein takes the position that the original title of the writing did not contain the number twelve but read only διδαχὴ τῶν ἀποστόλων or something similar. In case this is true—most scholars are not of this opinion—it is certainly by no means excluded that the unnumbered apostles in the superscription of the Didache are the twelve.

[112] Curiously, the Acts of Paul (see Hennecke-Schneemelcher-Wilson; cf. J. Wagenmann, *op. cit.*, pp. 180 ff.) also belong to this literary circle. Paul is never called apostle, but he can speak of "our predecessors, the apostles" (Epistle of Paul to the Corinthians, 4) who "were always with Jesus Christ" (*ibid.*). The Acta Pauli are constructed following the itinerary of the book of Acts which itself appears not to be used. In contrast to Luke, the author already had access to the epistles of Paul. The twelve apostles are also known in the Act. Joh. and the Act. Thom.

Papias also belongs to the middle of the century. The same time is rightly accepted by the exegetes throughout for our edition of the Didache and for the writings known to us as Barnabas, Jude, and II Peter, which are very difficult to define chronologically. Luke may be the earliest of this circle of writings,[113] but one must be careful not to place him too early.

Any use of the Gospel of Luke before the time of Marcion cannot be proved.[114] It is uncertain when Marcion, who left the church in Rome in 144, formed his canon. Since Marcion was active in the imperial capital as a heretic until about 150, one may accept 140-150 as an approximate date for his canonizing of the Gospel of Luke. But nowhere before him emerges a single item of unmistakable Lucan origin. Eusebius transmits to us not a single utterance of Papias about the Gospel of Luke, apparently because Papias is acquainted only with Matthew and Mark, not with Luke.[115] The book of Acts is indeed frequently cited by Irenaeus, but before him it is not attested at all. The four parallels with which E. Haenchen supports the acquaintance of Justin with the book of Acts (*op. cit.*, pp. 6-7) testify only to the common traditions, which are also abundantly present elsewhere, of the two authors. Whether Justin used the Gospel of Luke is uncertain. Thus there is no reason for placing Luke earlier than about 120-30.[116] In no case may one move it up into the first century; for then the special Lucan material could not have remained so widely unknown among the ecclesiastical writers before Justin or Irenaeus.

IV

1. Thus from about 120 onward we find in one definite literary circle a concept of the apostle which embraces the twelve, and only the twelve. The

[113] I Clement (see below) *possibly* appears as an earlier witness than Luke. It seems to me unlikely that Rev. 21:14 was written before 120.

[114] Even the use of Luke's Gospel by Marcion is disputed, e.g. by H. Raschke, *Die Werkstatt des Markusevangelisten* (1924), pp. 31 ff.

H. Köster, *Synoptische Überlieferung bei den apostolischen Vätern*, TU, LXV (1957), p. 121, thinks that he finds some traces of Lucan tradition in Polycarp of Smyrna. This is hardly correct.

[115] This is in any case the most probable assumption. Only if one regards such lack of acquaintance as impossible does one seek for explanations other than this, such as the suggestion that Papias' judgment concerning Luke was too unfavorable for Eusebius (W. Bauer [1], p. 187). That Papias must have been acquainted with the Gospel of Luke because Marcion used it in Rome at approximately the same time—unfortunately we do not know the exact dates for Papias—is an unfounded assumption on the part of A. Jülicher (*Einleitung in das Neue Testament* [6th ed., 1906], p. 289).

[116] Thus also Klein in his discussion of Haenchen's commentary on Acts in ZKG (1957), p. 371; *ibid., op. cit.*, p. 191. Further, the reasoning which A. Loisy offers in support of his placing Luke around 125-150 is by no means outdated in every respect. The book of Acts fits best into the first decades of the second century because its apologetic character sets it in closest proximity to the other early apologies. Cf. Haenchen, *op. cit.*, pp. 19-20.

fact that in contrast with earliest Christianity this is an innovation is as generally recognized as the fact that in this literary circle Paul no longer qualifies as an apostle. There is general agreement as to the reason for this remarkable development: Paul was so largely appropriated by the Gnostics that from the church's point of view one had to keep one's distance from him.

This explanation is at first glance very convincing. In his investigation of the relationship of Paul and the twelve in early Christianity, J. Wagenmann (*op. cit.*) first presents the earliest writings, which (according to his opinion) regarded Paul and the twelve as apostles. Then in a section on Paul and the twelve among the heretics the violent seizure of Paul by the Gnostics is shown; finally, in a third section he shows how because of the crisis which was evoked by Gnosticism Paul is repressed in favor of the twelve. W. Bauer ([1], pp. 216 ff.), for example, reaches the same conclusion.[117]

When one has recognized that originally the twelve were not apostles at all, one could patch up this explanation temporarily by saying that in anti-Gnostic interests not only was Paul's apostolic right contested, but the apostolate was at the same time transferred to the twelve disciples.[118]

But this explanation does not suffice. Why should they have given up Paul and surrendered him to the Gnostics? In the last analysis, as a matter of fact, the theology of Paul was eminently anti-Gnostic. In spite of the numerous Gnostic characteristics of the Pauline terminology, in its appeal to the apostle to the Gentiles the church always had the greater right and the better position. It did not need to reinterpret him. Is the church supposed to have been incapable of employing the instrument of the Pauline letters in the anti-Gnostic struggle, while Gnosticism, in spite of its more difficult position, understood how to use this instrument for its cause? This is unlikely.[119] In fact, it is impossible; for men of the church, and indeed most of

---

[117] The fact that "Paul enjoyed the favor of the heretics to a high degree" explains for W. Bauer "the reserve with which, toward the middle of the second century, the men of the church treated the apostle to the Gentiles. . . . Perhaps people would have preferred, as the circumstances developed, to keep Paul altogether outside the fold and to seek their support exclusively in the twelve apostles" (*op. cit.*, pp. 227-28).

[118] G. Klein now does this (*op. cit.*); on this, see below, pp. 265 ff.

[119] G. Klein (*op. cit.*, n. 982) refers to II Peter 3:15 ff. as to a *demonstrable* proof of the inability of ecclesiastical circles to make use of Paul. To me this is not sensible. The passage in fact shows precisely *how* one could use the letters of Paul in the ecclesiastical sense when the Gnostics appealed to them: The frivolous people twist the meaning of the difficult words of our dear brother Paul, *i.e.*, the church has the correct interpretation. Thus also Klein himself correctly says (*op. cit.*, p. 104): "By raising the Pauline theology to the level of an intellectual problem, it becomes at the same time the 'reserve' of the orthodox elite."

those who stood in the forefront of the anti-Gnostic struggle, such as Clement of Rome, Ignatius of Antioch, Polycarp of Smyrna, the author of the Pastoral Epistles, *et al.*, bring Paul into the battle against Gnosticism, sometimes with great skill and without any reservations; and this by no means happens only so early that one could introduce between this literary circle and the representatives of the exclusive apostolate of the twelve a development from Paul to the twelve. It was rather the other way around: The Gnostics had to appeal to Paul because he was an ecclesiastical authority who was constantly and continuously recognized (*vide* also pp. 235 ff.).

There is also the fact that the Gnostics by no means appealed to Paul alone, but no less also to the twelve or to individuals among them.[120] Occasionally they could even explicitly reject Paul.[121] But in view of this state of things it would have made no sense if the ecclesiastical authors around the middle of the second century had placed themselves at a distance only from Paul, although the Gnostics at this time already had long been appealing also to the twelve.

It would be remarkable also if people gave up Paul but did not oppose him with a single word. This would be an inconceivable attitude if one had come to terms with Paul. Either the heretics correctly appeal to him—then one would have to oppose him; or they falsify Paul—then one would have to present the true Paul in opposition to them.[122]

But even if one gives up Paul, whom one has earlier acknowledged—can one then so alter his own theological stance that nothing more in Luke or Justin will betray the earlier influence of Paul? And can one do this only because the Gnostics also make Paul a crown witness for their theology? All this is inconceivable.

Further, the writings which come into consideration in this matter

[120] Iren. I, 3.2-3; 18.3-4; 25.5; 31.1; II, 21.1; Hipp. 5.8; 7.20.1; Clem. Alex. Strom. VII, 17.106; Epiph. Haer. 3.13, 23; Ps. Clem. Hom. II, 23; Pist. Soph. 7 *et passim*; cf. also F. Haase, *op. cit.*, pp. 90-102; W. Nagel, *op. cit.*, pp. 70 ff.

[121] Iren. I, 26.2; III, 15.1; Epiph. Haer. 28.5; Eus., CH IV, 29.5. Also I Tim. 2:7 presupposes for the time of the Pastorals that the Gnostics against whom I Tim. is directed even now dispute Paul's apostolic authority, just as their predecessors disputed it in personal confrontation with Paul.

[122] With respect to this line of argument, G. Klein (*op. cit.*, p. 214, n. 982) refers to the variety in the early church. This variety is not questioned. But the line of argument offered above does not proceed from the supposition of a unity of the church, but from the fact that, according to the evidence of all the literature in which the present problem explicitly emerges, the church made use of Paul in the battle against Gnosticism. Even II Peter is no exception (see p. 256, n. 119). But then in support of the thesis that in certain ecclesiastical circles Paul was *disavowed* in the battle against Gnosticism, one cannot simply point to the variety that existed in early Christianity, but must present in specific details the evidence of the anti-Gnostic criticism of Paul. On the question of whether Klein has succeeded in offering this evidence, see pp. 265 ff.

contain not a single critical word about Paul.[123] The success of such a revolutionary concept of the apostle against Paul, however, cannot have occurred without resistance from that circle, still widespread within the church, which correctly held fast to Paul. We should remember that approximately at the same time in which Luke, who hardly betrays any anti-Gnostic tendencies, is writing his Gospel and his Acts of the Apostles, in which Paul does not qualify as an apostle, Ignatius, as a sharp contender against Gnosticism, is praising Paul to the skies. How, then, could Paul have been pushed aside in the interest of opposition to Gnosticism?

And how does this hypothesis of the abandonment of Paul in the anti-Gnostic struggle fit in with the fact that at just the time when this trial is supposed to have been in progress (Justin!), the whole church fixed, as its sharpest weapon against the Gnostics, the two-part canon, in which Paul *undisputedly* functioned alongside the twelve as crown witness of the church's teaching?

The solution of the problem, and with it the answer to the question as to how the apostolate of the twelve emerged, is to be sought elsewhere.

2. We are accustomed to dividing primitive Christianity into three streams: Jewish, Hellenistic, and Gnostic Christianity; and this is correct. The development which we are investigating takes place within the context of Hellenistic Christianity. If this forms a unity, then there is nothing left to do, in spite of all reservations, but to recognize that line of development which we have just indicated: the primitive Christian (Antiochian) apostolate—appeal of the Gnostics to Paul—transferral of the apostolate to the twelve and rejection of Paul. But Hellenistic Christianity was not a unity. If we leave out of account the Johannine writings, which represent, in the neighborhood of Gnosticism, a historically still completely unsolved case of ecclesiastical Christianity,[124] we may clearly distinguish, until well into the second century, two distinct thrusts of Hellenistic Christianity. I should like to call them the Jewish-Christian or Synoptic thrust and the Gentile-Christian thrust.[125]

The Gentile-Christian thrust starts from Antioch. Its special distinguishing marks are, among other things: no acquaintance with the traditions about the historical Jesus; from the beginning onward a strong Gnostic

---

[123] Only the Epistle of James, which belongs to this literary circle (see below) appears to criticize Pauline patterns of thought (James 2:14 ff.), though without betraying what is the source of acquaintance with this thought. In any case, James shows no anti-gnostic tendency.

[124] Cf. R. Bultmann, *op. cit.*, II, 10.

[125] By this I do not mean that all the expressions of Hellenistic Christianity can be neatly divided into these two categories.

influence on language and conceptual world; from the earliest time onward a zealous mission to the Gentiles; the authority is the exalted Christ who speaks through the apostles; a well-defined "dialectic" theology, which probably was formed in the main by Paul himself and even later is never completely denied; the delay in the Parousia therefore hardly becomes a problem; early anti-Gnostic struggle; for this reason soon a strong interest in office and tradition. Among the representatives of this thrust, besides the genuine Pauline epistles, are to be numbered the deutero-Pauline epistles and I Peter, as well as, at some distance, Hebrews, Ignatius, and Polycarp, and parts of I Clement.

The Jewish-Christian thrust starts from the congregations in Palestine. The special characteristic marks are, among other things: a strong interest in the expansion of the Synoptic tradition; from the beginning onward a strong influence of the Hellenistic synagogue upon language and the conceptual world; *originally* no mission to the Gentiles[126]; the authority is the exalted Christ, who speaks ever more fully in the Synoptic tradition; a diversified and, in some parts to be sure, a very modest theology which is concerned to replace the fading emphasis upon expectation of the end with a frequently moralizing ethic; the delay of the Parousia becomes a problem; at the outset no trace of anti-Gnostic discussions, but probably a strong interest in an explication of the relationship between church and state (Luke; the Apologists); therefore little interest in office and tradition. Matthew and Mark, together with their earlier forms, belong to the early representatives of this thrust; to these may be added the Lucan writings, part of the Apocalypse, (II Peter, Jude, James, Barnabas), the Apologists, Tatian, and Papias.

3. Both traditions, which naturally varied within themselves in several ways, have their own history independent of one another. We can no longer determine for sure where the beginnings of Antiochian Christianity are to be sought, even though it is certain that its christological kerygma is based upon the kerygma of the Hellenistic Jewish-Christian community. With all due respect for the moral authority of Jerusalem, Antioch always remained the independent and undisputed center of the Pauline mission, which was extended across Asia Minor and Greece to Rome and which left its traces everywhere.

The leader of the mission of Hellenistic Jewish Christianity was Peter,

[126] The Synoptic tradition is full of "traditions" in which there are several ways of handling the problem of whether and how the Gentiles are to share in the eschatological salvation, traditions which clearly show how for a long time people in the circles of Hellenistic Christianity of the Synoptic tendency wrestled with this problem.

as is indubitably evident from Gal. 2:1-10. We find him or his community certainly in Antioch (Gal. 2:1 ff.), Corinth (I Cor. 1:12), and Rome (Ign. Rom. 4:3; I Pet. 5:13; I Clem. 5-6). His wide-ranging missionary activity is also attested by I Cor. 9:5. The evangelist [127] Philip may also have had great importance for the Jewish-Christian Hellenistic mission. We find Philip first in Jerusalem (Acts 6:5), then in Samaria (Acts 8:5 ff.), near Gaza (Acts 8:26), in Ashdod (Acts 8:40) and on the Mediterranean coast up to Caesarea (Acts 8:40; 21:8-9). He was certainly the most important missionary of the Mediterranean coast of Palestine.[128] If he is identical with the Philip of the circle of the twelve or if the two traditions have been merged,[129] John also testifies to his significance: John 1:43-48; 6:5-7; 12:21-22; 14:8-9. The Mediterranean coast may have been his "Syria and Cilicia" (Gal. 1:21).

Later we find him with his daughters in Asia Minor,[130] just as we do Paul. Three of the traditions cited by Eusebius have him resident in, and then buried at, Hierapolis, the later seat of Papias: Polycrates of Ephesus[131] (Eus., CH III, 31.3; V, 24.2), Papias (III, 39.9) and Gaius[132] (III, 31.4) are the guarantors of these traditions, which certainly are reliable in their placing Philip at Hierapolis.

Still other relatively early traditions lead to Asia Minor, thus the letters in the Apocalypse and their author, the Ephesian John. Quite early the community in Ephesus, insofar as *ecclesiastical* Christianity was concerned, was wholly determined by the "Synoptic" Hellenism.[133]

Among the later representatives of this thrust of Hellenistic Christianity, Papias, like Philip, belongs to Hierapolis. Justin was probably born in Shechem and converted in Ephesus, where he remained for a considerable time. Quadratus, who certainly belonged to the circle of the Synoptic tradition,[134] is also native to Asia Minor, if he is identical with the Quadratus mentioned by Eusebius in CH III, 37.1; V, 17.2. Further, to Asia Minor belong not only the letters of the Apocalypse, but the Apocalypse as a

---

[127] εὐαγγελιστής is the title of the missionaries of the Hellenistic Jewish tendency; see p. 226.

[128] E. Haenchen, *op. cit.*, pp. 270, 538.

[129] This has happened in any case with Polycrates of Ephesus, who calls Philip "one of the twelve apostles" and also attributes to him the prophetess-daughters of Philip the Evangelist (Acts 21:8-9; Eus., CH III, 31). Cf. Th. Zahn [1], pp. 158 ff.

[130] See W. Bauer [1], p. 90.

[131] *Ca.* 190.

[132] *Ca.* 200.

[133] Cf. E. Lohmeyer, *Die Offenbarung des Johannes*, HNT (1953), p. 43; W. Bauer [1], pp. 87 ff.

[134] This is unmistakably clear from the only extant fragment of his apology (Eus., CH, IV, 3.2). Cf. Th. Zahn [1], pp. 45 ff.

whole. II Peter and Jude are also correctly and consistently placed by the introductions and commentaries in Asia Minor. James and Barnabas can be placed in Asia Minor at least as well as in other parts of the Roman Empire. In my opinion Luke also belongs there,[135] and there is nothing to hinder our placing Matthew and Mark also in Asia Minor or in the neighboring Syrian coastal region.[136]

On down to the middle of the second century the two streams of tradition of Hellenistic Christianity remained separate and developed separately from each other. This is shown, e.g., by the fact that to the Pauline and deutero-Pauline literature as well as to the later writings in the Pauline sphere of influence, the Synoptic tradition about the historical Jesus remained just as unknown[137] as did the Pauline letters and the Pauline theology to Justin.[318] Generally the collected special characteristic marks cited above for the two streams of tradition may still be shown around 150 as just such *special* characteristics marks.[139] This isolation on both sides was probably favored by local conditions. The Pauline congregations of Asia Minor had been in large part absorbed by Gnosticism quite early,[140] and had been able to assert themselves only locally in northwest (?) Asia Minor and perhaps more powerfully in Greece, while the Palestinian Hellenistic congregations of Asia Minor could counter Gnosticism with a much stronger resistance (*vide infra*). In addition, the fact that the Gnostics quite early appealed to Paul may have served to maintain the separation between the two traditions, even if, as we have established above, this fact could never have originally effected this separation.

4. But then it turns out that the development of the apostolate of the twelve involves an essentially independent development within that branch

---

[135] Luke has no impressions of his own of Palestine (H. Conzelmann, *The Theology of St. Luke*, p. 41, n. 1; pp. 66 ff.); Rome also fails to recommend itself as his native place (E. Haenchen, *op. cit.*, p. 106).

His writings appear to have been disseminated in the East earlier than in the West; cf. A. Strobel, "Lukas der Antiochener," ZNW, XLIX (1958), 134. Cf. E. Schweizer, *op. cit.*, p. 137, 14a.

[136] A. v. Harnack (*Chronologie*, I, 589 ff., 681-701; cf. BENT, VI, 48 ff.) has shown that it is likely that the original canon of the four Gospels was assembled in *Asia Minor*.

[137] Cf. p. 258.

[138] See pp. 250-51. It is therefore a short-circuiting of logic when Haenchen (*op. cit.*, p. 106) thinks that we have to assume the time of the emergence of the book of Acts and therewith of the Gospel of Luke as being still in the first century, because otherwise the epistles of Paul could not have remained unknown to Luke.

[139] Indeed Hegesippus still knows "the Lord," but does not show himself to have been influenced by Paul; see W. Bauer [1], pp. 216-17.

[140] W. Bauer [1], esp. pp. 81 ff.; cf. II Tim. 1:15. The *form* of Pauline theology made the communities of his mission territory very susceptible to Gnosticism, as Paul himself was forced to learn in Corinth, Galatia, and Philippi (Phil. 3).

of Hellenistic Christianity which was described above as the Synoptic branch.

At the beginning[141] of this development stood the growing appeal to the historical Jesus. His authority was at first mediated by his disciples in general. But already very early the δώδεκα were projected back into the life of Jesus and were elevated to μαθηταὶ κατ' ἐξοχήν. The "twelve disciples" now formed the authority to which all tradition was ascribed.[142] In the course of time their significance increased all the more as the presence of genuine recollections about them became less of a possibility. Thus they soon became also the first bearers of the mission, sent out by Jesus himself (Mark. 6:7 ff.), at first of the mission to the Jews in Palestine (Matt. 10:6, 17 ff.), but then also of the Gentile mission (Matt. 28:19),[143] to which the resurrected One sent them. Only after their missionary activity became a self-evident fact did they receive as missionaries also the title of ἀπόστολος.

This process is only natural and may in no way be dramatized. In the meantime, in the rest of Christendom ἀπόστολος had become a frequent term for the first missionaries who had still been witnesses of the resurrection (thus the communities of the Pauline tradition), and for the contemporary missionary envoys of the communities in general (thus the Gnostic communities; the Didache). How could one have better characterized the twelve than by the designation ἀπόστολοι? After it was once established that the twelve had been the decisive missionaries of the early days, they in fact fulfilled in ideal fashion all the conditions which might be established for an apostle of the church.[144] Moreover, at least in the

---

[141] "At the beginning" does not mean that this appeal was present from the beginning onward. I am convinced that the primitive community in Jerusalem at first had no more interest in the so-called historical Jesus than did the Pauline tradition much later still, but in this connection I need not argue this conviction more precisely. The imminent interest in the so-called historical Jesus is not *formally* different from the general Hellenistic interest in the θεῖος ἀνήρ or the Jewish interest in the "rabbi."

[142] The stressing of their having been eyewitnesses of the historical Jesus by Luke, for instance (Acts 1:21-22; 13:31), may have been derived from polemical interests; see H. Conzelmann, *The Theology of St. Luke*, pp. 37-38. But this is not certain.

[143] Justin (see pp. 250-51); Luke (Acts 1:8). Later the world is divided up among the twelve; each one had his special mission territory (Eus., CH III, 1.1 ff.; abundant documentation in F. Haase, *op. cit.*, pp. 25 ff.; Act. Thom. 1; A. v. Harnack [1], II, 19 ff.). This transferral of the Gentile mission to the twelve does not signify any "paulinizing of the total picture of the apostle" (W. Mundle, *op. cit.*, p. 52). The Gentile mission of the Synoptic branch in Hellenistic Christianity is explained without direct Pauline influences, and Paul is wholly innocent of the presentation of history of the book of Acts and the later period.

[144] G. Klein (*op. cit.*, pp. 62 ff.) objects that Luke sets forth the twelve precisely not as missionaries, and that therefore the title ἀπόστολοι within the twelve-apostle tradition can have no causal connection with missionary service.

circle of the Pauline congregations the leading personality among the twelve, Peter, had qualified since earliest times as an apostle. It is quite easily imagined that from him this title passed over also to the other members of the narrower circle of disciples,[145] all the more since Peter, because of the role of mediator which he actually played in primitive Christianity, possessed considerable significance also in Pauline Christianity (*vide* pp. 242 ff.).

Moreover, in the transferral of the apostolic title to the twelve a part may have been played by the fact that people had to come to terms with other kinds of apostolic claims, some of them heretical; and in the face of this fact one could not yield the title ἀπόστολος for the sake of the characteristic ἀποστολικός.[146] In this tradition it is not so much a question, then, of the tradition of the Pauline communities, with which the Synoptic tradition had only relatively slight contacts and against which it therefore (with the exception of James 2:14 ff.) hardly appears to have polemicized [147]

Now it is clear that already very early, even before the introduction of the title of apostle for the twelve, these were regarded as the world missionaries: Matt. 28:16-20. Within the twelve-apostle tradition this is their more or less *emphasized* position: Just. Apol. I, 39; 42; 49-50 *et passim*; Ep. Ap. 2; 19; 30; the apocryphal epistle of the Corinthians to Paul (from Act. Paul.) V, 4-5; Arist. Apol. (ed. Raabe, p. 3); Barn. 5.9; 8.3, and so forth.

Is Luke an exception? In a certain sense, yes. Luke shows himself not primarily interested in the missionary service of the twelve. They are rather the guardians of the true tradition and as such reside in Jerusalem. They indeed guarantee the orthodoxy of the world mission of the church, still this mission is borne more by Paul than by themselves. Here in Luke there prevails a closer approximation to historical reality, though unconsciously, in contrast to a dogmatic picture of the mission. Naturally not all missionary activity is denied to the twelve, as the first part of Acts shows, but their most prominent task is nevertheless to tarry in Jerusalem, in order in this way to guarantee the ecclesiastical tradition as the true Judaism (see p. 249, n. 86). Thus unintentionally a picture of the history which is closer to actuality fits in with the Lucan tendency which prevents Luke from presenting the twelve as world missionaries.

They were such, however, already in the tradition taken over and reshaped by Luke, as Luke 24:47 ff. and Acts 1:8 show! But this still means that Luke himself, for the reasons mentioned, loosens the connection between the circle of the twelve and the world mission, but that the connection was already present in his tradition, as it then in fact continued to be preserved in this tradition. This observation says nothing against our thesis of the causal connection between the apostolate of the twelve and the world mission, but on the contrary against Klein's thesis of the origin of the apostolate of the twelve in the theology of Luke; for that Luke both *denied* the missionary activity of the twelve and *ascribed* to them the title of apostle is hardly probable.

[145] Cf. A. Fridrichsen, *op. cit.*, p. 19, n. 12.

[146] It is no accident that the adjective ἀποστολικός is an obviously *ecclesiastical* construction which appears from Ign. Trall. inscr. onward (cf. Mart. Polyc. 16.2; Eus., CH IV, 15.39). The adjective contains *in nuce* the entire anti-Gnostic concept of tradition of the church.

[147] Luke is the best witness to the peaceful relationship of the two traditions (but cf. also the Act. Pauli; see n. 112 above). He knows Paul but none of Paul's letters and

(all the less since in fact Gnosticism was the common opponent of *both* Hellenistic traditions); it is, rather, a matter of the Gnostic tradition, which appealed to its own false apostles (Rev. 2:2) and later in increasing measure also to Paul (II Peter 3:15-16). It is self-evident that the Jewish-Hellenistic tradition also had to come to terms with Gnosticism, and this is witnessed to by the letters in the Apocalypse, by James and II Peter, by the Ep. Ap., by Justin's lost σύνταγμα κατὰ πασῶν τῶν γεγενημένων αἱρέσεων, and by others. Writings such as, e.g., the Epistle of Barnabas cannot deny external Gnostic influences. Moreover, the fact that Gnosticism itself soon began to appeal to the twelve "apostles" shows that it found itself in discussions with the tradition of Synoptic Hellenism.[148] That these discussions began relatively late is shown by the fact that the traditions of the Synoptics, including the special Lucan material, remained as good as untouched by Gnosticism. To the Hellenistic communities of the Jewish-Christian Synoptic stamp, quite in contrast with the Pauline communities, Gnosticism appears never to have become very dangerous. The historical Jesus and his overriding importance were the simplest and most certain means of protection against any Gnostic infiltration. Thus Gnosticism is throughout the opponent from without, not, as in the Pauline tradition, from within. But their competing existence certainly furthered the interest in the apostolicity of the circle of the twelve for the Hellenists who came from Palestine, and then also furthered the transferral of the title of apostle to the twelve, as the living apostolate of Gnosticism died out. For the more time passed, the stronger became the conviction in the church that the ecclesiastical is the apostolic. If the origin of this concept of tradition is also to be sought in the Pauline thrust of Hellenistic Christianity, then we can see how it became with good reason *the* anti-Gnostic weapon of the church. Where the twelve disciples served as guarantors of the church's teaching, they appropriated to themselves therefore the title of apostle which Paul, like Peter, had always borne.

We can no longer precisely ascertain when this naming came about. If I Clem. 42 already presupposes a twelve-apostle tradition, one must go back into the next-to-last decade of the first century.[149] Otherwise it would

---

therefore also no genuine theological traditions from the Pauline communities. Precisely this fact, that the relationship of the two traditions was potentially compatible, will have made it peaceable also.

[148] To be sure, corresponding to the essence of Gnosticism, this appeal came about less with respect to the traditions of the historical Jesus than in connection with the assertion that some possessed some common traditions about the resurrected One transmitted by the lips of the twelve apostles (cf. e.g. Iren. III, 3.1), a weapon in the battle of the spirits which the church then again later took over for itself (Ep. Ap.; see pp. 285-86 below).

[149] If, as is not impossible, one does not abandon the currently dominant dating of I Clem. at about 95, and place it on up in the second century.

suffice to assume[150] the beginning of the second century.[151] The latter is to me the more probable,[152] though I would not protest against an earlier beginning. The context of this development *then* was fairly certainly Asia Minor, if Gnosticism had a part in it; still, even Rome is not entirely to be ruled out.

V

Frequent reference has already been made to the above-mentioned investigation of G. Klein; at this point, it deserves and demands a comprehensive reference.

Klein's question is: Where is the origin of the apostolate of the twelve to be found? His answer is: The apostolate of the twelve is an original product of Lucan theology. Luke was the first one to deny the title of apostle to Paul and to give it to the twelve. The proof for this thesis is adduced in an investigation which was carried through with great systematic power.

First of all, we should mention the gratifyingly extensive agreement in the fundamental historical evaluation of the apostolate of the twelve, which sets apart Klein's study and the work presented here from the previous

---

[150] I regard neither Rev. 21:14 (see pp. 246-47), nor Matt. 10:2 and Mark 6:30 (see p. 72), nor Asc. Jes. 3.13 ff. (see n. 69) as earlier.

[151] The extant fragments of the Kerygma Petri still know the twelve disciples, but not the twelve apostles. The remnants of the Gospel of Peter also mention only (once) the twelve *disciples*. The title of apostle for the "disciples" appears to have remained still unknown to many other late writers whose authorities the twelve were: on Papias, cf. p. 253, on Aristides, pp. 253-54. Further, one must not overlook the testimony of John, who apparently still does not know the twelve as "apostles."

[152] Concerning I Clem., I should assume that for the author two traditions are intermingled: the Pauline one, familiar to him, which always had the concept "apostle" and from which he sets out in vs. 1 (cf. Gal. 1:11-12), and the Synoptic one, which he recalls in vs. 3 (cf. Matt. 10:7 with vs. 3; Matt. 10:11 with vs. 4a. The mention of the ἀπαρχαί in vs. 4 then apparently is again from Paul, but in any case the theory of succession expressed here is dependent upon the deutero-Pauline tradition), but which still did not have the concept ἀπόστολοι. Clement could then have been the first who in this way managed not to withhold from the twelve the title of ἀπόστολοι, without thereby testifying to a twelve-apostle *tradition*. At the same time it would become clear in what an uncomplicated fashion the title of apostle could be transferred, once the twelve were recognized as having been missionaries.

Therewith it remains possible that the Synoptic tradition to which the author of I Clem. had access still had not identified the whole group of the twelve with the historical disciples and primitive Christian missionaries, so that I Clem. calls the Palestinian missionaries who have seen the resurrected One "apostles," as does Paul in Gal. 1:17 ff. Then the concept of apostle of I Clem. would remain wholly within the Pauline tradition, which does not take the twelve into account.

G. Klein (*op. cit.*, pp. 84-90) treats in detail the concept of the apostle in I Clem. and comes to the conclusion that it is certain that for I Clem. the apostolate has no connection with the idea of the apostolate of the twelve.

investigations. Since Klein makes Luke the creator of the apostolate of the twelve and rightly places Luke in the second century (*op. cit.*, p. 191), the more or less obvious presupposition of previous research that at the latest Paul knew the apostolate of the twelve is completely overthrown; the same is true also of the thesis, occasionally asserted in recent times, of an early post-Pauline origin of the twelve-apostles idea. (Thus H. v. Campenhausen, among others, had already made a preliminary statement in his studies in the direction of an [early] post-Pauline origin of the apostolate of the twelve [*vide supra*, p. 232, n. 5], but he does not focus the problem sharply enough, since he does not adequately differentiate between the *transferral* of the title of apostle to the twelve and its *restriction* to them. The outcome is, therefore, only that toward the end of the apostolic generation the title of apostle had "been first *limited* [153] to the twelve alone." Cf. [1], p. 117; also *supra*, p. 234, n. 11.)

The above-mentioned fundamental agreement between Klein's investigation and the work presented here could be traced in part to the fact that the manuscript of my work was already in Klein's hands (cf. the position taken by Klein, *op. cit.*, pp. 62 ff.). It is, however, above all a sign that the question of the origin of the apostolate of the twelve calls for new solutions. In this one should no longer retreat behind the knowledge that only the late postapostolic time comes into consideration as the time of origin and therefore—this is the most important point in this new approach—the origin of the apostolate of the twelve cannot be sought in the controversy between Paul and Jerusalem.

The solution offered by Klein, to make Luke the originator of the twelve-apostles tradition which excludes Paul, is thoroughly original. The obviousness of this thesis indeed has long been seen (cf. H. v. Campenhausen [1], p. 117; *vide supra*, p. 256), but always with a negative attitude. G. Klein is the first to attempt to prove this thesis. Is this attempt successful?

If it is first of all the theological undertaking of Luke to suppress the apostolate of Paul and to elevate the twelve to apostles, there cannot have been an apostolate of the twelve *before* Luke; the later emergence of the twelve-apostles idea must be traced back to Luke.

Klein therefore has to contest all witnesses for an apostolate of the twelve before and alongside Luke: I Clem., Barnabas, Rev., Asc. Jes., Didache, Kerygma Petri, etc. Most of his individual exegeses in this connection are conceivable. They offer a solid and independent parallel to the above (pp. 235-55) review of the postapostolic literature and a new valuable and convincing demonstration that the origin of the apostolate of the twelve is

---

[153] Italics mine.

to be placed in a relatively late time. All in all, however, the elimination of all traces of the apostolate of the twelve before and contemporary with Luke—and thus Klein's thesis as well—cannot be carried out; cf. in particular, e.g., p. 247, n. 67; and p. 252, n. 96.

Strange to say, Klein has not even mentioned the problem which lies in the relationship of Luke to the other writings with an exclusive apostolate of the twelve. He lacks any attempt to show that the appearance of the apostolate of the twelve, which he recognizes, goes back to a use of the theological work of Luke: (Matt. 10.2;) II Peter; Justin; Ep. Ap.; Acta Pauli; etc. For example, I consider it not at all impossible that Justin was totally unacquainted with the two-part work of Luke. In this connection it is of little importance for our question whether Justin used the Gospel of Luke; for the Lucan picture of the apostle which excludes Paul is formed from Luke's *Acts of the Apostles*. But this was certainly unknown to Justin. It is true that Haenchen (*op. cit.*, p. 7) finds in Justin four echoes of the book of Acts, of which however only one appears to him to be convincing: Apol. I, 50.12 || Acts 1:8. But the slight agreement of these two passages is easily explained by the use of a common tradition, whose availability for Luke and Justin is indeed beyond question.[154]

In any case, it is impossible that Justin should have taken over the complete Lucan image of the apostle from the book of Acts and at the same time have practically ignored the book of Acts itself. In other words, Justin cannot have drawn his image of the apostle from Luke. But this means, further, that Luke was not the creator of this image.

This difficulty in connection with Justin repeats itself in Matt. 10:5, II Peter, etc., and makes the thesis of Klein appear untenable. Luke is not the turning point in the history of the concept of the apostle, as if before him one had to reckon with the apostolate determined by Paul and after him with that of the twelve. We must rather take into account the variegation in the early church in such a way that Luke stands in a tradition which

---

[154] The dubiousness of the method of deducing direct or even indirect dependence from echoes has been demonstrated in splendid fashion by Klein (*op. cit.*, pp. 192-201) on the problem of the relation of Justin to Paul. The following almost grotesque example may again show it. E. Peterson (*Frühkirche, Judentum und Gnosis* [1959], p. 252) affirms that a sentence from a catechesis of Cyril is found again almost *verbatim* in the Greek Physiologus. From this he concludes that the latter is dependent upon Cyril, without considering whether both could not be dependent upon a third source. But this is really the case. The sentence referred to is actually a literal quotation of Rom. 16:18*b*; the slight differences of the two quotations rest upon variants in the different manuscripts! This example clearly shows with what caution one must proceed when one proposes to find one writing attested in another and then makes such information the foundation for often far-reaching conclusions. In many cases the likely explanation is that both are dependent upon a common prototype, usually unknown to us.

did not *replace* the Pauline concept of the apostle, but existed *beside* it.[155]

Now it is true that even the *successful* demonstration that the apostolate of the twelve never appears *before* Luke and *after* him only in connection with an acquaintance with his two-part work would present only the indispensable presupposition of the thesis that Luke was the creator of his concept of apostle, and not a proof of this thesis. The major part of G. Klein's work is devoted to such proof.

To be sure, this proof can only be indirectly adduced. This is, of course, not favorable to the proof itself, but it is still understandable and perhaps even unavoidable. For if Luke wants to demote Paul to a nonapostolic level and in his stead bestow the title of apostle upon the twelve, he would surely not carry out so revolutionary an undertaking in such a way that one could catch him in the act, as it were, in his own writings. That the presentation of proof desired is possible only indirectly is thus quite demonstrable; but it still demands first of all the counterproof as to whether the state of the text at all allows the thesis that the interest of Luke is directed to the deliberate elimination of the title of the apostle for Paul and the introduction of the apostolate of the twelve. But this test turns out negatively, as has been shown (pp. 233 ff., esp. n. 144). Luke was *already living* in the twelve-apostles tradition, which is not interested in the apostolate of Paul.

In spite of this, it is rewarding to investigate Klein's specific indirect proof for his thesis. It is drawn from the image of Paul in the book of Acts. Klein describes this image of Paul in the following fashion: "The leveling of Paul's Jewish past and the abhorrence of his persecuting activity must, in the context of an 'Acts of the Apostles,' bring to a head the upsetting effects, precisely as the mediation of his conversion and his subordination to the pre-Pauline church can leave no doubt as to this subordinate position, and the ignoring of his writings in addition minimizes any effect of his original theology" (*op. cit.*, p. 211).

Klein thus presents four characteristics of the Lucan image of Paul:
1. Paul is represented as a typical Jew—contrasted, e.g., with Gal. 1:14 (*op. cit.*, pp. 115-44).
2. His persecuting activity is portrayed in excessive harshness—contrasted, e.g., with Gal. 1:13 (*op. cit.*, pp. 115-44).
3. He receives his gospel from the twelve and is strictly subordinated to them—contrasted, e.g., with Gal. 1:1, 11-12 (*op. cit.*, pp. 144-89).

---

[155] In the doubtless justified and gratifying attempts to work out the particularity of the Lucan theology, one still should not neglect to inquire about the rooting of Luke in his circle and in his time, to which Bultmann (*Synoptic Tradition*, pp. 366-67) has already explicitly pointed. Not everything which is presented to us as Lucan is also *originally* Lucan.

4. His writings are deliberately ignored; Luke *does not wish* to know them (*op. cit.*, pp. 189-201).

The main part of Klein's work is devoted to the demonstration of these specific points of the Lucan relationship to Paul. If we except Point 4, which appears to me not to be proved (*vide supra* p. 250, n. 91),[156] then the other three points hold their own against any critical examination. To be sure, the three points are not new, but they are newly and convincingly argued. In particular, the form in which Paul is connected with the tradition proceeding from the twelve is worked out in excellent fashion.

According to Klein the intention common to these three traits of the Lucan image of Paul is the downgrading of Paul. Here some questions arise. Is it after all a downgrading when Paul appears as a typical Jew instead of an especially zealous Jew with regard to the law? Hardly! The "leveling" of Paul, which after all occurs only incidentally, may not have resulted for the purpose of a downgrading; it rather betrays the dominant interest of Luke to represent Christianity as the true Judaism (*vide supra* p. 249, esp. n. 86). Besides, it may have been done unpolemically, since Luke may hardly have known how Paul himself evaluated his "conduct as a Jew."

And is it a downgrading when Luke stresses the persecuting activity of Paul excessively? This too is to be doubted. The contrasting effect achieved by the revulsion at the persecuting activity of Paul over against his conversion adds not only to the glory of God but also to the authority of the apostle. One may doubt whether the achievement of an edifying contrasting effect is indeed the only reason for the revulsion. But instead of going beyond this to think of a deliberate downgrading, one should rather observe that through such contrasts, the emergence, contradictory to Luke's tendency, of a Christianity distinguished from Judaism is made more understandable by reference to the sovereign intervention of God. Luke is also elsewhere concerned with this problem (cf. E. Haenchen, *op. cit.*, pp. 564-65 *et passim*).

But further, along with the criticism just made, it is not to be doubted that in the book of Acts Paul clearly is "downgraded." The arguments of Klein on Point 3 (*op. cit.*, pp. 144-89) are simply demonstrative of this. It is true that Klein does not go into the previous explanations of the long-observed fact of the "downgrading." So far as I can see, there exists a unanimity of opinion that through the fitting of Paul into the Jerusalem tradition, it was also and precisely the Christianity carried by Paul into the Roman Empire which was to prove itself to be the true Judaism. At issue

---

[156] However, Klein's statements on this point are significant throughout (pp. 192-201). They produce convincing proof that like Luke, Justin also was unacquainted with the Pauline corpus or did not use it.

is only the *interest* which Luke had in such demonstration.[157] Is it an apologetic interest? Or is what is under discussion in the two-part Lucan work a purely theological sketch without an actual "tendency"? We would be glad to have Klein's position with regard to such explanations. At any rate his own explanation goes in other directions. This is done with a certain propriety. The concrete tendency of the Lucan historical work, in fact, still has not been convincingly shown; the explanations given, including those of Conzelmann and Haenchen, are not adequate.

Klein's attempt at a more satisfactory explanation is ingenious and completely correct as to method: "The reason can only be found in the objective situation of the church in Luke's time" (*op. cit.*, p. 213). This situation is that of the anti-Gnostic struggle! What task did the two-part work of Luke have in this situation?

Here now Klein's argumentation wavers. One time it is apparently intended to make the appeal to Paul impossible for the Gnostics: Luke intends to make "Paul unsuited for Gnostic claims" (*op. cit.*, p. 214). But in another place Luke intends "to *preserve* Paul for the ecclesiastical tradition" (*op. cit.*, n. 982 end). These are certainly two sides of the same problem. Nevertheless it must be asked for whom the undoubtedly timely work of Luke was then specifically intended: for the hand of the Gnostics or for the congregation?

Let us test Klein's thesis under the first presupposition: Luke intends to make the appeal to Paul impossible for the Gnostics. But would not one have countered by saying, "But with his image of Paul, Luke confirms to the Gnostics precisely this, that when they appeal to Paul they also have the twelve disciples and even Jesus himself on their side"? Therefore one would already have had to determine more precisely the Lucan battlefront, that he is facing the Gnostics to whom the *historical* Jesus is an offense, and then see the chief attraction in the Lucan image of Paul in the subordination even of Paul to the authority of the historical Jesus. This is apparently Klein's meaning (*op. cit.*, pp. 210, 215; cf. pp. 213-14). But there is already the basic doubt that the Lucan historical work is intended for the hand of the Gnostics. Utterly impossible, however, is the assumption that Luke could have abandoned himself to the illusion that with the Gnostics, who possessed the *genuine* Paul, his image of Paul could evoke more than a disdainful smile. The whole Lucan construction could be carried *ad absurdum* at any time with a single sentence from the Galatian epistle.[158]

---

[157] Cf. p. 249, esp. n. 86.

[158] How one had to wrest Paul from the heretics is shown by Ignatius, the Pastorals, and I Clement, each in its own way: Paul is fitted to the *contemporary* ecclesiastical interpretation, the *current* office. But this is precisely what Luke does not do.

Further, the Lucan historical construction is hardly evaluated rightly if one makes the historical Jesus its pivotal point.

There remains only the possibility, the only one which is in itself probable, that Luke wrote for his *community*. According to Klein's thesis it must have been a community to which Paul is suspect because the Gnostics claim him, and which is on the verge of rejecting Paul. The existence of such communities has indeed long been called upon to explain certain traits of the postapostolic concept of the apostle (*vide supra* p. 256). It would be open to doubt whether there actually were such communities (on this *vide supra*, pp. 255 ff.). Of more interest here is the question whether the work of Luke is suited to preserving Paul for the churches. No question is required as to whether this Paul who is becoming suspect and is to be won back is the Paul of the *epistles*. What other Paul could it have been whom the church at the time of Luke was rejecting and whom he wishes to preserve for her? But now it is Klein himself who has emphatically stressed that Luke does not wish to know the Paul of the epistles, and in any case it is incontestable that Luke ignores the genuine Paul. Then, however, the book of Acts cannot have been written in order to preserve Paul for the churches! [159]

There is, further, the decisive consideration that an anti-Gnostic tendency is not exactly written on the face of Luke's work. The Simon Magus scene, which might easily have filled the bill with such a tendency, remains free from it. Luke appears to know nothing of the significance which Simon possessed in Gnosticism. So there remain only the anti-Gnostic characteristics of Paul's speech in Acts 20. I have already said (p. 249) that I do not consider this speech as originally Lucan. But even in the case of another opinion on this speech, it still could not carry the thesis of a dominant anti-Gnostic tendency of the entire Lucan work. Other than Mark and Matthew, no New Testament writer shows so little connection with Gnosticism as does Luke.

In other words, it appears impossible to interpret the Lucan image of Paul as anti-Gnostic, as I myself at an earlier time had considered possible.[160] Here we must remind ourselves of the fact that the thoroughgoing analysis of the Lucan image of Paul by Klein was supposed to produce the (indirect) proof for just this thesis of the Lucan origin of the apostolate of the twelve. This proof, which according to Klein himself even in the most favorable case could only achieve a "highest degree of reasoned probability" (*op. cit.*, p. 203), would only have been able to succeed if (a) the originality of Luke's

---

[159] But cf. further p. 285, n. 198.
[160] "Die Häretiker in Galatien," in ZNW, XLVII (1956), p. 62.

concept of the apostle were exposed to no other reservations, and (b) the formulation of the new concept of the apostle could be made understandable from the (according to Klein, anti-Gnostic) tendency of the Lucan work.

As to (a), we have seen that Luke apparently found his concept of the apostle at hand, all the more since the later emergences of the twelve-apostles idea cannot consistently be traced back to Luke. But Klein appears not to have recognized the necessity of the proof mentioned under (b), since he does not reflect upon the significance of the *concept* of the apostle within the anti-Gnostic controversy which he postulates for Luke. If he had done this, he would hardly have neglected the fact that where Gnosticism supported itself upon *tradition*, it never operated with the concept of apostolicity. The *apostolic* is always the *ecclesiastical*.[161]

VI

Of course despite all that, the problem, acutely seen and splendidly described by Klein, of the specifically Lucan concept of the apostle remains still unsolved. For it is characteristic of Luke that he is intensively concerned with the twelve as well as with Paul, but along with this he gives the title of apostle only to the twelve—and emphatically to them—while apart from Acts 14:4, 14, Paul is not called an apostle. Even if the use of the title "apostle" for the twelve in Luke can be explained by the fact that he stands in the already pre-Lucan twelve-apostles tradition, still the elimination of the Pauline *apostolic* claim must have a special reason back of it. But this reason then may be connected with the *forced* use of the title of apostle for the twelve and the fitting of Paul into the twelve-apostles tradition; for even if, as we have seen, Luke was by no means the first to call the twelve "apostles," still he apparently gives them this title with emphasis and in contradistinction from Paul.[162] But what concrete situation at the time of Luke has prompted the evangelist to such a manipulation of the concept of the apostle? This situation can be all the more convincingly defined, the more the specific features of Lucan theology find an explanation from within it. We list some of the major tendencies of the Lucan two-volume work:

1) The gospel of Jesus Christ is wholly rooted in the Old Testament; Christianity is the true Judaism; Jesus' suffering does not occur be-

---

[161] Of course later even this ecclesiastical concept of the apostle is taken over by Gnosticism, as for example the Gnostic acts of the apostles show.

[162] After Klein's study of "The Twelve Apostles" (*Die zwölf Apostel*), this should no longer be disputed. Even if it is asserted against Klein that Luke found the twelve-apostles conception already in existence, still it may not be questioned that he provides a central position for it. One who does contest this, as for instance J. Roloff does (*op. cit.*, pp. 169 ff., 232), cannot deal fairly with the problem of the Lucan concept of the apostle.

cause of a saving significance of the cross but "that the Scripture might be fulfilled," that is, to demonstrate the "salvation-history" continuity of the old and new covenants.

2) The true gospel is the gospel brought by the *earthly* Jesus; hence the church unconditionally requires the tradition-grounded connection with the earthly Jesus.

3) Normative bearers of the tradition are the twelve apostles as witnesses of the earthly Jesus, his resurrection and his ascension; Jerusalem, the seat of the twelve and the capital city of Judaism, is the only place of origin of the gospel and the center of united Christianity.

4) Before Paul's conversion the Spirit was given to the church at the beginning of her mission, and that through the twelve.

5) Paul preaches nothing other than do the twelve, for like all true Christian preaching his gospel stems from Jerusalem and in no way immediately from an encounter with the heavenly Jesus.

6) Paul's preaching accordingly stands in full agreement with true Judaism. Paul calls himself a Pharisee and *against* his wishes founds independent Christian communities alongside the synagogue. The expectation of the general resurrection of the dead on the basis of Jesus' resurrection forms the core of his proclamation.

7) Jesus arose bodily and ascended bodily to heaven. He will not return from thence until the Parousia, the time of which is not determined; Paul has only heard his voice.

8) Luke is not acquainted with a *theologia crucis*, even in his presentation of Paul.

These features are in large part not at all attested prior to Luke; they betray altogether a Lucan tendency. The position which Luke is opposing can be defined on the basis of his tendentious theologoumena as follows:

1) The Old Testament is rejected and Christianity is wholly separated from its Jewish roots; the resurrection of the dead is denied.

2) The normative witness and sole apostle of Jesus Christ is Paul. He was called directly by the disembodied Christ who is always present in his Spirit, and he was made conversant with the true gospel, which is not to be found with the twelve. Paul does not bear witness to the earthly One but to the One who was crucified for us and exalted, whose Parousia is not expected. His gospel marks the definitive break with Judaism.

3) The testimony of the twelve on the contrary has no fundamental validity. They did not possess the Spirit. The gospel does not stem from Jerusalem.

If the question arises where or by whom such a theology was represented in Luke's time, the name of *Marcion* suggests itself. Actually the *practically* anti-Marcionite character of the two-volume Lucan work has often been observed, thus for example always when people have marveled that Marcion placed Luke's Gospel, of all things, at the basis of his canonical Gospel, although the other Gospels, especially John, would have caused far fewer difficulties for his theology. In addition, however, not seldom even a *consciously* anti-Marcionite tendency of the Lucan writings has been asserted, in recent times above all by John Knox,[163] according to whose opinion the same basic writing underlies our Gospel of Luke and Marcion's Gospel. For his Gospel, Marcion edited this basic writing somewhat—but his was by no means an abridgment of our Gospel of Luke!—while the writer to Theophilus expanded the same basic writing in an anti-Marcionite fashion and published it together with the Acts of the Apostles. Thus Knox considers "Luke-Acts as being under one of its aspects an early apologetic response to Marcionitism" (*op. cit.*, p. 139), and this on the basis of the correct observations that for Luke, "the Apostle to the Gentiles, far from being independent of the Twelve, had acknowledged their authority, had been gladly accredited by them, and had worked obediently and loyally under their direction" (p. 119), and that Luke 1–2, for example, are especially well suited "to show the nature of Christianity as the true Judaism and thus to answer one of the major contentions of the Marcionites" (p. 87). With his literary construction of the relationship of the Gospel of Luke to Marcion's Gospel, Knox harks back to corresponding solutions which were quite widespread from Semler to Ritschl and Hilgenfeld, until after the victory of the two-source theory they properly disappeared from scholarly discussion. The Gospel of Luke is based on Mark and Q, not on a Proto-Luke related to Marcion's Gospel. But wherever in the course of early Gospel criticism the anti-Marcionite character of the Lucan work was observed, people discovered a set of facts which improperly escaped the consciousness of the scholars and was ignored to the detriment of the redaction-critical study of Luke in our own day. I have no doubt that one is fair to Luke only when one seeks to understand him in terms of an "anti-Marcionite" drawing of the battle lines.

Of course, "anti-Marcionite" must be defined more exactly. Luke obviously does not have before him a Marcionitism which holds a two-gods doctrine and correspondingly radically depreciates the creation. At any rate there are not any countering tendencies to these to be found in Luke. Thus he cannot be aiming at the late Roman Marcion or his followers. However,

---

[163] J. Knox, *Marcion and the New Testament,* 1942.

Irenaeus (I, 27.1; III, 4.3) and Tertullian (adv. Marc. I, 2) asserted that Marcion had adopted his outspokenly Gnostic doctrines in Rome from the Gnostic Cerdo,[164] and from the fact that in Rome Marcion at first belonged to the Great Church, it may in fact be concluded that his theological development in Rome increasingly alienated him from ecclesiastical Christianity.[165] Thus Luke has to do with an early Asia-Minor "Marcionitism." Since Marcion could have begun with his missionary activity soon after the turn of the century,[166] it cannot be ruled out that Luke is opposing him personally. But Marcionitism is hardly an altogether original creation of Marcion. One must rather regard Marcion as prominent representative of an ultra-Pauline theology which apparently arose in northern Asia Minor and which also had other representatives, as for example Apelles who, contrary to the schematizing accounts of the church fathers, must hardly be judged a pupil of Marcion but an independent representative of that theology from which Marcion also proceeded. When Apelles rejects the two-principles doctrine, he may not have been softening Marcion's position but rather maintaining a more original tendency of the school which comes very close to the position against which Luke is contending.

According to relatively reliable statements, Marcion was sent on his journey to the West, which from the outset was conceived as a missionary journey,[167] with letters of recommendation from brethren in Pontus. Thus he began his career as an emissary of an already existing community. And when Justin, around 150, states in his Apology I, 26.58 that the Marcionite false doctrine has already been spread abroad in all the world, this statement also presupposes that Marcion did not first begin with the founding of his communities after 144, but was a leading representative of an older anti-Jewish hyper-Paulinism which he had independently developed further.

In Acts 16:6 ff. Luke apparently concerns himself with the proof that at the direction of the Spirit of Jesus Paul had never personally preached in the centers of the "Marcionite" heresy, and that therefore the image of Paul of these circles could not be original. It has already often been conjectured with good reason that Luke himself wrote in Asia Minor; thus he

---

[164] Cf. A. v. Harnack, *Marcion*, pp. 28-29, 31*ff.

[165] Cf. A. v. Harnack, *Marcion*, p. 25*; J. Knox, *op. cit.*, pp. 12-13; H. Kraft in RGG (3rd ed.), IV, cols. 740 ff.

[166] Even if Marcion was first separated from the Roman community in 144, following the customary chronology, one can reckon with these dates; for in any case he did not work very long after this time. He apparently was a mature man when he came to Rome (cf. A. v. Harnack, *Marcion*, pp. 24 ff.). However, E. Barnikol (*Die Entstehung der Kirche im zweiten Jahrhundert und die Zeit Marcions* [1933]) puts the date of Marcion's *death* as early as 144. Cf. also J. Knox, *op. cit.*, pp. 11-12.

[167] Cf. A. v. Harnack, *Marcion*, p. 24.

must have come into contact with the early "Marcionitism." And when Marcion later shaped his Gospel out of Luke's Gospel, of all things, this state of affairs may be based simply in the fact that it was the only Gospel circulated in the ecclesiastical circles of his environs,[168] which he naturally, from his standpoint correctly, regarded as adulterated and first had to correct for his own use. The use of Luke's Gospel by Marcion, in any case surprising, thus testifies that relatively close relations in point of location must have existed between Luke and Marcionitism, connections which from both sides naturally bore a polemical character.

It cannot be said with certainty where the occasion and causes of the radical anti-Jewish Paulinism of the "Marcionites" are to be sought. If one wishes to connect Luke's anti-Marcionite tendency *causally* with his already often described [169] apologetic tendency, one must come to the following historical picture, which has in its favor also some internal probability:

The political imperiling of Judaism after the uprising of the year A.D. 70 necessarily drew the Christian fellowship into sympathy, for they too were in fact regarded by the Romans as a Jewish sect. Since the Christians, as distinguished from the Jews, pursued a deliberate and extended Gentile mission, their "Judaism" must have been especially offensive to the Roman state. The view that after A.D. 70 the Christians united closely with Judaism, and Luke accordingly developed his coupling of Judaism and Christianity in salvation history in order to gain for the Christians the governmental protection which Judaism allegedly possessed as *religio licita*,[170] therefore contradicts every historical probability. In the closing years of the first century, threatened Christian communities must rather have been concerned to put themselves at a distance from Judaism. Consequently, because he is setting forth the salvation-history unity of Judaism and Christianity for *theological* reasons, Luke sees himself as compelled to clear Christianity *politically* of the suspicion of intentions dangerous to the state, an undertaking which, as is well known, pervades his entire work and not infrequently has as a result an apparent contradiction of tendencies. In fact the (primary) salvation-historical theological connection with Judaism and the (secondary) apologetic-political dissociation from it mutually condition each other.

In this connection it deserves to be noted that the earliest reports of persecutions of Christians stem above all from the territory of Asia Minor, in

---

[168] Similarly also A. v. Harnack, *Marcion*, p. 42: "The first Gospel which came to Pontus probably was the Gospel of Luke; Marcion will have been familiar with it first, if it was not in fact for years his only Gospel in his homeland."

[169] Cf. H. Conzelmann, *The Theology of St. Luke*, pp. 137 ff.

[170] Thus Haenchen, *Die Apostelgeschichte*, Meyer Kommentar III (13th ed., 1961), *passim*.

which Luke composed his two-volume work: Revelation, 1 Peter, the correspondence between Pliny and Trajan; and that according to Dio Cassius (hist. rom. 67.14) Domitian, from whose time the first systematic persecutions are known, had his nephew, T. Flavius Clemens, presumably a Christian, executed because of an inclination to *Jewish* religious customs.

From what has been said there emerges the cause and tendency of the specifically Lucan concept of the apostle in itself. The "Marcionites" acknowledged only *one* apostle as such, namely Paul. His message represents the only authentic, i.e., the apostolic, gospel. In this sense Paul was *the* apostle, and it is not accidental in fact that the Galatian epistle which makes possible this concept of the apostle introduces Marcion's collection of Paul's epistles. Over against this, Luke refers back to the designation, to be sure scantily attested but undoubtedly already existent, of the twelve as "apostles" in the sense of "missionaries" and elevated this general designation to the level of a legal *terminus technicus*. Luke acknowledges that binding tradition must be apostolic tradition, but declares the twelve, because of their connection with the historical and bodily resurrected Lord, to be the only normative bearers of this tradition, that is, the only apostles in the technical sense, who as such reside in Jerusalem.

When Luke in Acts 14:4, 14, following a source, also calls Barnabas and Paul apostles, he therewith reveals that the concept of apostle for Paul was not unknown to him, but at the same time he tendentiously makes it clear that Paul bears this title *only* as does Barnabas, i.e., not in the sense of a fundamental authority that authenticates all tradition and goes back to Christ himself, but in the general and relatively unimportant sense of a missionary sent out by the community at Antioch. Paul's *title* in Luke's mind is, according to Acts 13:1, "prophet and teacher." [171]

While we earlier established that in the progressive transferral of the title of apostle to the twelve which came about in general independent of Luke, an interest in the *concept* of apostle for the sake of the anti-Gnostic *apostolic tradition* could have played a part, now at least for Luke—and for him likewise decidedly—an "anti-Marcionite" tendency must be reckoned as determinative for the development of the concept of apostle. To what ex-

[171] According to Klein, in Acts 14:4, 14 Luke is supposed to have allowed the concept of apostle for Paul to stand, with the cunning calculation that the readers might not notice that in actuality Luke had created the apostolate of the twelve and is denying Paul any apostolic right! It is true that Klein offers also the option of a more serious solution in the difficulty found in Acts 4:4, 14. Codex D offers a text in 14:14 without ἀπόστολοι. If one regards this text as the original one, then according to an opinion of G. Sass ([2], p. 235) which Klein follows, 14:4 would "no longer clearly refer to Paul and Barnabas." But who will seriously prefer the text in Codex D on 14:14? And to whom is the word ἀπόστολοι in 14:4 to be related? To the twelve apostles? Even Klein will hardly say this.

tent the same tendency also played a role in other representatives of the apostolate of the twelve cannot be said with certainty, but it may be assumed for Justin, for example. When Justin neither uses nor opposes Paul, but simply ignores him, such an attitude in an author who about 150 is explicitly debating in his Apology with Marcion can most easily be explained if Marcionitism restrained him, a man who had grown up within the "Synoptic" tradition, from seeking any positive contact with the Pauline tradition,[172] if however at the same time the existence of *church* communities of Paul forbade his taking a stand against *any* appeal to Paul and thus against Paul himself. Also the curious fact that the author of the Acts of Paul withholds from his hero the title of apostle, although he is acquainted with the epistles of Paul, can most readily be explained if the author of the Acts of Paul intended thereby to guard against a Marcionite understanding of Paul.

VII

The last necessary step in the development of the concept of apostle consisted, then, in a synthesis of the two conceptions at hand, after the Gnostic conception failed, indeed from the very beginning onward, to gain approval from the church; for already Paul is acquainted with only a limited apostolic circle. This synthesis supposedly took place in the West. The earliest provisional witness for this is possibly I Clem. 42 (*vide* n. 152), and the decisive witness is Irenaeus.[173] It is a remarkable synthesis which we encounter in Irenaeus; it consists of a simple combination of the two traditions at hand.

Paul is an apostle in the sense in which he had viewed himself as an apostle.[174] He preaches that which he himself received from the Lord (Iren. III, 13.2; 14.2). He is apostle to the Gentiles (Iren. IV, 24.1; III, 13.1) and as such has had more work than others (IV, 24.3). Beside him stands only

[172] Even Luke apparently was not acquainted with any epistles of Paul, although he shows himself to be very much interested in Paul and would have been able to become acquainted with the letters of the great apostle. For example, his presentation of the "apostolic council" and of Paul's journeys to Jerusalem unconditionally presupposes an ignorance of Gal. 1–2. Knowledge of Paul's letters also would have had to leave a deposit in the Lucan sketches of Paul's speeches, which however is not the case; cf. E. Haenchen, *op. cit.*, pp. 102 ff. Thus it is obvious that Luke is taking a stand against a definite interpretation of Paul which appeals to the collection of Pauline epistles.

[173] There is "certainty as to the fact that Irenaeus, although born in Asia and ultimately a bishop in Gaul, represented the Roman standpoint in ecclesiastical questions, on the basis of Roman education" (A. Jülicher, *Einleitung in das Neue Testament* [6th ed., 1906], p. 450).

[174] Of course knowledge about the wider circle of apostles which surrounded Paul as the most important of the host of apostles has long since been lost. From the other apostles people possessed no literary remains which could have kept alive the recollection of them.

Peter as an apostle of equal weight (IV, 35.2; I, 13.6; 25.2). The two have shared in the founding of the community in Rome (III, 3.2). When in more than fifty passages in his *Haereses* Irenaeus introduces citations with "apostolus ait" or something similar, this apostle is always Paul. Paul is also otherwise simply called "the apostle" (e.g., IV, 41.5); he is the "beatus apostolus" (e.g., IV, 41.6), and naturally also the "apostle Paul" (e.g., III, 15.1). According to one Irenaeus fragment[175] his apostleship is even foreshadowed in the Old Testament. Several times Paul's own expressions about his apostleship are cited (e.g., III, 13.2).

But the twelve are also apostles in the way in which they are portrayed to us in the book of Acts. Thus, just as Paul is spoken of as *the* apostle without regard to the twelve, the twelve apostles are mentioned (III, 13.2) without regard to Paul, or *the* apostles are spoken of in such a way as to exclude Paul (III, 13.3).[176] In his writing on the "Demonstration of the Apostolic Preaching" Irenaeus is able completely to describe the apostles with the qualifications of Acts 1:21-22, which exclude Paul (chap. 41), and also in chap. 46 apparently to rule out Paul as participant in the apostolic tradition. The twelve were self-evidently missionaries to the Gentiles (III, 2.7-8); *the* apostles went forth from Jerusalem (e.g., IV, 34.4).[177]

Finally, the apostles are frequently spoken of in such a way that Paul *and* the twelve are meant thereby (III, 1.1; 14.1,2; 15.1, 3; 24.1; V, 20.1); once Paul is explicitly placed as an apostle with the twelve (II, 21.2); and in IV, 35.2 (cf. III, 3.2) mention is made of Peter, Paul, and the other apostles.

Thus in Irenaeus (and in all the ecclesiastical writers after him)[178] we find precisely the concept of the apostle which dominates the unreflective thought of the Christian community, including her theologians, down to the present day. Without distinction of rank, the twelve and Paul, the dis-

---

[175] Ed. Stieren (1853), p. 836.

[176] In Iren. II, 21.1 the seventy disciples also are once indirectly called apostles; but no weight is to be attributed to this passage, since Irenaeus is guided by anti-heretical interests and apparently deliberately avoids giving the title of apostle to the seventy *directly*.

[177] Of course it is altogether unusual when *individuals* from among the twelve receive the title of apostle. For example, when John is given a title it is always ὁ μαθητὴς τοῦ κυρίου or something similar. Even Peter is given the title of apostle personally only in III, 12.1 and, together with Paul, in III, 3.2. In this refraining from giving the title of apostle to the individual members of the circle of the twelve, which can be observed also elsewhere, apparently a remnant of the original state of things is preserved. On all this, cf. Th. Zahn [1], p. 75, n. 1, and p. 142, n. 1.

[178] We have from Antioch at this time a testimony of Bishop Serapion (190-211), which is to be sure is not unequivocal: "As for us, brethren, we receive both Peter and the other apostles as Christ" (Eus., CH VI, 12.3). Of course Serapion has close connections with Asia Minor, with Hierapolis among other places, so that the tradition of the twelve certainly was familiar to him (Eus., CH V, 19).

ciples of the historical Jesus and the disciple of the exalted Christ, qualify as apostles; "apostolic" applies to the theology of Paul and to that of the Synoptics. Paul taught nothing other than what the other apostles taught.[179]

To reflective thinking this simple combination[180] of two completely independent traditions appears illogical. Thus J. Wagenmann (*op. cit.*, pp. 206 ff.) makes spasmodic efforts to give reasons for his judgment that in the opinion of Irenaeus Paul "bowed to the supremacy of the twelve, and that he was actually an apostle only by their grace, who acted upon commission from them and within their intention" (*op. cit.*, p. 215). It would take us too far afield to refute his arguments point by point. They are all untenable. Wagenmann places the chief stress upon the section Iren. III, 13-14, in which Irenaeus is battling the heretics who appeal to Paul against the twelve. In these two chapters Irenaeus shows that the twelve taught nothing contrary to Paul's teaching. Wagenmann turns this around: Paul teaches as do Peter and the rest of the apostles. Irenaeus argues: If the Gnostics accept the special Lucan material (which stems from Paul), they must logically accept also the other reports of Luke (transmitted by the twelve) (III 14). Wagenmann does not understand this argument and decrees: "The original apostles, who stand behind Luke, stand security for the genuineness . . . of the whole gospel" (*op. cit.*, p. 209). When Irenaeus III, 3.4 explains that the congregation at Ephesus is a true witness of the apostolic tradition because Paul established it and John spent a long time there, the passage still does not prove the subordination of Paul to the twelve, as Wagenmann (*op. cit.*, p. 211) proposes, but rather equality of rights. Irenaeus cites Gal. 2:1-2, 5 (III, 13.3) not in order to prove that Paul teaches nothing contrary to the twelve (*vide* Wagenmann, *op. cit.*, p. 215), but that the twelve teach nothing contrary to Paul, naturally without thereby subordinating them to Paul.

Thus it must stand, that Irenaeus allows validity as apostles to Paul and the twelve without any distinction as to their rank and their binding authority. One who finds this strange and asks how a person can allow validity to two such different traditions in close proximity and without connection, without noticing their discrepancy, should seek his answer among some contemporary theologians who are accustomed to speaking of the apostles in a way not at all different from the way in which Irenaeus did it.

Moreover, one naturally may not ask who then the first one was to combine these two traditions in such fashion, as if it had been a theological

---

[179] Iren. III, 13.3.

[180] In Irenaeus a combination is involved also to the extent that he in part only unites already existing sources which possibly still had a simple concept of the apostle (see p. 243).

achievement. Ever since the time of Paul, Rome has been in increasing measure a goal of *all* ecclesiastical currents. The community to which the Epistle to the Romans is directed is not Pauline and yet bears a Hellenistic imprint. But Paul is cordially received by it, as the existence of the Epistle and the testimony of Acts 28:11 ff. show. I Clement is evidently nurtured from both Hellenistic traditions. "Synoptic" people such as Justin can work in Rome and, without mentioning or using Paul, publish, in the same Rome in which the Pauline tradition has been active already for more than fifty years and in which the Pauline epistles are known. Rome had no occasion to play off the Pauline and the Synoptic lines of Hellenistic Christianity against each other, since it previously had been native to both of them. Rome could not decide for one of the two lines exclusively, since already at the time of Clement it had begun to fight the Gnostics with both of them. In opposition to these Gnostics—and this is the decisive point—Paul with his companions and the Synoptists with their literary circle could qualify, in fact, in the eyes of a generation not too keen in theological matters, as *one* apostolic tradition. Thus Irenaeus carries forward nothing other than what had been good Roman tradition all along and has remained so to this day, which at the same time was the precondition of the growing Roman influence: collection, synthesis, compromise. Irenaeus testifies to the fact that the Roman church never existed except as a *complexio oppositorum,* but that precisely this was her strength.

It still remains for us to take a look at earlier witnesses to the Roman synthesis, as it has been set before us by Irenaeus so perfectly and typically for all times. In doing this the fact of the formation of the canon comes immediately into view. Long before the two-part collection of writings of the New Testament emerged, there were the separated traditions of the Pauline epistle collection on the one side and that of the Gospels on the other,[181] both of which represented in their own fashion the authority of the Lord through the apostles; for the two traditions were at one in their conviction that the true tradition about the Lord can only be apostolic tradition. Jülicher[182] therefore correctly writes, "Hence the earliest canon of the New Testament was a one-part canon." But it is not correct to say, as Jülicher proceeds to argue, that to the one-part canon of the Gospels later was added that of "the apostles" by way of completing it. Rather there were originally two one-part "canons," which later were combined to make the church's two-part canon.[183]

---

[181] See A. v. Harnack [2], pp. 46 ff.

[182] *Einleitung in das Neue Testament* (6th ed., 1906), p. 441.

[183] In this the canon of the Pauline communities is certainly the older. The letters of Paul were already combined as an official collection in a time which still does not yield any

The first one who demonstrably does this is Marcion. His canon contains Luke (?) and ten letters of Paul in occasionally "purified" form. One can engage in a fruitless dispute over how far each of the two parts of his canon already earlier possessed for itself "canonical" recognition or whether an essential service in the process of canonization is to be credited to Marcion,[184] fruitless because the concept "canonical" is capable of several interpretations. It is undisputed that Marcion was the first to unite the two apostolic traditions in one collection of writings. This was a farsighted deed which could hardly have occurred anywhere other than Rome. To be sure, it was also a necessary step for one who intended to establish a world church. This combination, however, signified at the same time a joining of the two concepts of the apostolic. It is true that Marcion is obligated to Paul in a quite special way, but the twelve are by no means false apostles; in fact, Marcion instead explicitly distinguishes the twelve from such false apostles (Tert. adv. Marc. IV, 3-4; cf. I, 20-21). In contrast to Paul, the twelve indeed never understood Jesus, but they never consciously falsified his teaching. And they were not without any understanding, as for example Tert. IV, 26 shows. The—expurgated—Gospel of Luke (?) in fact contains traditions about the Lord which stem from them, the understanding of which, to be sure, Marcion's Paul first makes accessible.

Even without Marcion the church certainly would have united the two apostolic traditions into the ecclesiastical tradition and thereby sanctioned for all time the two concepts of the apostle which were at hand within them. But through Marcion, without doubt, the literary coalescence of the two separate traditions was considerably hastened.

Unfortunately we possess hardly any ecclesiastical literature which can be placed with certainty between Marcion and Irenaeus, i.e., between *ca.* 145 and *ca.* 180.[185] In these years, however, the two-part canon must have

---

traces of the Synoptic tradition (cf. Feine-Behm-Kümmel, *Introduction to the New Testament*, pp. 338-39).

[184] Marcion, who rejected the canon of the primitive church, the Old Testament, was compelled to canonize the apostolic tradition. In so doing he probably went beyond the estimate of the collection of New Testament writings which was common in the church up to that time. His decision then was not without influence on the formation of the ecclesiastical canon.

[185] II Clem. possibly belongs in this period. It still makes use of quotations from apocryphal Gospels, but probably also of the Synoptic tradition. Whether in II Clem. 14.2 the expression τὰ βιβλία καὶ οἱ ἀπόστολοι means Gospels and Paul's letters, or Old Testament and New Testament writings, is uncertain (cf. the passages from the *Acta Martyrum Scilitanorum* mentioned below).

G. Klein (*op. cit.*, p. 107) has shown that II Clem. does not contribute anything to the question about the origin of the apostolate of the twelve.

come to prevail in the church at Rome also,[186] and this aided necessarily in the general ecclesiastical recognition of the *two* existing concepts of the apostle.[187] To be sure, Irenaeus is still able, following the old tradition, to hold separate the Old Testament (= Writings), the Gospel, and the Apostle, at least in language—a fixed term to identify the two new authorities together is still lacking—but all Scriptures together form for him, without distinction in value, the binding Word of God; all are drawn into support of argumentation in the same fashion; Gospels and letters of Paul are apostolic.

The same attitude is attested at the time of Irenaeus by Athenagoras,[188] who cites the Gospels and the letters of Paul, and by the Muratorian Canon, which probably was written in Rome, but also by Theophilus of Antioch. Alongside the letters of Paul, which had already long been known in Antioch, Theophilus now also even more strongly invokes the Gospels, and thereby the traditions about the apostolate of the twelve, in his writing addressed to the pagan Autolycus. For North Africa the same is witnessed to, probably as early as A.D. 180, in the "Acta Martyrum Scilitanorum." According to these martyr-acts a member of the community answered the question about the contents of the book chest: "The books used by us and, in addition, the letters of the pious man Paul." If one does not wish to take the position, theoretically not excluded, that the Gospels were still unknown in North Africa at this time, then they must belong to the first-mentioned *libri*. Thus also in North Africa about 180 presumably Paul and the twelve qualify as bearers of the apostolic tradition. At the time of Tertullian (died 220) this is beyond question. Clement of Alexandria (died 215) gives for Egypt a corresponding testimony. From this time onward, the idea was unassailable in the church that the twelve and Paul are apostles of Jesus Christ.

Thus the formation of the two-part canon doubtless played a large part in the general and rapid recognition of the double concept of the apostle, and then has further figured in the removal of the concept from any debate; still we may not regard the formation of the canon as the actual cause of this combination of the two traditions concerning the ἀπόστολος. For even the formation of the two-part canon is only made possible by the fact that Christianity was open to a synthesis of the two streams of tradition. It is a very attractive conjecture, but nothing more than this, that the

---

[186] On the decisive role which Rome once again played in a characteristic manner in the formation of the church's New Testament, one may consult the splendid reflections of Harnack in BENT, VI, 64-76.

[187] The battle over the apostolicity of individual books, usually discussed in detail in the introductions to the NT and the histories of the canon, is of little significance in comparison with the basic ecclesiastical decision for the doubled tradition of the apostolic. For this reason we pass over these discussions.

[188] See A. Jülicher, *op. cit.*, p. 446, n. 169.

acceptance of the book of Acts into the canon came about in the intention of showing the doctrinal unity of the twelve apostles and of Paul.[189]

Even after 150, particularly in the heretical circles and in those circles within the church which stood close to various heresies, people naturally did not always join forces with the simple ecclesiastical line. The radical rejection of Paul by certain Jewish-Christian circles, for example by the Pseudo-Clementines, is generally well known.[190] The Gnostics have their own position,[191] which is of course influenced by the church's development in several respects. Fundamentally they reject the authority of the ecclesiastical apostles in general, who indeed are "apostles from men" (Gal. 1-2; Iren. I, 13.6; 25.2, 5; 30.13), precisely when they elevate the traitor Judas to be their authority (Iren. I, 31.1; Epiph. 38.1.3).[192] In order to be able to penetrate the Pauline communities, others soon appeal to Paul (Epiph. 38.2; vide p. 236, n. 20).[193] The increasing authority of the twelve compels the Gnostics also to use this circle as a support for their message (vide p. 257, n. 120). Then if the church refers to the inviolability of its apostolic tradition (Pastorals; I Clem. 42 ff.), they counter with the assertion of secret traditions,[194] which are supposed to have been transmitted in part by apostles, and in part by other personages of primitive Christianity.[195]

[189] In any case, it is certain that the book of Acts became "Holy Scripture" only in the course of the creation of the New Testament (in Rome), while the separate collections of the Gospels and of the letters of Paul already previously had enjoyed special spiritual recognition (cf. e.g., M. Karnetzki in ZNW [1956], p. 174). It is certain also that the title πράξεις ἀποστόλων, which first appears in the Muratorian Canon, presupposes the Irenaean ecclesiastical concept of the apostle which embraces the twelve and Paul.

[190] Ps. Cl. Rec. IV, 34-35; XI, 35; Hom. XVII, 14 ff.; Iren. I, 26.2; Epiph. Haer. 30.16; Eus. CH IV, 29.5; VI, 38; Orig. Cels. V, 65; Philaster Haer. 36.3; Epiph. Haer. 28.5.3 = Hol. I, 317.17 ff.; 25.1 = I, 366.7 ff.; Theodoret Haer. II, 1 = Migne, PSG 83, col. 388C; II, 7 = 393B. Cf. G. Strecker, Das Judenchristentum in den Pseudoclementinen, TU, LXX, 195-96.

[191] Again and again throughout the course of church history down to the present (new apostolic community) the original Gnostic conception breaks out in individual heresies, that there must be a present-day apostolic office (cf., e.g., Handbuch zur Kirchengeschichte, II [2nd ed., 1929], 121-22).

[192] Or they explain that the apostles did not know everything (Tert., de praescr. haer. 22 ff.).

[193] In addition, converts from Pauline communities might have brought their apostle along with them into the Gnostic communities.

[194] By no means did the concept of tradition in general develop within Gnosticism, as H. v. Campenhausen ([2], pp. 172 ff.) explicitly asserts in treating the testimonies, e.g., of the Pastoral Epistles. It is possible that the concepts παράδοσις and διαδοχή first acquired their technical meaning within Gnosticism in connection with the secret traditions (cf. ibid.).

[195] Orig., Cels. V, 62; Ptolemaeus in Epiph. Haer. 33.7; Iren. I, 3.1; 25.5; 30.14; II, 27.2; Hipp. 7.20.1; 5.7.1; 10.9.2; H. v. Campenhausen [2], pp. 172 ff.; W. Bauer [1], pp. 123-24, 192-93; A. Ehrhardt, op. cit., p. 108; Tert., de praescr. haer. 25-26.

The Montanists, on the other hand, appear always to have participated in the ecclesiastical development (cf. J. Wagenmann, *op. cit.*, pp. 134 ff.).

The "Conversations of Jesus with His Disciples After the Resurrection," known more briefly as "Epistula Apostolorum," is a writing of a peculiar kind difficult to define. This strongly gnosticizing and at the same time explicitly anti-Gnostic apocryphon counts the twelve among the apostles, but also concerns itself with the question as to what position Paul, whose letters are known to the author, can occupy alongside them. We have nowhere else encountered an explicit reflection upon this problem. The solution of the task posed here lies in a clear subordination of Paul, who is never called an apostle, to the twelve: "Teach and remind [him] what is said of me in the Scriptures, and what has been fulfilled, and then he will be a blessing to the Gentiles" (Ep. Ap. 31).[196] A similar relationship of Paul and the twelve is presupposed by the Acts of Paul, though in the extant fragments of this writing there is no conscious reflection upon the problem.[197] In the Coptic Andrew fragment, to which S. Morenz refers in ThLZ (1947, col. 295), Paul is expressly subordinated to the authority of the "great apostles," who "walked with the Savior from the time of his appearance." [198]

The so-called[199] anti-Marcionite Gospel prologues also perhaps belong to the transitional time before Irenaeus. (For the texts and relevant literature, see Huck-Lietzmann, *Synopsis of the First Three Gospels*, 9th ed., pp. VII-VIII.) In the prologue to Luke's Gospel, Luke is introduced as μαθητὴς ἀποστόλων γενόμενος καὶ ὕστερον Παύλῳ παρακολουθήσας. Here the twelve appear to be considered as *the* apostles. But later, when it is said: ὕστερον δὲ Ἰωάννης ὁ ἀπόστολος ἐκ τῶν δώδεκα ἔγραψεν τὴν Ἀποκάλυψιν, the writer seems to have been conscious that the circle of the apostles is not limited to the twelve.

The Marcionite prologues to the letters of Paul, which likewise may have developed before Irenaeus, are acquainted with *pseudo-apostoli* or *falsi apostoli* alongside the apostle Paul. Harnack's assumption[200] that by this the twelve Jerusalem apostles are meant cannot be proved.

In his letter to Flora, Ptolemaeus speaks of "[Jesus'] disciples and the apostle Paul" (Epiph. Haer. 33.3-7).

[196] Cf. the good presentation of the concept of the apostle in the Ep. Ap. in J. Wagenmann, *op. cit.*, pp. 172 ff. Cf. also F. Haase, *op. cit.*, p. 246, who assumes the anti-Marcionite tendency.

[197] Cf. J. Wagenmann, *op. cit.*, pp. 181 ff.

[198] It could be that the picture of Paul of these writings, which show themselves to be well acquainted with the genuine Paul of the epistles and quote him without embarrassment, serves to attest to the ecclesiastical congregations the orthodoxy of Paul in spite of the use which the Gnostics make of him, and thus to preserve Paul for the church.

[199] Cf. E. Haenchen, *Die Apostelgeschichte* (12th ed., 1959), pp. 8 ff.

[200] BENT, VI, 106 ff.; there also the text of the prologue.

Within the church itself insignificant secondary traditions are maintained, and later on the apostolic circle can be described very casually, without our having always to assume ancient traditions standing back of these descriptions. Occasionally one of the seventy disciples is called "apostle" (Eus., CH I, 13.14 *et passim;* cf. J. B. Lightfoot, *op. cit.,* p. 100, n. 1). Clement of Alexandria (Strom. VI, 106.1) can remark that whoever leads a perfect and gnostic life can be added to the list of the apostles. Later on, the names in the lists of the twelve apostles, especially in the Oriental traditions, show a remarkably wide diversity: Paul, Crispus, Titus, and others belong to them (cf. F. Haase, *op. cit.,* pp. 43 ff.; Hennecke-Schneemelcher-Wilson, II, 35-36). In these traditions, in general Paul definitely takes a place behind Peter and the twelve (F. Haase, *op. cit.,* p. 248), but occasionally can be given a preferred place ahead of them (*ibid.,* p. 247). In isolated cases some count thirteen (the twelve and Paul) or fourteen (the twelve and Paul and Barnabas or James) apostles (*vide* J. B. Lightfoot, *op. cit.,* p. 100, n. 5). E. Hennecke (2nd ed., pp. 111-256) offers much material on the concept of the apostle in this later time.

VIII

Finally, we must still note that the formation of the concept of the apostle in the Great Church, as we encounter it in Irenaeus, is accompanied, if hardly causally yet at least temporally, by the development of the monarchical episcopal succession.[201]

This succession idea has as its presupposition first of all the monepiscopate. Now Ignatius had already zealously attempted to introduce the monarchical office of the bishop as the chief weapon against the heretics in the communities which were close to him. In the middle of the second century this form of the highest ecclesiastical office generally carried the day, a development which certainly would have resulted, even without the Gnostic danger.

The other presupposition of the "apostolic succession" is the idea of tradition in general, which is already present early, in the Pastorals and in I Clem. 42 ff., and was further developed by the church in antithesis to the Gnostic thesis of apostolic secret traditions.[202]

It is the merit of one man, the Jewish Christian Hegesippus, to have taken up these two presuppositions,[203] and to have introduced the strict idea of

---

[201] On this, cf. H. v. Campenhausen [2], pp. 178 ff. and the literature listed there; *ibid.* [3], pp. 240 ff.; H. Stirnimann, *op. cit.;* J. C. Margot, *op. cit.;* R. Bultmann, *op. cit.,* II, 105 ff., 126-27.

[202] Cf. H. v. Campenhausen [2], pp. 176 ff.; A. Ehrhardt, *op. cit.,* pp. 109 ff.

[203] The concern by which he was prompted in this was an anti-Gnostic one (Eus., CH IV, 8.2).

apostolic succession into the church or at any rate to have brought it to an extensive recognition.[204] Irenaeus then pictures this idea with the following words: "Anyone who wishes to see the truth can find in every church the tradition which the apostles proclaimed in the whole world, and we can enumerate the bishops of the various churches installed by the apostles, as well as their successors down to the present day" (Iren. III, 3.1). This strict succession idea was not simply an extension of the principle of tradition long present in the communities of Pauline Christianity.[205] This is shown by the fact that—if one excepts Rome, where already since the time of I Clem. Peter and Paul always were taken as founders of the congregation (Iren. III, 3.2)[206]—Paul never stands at the head of a line of succession.[207] All the less can the Hellenistic Christianity of the Jewish-Christian Synoptic line have given the inner impulse to the formation of the strict succession theory; for this early Christian stream of tradition, as we saw, was never especially interested either in the idea of tradition or in that of the monarchical episcopate. Further, the succession theory still is not testified to at the time of Irenaeus in Asia Minor (H. v. Campenhausen [2], p. 185; A. Ehrhardt, *op. cit.*, pp. 67 ff.).[208] Thus the above-mentioned presuppositions for the introduction of the strict succession concept in the church are not the *source* of this new understanding of the office.

The source of the strict form of the monarchical apostolic succession is rather to be sought in the tradition in which Hegesippus is at home. It seems to me, in spite of the doubts of H. v. Campenhausen,[209] that we may presuppose that what is involved here is a mild form of Jewish Christianity.[210] Thus the origin of the succession idea of the Catholic Church is not to be sought in the prototypes of the ancient philosophical schools,[211] but rather in Judaism,[212] whose concept of *tradition* also Paul already had

[204] This opinion is so generally held by scholars today that I shall not argue it here. It is, of course, not undisputed (cf. most recently N. Hyldahl, "Hegesipps Hypomnemata" in StudTheol, XIV, 70 ff., esp. pp. 100 ff.) and in view of the paucity of our sources will always remain hypothetical.

[205] Cf. A. Ehrhardt, *op. cit.*, p. 158.

[206] Later of course, as in Antioch also, Peter leads off the list of bishops. The reasons for this in W. Bauer [1], pp. 118 ff.

[207] A. Ehrhardt, *op. cit.*, pp. 21, 67.

[208] It is true that very early a kind of prophetic succession seems to have been present among the Montanists, a succession in an unbroken series of names (Eus., CH V, 17; H. v. Campenhausen [2], p. 208; H. Kraft in ThZ [1955], p. 263). Unfortunately for us this phenomenon is completely without foundation. Cf. Th. Zahn [1], pp. 45, 168 ff.

[209] [2], p. 183, n. 4.

[210] W. Bauer [1], pp. 200, 216; A. Ehrhardt, *op. cit.*, pp. 63 ff.

[211] Thus H. v. Campenhausen [2], pp. 174 ff.

[212] See G. Strecker, "Christentum und Judentum in den ersten beiden Jahrhunderten," *Ev. Theol.* (1956), pp. 464-65.

taken over (e.g., I Cor. 11:23; 15:1 ff.; 11:2). We may agree to this argument of A. Ehrhardt in his book which in many respects is highly susceptible to criticism (*op. cit.,*),[213] and perhaps even to his more precise statement, "that the combined lists of Jewish royal and sacerdotal succession are the only type that can have been followed by the episcopal succession lists" (*op. cit.,* p. 48; cf. p. 61). But the circumstances within the Jewish Christianity of the second century are so obscure to us that only with great caution can one inquire behind the fact that Hegesippus was the champion of the apostolic succession within the monarchical episcopate.[214]

Sufficient to us is the point that at the same time in which with Irenaeus *the* concept of the apostle has become self-evident which embraces Paul and the twelve in perfect harmony and which has dominated the Great Church since that time, the content also of that which is to serve as apostolic in this sense was determined by the fixing of the canon and the practical application of the theory of apostolic succession. This concept of the apostolic, which is fixed by the end of the second century, still had to struggle for its victory in some places, to be sure; it was also further expanded; the canon was completed, the doctrine of succession was legally and sacramentally insured, the apostolic tradition was fixed in the rules of faith, and so on. But never again was it fundamentally called into question within the church.

---

[213] A. Ehrhardt seeks to prove that an "apostolic" succession in Jerusalem, proceeding from James, always existed (cf. *op. cit.,* p. 82).

[214] That he was not guided by purely historical interests is already shown by the fact that the early succession lists were collected and handed down without any indication of dates (see A. Ehrhardt, *op. cit.,* p. 39). Further, Hegesippus himself testifies to his interest in the succession of pure doctrine (in Eus., CH IV, 22; cf. also H. v. Campenhausen [3], pp. 246-47). It may have been altogether an original idea of Hegesippus to make fruitful for the early Catholic Church the custom which was known to him from Judaism of exhibiting lists of succession. In any case the present-day tendencies to revive the episcopal apostolic succession in the Evangelical Church by harking back to the first one hundred and fifty years of church history does not appear justified. In opposition to Gnosticism, Ignatius develops the (local) monepiscopate, and the Pastorals emphasize the doctrinal tradition, conceptions which cannot be obligatory for all time precisely because they sprang from a case of acute emergency and not from the necessary development of a theologically correct beginning. This is all the more true of the ideas, which are first witnessed to by Hegesippus, of the strict apostolic succession.